eddie jordan

# eddie jordan

## *An Independent Man*

THE AUTOBIOGRAPHY

First published in hardback in Great Britain in 2007 by
Orion Books
an imprint of the Orion Publishing Group Ltd
Orion House, 5 Upper St Martin's Lane,
London WC2H 9EA
An Hachette Livre UK Company

1 3 5 7 9 10 8 6 4 2



A CIP catalogue record for this book is available
from the British Library.

ISBN: 978 0 7528 7534 7

Printed in Great Britain by Clays Ltd, St Ives plc



www.orionbooks.co.uk

# CONTENTS


| | | |
|---|---|---|
| 1 | Sailing Away | 1 |
| 2 | Flash Jordan | 5 |
| 3 | A right Barney | 14 |
| 4 | Carpets and Cars | 19 |
| 5 | Marlboro's Irish cowboys | 29 |
| 6 | Marie the Meteor | 36 |
| 7 | Another few bricks in the wall | 43 |
| 8 | John Boy | 52 |
| 9 | Euro Star | 61 |
| 10 | Brundle v Senna | 68 |
| 11 | Riding a Camel | 77 |
| 12 | Managing my boys | 87 |
| 13 | The biggest chance of all | 99 |
| 14 | Nice car, no sponsor | 109 |
| 15 | Coming together | 118 |
| 16 | Talking the talk | 126 |
| 17 | By the time I get to Phoenix | 132 |
| 18 | Pushing our luck | 140 |
| 19 | Michael who? | 148 |
| 20 | Shafted | 155 |
| 21 | The Commitments | 164 |
| 22 | Almost pointless | 171 |
| 23 | Hart attack | 181 |
| 24 | Fast Eddie | 191 |
| 25 | An outrageous decision | 200 |

26 The blackest weekend 208
27 Pole position 214
28 Going Gallic 222
29 You owe me – big time 229
30 Yellow is the colour 234
31 Hissing Sid 240
32 Hijacking Hill 247
33 Oh, what a circus! 253
34 Losing the head 259
35 Taking the Michael 268
36 One two! 272
37 Back to reality 280
38 A brilliant victory 286
39 A win for the taking 292
40 A touch of theatre 298
41 Cut backs 308
42 Winning and losing 318
43 Slipping away 327
44 Saying goodbye 335
45 CLIC: another life 341
46 Driving with a difference 352
47 Breaking and entering 360
48 Bernie and the No. 414 368
49 Back to dealing 374
50 Conclusions 378

Index 388

To the two special people in my life – Eileen, 'The Matriarch' and Mother of all Mothers, so supportive; and Marie, 'The Mammy', who has continued that support through 28 years of marriage and is the mother of our four great kids.

Thanks to the three people who helped me on the racing side – John Walton and Bosco Quinn. The other, Maurice Hamilton, you have been a great friend and advisor to me during my F1 time. Thanks also for looking over my shoulder with my autobiography and keeping me in check whenever neccessary.

## Chapter 1

# SAILING AWAY

When 20 Formula 1 cars stormed off the grid in Melbourne on 6 March 2005, the only sound I could hear was the gentle lapping of water against the hull of a yacht. Instead of experiencing tension and a soaring pulse, I could feel only a gentle breeze coming off the Persian Gulf. I was several thousand miles away from Australia and a sport that had consumed my life for more than 30 years. To my surprise, it did not matter at all.

I have always thought it important for sports people to give up competition rather than the other way round. That is easier said than done because you are not always master of your destiny. I am also aware that it is just as difficult for racing drivers to reach that sometimes painful decision as it is for boxers or any other sports professionals living on the adrenalin produced by a dramatic business that has obsessed them for longer than they care to remember.

I often looked at retired racing drivers, struggling to come to terms with their existence outside the cockpit of an F1 car, and wondered if, when I finished my business in the sport, I would be the same. Some drivers would do commentary work on various forms of motor racing but in many cases, it seemed to me, they were not exactly happy about the sudden change in direction their lives had taken. I did not want that to happen to me.

I needed to make sure I was not wandering the paddock chasing something that was not there. I would only turn up if I had a job to do. Ironically, I had been approached about doing commentary work but I felt, even if I was any good, broadcasting would be for later. I had to make a definite break and look at other things.

I had read one or two seasonal previews for 2005 and realised I was rapidly losing touch. I no longer knew who was sponsoring whom, what deals were going down, which team was using what tyres. These were things that I would have been able to rattle off in the past because running an F1 team is like insider dealing – you know everything that there is to know. Now I had lost my power base. I had sold the team that had filled my every waking moment. I was in danger of becoming a prisoner in a vacuum of boredom.

My wife Marie was quick to realise that the weekend of the first grand prix in 2005 would be a killer. She quietly arranged a trip on *Burrasca*, a 183ft ketch built by Perini Navi in Viareggio. This magnificent yacht with 17,000 sq. ft of sail was based in Dubai and Marie knew there would be no motor sport there.

When we arrived in the Middle East, I could not believe how much was going on. It was proof of the insular world that F1 inhabits when a race weekend gets under way and you actually believe that nothing else is happening on the planet. You come to think that the grand prix is the centre of the universe. Dubai provided the perfect antidote.

Marie and I had dinner with Mark Knopfler and went to his open-air concert. The following day, we watched my friend Paul McGinley play in the Dubai Open. Without any apparent effort, I was involved with two of the loves of my life – music and golf. If there had been a soccer match taking place, my weekend would have been complete.

Nonetheless, motor racing was never far away. Nigel Mansell was in Dubai to watch the golf and the 1992 world champion stopped by for a drink and a look at the boat. There had been a suggestion that I should get involved in the newly formed A1 Grand Prix series. I had a visit from Sheikh Maktoum Hasher Maktoum Al Maktoum of Dubai, who had founded the so-called World Cup of Motor Sport in 2004. He brought along his business partners from South Africa to ask if Jordan would consider running the Irish team.

It was not something I wanted to do. In any case, there was confusion over who should be paying whom. I wanted $1 million for the right to use my name and they wanted the same amount from me if I wished to compete. Clearly, we were never going to meet in the middle, nor even come close, but all of this was a pleasant distraction from what was happening on the other side of the world in Melbourne.

Thankfully, at least from my point of view, coverage of the Australian Grand Prix was poor in Dubai. That probably had much to do with the fact that neighbouring Bahrain had a grand prix and Dubai did not. Local politics were in my favour as I walked the wooden decks rather than a concrete pit lane.

We set off on the Friday for the Persian Gulf and the Straits of Hormuz. This potentially dangerous stretch of water may have been littered with warships but it was a wonderful place to go diving, something I had never done before. There was an unavoidable feeling of freedom – and, in my case, escape – as we sat on the side of this monster of a magnificent sailing ship while it made the most of a favourable wind and cut through the bright blue sea. We would drop anchor at night, have dinner, talk and play cards. I detected the hand of Marie behind the fact that there was no television within reach.

It was not until Tuesday that I found out that Giancarlo Fisichella had won for Renault in Melbourne. Considering Giancarlo had won the last of four grands prix for my team, I was delighted, but it did not make me wish I had been there. Yes, I had thought about the race from time to time, but not as much as I predicted I would.

There was a definite feeling that my existence in the emotional and dramatic world of motor racing had reached a conclusion. That seemed bizarre, having spent so much of my life being a chancer in many respects while attempting to gain a footing and then make my way slowly but surely towards the peak. The climb had been difficult and, at times, painful but, along the way, the view had been magnificent. Now I was ready to see what lay on the other side. My base camp in Ireland seemed a million miles away.

Chapter 2

# FLASH JORDAN

Although I was born and brought up in Dublin, most of my younger days were spent in Bray, a seaside town about 12 miles south of the capital city. In the 1950s, Bray would be as popular in Ireland as Blackpool in England, but half the size and without the glitter, the tower and the trams.

My Aunt Lilian, who was unmarried, lived in Bray and doted on me. She loved having me there and we became really close. I felt at home in every sense because this house had been what you might call the seat of the Jordan family, where my dad had been brought up and my grandfather had practised as a dentist. Almost every weekend I would catch the train to Bray after school on a Friday, come winter or summer, sunshine or showers.

In truth, I enjoyed the winter months more, particularly when walking along the beach or the promenade while the wind whipped up the Irish Sea and battered the landscape around Bray Head. Despite the effect of the frequently raw elements, winter seemed more peaceful in Bray. The amusement arcades would be open on a Sunday only, whereas in the summer they would be busy seven days a week, and the place would be a madhouse.

The entire complexion of Bray began to change as the days grew longer and more visitors arrived. We local youngsters became Jack-the-lads, particularly when wonderful, gorgeous girls arrived from England and proved to be a bit wilder and noisier than the Irish women. They used more make-up and that must have added to the allure and sense of achievement if an Irish lad managed to pull. That was the challenge and most of us succeeded at some point. The English girls were more...accommodating...than their Irish counterparts because they were not shackled or influenced by the intense doctrine of the Catholic Church.

I had my first experience with alcohol when I was about 14. We would drink 'Black and Tan', a strange choice of name because, in terms of Irish history, the Black and Tans were very unpopular. They were mostly former British army soldiers brought into Ireland by the government in London after the First World War to assist the Royal Irish Constabulary. This was nothing to do with politics. It was simply a way of former soldiers earning money. There were not enough uniforms to go round and the new recruits ended up wearing a mix of khaki and dark police clothes – hence the name Black and Tan. They terrorised the locals and were deeply despised, even to this day.

You could not say the same for the drink, a heady mix of cider and Guinness. It had the desired effect at very little cost. My close friend at the time was Eddie O'Byrne. His father was state solicitor for County Wicklow. His mother used to have an account in the local grocers. Eddie would go into the shop, wait until the young girl rather than the suspicious owner was serving, pick up a couple of flagons of cider and have them charged to his mother's account as maybe a pound of butter and some bread and ham. That would be our fix for the day. We would go to the Monkey Pole, a tourist attraction located halfway up Bray Head, and sit there becoming increasingly goggle-eyed while watching the young girls go by. I have known less pleasant ways to spend an afternoon in the sunshine.

Everyone used to call me 'Flash', not because of my antics, but partly because Jordan rhymed with Gordon and partly because, if checked trousers were in, I would wear them; if drainpipes were the thing, I would have them; if flowery shirts were in fashion, I would be the first to parade up and down in one. The name stuck and a few people in Bray only know me as Flash, even now.

When I was younger, Bray provided another attraction in the form of pongo. No, it's not what you might think. Pongo was the forerunner of bingo and identical to it. Aunt Lilian would often take me to pongo on a Friday night and we would play for an hour. That was a big treat. Then she would bring me home and I would have Kimberly biscuits, do my studying and go to bed. Talk about the high life! But these are very fond memories and a prelude to an interest in a more serious piece of Irish culture.

By chance, Bray rather than Dublin became the place for local bands to do their stuff. This was where my love for music took root. In the wintertime, you had talented musicians such as Donny Deveney, whose father owned the newspaper shop, and a boy called Paul Ashford. Aunt Lilian taught in the technical college when Paul was expelled and I was under strict instructions not to mix with this boy, but he was a super guy and a brilliant bass player. We are still friends to this day. He played in a group called The Chosen Few and they would play in the All Stars Club on Albert Walk in Bray every Wednesday and Saturday. That is where I learned to play the drums and first got to hear Fran O'Toole.

Fran was a wonderful keyboard artist who played rock but whose passion was always a bit of jazz. He sounded just like Georgie Fame. He was so good that he was asked to join the Miami Showband, which was one of the biggest names, if not *the* biggest, in Irish music at the time. The Miami, whose lead singer was Dickie Rock, played five nights a week all over the country and in the UK. One Saturday night in July 1975, The Miami were returning from a gig in a ballroom in the North of Ireland when terrorists stopped their bus near the border and three of the eight band members were murdered in cold blood. Fran O'Toole was one of them.

We were totally devastated. Bray and the rest of Ireland went into deep shock. Yes, we knew all about the troubles in the North but no one ever expected the violence to include innocent people who brought such pleasure both north and south of the border. It was horrific and seemed so pointless. I could not get my head round this at all.

Partying and discos began to enter the social scene. I remember one night telling Aunt Lilian that I was catching an earlier bus back home to Dublin. Of course, being a chancer, I did a detour to the disco instead. My aunt, being an experienced teacher, was wise to these things. She marched into the disco, dragged me out, and gave me a verbal lashing. She threatened to put me on the bus – for good. I had to virtually get down on bended knee, apologise and plead to be allowed to come back to Bray. I would have been lost without the town and its music.

Not that there was anything wrong with home, of course. It was just that I was not spoiled as much. My father was an extremely quiet man who worked for the electricity board. My mother, in the typical fashion of an Irish house, ran the home and, to some extent, the finances. We lived for most of my childhood in St Kevin's Gardens in Dartry, Dublin 6, which was quite a respectable area, being slightly out of the city. Now, of course, Dartry is totally within the commuter belt.

We had a semi-detached property in a quiet cul-de-sac. My mum was very fussy about where we lived and she had saved night and day for this house. We had to make a lot of sacrifices because Mum was determined to move out of our previous place in nearby Ranelagh. This has become an area dominated by flats and apartments but, at the time, Mother wanted to move to a 'proper house'. It cannot have been easy because, based on my father's income, we were probably boxing outside our weight.

Mum somehow got the money and put the deal together. My parents were not inclined to have a big mortgage; that was not their style. They preferred to save and get the money first. They typified the philosophy of an older Irish generation – neither a borrower nor a lender be. Maybe in the next generation people will revert to that but, now, it is quite the opposite – you borrow and, if you cannot make 5 per cent on the money that you borrow, then you are a mug. My view has always leaned enthusiastically towards the latter philosophy.

Whatever Mother did, it was enough to get us into this house in

Dartry. I was about eight or nine at the time. My elder sister Helen was a very good student and worked really hard. When she was 19, she got married, which I think Mum and Dad considered to be a bit early. Not that it mattered because, after working with my dad for a while, Helen became an airhostess with Aer Lingus. That was a really cool job at that time. I remember watching as the Aer Lingus bus came to pick her up. She was off across the Atlantic to New York. In an aeroplane! Believe me, that was huge excitement.

Helen was always very sophisticated and stylish. There was a five and a half year gap between us, so we did not have much opportunity to be together socially. Once Helen started working, every Friday she would give me a small allocation of my pocket money. In my last years at school, it was always enough to go to The Templelogue Inn, which was better known as The Morgue. Everyone went there on a Sunday night. A pint cost two shillings and sixpence (12½ pence). So, for ten shillings (50p) you could have four pints. When you are 17 or 18, four pints have little effect. I would collapse in a heap if I had four pints now.

It was not my father's style to go down to the pub for a session. He preferred to come home at five each evening, read the paper, have tea at about 5.30 and be finished and washed up in time to see the six o'clock news. Then we would turn the telly off, kneel down in front of our chairs and say the rosary. It was the Angelus, which is recited at noon (which is not practical for most people) and in the evening. We did it without fail each night.

My dad's twin sister was a senior nun, Mother Rectrus of the Irish Sisters of Charity. This order was a huge part of Irish life and also one of the biggest in England. Every Monday at seven o'clock we would go to chapel for a special service. I liked that because we would meet my aunt and have tea and tiny slices of the most magnificent brown bread I have ever tasted. It was gorgeous, particularly with homemade butter. The trick was to make the bread with buttermilk that was slightly sour and on the point of going off. There was a knack to making it and every Irish mother knew how it was done. The other advantage of going to chapel on the Monday was it meant I could get away with doing less homework and studying. That was a difficult thing to do when you were a pupil at Synge Street School, arguably one of the best teaching establishments in Dublin.

It was a three-mile hike from our house. Synge Street was a state school where the academic standards were high – as were the fees at £6 per year. Not many people could afford that but, nonetheless, the roll call of soon-to-be-famous names attending Synge Street goes on forever.

Donnacha O'Dea was the son of the very famous actress Siobhan McKenna and an actor by the name of Dennis O'Dea. I went to school with Donnacha and he became an outstanding swimmer, doing his bit for Ireland. Then he became world champion at the age of 57, not at swimming, of course. By then he had moved on to poker, which he mastered with just as much ease. He was unbeatable and he is on television all the time, demonstrating his skills. Many famous footballers also went to Synge Street, as did the TV host Gay Byrne. I sat beside a guy called Brian Hurley, who went on to become a big singing star in Ireland and the United States under the stage name Red Hurley.

A bunch of us lived not far from each other and we would walk home together rather than take the bus. That way we could save two pence and use it to buy a cigarette and a gur cake. This consisted of all the bits that were not used in making confectionary, wedding cakes and fruitcakes. These odds and ends would be thrown into a bucket and mulled around before being compacted and sold off as gur cakes. The height of luxury was a Woodbine and a gur cake after a hard day at school.

The Christian Brothers who ran Synge Street made sure it was hard. You studied or you got beaten. So we got beaten – leather straps across the hand, usually once a day. The pain was wicked. It sounds terrible now but it never did us any harm. You received your punishment and off you went. There was no point in crying about it. And, not surprisingly, you studied and did your homework. If an essay had to be handed in by 12 o'clock, you made sure it was on time, otherwise you got two lashes. You soon learned that you were going to have to hand it in at some stage – so why not do it by midday? Why get two lashes for nothing? It was discipline.

On reflection, such an authoritarian regime sounds callous and cruel, but did it have the desired effect? Absolutely! The fear factor made you say, 'God, I've got to do this thing. I must do it. I have to finish it.' And you did. Whereas now, if you are not inclined, the reaction is, 'Oh fuck it. Who cares?' And, of course, no one does.

My life in Synge Street was made even more difficult by the fact that I am mildly dyslexic, but did not know it at the time. My two boys are the same, but the girls are not. Sir Jackie Stewart and others like him have proved that dyslexia is not the end of the world, far from it. Dyslexics adapt and find that they are better at things other than reading and writing.

I was always fantastically good at maths. If you have to add up 40 sets of figures, I will do it in half the time it takes you to punch the numbers into a computer – and I will be right. I see things in multiples, never singularly. For example, if there is a two, a seven, a nine and a six, you will probably add them in sequence whereas I am working in multiples of ten and measuring the zeros. I am looking for blocks of ten, which appear as a sequence and that brings up the answer every time.

That is probably one of the reasons why wheeling and dealing came so easily. I think I must have done that since birth because I have been at it for as long as I can remember. Conkers, marbles, books – I would be buying and selling continually. I was the youngest in the family and quickly realised that school books would not be retained at home, so I could sell them without saying too much. At the end of the year, I would buy books that had been kept much better than mine and flog them to the next class coming up. Why not? It seemed the obvious thing to do.

Of course, the big question was just what was I going to do with myself when I left Synge Street. There was one course that was obvious after being brought up and educated by the Brothers. I went to mass every morning of Lent, and had Sodality once a week with my aunt, usually at eight o'clock at night, which was mainly for younger people. During these occasions, the priest would bring up the merits of the priesthood. I would not want to say this was a form of indoctrination – but it was not far off. The priest would say, 'The Bishop is coming to confer you tomorrow and I just want to ask you the question: surely, boys, God has come into your heart and your soul, he has spoken to you and said that he wants to give you the calling, that he wants you to be one of his disciples – his apostle on Earth? And the fear and the love of God; surely everything he stands for, you can see in yourself?' On he went in that vein. Gentle persuasion!

During quiet moments of contemplation, you might think to yourself, 'Maybe I should be a priest?' Then you'd think some more and say, 'Hang on. That's ridiculous.' But then you'd consider it again. You might even mention your thoughts to someone and, reading your mind, they might say, 'Y'know, Edmund, priests don't have to be quiet. You could make a great priest.' I would say, 'Yeah, sure. Thanks very much.'

Towards the end of my time at Synge Street, I got as far as going to a retreat in Rathfarnham with the monks. They would set a target and you would go there for maybe three days and two nights. It involved mainly solitude and not too much talking with a bit of singing and reading. I remember it struck me as odd that there was very little bible reading. The bible, certainly in Irish Catholicism, never features strongly. Most places you go in the world, there will be a bible in the hotel room – and I have to admit that some of the bible stories are wonderful – but you rarely came across a bible in an Irish hotel room. When we went to mass, the priest would read from the prayer book. When I emerged from the retreat, I knew that was as close as I was ever going to get to the priesthood.

After that, there was the almost unspoken suggestion at home that

I should pursue dentistry, but only because it was in the family. There was my grandfather, of course, and I also had two uncles working in the dental college in Lincoln Place in Dublin. I went there, but only for a very short period. Various profiles that have been written about me say that I did six months in Lincoln Place. I did nothing of the sort. I went to a couple of lectures and quickly realised this was not going to work. So I stopped – or I ran out, if you like.

Banking and money seemed a much more logical calling but, even then, the Church would have its say. Some uncharitable people said my dad's twin sister, the indomitable Auntie Maureen – Mother Rectrus – got me into the bank because I could not possibly have made it with my qualifications. That is possibly true. I am sure it was no coincidence that I joined the Irish Sisters of Charity Bank, otherwise known as the Hibernian Bank before it became the Bank of Ireland. My aunt may have opened a few doors but, once inside, there was no danger of me making another rush for the exit. I was to the manner born.

Chapter 3

# A RIGHT BARNEY

We had two bank strikes in the space of four years in Ireland. During the first, in 1966, I was not affected. I was not yet working for a bank and did not have much money to transact. I spent the summer in Jersey doing odd jobs, trying to earn enough to keep me going. The second strike, in the summer of 1970, was more serious. By then, I was a bank employee and it meant there was no money in every sense. So, I returned to Jersey to earn some cash. Little did I know that this trip would have a profound effect on both my future and the spending and making of money on a scale I would never have dreamed of.

I did menial accounting jobs for the Jersey Electricity Company during the day and worked in the Bristol Bar at night. I was sharing the front room of a house with four people I had never met before, not that it mattered in those days. You put your case with all your belongings beneath your bed and just got on with it. The landlady would appear regularly to collect her money, which amounted to about 25 per cent of your earnings. No food was allowed in the house, so I made good use of the canteen at the electricity company and, thankfully, there was a bit of food to be had in the bar. I began by washing glasses and cleaning tables. When the bar became really busy – which was often – I would pull pints and generally enjoy the mayhem. It was manic at times in that pub.

Bars did not open on Sundays in Jersey. With nothing better to do, I tried my hand on a go-kart at a small track at St Brelade's Bay. The sense of excitement was immediate. I could not believe how close you were to the ground, and the cornering ability of the kart amazed me. I had no idea that this sort of exhilaration existed, and all for a relatively small amount of money. I was earning enough to be able to spend a couple of hours each Sunday at the track. Unofficial races would develop with the local heroes, who knew the karts and the track very well and were difficult to beat.

It was not the racing that mesmerised me at the time; it was the thrill of driving these buzzy little things quickly. The absence of suspension on a kart meant you would be bouncing and jumping all over the track, feeling most of it through your backside, which was an inch or so from the pavement and often in contact with it.

That basic sensation was repeated in all subsequent formulae as I worked my way through motor sport. You can learn so much about a car just from how it feels. Jockeys will tell you the same thing. They may never have ridden a particular horse before they canter to the starting post, but that short journey will tell them exactly what the horse is likely to do, whether he pulls this way or that. They get the feel for the horse and will know whether he is a good one or a bad one. It is the same in motor sport, from a kart through to a sophisticated racing car. You can tell a great deal by the sensation coming through your backside and I was experiencing it for the first time on the kart track in Jersey.

Having got the taste, I was very keen to go racing when I returned to Ireland at the end of the bank strike. I had been posted to Mullingar, where I met Dennis Shaw, a solicitor with a practice in the town. We established the Mullingar Karting Club in association with the local council. Our 'track' consisted of a few roads with straw bales marking out the course and protecting us from lampposts and other potential hazards. It was very basic. No, it was worse than that – it was agricultural. If the safety people evident in racing today saw what we were up to three decades ago, they would have a fit. At the time, no one cared. It was huge fun because we were racing and the local population, for whom life in Mullingar was pretty still, loved the spectacle and the noise. And it cost them nothing.

At first, I shared a kart with Dennis but we quickly realised we needed one each. I cannot remember the detail of the transaction but I bought mine locally. It was prepared for racing by Michael Tunney, who went on to become an outstanding businessman and, some 40 years later, remains one of my closest friends.

The trick was to have Alan Johnson tune the engine. Alan was known as 'The King' because he also won most of the races, but just being on the scene, having a kart and racing regularly was enough to qualify for a major championship event. That must have been the criterion because I was selected to represent Ireland at Heysham in Lancashire, despite not having achieved much in terms of results. It was at this event that I met Terry Fullerton, probably the only kart driver in the world who, ten years later, had Ayrton Senna's total respect. Karting was a natural proving ground for young racers and many of the faces I saw and competed against at the time reappeared as I moved through Formula Ford and F3. There were some outstanding drivers, including Austin Kinsella and The King.

We would load the karts in a van and go to places such as the Isle of Man, where we would get a race after the bikes had finished. Providing added entertainment at a motorbike race was always tricky because the circuit would be far too big and fast for a kart. In some places, it was suicidal.

It was also costing me a fortune. There was no prize money – I mean, who was going to pay when we were willing to turn up and race on anything that remotely resembled a track? The best you could do was ask the local council if they would provide a couple of trophies. That was it. You had to fend for yourself. The last thing you needed was an accident because of the damage to the kart or, worse, yourself. I was to find out all about that thanks to a major shunt at a place called Monasterboyce.

We used to go there often. Monasterboyce was a village about an hour north of Dublin on the road to Belfast. Everything used to close in Northern Ireland on a Sunday – they even went so far as chaining the swings in the public parks – so the karters, bored stiff and itching for a race, would drive south. We had some wild races as a result. My accident, however, occurred during a practice session.

One renowned karter, Barney, was famous not so much for his results as for the fact that he had one useable arm. The other was a stump with which he could do very little while driving. I do not know how he got a licence. In fact, I don't think anyone ever saw his licence. Administration, if you could call it that, was fairly lax in those days. Despite this handicap, Barney was amazingly good. He was also a bit of a lunatic. On this particular day, he got bored with lapping in the same direction. So, without saying anything, he decided to go the wrong way, just for the hell of it. I was the one who found him first.

It is one thing coming across another competitor who has spun and stalled in the middle of the track, and quite another suddenly to find someone coming at you, flat out. We collided head-on. It was an horrific accident and I came off worse. Barney had a few scratches but I had gone head-over-heels and was lying on the road with a big piece of bone sticking out of my left leg.

There was no medical back up worthy of the name at the track, not that anyone could have done much on the spot. I was in a bad way. Someone took me to The Lady of Lourdes in Drogheda which, fortunately for me, is a really famous hospital. Normally, with a broken leg, everything would be set right, plaster applied and away you would go. I was detained for at least three weeks.

I had a fairly serious compound fracture that became infected. I needed a couple of operations and, at one point, there was concern that I would lose an inch off my leg. My nervous system was affected and, as a result, I developed alopecia. Talk about a double whammy.

When I had recovered enough to return to work, I found that I had been transferred to Galway. Although I did not ask, I was fairly certain that the accident and its aftermath had prompted my aunt, the nun, to persuade the bank to move me as far away as possible from all this nonsense with karts and racing in the hope that I would give it up and do something less hazardous. If anything, it made me more determined to progress. Racing was truly in my blood.

## Chapter 4

# CARPETS AND CARS

Looking at me now, you would think I would know better than to pay £450 for a racing car that was an old dog, but that's what I did when searching for my first single-seater. Much as I enjoyed karting and the friendships that came with it, I could see that single-seaters were the way forward for any young racing driver keen to make his mark. I bought a Lotus 61 Formula Ford from a guy in Northern Ireland who wanted rid of it. I quickly discovered why. The car was crap.

A Lotus had been the one to have but that famous name was in decline in the junior formulae and the 61 model was a good – or a bad – example of that. It kept breaking down and I eventually moved it on to a youngster from Dublin who seemed to have a similar passion for the sport. I took his souped-up Ford Anglia in part-exchange and then watched with some discomfort as he began to do rather well with the Lotus. In fact, I would not have been surprised if someone had told me then that the guy in question would go on to become a grand-prix driver. His name was Derek Daly.

I put Derek's hard-earned cash towards a Crossle 20F, which I bought from Richard Parsons, another driver from the North. This was an altogether better deal because the Crossle was a fine car – not as good as the brilliant 25F, which came later – but a useful Formula Ford racer nonetheless, and I made good use of it on the Irish motor-sport scene.

Despite the so-called Troubles that had flared up in August 1969, in the early 1970s it was still possible to cross the border with relative ease and go racing in the North. Bishopscourt and Kirkistown were two fairly similar circuits based on airfields in County Down, the former still being used at the time for military purposes. Races in the North were always held on a Saturday, which was very handy because events down south at Mondello Park and, occasionally, Phoenix Park, were usually staged on a Sunday. The least said the better about some of the driving in the convoy that rushed south on a Saturday night.

The trips to Northern Ireland were always great craic. We would catch a ferry between the villages of Strangford and Portaferry to reach the southern tip of County Down and then drive to a bed and breakfast in the fishing village of Portavogie. Even though our heads were full of racing and we were always in a hurry, it was impossible not to admire the beautiful scenery around the southern reaches of Strangford Lough.

The usual plan was to finish work at 5.30 p.m. in Dublin, wait for the traffic to die down and leave at 8 p.m. If you did it right, it was possible to complete the journey in under three hours and reach Portavogie in time for a pint. Then it would be a 5 a.m. call on the Saturday and off to Kirkistown to prepare the car, get through scrutineering and go racing, hopefully through the heats and into the final. You had to be careful during race meetings when the days were shorter at the beginning and end of the season. The last ferry would leave Portaferry earlier than usual and you had keep that in mind if you stopped off with the lads for a pint. The trick, of course, was to get to know the man on the ferry, slip him a couple of quid and have him wait for you. There was always a deal to be done!

The Troubles may have begun to turn nasty in certain parts of the North but racing people made a conscious effort to encourage terrific camaraderie, regardless of your background or religious persuasion. I raced against some really great people – Brian Nelson, Tommy Reid, Patsy McGarrity – during those wonderful summers and I have to confess it was often difficult to return to work on the Monday.

I was still at the bank at that stage and I remember being sent to work in a branch in Portumna in County Galway. That made life very difficult for me because it was a desperately long trek with the car and trailer all the way across Ireland to County Down. I applied for a transfer back to Dublin but it so happened that I had to take time off work in any case after breaking my ankle for a second time. I had broken it while racing karts and now I had broken it again while testing a Formula Ford.

My main worry was persuading the people in Human Resources that I should be back in Dublin. I threatened to become a pain in the arse if they didn't transfer me but, as it turned out, there was no need for that because I had been earmarked as someone worth watching – for all the right reasons, which made a nice change. I always received a bonus each year for opening more accounts than anyone else and was already aware that I seemed to be a bit of a sales person. This would stand me in good stead, not only with the bank, but also when it came to raising enough cash to go racing. I was always on the look out for a decent deal.

My sister, Helen, had just married Neil McCarthy, who was in the fish business. Neil had struck gold by exporting smoked salmon that had been vacuum packed. For me, this was perfect. I would stand at the top of Grafton Street, which is one of Dublin's main shopping streets, and flog smoked salmon. Over the years, a bit of spin has been applied to that story by insinuating that some of the packs of salmon were past their sell-by date, which I had scratched off. I can say categorically that was not the case because there was no dating system in those days, although I suppose that will not stop the suggestion that all of it was out of date in any case. I doubt that it was but I cannot say for sure. All I know is that it raised cash towards what was, in my view at least, an extremely deserving cause.

Other methods of finding finance emerged from the strangest places. I came across a guy called Joe Eustace who was in the carpet business. He really had the gift of the gab and he was making hay at a time when a lot of new houses were being built and the Irish people really felt they were going places by having fitted carpets in their homes. Joe was doing deals with the developers for the provision and fitting of these carpets and I persuaded him to give me a small amount of money in return for having The Flooring Centre advertised on my car. One thing led to another, particularly during the off-season of 1972–73. I did a deal with Joe to take his remnants and all the carpets and rugs that he couldn't sell. The remnants were free and I took the rest of it – which was quality stuff – on a sale or return basis.

If you were into trading, the place to be was Dandelion Green. It was cool to have a stall there and I loved it. Every Saturday morning I would arrive with a flask of something hot, ready for the day ahead, which involved going for a pint at lunchtime and returning to the stall in the afternoon. You might not sell a thing but there would be great craic among the stallholders.

Occasionally, I would ask a really good friend, Dave Meek, who used to come to the races with me, to help out on the stall on a Sunday. In return for going 50–50, Dave would look after the Dandelion pitch while I headed out to the main Belfast road. At one time, gypsies used to sell pots and pans alongside this road and the market they started had grown into a massive affair, a precursor of the Sunday markets and car-boot sales you see today, except this was a serious place. I was as happy as a sandboy, playing the chancer and loving every minute of the buzz, the banter and the bartering.

One Sunday, I was spotted by the father of Martin Donnelly, then involved with Formula Ford and later to become one of my drivers in F3000. Donnelly Senior was a potato merchant from Belfast and he could hardly believe his eyes when he saw me flogging carpets by the side of the road. It did not take long for that tale to circulate within Irish motor sport. I did not rush to refute the story when asked and this quickly became a piece of Jordan folklore, particularly later on when I was arguably the only team owner in F1 who had once resorted to selling carpet remnants. It was part of some very happy days spent raising money. It was also a source of revenue that was limited to the weekends. There was a different scam during the week.

I was developing a brisk business in private car sales through adverts in the local newspaper. For some reason, Irish people refused either to trust the main dealers or to pay the price when buying second-hand. I propagated that image by advertising in the paper and telling prospective punters that the dealers were selling exactly the same car for a couple of hundred pounds more. In fact, it was usually a slightly different model, but who could tell the difference?

I built up my stock through contacts made in the world of trial biking. Dave Meek was a trials rider in the winter and I would go with him and have a ride from time to time. Trials riding attracted many of the sales people from the bigger garages in Dublin, and I got to know them well enough to be able to ring up after scanning their stock and say, 'I'll have those two or three cars as they're seen!' I would choose trade-ins that I knew the dealers would want to get rid of as soon as possible; or, if they had too many of one particular model, I would offer to take three away at a knock-down price. I would try to sell two for the price of three, leaving the last as profit. It did not always work, but the game plan was to sell on Tuesday, Wednesday and Thursday, hoping to get rid of the last one on Friday before going to Dandelion Green the next day.

The bank would often provide a source of potential customers. Someone might come in for a loan to buy a car. I would ask them what particular year and model they had in mind. Then I'd say, 'Well, that's a stroke of luck. I know where there's a car exactly like the one you want. Leave it with me.' Once they had gone, I would be on the phone to the dealers until I found a car that matched the requirement and away we would go.

Sometimes I might have as many as ten cars in my 'stock'. The problem would be finding somewhere to put them. I had some in the bank car park, some in the driveway of a house where I was living, some here and some there. The winter brought another snag when the cold weather would cause difficulty with starting some of these very fine cars. The batteries would go flat, so I had to make sure that the worst offenders were parked facing downhill.

Of course, this was playing havoc with my proper job in the bank, but I had a wonderful ally in Margaret Nevin. Margaret would cover for me when I was out and about, either moving and selling cars or buying clutches and bits and pieces for my Formula Ford. Just to keep it in the family, Margaret had a brother, Liam, who was an electrician, a really gifted guy who could turn his hand to anything. He ended up preparing my race car. Liam became part of an important group of mates, including Dave Meek and Jim Woods, known as 'Woody', who built my race engines.

It was important to have good support because the racing was ferocious. With drivers such as David Kennedy, Derek Daly and Bernard Devaney from Dublin up against Gary Gibson, Richard Parsons, Jay Pollock and Jim Sherry, the competition was intense. They were quick, believe me, and a better bunch of people you could never hope to meet. They were all diamonds.

We wanted to beat each other so badly that all sorts of muttered accusations were heard among the losers. If I did well, there would be complaints that Woody was building dodgy engines. Of course, he was doing nothing of the sort. Woody was a very clever guy with a great understanding of what made an engine work. He was in demand and the others were trying to tempt him away but, for whatever reason, Woody just wanted to look after my engine, and I was really grateful for that because the competition was so fierce.

I received an interesting measure of just how good the Irish guys were when I took myself across the water for a couple of races in England. Dave Meek and I went to Longridge, near Preston, one of the reasons being that Dave's aunt lived in Preston, which meant we had a place to stay. It cost quite a bit to take the car and trailer across the Irish Sea but, as ever, there was a deal to be done. A guy I grew up with in Bray had become sales and marketing manager for B+I Ferrries, which was very handy because we could travel from Dublin to Liverpool for the very best price.

Having raced at Longridge on the Saturday, we went across to Yorkshire the following day and raced at Croft. I did rather well on both occasions and I was immediately struck by the fact that racing at places such as Mondello and Bishops Court was a hell of a lot more difficult because there were so many good guys competing in Ireland.

Various places often develop a stranglehold on a certain subject, for no particular reason. It could be music, it could be sport. In the early 1970s, junior motor racing in Ireland had gathered terrific momentum. The level of competition was so fierce that it pushed us all on to a very high level. Derek Daly went to England and was massively successful. David Kennedy did the same. I eventually followed suit and we all wound up in F3.

We were very similar in many ways. Our parents were hard-working, good people but none of us had any money. David Kennedy used to work for a garage delivery service, the deal being that he could have a car and a trailer at the weekends. That was important to him so he was happy to work for the car delivery man throughout the week. Derek Daly made ends meet by doing up cars for banger racing. You did anything that would earn money to allow you to go motor racing.

I had no time for girlfriends because I was too busy. Any socialising was done in the pub, usually Johnnie Fox's, which was about half an hour from the city centre, heading into the Dublin Mountains, or the Step Inn in the nearby village of Stepaside. We used to go there because of the late drinking. In fact, once you went in, it was very difficult to get out. That seemed to be the way of it in almost any pub outside Dublin. There were strict licensing laws about closing at 11.30 p.m. The trick was to be inside at 11.29 p.m. Once the door was locked and the lights turned down, you could stay for most of the night and early morning if you felt so inclined.

The Step Inn decided to serve food, only because it meant they could get a longer licence and stay open – officially – until 12.30 a.m. It was a perfect place for motor-racing people and anyone who was anyone on the motor-racing scene would be there. The craic was great but the thing I could never understand was that people would fall out of that pub at all hours – and it was right next door to the police station. It did not make a blind bit of difference.

Dublin was a really great city in which to grow up and, from what I hear, that remains the same 30 years on. My second born, Michele, better known as 'Miki', went to university there and Zak, my third born, is still there. By all accounts, nothing has changed – although the tempo seems to have moved up a scale or two! For me, the early days were blissfully humorous and carefree. Life was just a joy and my priorities, as a wannabe racer, were clear-cut. The first question was do I have the money to go racing this weekend? If the answer was yes, the second question was do I have enough to buy a proper set of tyres for the car? The next question was what state is the engine in and can I afford to have it rebuilt or, at least, get the head done? Even if I did not have all my financial ducks in a row, I still went ahead and raced. It was the same for all of us. That's what we were like. Racing was the beginning and the end. Nothing else mattered.

In the winter, of course, there would be no racing, so we went rallying instead. It was a different bunch of people but just as much fun. In fact, doubly so because this was more of a laugh than racing, which had a serious edge given that we were all would-be world champions, at least in our own minds. I rallied all sorts of weird and wonderful cars that I acquired by doing deals in the pub.

On one occasion, I bought a Vauxhall Viva 2000 with a V6 engine from a journalist and the radiator burst. The thing about rallying is that you keep going at all costs. Everyone is there, doing their bit and willing you on. Spectators were pushing the Viva down the road, water spewing from the radiator, when someone produced a couple of eggs and popped the whites into the hot radiator to seal the leak. To my amazement, it worked. That was typical of the little tricks of the trade perfected by the rally brigade to bring a lame car home. Rallying was a major sport, an important part of motor-sport culture. The Circuit of Ireland at Easter was *the* event and attracted top international names.

During this time I met Martin McCarthy, who was starting in Formula Ford and who was also keen on rallying. He gave me the best insight into aerodynamics, which, as an incredibly talented engineer, came naturally to him. He was one of the consultant engineers who designed and built the hugely impressive Du Pont chemical plant in Northern Ireland.

I moved on to a green Triumph 2.5pi but this got me into trouble even before I had used it for rallying. The Triumph was a fine big car and I would use it for towing cars and carrying all the lads to and from the races. We were travelling back and forth between Dublin and Mondello Park one weekend when the police stopped me for a serious case of speeding. I told the boys to sit tight while I got out and chatted up the Garda officer. After about five or ten minutes I got back in the car, said everything was sorted, and drove off. The boys couldn't believe it. I had found out that the police officer was looking for a second-hand car. A few days later, I sold him exactly what he was looking for and everyone was happy.

We took the Triumph to the west of Ireland for the Galway Rally. Liam Nevin was my co-driver because he was a local lad and, as I've said before, really handy when it came to fixing things on the car – quite literally in this case. Rally cars needed sump guards and the Triumph did not have one. So, what did Liam do? He took a square manhole cover from the road, modified it and proceeded to weld the result to the bottom of the car in the hotel car park. All the professional guys had these titanium sump guards and there we were with a manhole cover. The extra weight did not bear thinking about but at least we had proper protection for the rough roads and the humps and jumps. We were lying third at one point but I can't remember where we finished. All I know is that I sold the car for a profit the following Wednesday on the basis that it now had a decent competition pedigree. The bottom line, as always, was being a chancer and finding cash to go racing. Rallying was a light-hearted diversion. Racing single-seaters continued to be the main aim.

## Chapter 5

# MARLBORO'S IRISH COWBOYS

Both legs were broken. One was at a horrible angle and the ambulance ride to the Leicester Royal Infirmary gave me time to consider that my racing career might be over. The irony was that I had finally got my hands on a Crossle 25F, a brilliant Formula Ford car that was allowing me to win a few races in England. However, being fast was one thing but, as I had just learnt, you also needed to be able to stop the car. Going into the hairpin at Mallory Park, I suddenly discovered that I had braking on the front wheels only. The brakes locked and I ploughed straight into the bank.

No one was to blame. It was one of those things. The position of the brake pipe was a bit marginal at the point where it went into the back of the chassis. If the rear anti-roll bar was not done up tightly, it could touch the brake pipe, which is what happened. The pipe eventually broke and I had no rear brakes and two broken legs.

I was in hospital for quite some time and it was clear that I would not be racing for the rest of 1975. The compound fractures to the left fibula and tibia were pretty ugly and the surgeons had to do some grafting. I did not want to tell my parents. When I rang home a few days later and my mother asked how I was keeping, I pretended that everything was normal. I was living in the home of Ian Smith, the treasurer of the Aintree Car Club, and it was several weeks before I told my mother what had actually happened. I was on the verge of giving up completely, my view being that I'd given it my best shot and had a pretty good time. I had damaged my legs and ankles before, so perhaps this was the point at which I ought to stop.

It is funny how things happen. Towards the end of that summer, I received a call out of the blue from Terry McGovern. Terry looked after the cars driven by Ken Fildes, a well-known Irish racer. Ken had decided to move on and do other things and Terry wanted to know if I would be interested in racing Ken's Lotus 69. The Lotus may have been a bit long in the tooth but it was a beautiful car helped, in my patriotic view, by the fact that it was painted green and orange. Better than that, it was a Formula Atlantic car that, regardless of its age, represented an exciting leap from Formula Ford. I didn't need much persuading to accept the drive at Mondello Park.

I went very well that weekend and they decided to let me have another outing. This was, in effect, my first 'drive' as opposed to running my own car and doing everything myself. The deal was that I would pay for certain things, so I enlisted sponsorship from The Flooring Centre and from an old school mate from Synge Street, Tommy Hogan.

Tommy owned a chain of butcher's shops. He was quite an operator and very trendy – a new breed of butcher in the way he revolutionised the sale of meat in Dublin. The big hoteliers began to use him and, before we knew it, Tommy was the first of our local lads to be driving a nice Porsche. Tommy simply liked to be associated with cars, we were good friends and sponsoring my racing was an extension of his interest. It worked well because he would always be working on a Saturday and yet he was able to take the Porsche to Mondello on a Sunday, watch the racing, have a drink, meet a few girls and then go home.

It was very satisfactory all round, so much so that Terry moved the Lotus on and, between us, we managed to buy a March 74B. This was a Formula Atlantic car that had previously been raced by Alan Jones. The car may have had a fine pedigree, given that it had been driven by a man destined to become world champion with Williams in 1980, but it had a bent chassis that we knew nothing about until it was too late. Nonetheless, that did not stop me having fun in 1977 and, almost before I knew it, all of this had led to a sponsorship association that would have a massive effect on my life in racing. It also introduced me to one of the craftiest salesmen I have ever come across – and I've met a few.

It all began with Vivian Candy, a very clever guy who worked in the advertising world. Vivian raced saloon cars but, like everyone else, he wanted to progress and needed the money to do it. Vivian got wind of a possible deal with Philip Morris – David Kennedy likes to take the credit for tipping off Vivian, but I really don't recall that. Philip Morris knew all about the strength of advertising in motor sport since they had been associated with BRM and then McLaren in Formula 1. Their Marlboro brand was popular in Europe, and the UK was a growing market, but Philip Morris wanted to get into Ireland, which they knew would be a tougher nut to crack because the Marlboro cigarette, with its roasted tobacco, had a completely different taste from the more traditional Virginia blend that was popular in Ireland.

Vivian was very experienced in making presentations but he knew that his record in racing in the lower formulae was not strong enough to attract Marlboro. He needed a package of two cars, which is where I came in thanks to my profile in Formula Atlantic.

We put a proposal together and the key to it was that Philip Morris would come in on the back of a well-known name in Ireland. Vivian's suggestion was that Marlboro should join with another, like-minded, red and white sponsor known as Captain America, a burger chain. We went to Great Western House, near London Heathrow, to see George Macken, who was the sales and marketing director of Philip Morris UK, with responsibility for the budget for Ireland. A deal was agreed eventually – I would compete in Formula Atlantic while Vivian would race in Formula Ford – and we launched the programme at the IRAC in Dublin.

As an aside to all of this, Philip Morris appointed a sales manager in Ireland, Michael O'Flaherty. He was some operator, particularly when George came to Dublin to see how things were going. There is no doubt that this was a very difficult sales market to penetrate and Michael had his work cut out, but he was certainly not going to let George know about his lack of progress.

Every now and again Michael would say, 'Right lads, George is coming next week and I want you to get everything ready. Let's arrange to go to this nightclub and that place,' and so on. Michael would pick up George at the airport, drop him at his hotel and arrange to take him out for the night. That's when the fun would start because, of course, George would be looking for evidence of Marlboro's presence and, truth be told, there was not a great deal of it. So Michael went in to overdrive.

He planned the route he was going to take and, surprise, surprise, they would pass shop fronts carrying the Marlboro trademark cowboy and horse. Michael was the chippiest salesman I ever met. He was just dynamite, but George was no fool.

Michael would collect George at Jury's Hotel, the plan being to start the evening with a couple of pints at O'Donoghue's, a well-known pub on Merrion Row. Of course, Michael would have been there in advance, found the barman due to be on duty that night, slipped him a few quid and said, 'I want plenty of these cigarettes in stock over there, and a banner up here.' The barman would be quite happy to play along. That worked for as long as George actually went into O'Donoghue's but he soon got wise to Michael's tricks. The conversation would often go like this:

'No, let's not go in here, Michael. I want to go to that pub over there.'

'No you don't, George. Let's go in here because it's too rough for you over there.'

'No, it's all right. Looks OK to me. I'll take a chance. C'mon. Let's go to that one.'

Of course, I was in on all of this and knew my job would then be to divert George as much as possible while Michael went to work on the bar staff. I recall one particular occasion when we were suddenly diverted into O'Brien's, a legendary pub on Leeson Street. There was not a single sign – no sales pitch for Marlboro. I remember wondering, 'How on earth is Michael going to get out of this one?'

It got worse when George asked for 80 Marlboro and the barman said, 'Jayzus! Eighty did y'say? Hang on a sec, I don't think I have that many. Let me go and check.' Michael had already slipped him 40 to put up on the rack, knowing George would ask for them. The barman, a chancer to the manner born, was on to the scam immediately. 'Jayzus sir, would y'know, I'm down to my last forty. They're a great seller, grrrreat seller! Walkin' outa here like you wouldn't believe. Can't get enough of them.'

That barman became a legend. I don't think George was taken in but you had to admire the typically Irish way the game was being played. It was hilarious. Michael would stop at nothing. His eventual successor, Michael Brady from Belfast, was just as mad.

O'Flaherty knew George had a taste for Irish music and he arranged to have all the top musicians in town pitch up at whatever pub he had earmarked for George's visit. It was the usual story – just like Johnnie Fox's and the Step Inn – where, if you were inside at 11.30 p.m., they shut the door and you were there for good.

On one particular night, we were locked in a certain pub at 3 a.m., the music and drink were flying and the owner's son was with us in the bar. The family lived directly above the pub and the mother arrived downstairs, dressed in her nightdress. You could tell from her expression that this was not a social visit, far from it. Bear in mind that this was when the Troubles were really getting into their stride in the North and there was a fair amount of ill feeling in certain quarters. It turned out that this woman was a staunch Republican and she took exception to hearing George's English accent in her bar at 3 a.m. She was a ferocious woman, so we thought it best to make as quiet and as dignified a retreat as we could muster at that hour.

You could never be too careful, no matter which part of Ireland you were in – as I discovered during a hair-raising visit to Belfast. Marlboro Team Ireland had really taken off and, while Vivian was struggling a little in Formula Ford, I was going places in Formula Atlantic and taking a serious run at the Irish Championship in 1978.

The drivers I was up against included Patsy McGarrity, Brian Nelson, Richard Parsons and John L'Amie – serious competition that required me to have the best available car to take them on. I bought a Chevron B28, a really great racing car that was powered by engines built by Alan Smith, one of the best engine specialists in the UK. (As a demonstration of the small world we racing people live in, my engines were actually prepared in Derby by Mick Ainsley-Cowlishaw, who went on to become chief mechanic with Benetton when Michael Schumacher won the championship in 1994 and, more recently, reappeared as team manager with Super Aguri.)

At one point during the season, at Kirkistown, I had blown a head gasket by running the engine too hot and I needed the head re-ground. I whipped the engine out of the car and headed for the premises of Gerry Kinaine, a former racer who had promised to turn round the job in double-quick time, but I had overlooked two small details.

Part of the Marlboro Team Ireland package included a truck that I had bought and proudly painted in team colours, with an Irish Tricolour emblazoned on both sides. Kinaine's premises were on the Falls Road and I hadn't bothered to get proper directions. I took a wrong turning and found myself on the Shankill Road, the centre of the Protestant universe. I was so focused on getting the engine sorted in time to go racing for more championship points, that I never gave the political situation a second thought as I passed the Union Flags and the red, white and blue bunting while driving the truck deep into the heart of the Shankill. The Falls Road is the Catholic stronghold and the two areas are back-to-back. When I finally made my way to Kinaine's, one of the guys came out of the workshop and the blood drained from his face when I explained where I had been.

'Bloody hell!' he exploded. 'What the fuck did you think you were doing? This,' pointing to the truck with its Irish Tricolour, 'would've been torched, no problem, if the lads had seen it! They'll be waiting for you if you go back that way.'

I had absolutely no idea of the implications. I got the engine out, had the job done and hurried away. My heart was in my mouth as I followed the route back in case I took another wrong turning, but it was worth it because I was able to race and go on and win the championship. Not bad for someone who, at one stage, had been lying with his legs in the air contemplating retirement.

## Chapter 6

# MARIE THE METEOR

Even though I had no time for girlfriends, I did have an eye for a good-looking woman – my mother was always saying I paid too much attention to the fair sex, usually at the expense of my studies or work – but this passion for racing and doing deals was all-consuming. I enjoyed having a fun time and girls were part of that.

One of my earlier casual relationships was with Gill, the sister of a very great friend, Des Large. Des was a musician and we were as thick as thieves – an appropriate analogy, perhaps, given some of the tricks we got up to when I was buying and selling cars. I recall going to his house one Christmas Day. The Large family were Protestants, who were obviously in the minority in Dublin, but they stuck to tradition to the extent that everything in the household stopped at 3 p.m. in order to listen to the Queen's speech.

I had spent the day with my extended family, running around Dublin in my car and then visiting Brian Wallace – known by one and all as 'Wallier' – an advertising executive with two very impressive accounts, Nissan and Beamish, a competitor of Guinness. It goes without saying that one of the attractions of visiting Wallier was a barrel of Beamish that was on tap all day. I don't know what came over me but I was wearing a browny green velvet suit and a dickie bow. I must have looked a complete idiot. I would hate to see a photograph.

In due course, I went to the Large house to meet Gill. Mrs Large and most of the family were present and I was keen to impress. I had not met Gill and Des's mother before and when, in polite but curious conversation, she asked me where I went to school, I said, 'Sandford Park.' Des almost choked on his drink. He could not believe what he was hearing. Sandford Park was a small, very select school – for Protestants. I only knew of it because a friend of mine, Tom Jenkinson, had gone there. I have no idea what possessed me to say that. It was like Billy Connolly saying he had been to Eton or Harrow.

I was a chancer and thought I could get away with anything. So, I just spat it out. Des was in convulsions. It was so stupid because Mrs Large, being a member of the comparatively small Protestant community, could have asked me if I knew such-and-such a person and I would have been completely exposed and made to look an even bigger clown as I sat there in my dickie bow and browny green velvet suit. It was one of the stupidest things I've ever done, but another example of me taking a flyer and it working.

When I met Des a few days later, he said, 'I can't believe what you did!' He then told me his marriage was breaking up and he would like to sell his house in Greystones, a small town farther down the coast. Quick as a flash I said, 'I'm the man to do that for you. I'll do it for half the commission charged by anyone else.' Whether through shock or resignation, Des agreed.

I placed an advert in the local paper, saying that viewing would be on Sunday. I spent the whole day there, sold the house and met Des in Jury's Hotel. He got together with the prospective purchaser and they had exchanged and completed in about five weeks. Job done. The next step was to find Des a new partner.

We used to frequent a disco every Friday night at Leopardstown, the horseracing course south of Dublin. A friend, Peter Lynch, turned up one night with a young blonde. I say 'young' because I was 28 at the time and this girl was only 18. I had spotted her before with Peter at an auto test somewhere and I remember him saying she was not really my kind of girl. Whether he could see what was coming, I don't know but I do know that when I saw this tall blonde again at Leopardstown, I made further enquiries. I discovered she was Marie McCarthy, a basketball player for the Ireland Under 21s, which figured because Marie was seriously fit.

I had a girlfriend at the time, Mona O'Reilly. Mona would accompany me quite regularly to the races and make the sandwiches and so on. She was a really nice girl and her family were rallying people with a very successful agency for the motor oil STP.

One evening, Mona and I were at Stella House, a regular haunt because there would usually be live music, which was another important part of my life. Marie was there on her own – well, not exactly on her own. She was with her sister, who was going out with Paul Ashford, another friend who was also playing in the band. There was no sign of Peter Lynch. I discovered that Marie was leaving later that night for a cheap holiday in Greece with her sister and another friend.

I took Mona home and headed straight to Dublin airport, arriving in time to learn that Marie's plane had been delayed. I blagged my way through customs and immigration and what security there was in those days, particularly at around midnight, finding it no trouble at all to get into the departure lounge and down to the gates. I had an announcement made, asking Marie McCarthy to come to the information desk. Marie had the shock of her life. Being the youngest of the group, she was quite shy and highly embarrassed. Nevertheless, even if she did not admit it at first, she was rather impressed by this little episode, although less so when she later discovered that I had more or less ended the relationship with Mona that night. Marie and I wrote to each other while she was away and I was waiting at the airport when she returned two weeks later. That was the start of the relationship.

Marie played basketball for the Meteors, who were Irish champions. Despite the difference in their ages, Marie's three sisters were in the same team. Several of the Meteors' players made it to international level, including Marie, who was probably one of the youngest full internationals ever at that time. I used to go to watch her play and as the team used to travel quite a bit to matches, it seemed only natural that she should come with me to the races. In fact, one of our earliest trips was to a rally in Cork but such was the delicacy of the situation that Marie brought her neighbour, Katrina Bramach, along for the ride. I slept in the bath, my only company being a pillow.

By the time the Phoenix Park races came round in the late summer, Marie's parents made the trip specifically to meet me. It was the first time they had come to a motor race. Marie and I were more than just mates at the time and I remember this being seen as quite a serious development. That's the way it was in those days. In the meantime, I had introduced Des to Marie's sister, Ann, saying if anything came of it, he would have to buy me a set of tyres for my Formula Atlantic car. He married Ann. I had saved him money on the sale of his house but the little introduction to his new wife cost him about £350!

Marie and I were very happy because I had my racing and Marie was really into her basketball. Whereas Mona had been smart appearance and neat sandwiches, Marie was jeans and bacon butties. We would meet at lunchtimes, usually on a Friday, and go to the Hibernian Hotel. Being a Friday, the day that *Autosport* arrived in the shops in Dublin, this was my first opportunity to devour the weekly motor-sport bible. The time might pass without either of us saying a great deal but we enjoyed each other's company, shared our interests and had a great time together. One trip, however, was usually reserved for the boys – the annual pilgrimage to the British Grand Prix at Silverstone.

There would be a massive exodus of Irish fans and we would join them, usually in a Transit van that could hide a multitude of sins. Not only would this be our mobile home – and I will not begin to describe the state of the interior once we had finished with it – but the van would also be a kind of Trojan horse. We would pool the cash we had in order to pay the entrance fee for the two occupants of the front of the van. Meanwhile, half of Dublin would be buried beneath the sleeping bags and rubbish in the back. There was not the rigid security you see now at Silverstone and I reckon the amateur gatemen did not dare venture too deeply inside a rickety van driven by a couple of ragged, unwashed Irishmen.

Silverstone was Mecca, the place of our dreams. If you had told me, as we drove through the main gate, that the field behind me would one day provide the headquarters for my grand-prix team, I would have said you had been drinking too much the night before in Silverstone village – which we usually had. The craic was great and you can imagine a bunch of fast-talking Irishmen – would-be world champions all – moving among the local girls in the Silverstone pubs.

Come the next day it was down to serious business as we watched the men we aspired to be, if we ever grew up. It is hard to believe now that such pillars of motor-racing society as Derek Daly, David Kennedy and Eddie Jordan were engaging in such shenanigans. Our favourite vantage point was the advertising hoarding overlooking Copse Corner. Apart from providing an uninterrupted view of this very fast right-hander at the end of the pit straight, it cost nothing and was high enough to keep us out of security's reach – thanks to the noise on the track, we pretended not to hear the official's plea to come down. In later years, all of us had to pay to get in, but it was worth it because, without question, this was the highlight of our social year in motor sport. We would head for home more determined than ever to make the grade on this side of the Irish Sea.

Boosted by winning the Irish Formula Atlantic Championship in 1978, I made plans to race in the British F3 Championship, which would mean basing myself in England, but I had a much more important mission before I could even contemplate racing another mile. On 25 January 1979, Marie and I were married at St Joseph's Church in Terenure, Dublin.

I took six months' leave of absence from the bank but Marie was being trained as a computer programmer with Price Waterhouse and she had to see out that month of training before coming across the water. Marie was leaving all her friends behind and giving up a great deal.

We rented a house in Brackley and stayed there for six months but, having gone back to Dublin for Christmas, we found we had nowhere to stay on our return. Alan Docking gave us a bedroom in his house and we joined the scrum at breakfast each morning because Alan, being an Australian team owner, always had plenty of people passing through. It was a concept Marie and I would come to understand very well.

We bought our first house in Silverstone village for £3,000. It was an old property with two small rooms upstairs and a living area below. Built on to that was the kitchen and the outside bathroom. There was no central heating and animals in every corner – spiders, flies, you name it. We kitted it out for about £5. We paid 50p for the fridge and maybe as much as a pound for the sofa. The wardrobes were 50p and the bed another pound. That might sound bizarre now but this was house-clearance stuff from a Northamptonshire auctioneer.

It was so cold that ice formed inside the house and we would fight over who was going to be first to get into the freezing bed. We lived there for about two years and, during that time, Marie worked as a packer for General Foods and then an electrical company, earning around £1.25 an hour, which helped to pay for the food.

A large, derelict garage at the bottom of our garden had its own driveway, and I realised that it would be suitable for a barn-type conversion. A planning application was lodged and, when we were later offered £13,500 for the whole property, we jumped at it. Allied Irish Banks had just opened a branch in Northampton. I was their fifth customer. Based on the profit we had just made, the bank was more than happy to bridge the gap to allow us to pay £23,000 for our next house in Hillside Avenue in Silverstone.

This took us into the role of landlords. The house was modern, semi-detached and had five bedrooms. We offered bed and breakfast and took in lodgers, nearly all of whom were teenaged wannabe racing drivers, some of them a long way from home. Marie did all the cooking, washing and ironing for our guests, in return for which we received about £40 a week from each and enjoyed the benefit of having built-in babysitters for our first child, Zoë.

It was a shoestring operation that just about paid for itself. Our payday was the British Grand Prix, when we would pack as many as 17 people into every conceivable space. It was hard work but fun. Our hope was that it would be worth it in the end. However, even allowing for my sometimes wild ambition, I could never have imagined what lay in store.

## Chapter 7

# ANOTHER FEW BRICKS IN THE WALL

It seems ridiculous thinking about it now, but Marlboro Team Ireland went racing in 1979 with Stefan Johansson, a Swede who looked and sounded as Irish as Zinedine Zidane, and the team rarely raced inside the Irish border. That was the result of some fancy footwork designed to get me across the water to the UK. I had done well at home but it was obvious that the way forward had to be competing against the top names in England and beyond. The problem, as ever, was finding someone to pay for it.

A possible solution had come to mind the previous year. Attempts to give the Irish Formula Atlantic Championship an international edge had resulted in races being held in England. I won the first Atlantic race at Donington and it struck me that this race actually generated more publicity for Marlboro in Ireland than the all the Irish races put together when we had won the Atlantic Championship at home. It took a while for this to sink in but Marlboro eventually grasped it.

For me, this seemed to be a crafty way of receiving a budget allocated to Ireland without actually having to race there. In fact, it would turn out to be very satisfactory all round. Marlboro were able to make much of the fact that they were behind what appeared to be a scholarship programme. They had supported a driver at home and then given him a chance he might not otherwise have had to go racing outside Ireland. It was also useful for Marlboro to follow this line because concerns were beginning to be raised in certain quarters about the rights and wrongs of tobacco advertising.

From where I stood, it was good from more than just a financial point of view. I was bringing a big name into the lower levels of the sport. That image helped attract television documentary makers to film Marlboro Team Ireland. Marlboro were quick to promote the strong human message along the lines of: 'We've seen someone who is promising, we've given him a chance and now we're going along with him as part of the Marlboro World Championship Team to see just how far he can go.' All of that meant that later I was able to go off to Australia and New Zealand to participate in some small races there. I also went to Trinidad and Tobago, as well as Guyana and Brazil. It was cool for Marlboro to have a driver in the junior category of motor racing world wide, never mind what it was doing for the career of Eddie Jordan as he grabbed his chance in Formula 3.

The British F3 Championship was the only place to be. Chris Witty, a former journalist, became team manager, looking after Stefan, Irishman Bernard Devaney and me, all three of us racing for the Donegal oil baron, Derek McMahon, but with that vital support from Marlboro Ireland.

There was only one other Marlboro driver in the championship – Andrea de Cesaris. He had enjoyed the backing of Marlboro Italy for most of his career because of his father's links in the Italian tobacco business. Ranged against us were a number of British hopefuls, among them a driver destined to become world champion, not that you would have known it at the time. In 1979, Nigel Mansell was considered to be no more than average, certainly no better than most of us. The quick drivers of the day were Mike Thackwell from New Zealand, Kenny Acheson from Northern Ireland, Chico Serra from Brazil, and de Cesaris. Serra and de Cesaris were pushing for the championship – quite literally, in the case of Andrea.

The season was coming to a close when we went to Oulton Park in September. A shunt in the early stages of the race meant a restart, and Thackwell led from Serra, Acheson and me. Having got ahead of Serra in the first part of the race, de Cesaris was keen to do the same again and I was watching out for him because I knew he would be getting desperate if Serra was ahead and looking good for the championship.

Mansell was behind me, with Andrea climbing all over the back of his car. It was incredible. Each time I looked in the mirror, I would see them side-by-side, first one in front, then the other. I knew de Cesaris was going to have a shunt with someone and I just hoped it would be Mansell, because I was next in line and there was no way I was going to let him through, particularly as I was going so well.

The inevitable happened – and I would not have wished the accident on my worst enemy. De Cesaris must have tried to get alongside again because his front wheel went under Mansell's rear. When that happens, the car in front goes cartwheeling into the air. It was a massive accident. Mansell suffered a crushed vertebra but, when I saw the wreckage, I thought it would be a lot worse. I lost concentration for a short while but managed to hang on and finish fourth. Serra clinched the championship and all de Cesaris had to show was another damaged car.

It was typical of Andrea at the time. He was incredibly quick but very inconsistent. All sorts of theories went round about why this should be, the most popular being that de Cesaris couldn't see where he was going for some of the lap. He had a small problem with an eye defect. His pupils would sometimes roll into the top of his head, leaving literally nothing but the whites of his eyes showing for a fleeting second. Thankfully, the problem disappeared later in life but, at the time, there was a view that he should not be driving on the roads, never mind on a racetrack.

Whatever the reasons were, he had a lot of shunts and earned the nickname 'De Crasheris'. Right enough, there were some pretty spectacular incidents. The one I recall, over and above that incident at Oulton Park, was when he barrel-rolled his McLaren in spectacular fashion during the race morning warm-up for the Austrian Grand Prix – and this after his mechanics had been up half the night rebuilding his car following another crash the previous day.

I don't believe he ever broke a bone in his body. Andrea had a miracle approach. He went into everything at a million miles an hour, hoping that he would emerge intact at the other end, which he usually did, albeit it sideways and perhaps on the grass. He was, to put it mildly, a very exciting driver and he did calm down and mature to such an extent that we had no hesitation in using him later on as one of our drivers when Jordan went into F1. He was such an adorable guy and he did an absolutely first-class job for us, but in 1979, he was a bit wild, as that incident with Mansell proved.

We were very fortunate to have some brilliant circuits as part of the F3 Championship. Oulton Park was one, Cadwell Park another. Cadwell was one of my all-time favourites. We used to go up to Lincolnshire the night before and stay at Skegness. Stefan and I would often have a few drinks and go clubbing – drivers used to do things like that, even though they would be racing the next day. You often needed a drink to steady yourself after the race at Cadwell because it always seemed a miracle if you managed to get through the first corner without incident. And, when that corner was safely negotiated, there was the Mountain, a steep hill where cars became airborne at the crest. It was massive. The car simply took off.

In 1979, they stopped the race and we could not understand why because there was no sign of anyone having had an accident. That was because de Cesaris had disappeared off the road, left the track completely and dropped into a hollow with a marsh at the bottom. He almost sank without trace. The only clue was steam rising from the hot, semi-submerged car. Once again, he walked away completely unharmed.

We had started off in 1979 with Chevrons, changing to the more competitive March as the season went on. The following year, I switched to a Ralt. Designed and built by Ron Tauranac, former partner of Jack Brabham, the Ralt was to be the backbone of many a championship thanks to its straightforward and reliable engineering. It was a move forward for me and marked the beginning of an association with Ralt that would continue through most of my days as an entrant in F3.

Nigel Mansell, meanwhile, had stuck to March but that became irrelevant when he made the massive step into Formula 1 during 1980. This was due to the foresight of Colin Chapman, the boss of Lotus, who saw something in Nigel that I have to confess escaped me – and many others – at the time. It was typical of Chapman's intuitive genius, an instinct that was particularly apparent when it came to designing and engineering racing cars.

Known affectionately as 'Chunky' because of the few extra pounds that would appear from time to time around his waist, Chapman was, in my view, one of the cleverest men ever to sit at a drawing board. Some said he was perhaps a bit too clever at times, but I wouldn't know about that. His innovative ideas – the monocoque chassis, the aerodynamic wedge-shaped car, the introduction of 'ground effect' that rewrote the thinking on a car's aerodynamics – put him streets ahead of his rivals. It was a complete travesty when he died of a heart attack in 1982 at the age of 54.

His death was a serious blow to F1 for lots of reasons, not least because Chapman was one of the few individuals to have the complete respect of Bernie Ecclestone.

You would frequently hear Bernie mutter, 'If Chunky was alive now, he wouldn't have stood for that,' or, 'Colin wouldn't have done that,' or, 'Chunky wouldn't have given a fuck about this, that and the other!' Bernie would never talk like that about people for whom he had no respect.

Chapman had what we thought was a curious respect for Mansell. I was one of the sceptics because I felt that Mansell, at that stage, was not much better than I was. But Chunky had seen Nigel's will to win, a total self-belief that would carry him through. The strange thing was that his extraordinary determination was not matched by ability on the track. He seemed to be injury and incident prone but, 12 years later, Chapman was proved correct when Mansell became world champion.

In the meantime, I had not been making the progress I had hoped and began to realise I would never be a top-line driver, but that left plenty of scope to pick up drives in sportscar racing. This, in turn, led to a shared drive in a twin-turbo Porsche 908, one of the most awesome cars it has been my pleasure to drive. Apart from brute power, it was not exactly state of the art. The chassis was tubular frame, a form of construction that was rapidly becoming old-fashioned. Nonetheless, I put this rocket ship on the front row at Monza and drove about four or five races. At the Nurburgring, the veteran German driver Herbie Muller was driving the Porsche. During the race, he collided with the Coca Cola Porsche of Bobby Rahal. The impact ruptured the fuel cell and, within seconds, the Porsche was an inferno. All they were able to find of Herbie was his gold tooth. He was a great character and a terrible loss.

The Le Mans 24-Hour race was not long after this and I found myself at the wheel of the Pink Floyd entry thanks to Nick Mason having to miss the race. This had been a dilemma for Nick because he had to give up his love of racing in order to take his more familiar role of drummer at the Brick In The Wall concert at Earls Court.

Steve O'Rourke, Pink Floyd's manager, wanted money from me to drive the car, a BMW M1, and I wanted money from him to drive the car. We never did resolve the problem and, many years later, we still joked about who owed who. Ssdly, Steve died but he could never understand how some of my sponsors wound up on the nose of his car without the team actually receiving any money. I told Steve that this was normal with me and, in any case, it was better to have sponsors on the car than none at all. I'm not sure he was convinced.

Le Mans is extraordinary for a number of reasons, not least the Mulsanne Straight. There is nothing like it anywhere in motor racing. It is unique because this is a public road for 51 weeks of the year. On a motor-racing circuit, there is no crown in the middle of the track but at Le Mans, it is very different. In a road car, you would think of it as an ordinary piece of highway. In a Le Mans car doing 200mph, you suddenly realise that, unless you are absolutely in the middle of the road and on the crown, the car will be pulled to one side or the other. You are focusing on getting past cars that are travelling perhaps 30mph slower and, at the same time, coming up behind will be someone like Derek Bell in a Porsche 956 doing 230mph. If you move off line, it's a struggle to stay on the road. As a result, the driver about to be overtaken never really wants to move away from the central line. The attitude is: 'If you wanna come by, find your own way. Good luck.'

You try to play the game and move off your line a little but, all the while, you're telling yourself not to lift off the throttle. In addition, there are all sorts of variables that need to be taken into consideration. You might have rejoined after a pit stop and have a lot of fuel on board. Maybe you have new brake pads and are trying to bed everything in while, at the same time, getting your eye back in. Meanwhile, you are running in company with someone who is coming to the end of his run. His car is light on fuel and he's in the groove, totally pumped up and really pushing on. It's scary, very scary.

Le Mans in 1981 turned out to be one of the hottest on record. I was sharing with David Hobbs and, unfortunately on this occasion, we were in an enclosed car. It was hideous in that cockpit. The mood was not helped by a number of fatal accidents. In one, Frenchman Jean-Louis Lafosse was killed, while another took the lives of two marshals.

Usually, there are three drivers per car, but David and I could probably have managed reasonably comfortably had it not been so hot. The trouble was that there was a difference in height, David being quite a bit taller than me. So we each did three stints in succession in order to avoid having to lift seats and padding in and out of the car. We really suffered as a result. Two stints would be normal in order to give one driver a break and yet not cause too much fatigue for the driver at the wheel.

I was completely dehydrated and there was very little air getting in to the cockpit to chase away the fuel and oil fumes and the dust from the brakes. Then I arrived on the scene of the Lafosse accident not long after it had happened. There was debris everywhere. It was a terrible mess. I remember vomiting my guts up, one of the very few times I've done that in motor racing.

I really did wish we had three drivers. That would have meant driving for an hour and a half, which can be really enjoyable, and then having three hours off. David and I could have done 90 minutes on and 90 minutes off, but that doesn't work. The problem is that you may be out of the car but your adrenaline remains high for some time and yet you need to have something to eat, rehydrate yourself and have a massage. All the while you are looking at your watch because the 90 minutes goes really quickly. The other difficulty is you have to be continually at the ready in case the other driver comes in early and the team decides to refuel and start another stint. Having said all that, when the engine failed with two hours remaining, we were all massively disappointed. Having endured everything thus far, we felt cheated.

As soon as our race was over, Marie drove us back as quickly as she could because we wanted to make it to the Pink Floyd concert that night. We got to Earls Court in time and went backstage. James Hunt was there and so, too, was Alain de Cadenet who, like me, had dashed back from Le Mans.

Alain and I had been involved in an incident during the race and things became a bit heated that evening in the aftermath of Lafosse's fatal accident. We had been running behind the pace car at one stage. On these occasions, drivers are supposed to behave themselves and run line-astern at slow speed behind the official car. The race is on hold, as it were. Overtaking is not permitted. De Cadenet had tried to pass me, but I wasn't having it. I smacked into his car, which was my way of saying, 'Get back and behave! These are the fucking rules! OK?' I had been hardened during my time in F3 and if Alain wanted to pass me with an illegal move, I was going to get stuck into him, which I did.

Backstage, de Cadenet started slagging me off for blocking him. I remember James saying '15 Love' and then shouting '15 All!' when I replied. There was some outrageous behaviour between Alain and myself that night and, for all of James's efforts to lighten the debate, it took quite some time to mend our relationship.

Everyone in the band wanted to know how we had got on in the race but I found it difficult to answer. Everything seemed a blur to me. I was so exhausted. The concert was wonderful and it was a privilege to be there but, despite such an incredible distraction on stage, visions from the race kept flashing back. It was a sign that Le Mans was one of the toughest things I have done in racing and in life. I did it a couple of times and each time I thought, 'Why am I doing this? I don't need to do this!' It is one of those things that you savour after the event rather than during it. It was also no coincidence that I had begun to think about stopping. It was time to concentrate on the guys who really could drive.

## Chapter 8

# JOHN BOY

I had a meeting with an extraordinary woman in the Granby Bar in Parnell Square, a strong Republican area of Dublin and a place where the ladies of the night looked their best. Mrs Walton, in her fifties, was tiny, very slim and slugging down pints of Guinness with whiskey chasers like there was no tomorrow. The bar was a stopping-off point on her way from Coolock to The Irene, a well-known dance hall in the city centre. Coolock is a tough area on Dublin's North Side and going to a dance was clearly a great means of escape. I had rather the same thing in mind for her son and I was trying to persuade Mrs Walton that it would be a good thing if he came to England and worked for me as a mechanic.

I had first met John Walton when a friend brought him along to Phoenix Park and he helped with my Atlantic car. There was something about him. As well as being a gifted mechanic, he was a good-looking boy with a twinkle in his eye that would lead to all sorts of trouble. 'John Boy', as he quickly became known, was clearly his mother's son – if it's in the ram, it's in the lamb', as they say. John was a laid-back but determined individual, a survivor brought up the hard way. His father had died some time before and he and his mother had worked hard to make ends meet. We had kept in touch and I very much wanted him to come with me to England, but first, I had to make sure that 'The Mammy' was in favour. Fortunately, she was. John Boy and I were about to start an incredible roller-coaster ride, a frequently hilarious and sometimes stormy relationship that would last for more than 15 years.

There was no doubt in my mind that I was going to stop racing. When I bought a Ralt Formula 3 car for 1981, I never intended to drive it. I had named my team Eddie Jordan Racing in 1980 and now I was going to run it rather than simply do everything, including the driving. I picked up drivers here and there, quick guys who had a bit of money or a bit of promise. David Sears was one and David Leslie was another. David Sears had actually driven our first race at the end of the previous season at Thruxton. David Leslie was a really good driver who did not have enough belief in his own ability, which was a pity because he had so many good things about him.

I was working closely with Tim Clowes, an insurance broker who loved and understood motor racing. Tim was a huge fan of James Weaver, a young Englishman who had shown a great deal of promise. I put him in the car for the 1982 Marlboro British F3 Championship. James turned in some great performances particularily towards the end of 1982, not in the British F3 but when we entered the non-clashing European championship. He won at Donnington, came second at Silverstone and finished the season with two wins at Nogaro and Jarama. But the man of the moment turned out to be Tommy Byrne, arguably one of motor sport's greatest unrealised talents. Unfortunately for me, the Irishman was driving for a rival team run by Murray Taylor.

We had no money and ran the team on fresh air. Murray Taylor had decent backing, so much so that he could often afford to install new gear ratios for the race. We would wait until his used ratios and dog rings had been thrown in the trashcan and then fish them out because, whatever their condition, they would be in a better state than those fitted to our car. Failing that, we would sift through our collection of well-worn ratios and choose the set we thought might have the best chance of lasting the race. Despite this shortfall in decent equipment, we had our moments with James. One of them, however, was memorable for all the wrong reasons.

Monaco was not only the most important race for F1 people, it was also the showcase event for F3, precisely because anyone who was anyone in motor sport would be present, and it was such a difficult race to win. We had entered James and travelled to the south of France, very hopeful of a good result. James had won the Donington round of the European series when that championship visited Britain, and there seemed to be no reason why we should not be in the running for the so-called Jewel in the Crown.

There was only one problem – James failed to sign on. For a racing driver, signing on should be as routine and automatic as putting his trousers on in the morning. James arrived just as they were closing for the day and was told to come back the following morning. Whatever the distraction was – he was doing sponsorship work or some such – he completely forgot.

I was furious. We tried every trick in the book and eventually looked for the sympathy vote, pleading that we had come a long way, but the organisers would have none of it. James's girlfriend, an excitable Kiwi at the best of times, even went so far as to seek out Bernie Ecclestone and tell him she would 'do anything to get James into the race', but to no avail. Weaver was out. Then, just to add to our misery, a second car I had entered for Philippe Colonna blew its engine during qualifying and he failed to make the race as well. This was massively disappointing for all the obvious reasons. I was particularly upset because Eddie Jordan Racing was trying to make its name as a competitive and respectable team.

I had managed to get backing for Weaver from Racing for Britain, a scheme designed to foster young talent. The idea was to invite members of the public to join the club and do their bit for future British champions. The British Racing Drivers' Club was also involved and I was in the process of building up a good relationship with the BRDC and with Jimmy Brown, chairman of Silverstone Circuits, the BRDC's landlord. For various reasons – not the least being a sponsorship cheque for £20,000 made out to Eddie Jordan Racing – I was a huge fan of the scheme, which helped everyone and involved the much-abused spectators. I knew that there would be a considerable number of British enthusiasts making the trip to

Monaco, many of them members of Racing for Britain rooting for James in the F3 race as he took on the vast numbers of French and Italians. After such a frustrating and embarrassing cock-up, there was only one thing to do.

At least at Monaco, there was no shortage of places to have a beer, albeit an expensive one. Choice was dictated by the size of your wallet although, the previous year, Marie and I had shown just what could be done. I had used my Marlboro connections to wangle two free tickets to the Grand Prix Ball, supposedly an exclusive reserve for F1 people and the high rollers who could afford to pay the outrageous admission.

We did not have two French francs to rub together but I was determined to go. Marie had come down to Monaco with our first-born, Zoë, and we were living in a caravan. When I say 'we', I mean the entire team, such as it was. John Boy and another mechanic, Mal, were staying with us. Mal, a Kiwi, was travelling Europe and he loved motor sport. He worked for nothing and lived under the caravan. John had more luxurious accommodation – a hammock slung inside the caravan. There was no running water, of course, so we showered in salt water on the beach.

Our car that weekend was being driven by Brett Riley, a very quick New Zealander. This was a deal arranged with another entrant, Dave Price. The going rate to enter the Monaco F3 race was about £5,000. Dave called me and said Riley was a very useful guy – 'a potential winner', I think were his words – but Riley had only £1,500 to pay for the drive. I thought I would take a chance, although I felt sure someone – probably Pricey himself – was having me over. Brett's gearbox blew up on the first day of practice and John Boy had to get stuck in and fix it. As John and Mal were doing that, I emerged from the caravan wearing a tuxedo, with Marie alongside looking a million dollars in a fabulous red dress, which cost her 50p in Oxfam. You can imagine the comments from the other team bosses who had not been invited.

While I was networking like mad at the ball, John Boy was up most of the night working on the car. It was worth the effort because Riley qualified comfortably, a good enough reason to have a decent meal that night in Pulchinellas. Dave Price had found this Italian restaurant tucked away in a side street within earshot of the track. Run by Carlo and Angie, Pulchinellas became – and has remained – a great favourite of everyone in motor racing.

Dave and his business partner John Bracey would usually accompany us. We got on well and I think they had a soft spot for Eddie Jordan Racing. We could never boast the kind of equipment David Price Racing had available, but Pricey would always help out. At times, certainly during my early days as an entrant, Dave would have thought you had received a bang on the head if you suggested that Eddie Jordan would one day run an F1 team – and win four grands prix. Every time we had dinner together, and this meal in Pulchinellas was no exception, Pricey would remind me of some the more lurid tales of our early days. His favourite concerned a F3 race the previous year at Dijon.

This was in 1980, when I was doing less driving but taking part in a fun event in Tobago for Marlboro. While I was away, I received a call from Wyatt Stanley in Birmingham. Wyatt, a great friend of the UB40 group, was an amateur racer and he wanted to drive our F3 car at Dijon. We agreed a deal and John Boy was waiting with the truck and racing car when I flew back to Heathrow. We drove to Dijon where we discovered the hotel room was so small that there was nowhere for John to sleep. Fortunately, one of Dave Price's mechanics offered him space on the floor of his room.

Wyatt qualified near the back of the grid and I was with him just before the start. John Boy had left us to it and when the call came to start engines, I realised he had gone off with the jump battery. I went into a mild panic. Pricey likes to tell everyone that I was shouting, 'John Boy! Where's the fucking jump battery?' I am not sure that is true because, as Dave says, I would have been hard-pressed to know how or where to attach the leads of the battery, had it been there. That side of things was, shall we say, not my territory.

I would talk to the driver and he would say that the car was understeering or oversteering. I would rattle a few spanners around and make small adjustments here and there and that would be it. The driver would return to the track and immediately go faster, thinking I had been the mechanical equivalent of Einstein when, in fact, I had done next to nothing. Having been a driver, I know how important motivation and self-belief actually are, a fact that many technical people tend to overlook as they bury themselves, almost literally, in the nuts and bolts of making a racing car go quickly. The best adjustment can quite often be in the driver's head.

In any case, I had quickly become a legend for my lack of mechanical sympathy, Dave Price never hesitating to remind everyone that I once sent out a car with the jump battery still attached and dragging along the pit lane. On another occasion, when I was 'engineering' Stefan Johansson in Macau, I failed to tighten the wheel nuts and he reappeared after one lap with three wheels on his car. My speciality was the dealing and the finance, which brings us back to Wyatt Stanley at Dijon.

Wyatt had agreed to pay about £1,700 but he failed to tell me that the money would come in tenpence pieces! Wyatt owned a number of bingo halls in Birmingham and, as he did not have time to go to the bank before leaving, he brought his stock to France and handed over sacks of coins.

'Jayzus, Wyatt!' I exploded. 'What the fuck am I supposed to do with this?' Everyone fell about.

We found a home for the money surprisingly quickly, being absolutely skint at the time. I used the cash to pay for tyres, fuel – everything. It vanished instantly. Despite all that, I had great affection for Wyatt. He was a very honourable man, very 'old school', and he had a few more races with us.

Those stories came out round the table at Pulchinellas in 1981. After dinner, we walked to the Tip Top bar, which is actually on the side of the racetrack, on the downhill plunge from Casino Square to Mirabeau corner. The Tip Top had great years in the 1960s and

1970s but I always felt we were being ripped off there. My personal preference had always been Rosie's Bar, farther down the hill towards the harbour. Rosie was a little darling and it was a great shame when she was forced to sell. Like it or not, the Tip Top had become an institution and it was the obvious place to go for a nightcap, but I could see that John Boy had more of a twinkle in his eye than usual. Just was we were leaving, he pointed to a smaller, more sophisticated bar farther down the road.

'I'm just going to nip in there for one more,' he said.

I reminded him that the race was the next day and he had been up for most of the previous night working on the car. I may as well have talked to the immaculately whitewashed wall outside the bar.

The following morning, the hammock was empty. That was not unusual because John was a good-looking guy and sometimes he would get lucky, but as the deadline approached and there was still no sign of him, I began to get annoyed. There was work to do and, as I've said, my mechanical skills were limited. By the time the drivers were getting ready to leave the paddock, I was fit to be tied. People were giving me a wide birth. Now I was worried for reasons other than getting on with this race. Where was John Boy? Had he been in a fight? Had he been knocked down? Was he lying in hospital somewhere, unable to communicate? Should we get the police?

Meanwhile, I was quickly going mental just trying to add the right amount of fuel to the car. I had to ask whether this was actually the correct fuel and I remember having to siphon some of it back out of the car because I had lost track of how much I had put in.

John arrived at the last minute. I could see everyone grinning and looking our way because word had got out and they thought I was going to explode. John Boy was still dressed in his gear from the night before and it was clear that he had not been to bed. I was thoroughly pissed off and not in the mood for pleasantries. I did not say a word. When I'm *really* angry, I go quiet.

Brett Riley finished the race in eighth place, which, for us, was a fantastic result because the French and Italian drivers filled most of the top places and we were the best of the British entries. I still had not spoken to John about whatever he had been up to prior to the race. That would be settled almost immediately by an unexpected turn of events.

As a result of the team doing so well, I was approached by John Vos, a driver who was interested in racing our car on his home track at Zandvoort in Holland. We settled on a figure. The only problem was the race was the following weekend and the deal included a test session at the track on the Tuesday. Zandvoort was not exactly next door. Since I would be towing the caravan with Marie and Zoë in the car, John Boy faced a very long drive in the truck – and he would have to leave more or less straightaway.

This was important because, not only had we won some much-needed prize money at Monaco, the Zandvoort trip would be a good little earner. Fortunately, all of this had helped calm me down when I opened negotiations with John. We got talking about what had happened.

Sure enough, he had met a woman. Even though she spoke very little English and he spoke no French, they had a great time and ended up at her place. That was fine until the morning, when John left for work and discovered that her apartment was outside the boundary of the circuit. Of course, he had no pass, no means of getting through the gate. So he had to blag his way all the way back to the paddock. Knowing John Boy, this sounded very plausible indeed.

Now I had to ask him to sort out the car, change the gearbox and drive the whole lot to Zandvoort by Monday afternoon so that the car would be ready to run first thing on Tuesday morning. John said he could do it, and he managed to get there despite no sleep on Thursday night and, I assume, very little on Friday, the night before the race.

John Vos paid his money up front. He was involved with a chain of what might best be described as clubs, involving all sorts of things. John Boy was taken to one of them and he said you really did not want to go there. Apparently, it was unbelievable.

We stayed in a small guesthouse for a few days and it was like a mini holiday. Zandvoort is by the sea and you could sit outside, enjoying a beer and the most delightful chips and mayonnaise. The Dutch are lovely people, very proud of their country. They reminded me in many ways of the Irish, and John Boy was about to give us a reminder of how the Irish could operate. We were in for a repeat of Monaco.

It started in exactly the same way. We were making our way back to the guesthouse when John excused himself and sidestepped into a bar. There was no sign of him at breakfast and no sign of him at the track. At around lunchtime, a soft-topped BMW – one of the first I had seen – arrived with a very grand blonde girl at the wheel. Perched beside her was none other than John Boy.

John had the most 'come-to-bed' eyes anyone had ever seen. Girls fell for him so easily – they just ran away with him. This girl turned out to be a pharmacist in the town and John was with her for the rest of the weekend. His work did not suffer one bit. That was the point. John Walton was able to work all night, then drink copious amounts of Guinness, smoke like a train and stay out most of the next night. He was of slight build, but he had the constitution of an ox.

The guy was a legend. He was young and carefree – well, reasonably so. John had a wife and twins back in Ireland. Then he had a child with another woman, who came after him with a vengeance when he moved out and came to England. He was continually sending money back for his kids, but he was on the road having the time of his life going motor racing. Despite not being formally trained, John Boy was a brilliant mechanic and a good organiser. I was very lucky to have him, and our story together was just beginning.

## Chapter 9

# EURO STAR

One way or another, I was enjoying racing in Europe. It seemed to me that this was more fun that racing in Britain despite – or, perhaps, because of – some colourful incidents along the way. A F3 race at Zolder in Belgium was a case in point.

Michael Bleekemolen, a Dutchman with F3 experience, wanted to race our car there. With increasing interest in Eddie Jordan Racing, the price was naturally going up rather than down. Where possible, I worked along the lines of having one driver who was perhaps in a position to win, or at least collect championship points for the team, while the other brought in sponsorship. The second drivers might do well, they might not, but having money available allowed them to race and my team to survive. Bleekemolen said he could get a good deal on tyres and he had some other bits and pieces to contribute to the effort. So we shook hands on a deal and headed for Belgium.

Michael did a really good job during qualifying and, to our absolute delight, he got on the podium. In my ignorance of local politics, I did not know that the Dutch and the Belgians are not necessarily the best of neighbours. When the Dutch flag was hoisted behind the podium, it received a rather cool reception – which was more than could be said for what was going on at the paddock gate.

Needless to say, Michael's family and friends were very excited, but they could not get into the paddock because they did not have the right passes. In any case, the gates had been bolted to prevent unwelcome visitors. Bleekemolen's friends decided to have a chat with the Belgian guy on the gate. The word 'Non' was used a few times and the situation became a bit heated. The podium was tucked away in a strange place and, of course, John Boy and I were at the foot of it, jumping up and down like eejits while celebrating a great result abroad. We were nobodies, a pair of chancers from Ireland who had blagged a car and a good engine, got a result, made a bit of money and John had probably shagged himself stupid along the way. We were ecstatic. We were also completely unaware that all hell had broken lose at the paddock gate.

There had been a major punch-up, during which one of the security guards had been hurt. I was soon to learn that, if there is a row, you want Dutch people on your side because they know how to take care of themselves. This free-for-all had been taking place at one end of the paddock while two Irish guys had been going mad at the other end where they were celebrating the raising of the Dutch flag in Belgium. Michael, a really good-looking guy, was beaming on the podium while one of his close friends had just knocked a complete stranger's teeth halfway down the man's throat. Not ideal for cross-border relationships. You would not have seen the like in a comedy show.

The police eventually arrived in large numbers and calmed everyone down. There were official complaints and word spread that the trouble had been connected with the Jordan team. The next thing I knew, our prize money was being withheld. Now that *was* a problem.

Under normal circumstances, you would be paid immediately after the race, but these were not normal circumstances and we would not – could not – leave until we received our money. It was difficult getting money out of organisers at the best of times. That is why I could appreciate how F1 had evolved under Bernie Ecclestone. It used to be that each F1 team had to deal individually with the race organisers. Never mind the fact that they might pay one team more start money than another, Bernie's collective bargaining also rid the teams of having to queue at the promoter's door to wait for their money once the race had finished. In the junior formulae, however, it remained – and still does – every man for himself. After much talking and a considerable wait at Zolder, I was eventually paid what was owed and we made our escape.

Despite that problem in Belgium, I was building a kind of love affair with Europe because it was easier to win there, rather like it was in England when I came over from Ireland to race. That gave me the confidence to build a team in Europe as well as in England. For 1983, in England I had Allen Berg, a Canadian who was paying substantial money, and Martin Brundle. In Europe, I had Tommy Byrne, who had just won the British title with Murray Taylor. Tommy had massive talent but whereas Brundle turned out to be the epitome of common sense and control, Byrne was the opposite. A race at Misano in Italy demonstrated that fact.

Misano is next to Rimini on the Adriatic coast and this was in the middle of July. Tommy had arrived early – which was unusual, to say the least – and I soon discovered why. Tommy was absolutely deadly. He had met this much older lady in the hotel. She took pity on him, fed him, watered him and whatever else – I really did not want to know. They would take a walk along the beach in the morning and somehow you knew it would lead to no good. Added to the mix was Joe Stoop, Murray Taylor's brother-in-law. When Joe and Tommy got together, they were dynamite. Apart, they were not too bad; together, they were always in trouble.

So, there I was in Italy, trying to take on the big operators in the European Championship – top drivers such as John Nielsen, Emanuele Pirro and Pier Luigi Martini – and I had this lunatic and his mate to keep an eye on. In many respects, we were babes in arms. We went to Misano without even knowing the basic fact that the circuit bucked the usual trend and was run anti-clockwise. That can be a killer for the driver's neck because he is using muscles that have not been toned to cope with the predominant number of left-hand corners – not that Tommy cared about that. He did not seem to worry about anything, as I was about to discover.

During the first qualifying session, Tommy went out and set the fastest time straightaway. Gradually, the other drivers overhauled us. Just before the end of the session, calm as you like, Tommy put on a fresh set of tyres and, bang! Fastest lap. No trouble at all.

We were looking good for the second and final qualifying session in the afternoon, except for one thing. I could not find Tommy. He had vanished. Eventually I discovered he had gone to the beach with Madame. His argument was that the temperature was rising, no one would be able to go any faster, so why put unnecessary miles on the car and engine? He turned out to be correct. Nevertheless, I was furious. I wanted to sack him on the spot. Meanwhile, another problem had arisen, and that also involved Tommy.

This being the height of the summer in Italy, it was extremely hot. As a means of letting off steam and keeping cool at the same time, a water fight had broken out in the paddock after the first qualifying session. During the course of this, the sister of Cathy Muller – a good driver in the European Championship – had slipped and hurt her foot. This woman had been what might best be described as friendly with one of the British mechanics. Tommy and Joe got involved with loading her into a car to go to hospital but, during the process, they closed the door on someone else's foot and broke his leg! Suddenly, there was chaos. The police became involved and wanted to speak to Tommy Byrne. By now, he was on the beach and I was having to explain that I had no idea of the whereabouts of my driver. It did not end there.

Tommy at least knew what time the warm-up started on race morning, but before that, there was a drivers' safety briefing. Of course, come the hour and there was no sign of my driver. This was serious because there was the risk of exclusion if the driver was not present. I went along and, when Tommy's name was called out, I said, 'Here! Si!' Of course, the other drivers, led by that well-known prankster Gerhard Berger, started shouting and saying I was not Tommy Byrne. I was getting madder by the minute. I did not need this and suddenly there was a war going on with the race director on his feet, calling for calm.

Tommy did not appear until 20 minutes before the start of the race – no briefing, no discussion about the set-up on the car or tactics in the race, nothing. I was apoplectic. Tommy calmly climbed into the car, made a slow start but grabbed the lead during the opening lap. Here was the trick – we had kept him on qualifying tyres. This was a big gamble because although these soft tyres had the speed, we did not know how they would hold up for 26 laps in the heat.

Tommy was pushed all the way by the similar Ralt of Martini. They were rarely more than a second apart. He somehow held on to set the fastest lap and win by just over a second. It was an incredible performance, truly outstanding. That is why I say that Tommy Byrne had massive potential that went unrealised. He was cocky and irreverent and, ultimately, in the minds of some F1 people, that overruled the plain fact that he was very quick indeed, a future world champion in the right hands.

Of course, the rest of the F3 entry at Misano was stunned. How was it possible for this rag-arsed combination from Ireland to come to a track they had never seen before, do the minimum of qualifying, not bother with the briefing and then win the race? There had to be something funny going on, surely? It was hardly a surprise when the organisers demanded to strip the engine in Tommy's car. If an Italian outfit had come to Silverstone under similar circumstances and blown us into the weeds, I would have been muttering about illegal engines too. It was also unfortunate that our engine was a Toyota and the next three cars were powered by Alfa Romeo – the local force.

The good news was that the Toyota had been built by Novamotor, an Italian firm. So we had someone who spoke the language batting on our behalf. Nonetheless, I was not going to let the organisers off lightly, because I knew we were 100 per cent legal. I said, 'I think you're wrong. Can you please pay me!' They refused to do that until the engine was proved to be legal. I told them this was out of order and the rules said I had to be paid beforehand. They said they could do whatever they liked but I argued that they were taking apart a very good engine that I wished to continue racing. If they were going to take it apart, I would need to pay Novamotor to have it rebuilt. That was why I wanted compensation agreed before they started.

The people from Novamotor backed me up. Novamotor was run by the Pederazzani brothers and one of them finally said, 'OK, let them do what they want. Let them take the head off, measure the bore, whatever they want. I'll be here to make sure everything is done properly.'

The scrutineers took the engine apart and found nothing. By the end of Sunday night I had a box full of bits. The Novamotor people were still rebuilding it on Monday morning. I got my money but that engine was never the same and there was nothing I could do about it. However, if this was the price of success, then fine. I could live with it.

While going from race to race at home and abroad, I was also keeping my eye on the up-and-coming drivers, and one name kept coming up time and again – Ayrton Senna da Silva. In the summer of 1982, he was sweeping the board in the 2-litre Formula Ford series. I was giving some thought to getting into driver management and it seemed da Silva was exactly the sort of young talent I needed on board.

I gave him a call and offered him a test drive in our F3 Ralt. He said he first needed to get permission from his team, Rushen Green, which was duly done. We agreed that he would come to Silverstone with his father one Wednesday afternoon in June.

We had been racing the previous weekend on the Silverstone short circuit and James Weaver had qualified on pole with a time of 53.58 seconds and set the fastest lap of the race at 54.40. Ayrton arrived and did about 20 laps. This was his first outing in an F3 car and he looked amazingly good. He came in and asked for a few adjustments to the car. If I remember rightly, there was a bit too much understeer. These were not major changes; just enough for Senna to have the car more to his liking. Then he completed another ten laps, during which he went faster than James's pole position lap. It is important to remember than the qualifying lap had been done in the morning, when the track and conditions are usually faster, and here was Senna, in a car he didn't know, bettering those times. It was absolutely astonishing.

I could see that he was something very special – only an idiot would have missed that – and I would have done anything to have him on board. In my heart of hearts, though, I knew he probably would not drive for me. At that time, Eddie Jordan Racing lacked the pedigree he was looking for. Normally, I would charge drivers for a test like that but I gave Senna a free run. Ayrton appreciated that and we got on well. However, 12 months later, when we were neck-and-neck in arguably one of the greatest F3 championship battles ever, he would hardly speak to me at all.

## Chapter 10

# BRUNDLE v SENNA

This is going to sound bizarre given the reputation I seem to have acquired for financial wheeling and dealing, but when it came to having paying drivers in the team during our years in F3, I always had difficulty in demanding the right fee. For instance, Martin Brundle had very little backing when he drove for me in 1983. Martin and his father, John, put what money they had on the table. A season would cost £65,000 and the Brundles had been able to raise about £16,000. We went to Tom Walkinshaw, who was a big fan of Brundle's and with whom Martin would win the World Sportscar Championship for Jaguar. Tom came up with a few thousand and we raised some extra cash here and there.

For the lion's share of the money needed to put Martin on the F3 grid, I went back to Jimmy Brown and the British Racing Drivers' Club. I convinced Silverstone Circuits and the BRDC that Britain was falling behind the French and the Italians when it came to encouraging home-grown talent. The national clubs such as the BRDC, the British Automobile Racing Club (BARC) and the British Racing and Sportscar Club (BRSCC) were too busy running races to notice or, come to that, care about the absence of young British drivers coming through to the mainstream. It is true that these clubs were flat out every weekend but I felt they were missing the point and failing to arouse awareness outside the narrow confines of the sport itself. The British press were losing interest because the potential stories surrounded Brazilians, such as Nelson Piquet and Ayrton Senna da Silva, who were winning all the national championships. Where were the Brits? At the end of 1982, there was not a single UK driver in a position to earn newspaper ink.

I made a presentation – something that I enjoy doing – to Jimmy Brown and the board of the BRDC. The key figure was Jimmy, a tough old Scot who knew which way was up. Jimmy was aware of the business angle in the long term. The BRDC had plenty of funds raised by its membership but the source of income would gradually diminish if there were insufficient drivers qualified to join the club. It was a Catch 22 situation. I must have got the point across because I succeeded in getting £20,000, which, in 1983, was a sizeable amount.

When racing in Formula Ford and F3, I had always wanted to be a member of the BRDC but believed that my Irish nationality would exclude me. Duncan Hamilton, a legendary character who had won for Jaguar at Le Mans in the 1950s, explained that he had been in a similar position but found a loophole. Apparently, if I was born in Ireland before a certain date – I think it was 1950 – I was eligible because of some ancient clause involving British control of Irish motor sport. I was delighted to exploit this and become a proud member of the club.

Having secured that handsome cheque, I focused on the fact that John Brundle was a Toyota main dealer in Norfolk. I approached Toyota in Japan. They said that they were not making engines for F3 but suggested that I speak to the Pedrazzani brothers at Novamotor in Italy. I flew to Turin and did a deal that would quickly irritate our main rival, Senna.

Ayrton was driving for Dick Bennetts and their Novamotor engines were built in England. Almost from the start, Senna became very upset because, although we had more or less identical cars from Ralt, he always claimed that we had a better engine. Just to rub salt into the wound, part of my deal with Novamotor in Italy was that they could not build an engine for anyone else in England. I argued that Martin was a Toyota dealer and the name needed to be protected. I was being a chancer and it took a lot of persuading. The net result was an exclusive deal between Novamotor (Italy) and Jordan for the British Championship.

This was typical of the mind games that could be played in order to manipulate your position. You did it in the knowledge that, given half a chance, the opposition would do everything to screw you. I loved it! This was to be the opening gambit in a brilliant season of F3 racing.

There was no doubt that Senna was the favourite and he backed that up by winning the first nine races. When Martin finished second on all but one occasion, the championship trophy was certain to be going back to Brazil with its superstar young driver. Then we came to a race at Silverstone in June and that's when the picture began to change dramatically.

This particular race was eligible for both the British and the European Championships. You were free to choose which series you raced in. If you took part in the Euro round, your driver would not be eligible for British points, but the plus side of the European Championship was that competitors could run with the softer and faster Yokahama tyres and go for outright victory as a result. Senna was so far ahead in the British series that he could afford the luxury of opting for the European Championship and increase his chance of winning such an important race.

Martin needed the points, so we chose to stick with the British Avon tyres, but we seriously began to doubt the wisdom of that when he qualified 12th. With about 20 minutes of practice remaining, we made the decision to switch to the Euro Championship, grabbed some Yokahama tyres and Martin stuck the car on pole. It was an incredible performance, one that did not go down well with Mr Senna. That was the start of the fun.

In the race itself, Martin took off and Senna could not get near him. Now the boot was on the other foot and, to our amazement, Ayrton cracked. He spun twice and, on the second occasion, damaged his car. Even worse – or better, depending on your point of view – he did it at the final corner and right under the noses of the press corps who had come to praise the next F1 genius.

As an aside to that, Jordan created, if not history, then a question that you will hear in motor-racing quizzes. Name the team that finished first and second and first in the same race. We had put Tommy Byrne in a car for the Euro series and he finished second. Meanwhile, Allen Berg, who had been driving alongside Martin in the British Championship all year, won that category. We had gambled and won, and that was to be the hallmark of Jordan. It was a fantastic day and the rock'n'roll bash that followed is still talked about.

The party was a great opportunity for the team to welcome a lot of European guys who looked after us when we raced abroad. We were based in a small lock-up unit in the circuit's industrial complex but 'Silverstone Sid', the well-known and highly respected safety car driver and the man who got things done, organised a huge barbecue for us. The whole thing was absolutely massive, unbelievable. Loads of people from the BRDC and Silverstone Circuits stopped by. Everyone was pissed out of their heads. It was a great way of repaying people such as Hamish Brown (Jimmy's son), Sid and his mate Les, who had let me in and out of the circuit, night and day. I owed the Silverstone staff a great deal and this was but a small means of saying thanks. Whether they agreed with that when nursing hangovers the following morning, I wouldn't like to say.

Reflecting on it now, that race at Silverstone marked a turning point. The cars and the team had not only looked the part but we had performed on the track. We were seen as being on top of our game, an operation to be reckoned with. It was a wonderful feeling. The euphoria stretched through the night but most people thought that, despite such a dominant result, it would be business as usual for Senna when we went to the next round of the British Championship. So Ayrton and most of the paddock were in for a big surprise. Martin and the team had been truly fired up by exposing the chink in Senna's armour and we were determined to make the most of it.

Martin won three of the next four races, and increasing desperation seemed to creep in to Senna's driving as a result. He left the road a couple of times, on one occasion, at Oulton Park, landing on top of Brundle's car while trying to overtake. I have to admit that we added to his frustration by playing more mind games.

There was a lot of horseplay over the legality of the rear wings teams were using and how these wings could be made to flex in order to improve performance. Each team was watching the others like a hawk. We tried to have Ayrton's car excluded from a couple of races on dubious technicalities, and we would feed non-attributable stories to the motor-sport media about naughty things we were allegedly doing to our car, knowing that Ayrton devoured every written word because he had absolutely nothing else to do with his life at that time.

We would employ the simplest of moves to upset Ayrton. Each car had to undergo scrutineering at the start of a race weekend. The trick was to be first in the queue in order to avoid wasting time. I knew Ayrton had a thing about that, so I drilled it into my guys that it was essential our cars were first in the queue – even if it meant staying up all night. In fact, we used to arrive early, at about 6.30 a.m. This would really irritate Ayrton and mess with his head. First in the queue for scrutineering would do it to him, let alone being first cars on to the track. Then we would do the business, scrub in tyres, bang in a fast lap time, put it on our pit board and leave the board sitting by the wall where Ayrton could see it. Little things like that really infuriated him.

We discovered that he hated coming to Silverstone because he knew it was Jordan's 'home' circuit and he thought we had some sort of advantage there. It was true that we knew everyone very well and got on famously with the scrutineers but, despite that, the officials were 100 per cent professional and would throw us out as quick as look at us if they thought we were doing something wrong. Ayrton couldn't quite believe that. The worst part for him was that no less than eight of the races were held on the various tracks at Silverstone.

We did have a big advantage because we would test at Silverstone.

I would turn the screw by hiring the circuit exclusively and charging the other F3 teams if they wanted to join in. They knew I was making money at their expense but the reality was that I was keeping the track for F3. On a general test day, you would be sharing the circuit with Mini Sevens and all sorts of cars. Apart from anything else, it was not safe to have cars with such variations in performance on the same piece of road. So I used to block book it and anyone could come. I would say, 'Whether I like you or I don't like you, you are welcome to come. But this is the price. Instead of £70, it's £150.'

I needed about 20 cars to break even. If 30 turned up, Dave Price and the others complained that 'Jordan is thieving us!' I didn't realise it at the time but my methods were no different from those employed by Bernie Ecclestone in F1. A collective deal made far more sense for the teams but, as Bernie found in F1 in the early 1970s, no one was prepared to do it. So Bernie took charge and made a lot of money for the teams, but when they found out how much he was taking as his agreed percentage, they moaned like hell.

This was what was happening, on a much smaller scale, with my dealings in F3. I would say, 'Look, I'll buy the day and if only one car turns up, I'm stuffed. But I know your loyalty to the F3 cause, so I'll make some money out of it for my time and effort.' However, I was not prepared for the number of people who did not want to pay. They thought they were being clever by adopting the attitude, 'I haven't paid and I'm not going to. Fuck EJ. How's he gonna stop me?' This became such a serious problem that it jeopardised the entire running of F3 testing. There was only one answer – I made a deal with Silverstone Sid.

I said, 'Sid, I'm gonna give you a little drink. Here's how it works. Everyone has to have a pass. You put one of your guys at the end of the pit lane with a flag. If a car turns up and it hasn't got a pass, the driver gets turned away. Simple.' It was fun to watch a car reach the end of the pit lane, only for the driver to be told, 'Sorry, park your car there. Your team hasn't paid, you haven't signed the form, therefore you're not insured. You'll have to forget about running today.

Sorry, mate.' The realisation dawned that there was no option but to pay. So I had them!

As a lovely aside, this was something else that really got under Senna's skin. Normally, a driver would not care about such details. All he wants to do is drive the car. That worked in my favour because, having got kitted out and pumped up, ready to go testing, a driver would usually react angrily when he reached the end of the pit lane, only to be prevented from going about his business. The sound of other cars roaring into Copse Corner would heighten the frustration enormously.

Ayrton got involved in everything. He wanted to know every detail about the colour of the car and how the entire operation was working. He had a fixation about certain things. His helmet had to be in a certain place, for example. He had to be able to say, 'That's where we park. That's where we keep this, that's where you put that. This guy only does that,' and so on. So you can imagine the explosion if he discovered that someone – particularly a rival, particularly Jordan – was preventing him from doing the one thing in his life that mattered most – driving a racing car.

Poor Ayrton was easy to play mind games with; you could see it in his face. We would put the word around that we had people watching him and it would get back to him. Of course, we were doing no such thing, but if a person happened to be standing in all innocence by his garage door, Ayrton would start getting twitchy. You could see it happening. Now that was extending to his driving. We realised Senna was suspect under pressure, so Martin pushed him like crazy, and it worked.

We should not have been within a point of Senna going into the last race at Thruxton because Ayrton was an extraordinary driver with a great team. Dick Bennetts is an exceptional guy, very talented. By rights, they should have walked that championship. They clinched it in the end when Ron Tauranac came up with two developments for the Ralt, but there was only one of each. We were given the front suspension modification but the sidepod development on

Senna's car turned out to be the better tweak of the two. That is why Martin forever afterwards playfully referred to Ayrton as 'Sennapod'. It had been an enthralling contest, particularly during the second half of the season. I desperately wanted Brundle to win. However, we knew how good Senna was and I think we did a blinding job to push him as close as we did.

Having come so close, I was also sad not to win the title for another more personal and emotional reason. As I say, 1983 had been a fantastic year but, as far as Jordan was concerned, there had been a dreadful black spot in the middle of August.

A F3 support race had been staged at the Austrian Grand Prix. The long trip was worthwhile because anyone who was anyone was taking part and the organisers paid well. It was a prestigious event, second only to the F3 race at Monaco. The Österreichring was a fantastic circuit and this is where I got to know Gerhard Berger better and formed an enduring friendship.

Allen Berg had enough money to pay for his entry, so I threw in the Brundle car as well. It meant a bit of financial ducking and diving but everyone was happy. Martin won the race and, all told, it had been a very satisfactory weekend. That, of course, is when you should be ready for the unexpected to come and bite you on the backside, but we were much too happy to think about life's sometimes cruel turns.

On the return journey, the truck had an accident. The entire articulated lorry went over the guardrail and into a ravine on a steep mountain pass. The two mechanics in the cab were thrown through the windscreen and somehow survived but Rob Bowden, our chief mechanic, was asleep in the back of the cab and was killed. The effect of such a thing on a small team can be imagined. We were totally devastated. The whole thing reduced me to rubble.

We had a race two weeks later at Silverstone, so in the midst of the emotional turmoil, we had to gather our thoughts and get sorted. I do not think anyone slept for a week. Rob's wife Kate was incredibly strong. We helped her prepare for his farewell. Ron

Tauranac, the boss of Ralt, and Tim Clowes, our insurance broker, disregarded all the normal procedures and all the usual red tape, of which there seemed an insurmountable heap. Tim was magnificent. He went straight to Ron and said, 'Whatever needs doing to get Jordan on to the grid, never mind the cost, just do it.'

We had to deal with the wreckage that arrived as a heap of scrap on the back of a truck that we had somehow found was returning empty from Austria. Alastair Macqueen, who had been with me for a couple of seasons, was instrumental in overseeing the rebuild programme and keeping morale high. I will never forget the moment when we wheeled the cars on to the grid at Silverstone. Ian Titchmarsh, the commentator, made mention of what had happened and the entire grandstand rose as one. It was incredibly moving. We were ready to race because this event was a vital part of the championship and it was exactly what Rob would have wanted us to do. Senna won and Martin finished second, with Allen taking fourth. It was a huge moment because we all did it for Rob.

People think motor racing is merely a sport and therefore nothing more than a joyride all the way through. People also talk about how horrible individuals can be in motor racing or sport. Nevertheless, in times of real adversity, you discover the fundamental truth about this business. Ron Tauranac came up trumps and Tim Clowes made sure that the money was delivered so that Ron could be reimbursed. There was never any question or doubt. It was simply a case of 'let's get it done'.

If we could have beaten Ayrton Senna at the last round, that would have been the icing on the cake. It was not to be but we had given it our very best shot and, in the end, we had been beaten – only just – by one of the greatest talents the sport has ever seen. It had been massive fun and a memorable year for reasons both good and very sad.

## Chapter 11

# RIDING A CAMEL

One of the great things about going motor racing is that you meet such an interesting and varied bunch of people. Among them during my early days behind the wheel were Adrian Reynard and Rick Gorne. The pair of them were very quick on the racetrack and they were to prove just as sharp when starting up a business building racing cars. I knew all about the quality of Adrian's design work when a Reynard driven by Andy Wallace beat us to the F3 title in 1986.

Prior to this, Jordan had been experiencing a difficult time. I had run David Hunt – the younger brother of James, the 1976 world champion – and Allen Berg in F3 during 1984. David had brought money from Acorn computers but we did not have much to show in results. The following year, I had made a move into Formula 3000 with the Belgian driver, Thierry Tassin. F3000 cars were a step above F3 but nowhere near as sophisticated as F1. Results were once again few and far between and I felt we had gone backwards for the first time. At the end of 1985, I had been asking myself a number of serious questions about whether or not it was worth continuing. It had been difficult to attract the right sort of people and the necessary amount of money. F3000 proved to be a very steep learning curve. Our F3 campaign had suffered, perhaps as a result of that, with Harald Huysman finishing ninth in the British Championship.

Huysman had been the choice of Marlboro and I went along with that because I had been impressed with him during the Formula Ford Festival. He had the speed and I reckoned, if I could control him, everything would be fine. He finished fourth in the first race of the season but, after that, progress seemed to be halted by one crash after another. It became so bad that I feared this was going to bankrupt the team.

Huysman was a Norwegian based in Brussels and he had incredible style and a gift with languages. I remember saying to him, 'Harald, you cannot imagine what talent you've got – but not in a racing car. Or not as much in a racing car as you have outside it. You've got a great marketing brain, you look very good, you speak well, you've got a fabulous way with sponsors. I think that you'll do well. But, sadly, not as a driver.' I was proved right because Harald made a great success of business management in various branches of sport. Meanwhile, the Jordan team had to regroup after a disastrous year and, as it turned out, 1986, or the final part of it, proved to be a new beginning, courtesy of the intervention of Reynard and Gorne.

I had loved working with Ron Tauranac. I always thought he was the most talented engineer when it came to producing fast but practical F3 cars but, I have to confess, I began to feel that Reynard was a more polished operation. The car looked slicker and the company had a proper marketing programme. Adrian Reynard was a very clever guy but the trick was that, in Rick Gorne, he had the most gifted sales person I have ever come across in motor racing. Rick could sell cars to men without limbs.

Rick had great vision and the balls of an ox. During the 1986 F3 season, he approached me and suggested we switch from a Ralt to a Reynard. He said this was the way forward because Reynard were going to build a F3000 car for 1987 and I ought to be moving up and doing it with them in Europe.

'What?' I responded. 'You want me to change cars mid-season? No way. In any case, I'm not giving you one penny for that piece of shite!'

'Jordan, you don't have to,' Rick replied. 'Take the car and win the race, and when you've done that, you'll be wanting the car – and *then* you'll have to pay for it.'

It was a big decision to make at that stage in the season. I was not 100 per cent happy with Ralt. The business over Dick Bennetts and Senna receiving the aero update for the last round in 1983 continued to rankle and I did not want the same thing happening again. I agreed to run the Reynard in the last few races, even though it meant I was burning my bridges with Ralt to a certain extent.

Maurizio Sandro Sala finished second in the championship for Jordan and there was no doubt now that the Reynard was the car to have. It was a clever move by Gorne. This was Reynard's first season in F3. Andy Wallace's car was run by Robert Synge and Madgwick Motorsport but we had been the biggest thorn in their side, Sandro Sala leading the championship more or less all the way to mid-season. Sala was an outstanding young driver. He was small and light – perfect in a Formula 3 car in terms of the power-to-weight ratio. Unfortunately, Maurizio seemed to lose a bit of mental momentum – there was a lot of argy-bargy over the type of fuel being used and he felt we were losing out – and Wallace began to ease ahead. Then, by encouraging the swap, Adrian and Rick not only caused a blip in our challenge, they also had us on their side. Two very smart guys.

I was now going down the Reynard route for F3 in 1987. Johnny Herbert was the driver – and he did not have two pence in his pocket. I owned part of his future contract, so I let him have the drive free because I could see Johnny had vast natural talent.

Having made the switch from Ralt, I was now about to make another fundamental change by moving from Toyota and Novamotor to Volkswagen and Spiess. I had seen their engine in Germany and been impressed by how small and light it was, with performance to match. The Toyota was becoming quite heavy with its steel block. Alfa Romeo, with a cast block, were making inroads and it seemed to me that VW was the answer for the British F3 championship. I convinced Volkswagen-Audi at Milton Keynes to help pay for the Herbert engine and repaid them by winning six races and the championship. It was a dream year for Eddie Jordan Racing.

I did not pay for the car. I blagged it from Rick at Reynard, and because we were winning races, I had, within reason, as many spares as we needed. Adrian could not cope with that. He wanted to charge me the same as everyone else, whereas Rick saw things differently. His view was, 'Keep the car winning, keep it up there. Give the winning team all the spares they need. What have we got to lose? Only a comparatively small amount of money but, in return, we will be able to use this as a sales tool. We can say to potential customers, "Look at Johnny Herbert, he's doing all right in a Reynard." '

On the back of a winning team, Reynard sold more cars than they ever believed possible. Naturally, I was keen for this to continue as we moved into F3000 with them, and so was Rick but Adrian was not happy, not happy at all. I was trying to negotiate with Rick but he had to stop discussions. 'Listen EJ,' he said. 'I'm in serious shit here. Adrian's gone mental over my deals with you. I think you need to talk to him directly.'

This came at a time when I was more or less living out of a suitcase and staying in the Green Man pub near Silverstone. Marie was in Spain because our second girl, Miki, was suffering from chronic asthma, but at least my home life was stable. In the early days Rick seemed to marry a different girl every few years. It became so confusing that we called them all 'Jane' to make a joke of the situation and save embarrassment. That said, I introduced him to his latest wife on a transatlantic flight. Reynard had just won a Champ Car race in Detroit and, on the same weekend in 1995, we had finished second in Canada. Their plane stopped in Montreal on the way back and I made the introduction – at no charge to Rick. That was how our relationship had grown from those early negotiations but, for the moment, things appeared to have stalled because of Adrian's unhappiness. We met at his house.

'Adrian, why are you so bloody grumpy?' I asked him. 'You've got everything going for you. You've just won the F3 championship with Johnny Herbert, you're selling all these cars in Europe on territory that used to be the preserve of Martini and Dallara, you're crucifying Ralt with a car that's clearly not got as nice a design…' – I used to say that just to annoy him – 'I'm only using your car because it's free. I could easily go back to Ron if that's what you want.'

'Naaaaaahhhh, you don't need to do that,' said Adrian, 'but Rick has done this ridiculous deal with you.'

'Adrian!' Rick interrupted. 'Would you just concentrate on designing the car and leave the commercial aspects of this company to me? That way, by sticking with what you know, you might find that you make an awful lot more money!'

It was that kind of conversation. Drink was put on the table and we had a few. Then Adrian said, 'Listen, why don't you come back and stay with me. I'll get Gill to make us some grub.' I was happy to agree and avoid another night of B&B. During dinner, I told Adrian that Marie would be returning soon and I would have to start preparing to buy a house. Quick as a flash, Adrian said, 'I have the house for you.' I thought he was having a laugh at my expense because of all the grief I was causing over the cars.

We drove to Oxford. Now I was sure he was having a laugh because the house he took me to in Northmoor Road was virtually derelict, but it had a magnificent central location, backed on to the river and was close to the schools. It had been a don's house, which she shared with 24 cats. When she died, it was an absolute mess. The smell was disgusting. Before I knew it, I had agreed to buy the house. That gives some indication of the strength of both our relationship and the drink I'd had beforehand.

This seven-bed town house would make a wonderful home. It would also be very different from the house we had moved to in Westbury, about two miles from Brackley, in 1983. That was two old cottages, built with Cotswold stone and knocked together to form a beautiful dwelling in its own ground, with a swimming pool and tennis court. Miki and Zak were born there but we sold Westbury after about four years so that Marie could take Miki to Spain. All the while, we had been making the most of the continuing rise in property prices, and large loans, to take us on to the next level.

Discussions with Adrian continued. He was saying, 'We're gonna do this Formula 3000 car and we've got to beat March.'

'New car! Big series! But with March down the road, forrrgetit,' I told him. 'You won't spend the money because you're a bunch of tight-arses. Stick to what you know and you'll be fine. But not Formula 3000.'

Adrian would have none of it. 'It'll be great. Our car is a winner. Will you come with us? You have control of Johnny and he's the guy we want on board.'

I said I was trying to get Johnny into F1 but was having no joy. That merely strengthened Adrian's resolve. 'Come on, let's do this!' he said. I was wavering. I knew that if Adrian felt he was not making much headway, he had some heavy hitters to call on. One was his great mate Richard Branson, and the other was Alex Hawkridge, a former racer who was behind the Toleman team. Toleman, having moved into F1 in 1984, were eventually bought by Benetton and finally changed into Renault.

Hawkridge got in touch and said that, through his involvement with Zytec, he would sort the engines out. I said I would pay the running costs but Reynard had to supply the cars. They did not seem to notice that I used the word 'cars' – plural. My plan was to run another driver at more or less full money if I could get him into a new car.

I had persuaded Trevor Foster to join me to run the F3000 team. Very experienced in Formula Ford and F3, as well as being a good friend of Johnny's, Trevor was less than impressed when he arrived at our workshop to find very little in terms of equipment. I had, for example, bought a trailer from the Williams F1 team but had nothing to pull it. When it came to stepping up to the bigger formula, we were starting from scratch in many ways.

The greatest difficulty proved to be selling the sponsorship, which was hardly surprising when you considered the facts. This would be a new start for Jordan and a new car for that championship. The driver had never driven in F3000 before and was totally unfamiliar with Jerez, host of the first round. Forget it. Who was going to be interested? Most people thought that, at the very best, we would be midfield.

We were going nowhere fast and I could not see how we were going to pay for this. Above all, I did not want to jeopardise Johnny's career. He was like a son to me and he had a contract. My feeling was that this was catastrophic and the whole thing was going to collapse in a heap and take Johnny and Eddie Jordan Racing down with it. So it was with some trepidation that I put together plans for the opening round in southern Spain.

Johnny took pole position! This stunned everyone – not least myself. There we were on pole position with not a sponsor in sight. The car was as white as the driven snow and the race was being televised. We had barely enough money to get us home, never mind take part in the next race. My mind went into overdrive.

I started thinking about Camel cigarettes. They were sponsoring the Lotus F1 team and word was that Camel – or, to be precise, R.J. Reynolds, the tobacco company – were not happy. I discovered that the person to speak to was W. Duncan Lee, who was responsible for Reynolds in Europe. On the Saturday night, I called Mr Lee out of the blue. I said, 'I'm sorry to disturb you. My name is Eddie Jordan and I think you may know who I am. I know who you are and well done with what you're doing at the moment. I'm not looking for any money but I'd like to have a little chat with you because I have an interesting proposition.'

He said that he was going out to dinner, so I told him it would take two minutes. I explained that this was the first F3000 event of the season and it was being televised from Spain, which I knew to be an important market for the Camel brand. I said, 'There's no sponsor on our car and we're on pole position. I'd like to have your permission to put Camel on both side pods, the rear wing, the front of the car and on the driver's visor – for a consideration.'

You could almost hear the resignation in Duncan Lee's voice when he said quietly, 'And what's the consideration?'

'If we win, you'll meet with me on Tuesday.'

'Sorry? Is it money you're after?'

'I don't want a penny right now.'

There was a pause before Lee said, 'Run me through this again. You're in a new car, the Reynard. You're on pole. The race is on TV. And you want to put full Camel stickers all over the car?'

I confirmed that that was the deal. I told him that I had actually gone ahead and had the stickers made because it was such a mind-blowing deal with no downside for Camel. 'But you have to hear me out if we win. You won't hear from me again if we lose, but if we do win, you have to agree to see me on Tuesday.'

'OK,' he said. 'No problem. I'd like to do that anyway. Good luck.'

So far, so good. Now there was the small matter of winning the race, our first in F3000 with a new car and a driver unfamiliar with either the track or the championship. Here we were, one step away from F1, a move that was cheeky, brave and mad. I was being a chancer in the extreme. I had a fitful night's sleep on Saturday.

I need not have worried. Johnny led all 47 laps – the last of which was probably, in my view at the time, the longest and slowest in the history of motor sport. He gave Reynard a victory first time out in F3000 and W. Duncan Lee an appointment in his diary for Tuesday, 19 April 1988. It had been a gamble where, in truth, neither side had anything to lose, but now I had to make it stick.

We spent all day Monday doing the artwork and worked most of the night on the presentation. I went to meet Duncan Lee and his assistant, David Warren, whom I had met before. We signed a deal and agreed that the car should be sprayed yellow, Camel's colours. The car could have been painted pink if that's what the sponsor wished but, in this instance, I was delighted because yellow had always been a lucky colour for me. Although nothing was said, I had the impression that Camel were very disappointed with Lotus. Colin Chapman had been dead for nearly six years and the team was going nowhere. Jordan was like a breath of fresh air. Having made the deal stick, now we had to deliver.

That was easier said than done in such a competitive series. Johnny, after being unable to restart his engine after a stoppage during the race at Monza, put in the drive of the year to come through the field and finish third. Although the championship was being led by Roberto Moreno in a Reynard, engineered by Gary Anderson – two names that would figure in Jordan's future – Johnny was the man many of the F1 team owners were watching closely.

Ken Tyrrell was interested and so were Benetton and Lotus. Although we had Camel sponsorship, the money was tight. Duncan Lee kept explaining that their budget was tied up with Lotus but he managed to find money, a little bit here and a little bit there, which he would scrape together from the various countries we were racing in. Camel was not big in England but they wanted to be big in Italy, Spain and France. Thankfully, we raced there but I could understand why Camel did not particularly want a British driver. It was up to me to make sure I used the F3000 opportunity for Johnny to showcase his talent and win an F1 contract. Some of the F1 team owners came to Brands Hatch, Johnny's local track, on 21 August. This was going to be an important event for us all.

Although Camel were not particularly in favour of British drivers, I had two entered for that race. The reason was that I'd had to sack Thomas Danielsson, our Swedish second driver. He had brought some money, but not all that had been promised, and unbeknown to me, he had received a knock on the head and was having difficulty with his eyesight. I replaced him with Martin Donnelly, who had been turning in some sensational performances in F3. The Ulsterman grabbed his chance at Brands Hatch, where he put his car on the front row, alongside Johnny. This was going to be interesting.

Johnny led easily until Moreno crashed at Paddock Bend and caused the race to be stopped. At the restart, Herbert had too much wheelspin and Donnelly shot into the lead. Johnny, third, became embroiled with Gregor Foitek as they accelerated along the back straight and there was a massive accident. The front of Johnny's car was destroyed by a double impact. His driving boots, complete with laces still done up, had been wrenched off and lay in the middle of the track. A marshal, who came to the rescue, collapsed when he saw the remains of Johnny's feet protruding from the front of the car.

The race had to be stopped for a second time. Donnelly finally won the restart but, with the greatest respect to a very fine drive by Martin on his debut, our thoughts were with Johnny. The crash had been so severe, there were doubts that he would survive, never mind walk again. Immediately after the accident, I went to the hospital in Sidcup.

Johnny was having terrible problems. One of his feet was hanging on only by the skin. Two or three doctors were present and one of them, an Asian guy, said he thought he could save the foot. The other doctors were of the opinion that there was no alternative but amputation. Either way, there seemed little chance of a full recovery. The fact that Johnny was able to race again and win three grands prix is a massive tribute to the team at St Mary's Hospital and Johnny's personal resolve.

At the time, though, the situation looked very grim. It took a while to sink in and then the full and far-reaching reality hit me. Johnny was out of danger but we were absolutely certain he would never race again. A brilliant career was over and, being brutally honest, once I knew Johnny would survive, I went home and thought, 'My star driver is out and I'm in debt. What the hell do I do now?'

## Chapter 12

# MANAGING MY BOYS

Johnny Herbert's horrific injuries aside, I have to be honest and say that, when it came to racing drivers and risk, my thoughts were usually focused on the financial gamble rather than the hazards associated with driving quickly. I would let the drivers take care of what they knew best and I would concentrate on what I knew best – doing the deals. That was why I started Eddie Jordan Management (EJM) in 1983.

A number of drivers clearly had bright futures but very little money. There was no point in taking on someone with financial clout if he was not quick enough. Herbert and Donnelly are good examples. One was from Essex and the other was the son of a potato merchant from Belfast – two very quick guys but not ten pence between them. If I wanted the best drivers, I would have to fund their racing initially and recoup my investment when they became the good racing drivers and earners I hoped they would be. If they failed, I would lose. There was a fair element of risk involved, but I was not doing this alone, and neither would the driver be continually fighting the financial odds on his own.

The deal was that we would hire the driver and commit to him, pay for his racing, his future, but there had to be some form of payback. It was not long before I received tentative enquiries from IMG (International Management Group). I probably should have sold EJM to them because IMG were familiar with this type of work whereas I was only thinking of it as a secondary business. My main aim was to win races. I liked the glamour of the management side but, really, did I know enough about it? Our discussions with IMG were informal but, in the end, I decided to stay put for two reasons – it was the type of venture that I loved, and I had a very good man to help me.

I first met Fred Rodgers in 1982. Soft-spoken and passionate about motor sport, Fred was a partner in a law firm. When we had the terrible accident with the truck in Austria in 1983, Fred looked after our legal interests. He was enthusiastic and diligent, the perfect man to help me handle the paperwork and legalities involved with EJM.

Fred moved that side of the operation from Silverstone to his office in Highgate, and with him went a young lieutenant by the name of Jim Wright. Jim had worked for me, on and off, in 1982 and came on board the following year doing what might best be described as a bit of this and a bit of that. Jim was as keen as mustard and a terrific guy to have around. He took care of what we would now call logistics and would pick up a spanner if the mechanics were pushed. It became clear, however, that Jim's talents lay with the commercial side of the operation, which was why he began working with Fred in that small office above an estate agent's in Highgate. Jim must have learned a fair bit because he later started his own company before becoming the head of marketing at Williams and, more recently, at Red Bull/Toro Rosso. However, at the time, he dealt with most of the action at the sharp end of EJM as we handled Martin Brundle and Tommy Byrne, our first major clients united by the fact that Martin had very little money and Tommy had none at all.

I really had very little to do with the day-to-day running of EJM. I would give my view on the drivers I thought we should have, and how we should manage them. I would sit in on the meetings but the reality was that Jim was doing all the graft. I loved working with 'Jimbo' because he was absolutely dedicated. He just could not see anything outside his life other than motor racing. The same had to be said for Fred because his practice probably suffered as a result of his complete and utter devotion to motor racing.

With Marie on our wedding day, 25 January 1979.

My mother Eileen has been so supportive of me throughout my life and career. (Pip Calvert)

The two ages of my children. (Above) Miki, Zoë, Kyle and Zak together in 1991; and (below)

(Above) Skiing in Courchevel in 1999: me, Kyle, Marie, Zoë, Miki and Zak, while (below) we all get away to the sun in 2004. (Ben Wright, *F1 Racing* magazine)

Marie on a Harley that had been donated for a CLIC event; the charity does some wonderful work for children, and I have been thrilled to support it. (Hugo Burnand)

Marie and me at a CLIC charity event in St Petersburg in 2005 where Elton John sang and Bill Clinton spoke, and a lot of money was raised.

With Frank Lampard, his partner Elen Rives and Bono in St Tropez in the summer of 2005. (Jean-Pierre)

Music and golf are two of my passions away from motorsport. (Above) My band plays after the British Grand Prix at Silverstone in 2003. Producer Chris Thomas is on keyboards, writer Jonathan Perkins is singing, while Pete and Matt man the guitars, and I'm on drums. (Below) A proud Paul McGinley displays the Volvo Master trophy in 2005 – undoubtedly a better golfer thanks to my caddying advice earlier in the season!

Messing about in Cannes in 2006 with Liam Cunningham, one of the stars of the film *The Wind That Shakes The Barley*, which was to win the Palme d'Or. (Jean-Pierre)

Receiving my honorary doctorate from Dublin Technology Institute, along with Pierce Brosnan. (Jason Clarke)

You meet the strangest people in the pits. (Above) Marie, Catherine Zeta-Jones, me, Kathy Ojeh and Michael Douglas get together ahead of the 2001 Spanish Grand Prix. (Below) Dave Marren, Brian O'Driscoll, Bono, Nigel Northridge, Gary Alexander and I pose together in 2003. (Sutton

Posing with the Bongo Man. I'd bumped into Ronnie Wood during a holiday in Barbados as we both walked along the beach, and our encounter with the Bongo Man had inspired this wonderful painting.

The promo shot for Eddie Jordan's Bad Boy Racers, the TV show I did to try to help some lads who were heading for trouble to find a way forward to a better life.

I would hold most of the initial discussions with drivers. The conversation would go along these lines: 'I'll take you on, but I want a three-year or perhaps a five-year contract with you. I will sell you and get you into all the different places. You drive the car but I own your contract. Part of the deal is that we will claw back the money out of the driver management. So, for instance, if your season costs £70,000, I will charge you a commission until such time as the money is paid back, and 10 per cent thereafter, for the period.' I would have to work bloody hard, and there was always the risk that the driver might not make it. In the end, very few of these contracts actually made financial sense, because of the overheads.

Jean Alesi was one driver about whom I had my doubts initially. Jean had been signed by Marlboro with the French Oreca team and I could see that he was fast, but very erratic. Jean was part Sicilian, part French and, frequently, the Latin blood would rule. A close mate of mine, Bosco Quinn, was friendly with José Alesi. Bosco asked me to meet José, who tried to persuade me that his brother could be tamed. I told José that I did not think that was possible because Jean was quick but inconsistent. José would not be put off and insisted that Jean would be available if I wanted to do a deal. I declined.

Then I heard through the motor-sport grapevine that Marlboro had had enough of Jean and were sacking him. That was perfect because now I could have Jean under my terms. If I had been seen to be taking him away from Marlboro, the impression would have been that Jean, despite a terrible season, was a future star and Jordan was desperate to have him. That would not have worked simply because it would have sent the wrong message to Jean and Marlboro. This was a critical moment.

Jean knew how important this drive was to him. On the face of it, his career was washed up after finishing tenth in the 1988 F3000 championship and effectively being booted out by Oreca. We had a test at Vallelunga and Jean was faster in the 1988 Reynard than other quick guys in 1989 cars. He was also faster than Martin

Donnelly in our other car. That did a lot for Jean's confidence – and mine.

The first race of the 1989 season was at Silverstone. I had high hopes because I reckoned we had the strongest pairing on the grid. Sure enough, Alesi was incredibly quick in the opening practice session but he failed to replicate it when it mattered and finished fourth. Donnelly had to retire with an engine problem.

Martin outpaced Jean at Vallelunga and went on to win – on the track, at least. Our car was disqualified for running a nose that had not passed a crash test. We were not alone in using this particular nose on the Reynard but we were the only team to have scored points and were therefore subject to a protest from a rival.

A hearing was held at the FIA headquarters in Paris not long after, and the trip seemed to be fraught from beginning to end. Having had our appeal rejected, I was running late to catch my flight back to the UK. By the time I reached Charles de Gaulle airport, the flight had closed and there was a waiting list. My seat had gone – for the moment.

Digging into my briefcase, I whipped out a dodgy press card I'd had for many years. According to the press card, I was with the *Irish Times*. It so happened that the Paris Air Show was on at the time and I said I had to get back urgently to file a story. The only story I was telling was the one to the girl at check-in. She not only believed me but also gave me an upgrade. That was the only bit of good news connected with that trip. Donnelly had lost a perfectly good win and, in retrospect, he never really recovered from that for the rest of the season.

What about Alesi? He had crashed out of the Vallelunga race and things were not looking good. I had to get a grip on the situation before Jean lost the plot completely. I told him in no uncertain terms that he would have to leave his home in Avignon and come to live in England, near the workshop. 'You'd better get over here and learn what these mechanics are doing for you,' I told him. 'You're crashing this car all the time.'

Jean had a room in our house in Oxford. I wanted him to take in the British way of doing things. Just as important, he needed to improve his English dramatically because, until now, José had been doing all the talking on Jean's behalf. Had Jean been left to his own devices in Avignon, goodness knows what state he would have been in had things continued to go wrong at each successive race.

Jean won the next race at Pau where, ironically, it was Martin who made a mistake on that great street circuit. After finishing second to Martin in the sixth round at Brands Hatch, Jean was leading the championship. That one-two was appropriate because, a month before, both Alesi and Donnelly had been propelled into the F1 limelight – courtesy of Eddie Jordan Management and an extraordinary sequence of events.

I had been close to the Warwick family ever since Paul Warwick had driven for me in F3 in 1988. Paul was a really nice guy, and quick, too. The family was devastated when he had a fatal crash in a F3000 race at Oulton Park. Derek Warwick was driving for Arrows in 1989 and I heard that he had hurt himself in a karting accident. Derek got in touch and said I might want to have one of my drivers standing by in case he was not fit to race in the French Grand Prix.

Meanwhile, I also heard that there had been a disagreement between Ken Tyrrell and Michele Alboreto. Michele had returned to Tyrrell after five years with Ferrari, bringing with him personal sponsorship from Marlboro. This led to increasing problems for Ken because the team received support from Camel. It came to a head just before the French Grand Prix when Alboreto and Tyrrell parted company.

My brain went into overdrive. Here was an unbelievable opportunity to get not just one but two of my drivers into F1. Donnelly could replace Warwick and Alesi would be ideal for Tyrrell given Ken's Camel connections and the fact that the race would be in France. It seemed a very long shot indeed, but I was going for it.

My immediate priority was to contact Camel. I could not believe it when I discovered that Duncan Lee, and everyone else I needed to speak to, was in Siberia for the Camel Trophy and completely out of communication. I couldn't even raise Tony Jardine, whose company was handling Camel's PR. I went berserk. There was only one answer – I had to go straight to the board of Camel. Fortunately, a few weeks before, I had been at the Monaco Grand Prix with some members of the board, including Irishman Ed Horrigan, who became famous through the bestseller *Barbarians at the Gate*. Nonetheless, it was still important to speak to Duncan Lee because he was the man controlling the F1 budget.

Eventually, I tracked him down by satellite telephone. It was a terrible line and I explained that here was an opportunity that was too good for Camel to miss. Everything was ready to fall into place – Tyrrell and Camel, Alesi and Camel, a Frenchman making his debut in France. Predictably, Lee responded that he had no money in the kitty because most of it was being soaked up by Lotus. I pointed out – not that Duncan needed reminding – that Lotus were tenth in the F1 championship with three points. Tyrrell were ahead of Lotus in seventh. Duncan knew what I was getting at and he got in touch with Tyrrell. Ken immediately suspected my involvement behind the scenes and I knew my next discussion with Tyrrell would be difficult, even allowing for my supposed gift of the gab.

Ken was what you might describe as 'Old School', a man who had come up the hard way. He raced in the 1950s, but purely as an amateur because his income came from running a timber business with his brother. They operated out of a wood yard in deepest Surrey and, although Ken did not know it at the time, that very rural address would become famous in the world of motor racing. Ken gave up driving to become an entrant. One thing led to another and, before long, he was forming his own grand-prix team with Jackie Stewart as the driver. They enjoyed a wonderful golden period between 1968 and Jackie's retirement at the end of 1973. From that point on, the Tyrrell team began a very slow but gradual slide into decline.

By the time I came into contact with Ken in the early 1980s, his team had passed its best – not that you would have known it, talking to Ken. He remained as bullish as ever and, to be fair, Tyrrell Racing continued to be one of the most professional outfits in the paddock. It was certainly an excellent place for a young driver to cut his teeth. Ken was set in his ways and did not suffer fools gladly, which was great for F1 novices because they would learn the hard way. Nevertheless, it was difficult for anyone else to hold a discussion because it would inevitably become a one-way conversation, with Ken having his point of view at the expense of yours.

I had helped Martin Brundle find a drive at Tyrrell in 1984 after his F3 season with us. Five years later, here I was trying to negotiate with Ken to take Jean Alesi. It was just ridiculous. I was talking, but I don't think Ken was listening. With the exception of his wife, Norah, I do not think Ken listened to many people in his entire life.

He was great value, particularly when the F1 team principals got together. At the start of every meeting, Ken would shout at Bernie Ecclestone. 'Bernie!' he would bellow in that gravelly voice. 'You stole our fucking business!' That contentious issue aggravated Ken right up until he passed away in August 2001. Ken was not alone in believing that Bernie had taken more than his fair share of the income generated by F1. I was not surprised the first time I heard Ken say that, because he was the one person alive whom Bernie could not quite control. Colin Chapman had been another. Bernie revered Chapman because he felt that the boss of Lotus was incredibly clever and bright. Ken was something else.

I had to steel myself before picking up a call from Ken. I would almost have to bang my head on the wall just to make myself angry, mean and tough because, if I went in to bat against Ken without being fully prepared, I would be trampled on. That is not an exaggeration. I would work myself into an almost violent state. When this particular call came through, Ken was typically to the point.

'Jordan,' he said, 'don't fill me with bullshit. This bloke isn't going to qualify, never mind finish the bloody race. D'you understand?'

'Are you sure about that, Ken? Which bloke have you got in mind?'

'You know exactly who I mean! You've been ringing the Camel people in Russia about your bloke Alesi. As it happens, I don't have too much time. Can he drive the car?'

I said that of course Jean was capable of driving an F1 car, and he was available. Ken knew he was being eased into a corner but, even then, he and his son Bob seemed reluctant to accept it. Ken never put anything in the subsequent agreement to cover the eventuality of Jean doing well. He was so convinced Alesi would be off the pace that he did nothing.

Bob arrived at our workshop at Silverstone and had a look around. His view – probably quite rightly – was that this was a tip, even worse than the Tyrrell timber yard at Ockham. Bob came out with all the reasons why we were so lucky, adding that this was Alesi's big chance and we should not read too much into it because they would have Alboreto back at the next race. They would get Jonathan Palmer (Tyrrell's number two driver) to help Alesi as best he could, but we had to accept that Jean probably would not qualify.

I had heard more than enough of this nonsense. I remember being incredibly rude to Bob and telling him to get the f*** out of my office because he did not realise what this was all about. If he thought that negotiating to have Alesi was like haggling over a piece of meat, he was making a huge mistake because this was not an abattoir. I wanted the best for Jean but I was genuinely annoyed because the Tyrrells were trying to get their hands on Jean for next to nothing. I wasn't having it. Not by any means. I had had a huge stroke of luck with the way my association with Alesi was working out and I was not going to be bullied into releasing him.

Eventually I said to Bob Tyrrell, 'Fine, just forget the bullshit. How much are you paying us?' We had to wangle a few quid out of Tyrrell and then argue over Alesi's overalls and the stickers we wanted on the car. Ken Tyrrell had always been notoriously difficult over things like that but we needed the patches and stickers in order to earn some money. Agreement was reached. Alesi had the drive.

The mission with Donnelly turned out to be much simpler. I persuaded Arrows boss Jackie Oliver to ring Derek Warwick to canvas his opinion on Martin. I knew Derek was on our side. He did not want a star name filling his seat and he told Oliver that Donnelly would be the perfect choice.

Martin qualified 12th at the Paul Ricard track but, due to a technical problem, started from the pit lane and went on to finish 12th. Alesi qualified 16th and finished fourth to score three championship points in his first grand prix – not bad for a novice who apparently had no chance of making the race.

On Monday, the Tyrrells were beating down the doors of my office, looking for a contract. They wanted me to let Jean go for the rest of the season, but I said I wanted to win the F3000 championship. Ken spluttered, as he always did when getting annoyed or excited, 'You can never win the championship. You've only won two races!' I said that may be so but Jean was staying.

Alesi won the Birmingham Superprix and the race at Spa and took the title. In fact, only two of the remaining grands prix clashed with F3000, which allowed Jean to drive another seven F1 races. He covered himself in further glory by finishing fifth at Monza and fourth in Spain. The next time we saw Alesi in action was when he was fighting with Ayrton Senna for the lead of the first race of the 1990 F1 season in Phoenix.

There had been quite a pantomime following Jean's mercurial debut in France. Fred had been going from motorhome to motorhome at the final few grands prix that year. At one stage, Jean had contracts from Williams, McLaren, Ligier and the one he would drive for, Tyrrell. Then Jean got himself into a right old mess. Having signed the Tyrrell deal for 1990 and blown everyone's mind by fighting for the lead with Ayrton Senna in the first race, Jean was the centre of attention. Suddenly, Frank Williams was pestering me, continually asking if a deal could be done for 1991. A deal was eventually agreed and everything was fine until it got to the British Grand Prix in July, where Jean was approached by Cesare Fiorio, manager of the Ferrari team. Being half Sicilian, the thought of driving for Ferrari was too much for Jean and he agreed to sign, more or less on the spot. Then he came back to me, saying I had to get him out of the predicament he had landed himself in. I told him there was no way.

However, I explained to Frank what had happened. Naturally, Frank wanted compensation from Ferrari, which he duly received in the form of a cash payment and the Ferrari that Nigel Mansell had raced in 1989. I was pleased the matter had been resolved, thanks, in no small part, to the work of Eddie Jordan Management.

Having had one Ulsterman driving for me in 1989, I went and signed another for the following year. Martin Donnelly, after starting the season as one of the favourites, had actually finished it in eighth place, an unfair reflection of his talent. Just two points behind Donnelly came Eddie Irvine. Although Eddie's best result had been a third and a fourth, like Martin, the bald facts did not tell the full story. Irvine had been disqualified twice in the first three races through no fault of his own and what impressed me most was that his head did not go down. He remained as forceful and committed as ever and the man from County Down was the ideal replacement for his former neighbour from just up the road in Belfast. The career paths of these two really promising drivers then took wildly diverging paths.

Donnelly had just the one F1 outing for Arrows thanks to Warwick's return to fitness. Nonetheless, Martin had done enough to attract a drive with Lotus for 1990. It would prove to be a catastrophe that almost killed him.

The yellow car was an even bigger disaster than the one that had left Lotus languishing in sixth place in the 1989 championship. Donnelly struggled but at least his efforts stood the test of comparison with his new team-mate, Derek Warwick. Martin was beginning to put Derek under pressure as the season wore on but the thing that broke first was the front suspension on Martin's car during qualifying for the Spanish Grand Prix at Jerez. The car slammed into the barrier at 140mph and more or less disintegrated. That is what probably saved Martin. He was flung from what was left of the cockpit and ended up on the track, unconscious, with the seat still strapped to his back. He looked like a rag doll. It was the most terrible sight.

The initial impression was that he was dead, for it seemed that no one could survive an impact like that. Professor Watkins, F1's medical supremo, was on the scene just in time. The accident had occurred towards the end of a lap and it took the medical car that bit longer to reach him as a result, and Martin was choking on his tongue. The Prof sorted that out and had him removed to the circuit medical centre but the prognosis was not good. It was only after some time in intensive care in the London Hospital – and a couple of scares along the way – that Martin began the slow recovery to his cheerful, cheeky self. Unlike Johnny Herbert, however, Martin's F1 career was over. The injury to his leg prevented him from being able to evacuate the cockpit of an F1 car in the required time. It was such a waste because there was no question in my mind that Martin Donnelly had outstanding talent and was a hard racer.

Eddie Irvine was showing similar traits, and similar results in F3000 in 1990. He scored just one point in the first four races, due to a combination of circumstances, including an accident and being ill. However, once he got going, Irvine regularly scored points and won at Hockenheim at the end of July. By then, it was too late to think about the championship. I wasn't having much luck, either, with Heinz-Harald Frentzen who was failing to deliver in the other car, but at least Heinz was doing better than a third driver, Emanuele Naspetti, whom I sacked before the end of the season.

Overall, it had been a disappointing year for Jordan as reigning champions, and it was made worse by Irvine becoming upset because he was not getting in to Formula 1. There was disagreement over who said what, Eddie contending that I had promised him F1.

I agreed that was the goal but I had not – could not – guarantee it. So Irvine took himself off to race in Japan where he began a successful money-making career. Meanwhile, big plans were fermenting at the back of my mind, and they resulted in a scheme that would ultimately bring Irvine and Jordan back together a few years later.

## Chapter 13

# THE BIGGEST CHANCE OF ALL

I cannot pinpoint an exact date when I considered racing in Formula 1. I suppose the thought had always been at the back of my mind, a dream that, one day, Jordan might have a car in grand-prix racing – but it's such a big step. Buying a car from Ralt or Reynard and racing it is one thing. Actually designing, creating, building, testing and developing your own, and then taking on Ferrari, McLaren and Williams, is something else. It costs nothing to muse about such a thing while having a quiet glass of something in a reflective moment. In any case, I was never one to let hard facts stand in the way of doing something different or special. F1 would be very special.

Those thoughts had begun to take a more substantial form during 1989. When we won the F3000 championship, Eddie Jordan Racing was at another crossroads and one of the options had 'Formula 1' marked on it. I had always tried to stick to a philosophy of not moving out of a series until I had won it. Jordan had won more races in F3 and F3000 than any other British team. Having successfully put F3 to bed with Johnny Herbert, and following Jean Alesi's success in F3000, the obvious question was, 'What next?'

I had a significant amount of money – about £5 million – in the bank as the result of our success in F3 and F3000, EJM and buying and selling in areas not directly associated with motor racing over the previous few years. The question I asked myself was this: 'Do I hang on to the money and do Formula 3000 again? I can be at the top of this for some time and make a couple of hundred grand, or thereabouts, each year. Plus, the team's value is going up. As a useful aside, I can bring drivers into F1 and there is no conflict. It would be safe.'

But was that what I wanted? Did I want to invest the money and make it grow? Or did I want to risk all and blow not just the five million but whatever sponsorship I could raise, and then have debt at the end if it all went wrong? I was either going to make a success of this or go bankrupt and go back to Ireland. For what?

When I gave up driving, I took a risk in creating the Formula 3 team. I knew I could gather people with technical experience together. Jean Alesi, to whom I had become very close, would tell me what was going on at Tyrrell. He would say, 'Eddie, there's nothing special that you can't do here!' Putting common sense aside for a moment, there was only one answer.

The move into Formula 3000 had formed the catalyst for adventurous thinking. This was a sophisticated formula by our standards and yet we had come in more or less as a bunch of rookies with Herbert and Reynard in 1988 and won our first race. I may have been busy grabbing Camel's attention in the immediate aftermath, but I felt very proud about what we had done. Perhaps subconsciously, I started to peer across the next fence and look at F1. It was difficult to ignore, for instance, the fact that a good F3000 team could probably sit comfortably on the back of an F1 grid. All you needed was a decent car, engine and driver.

On the other hand, when in F3, I had looked at F3000 and doubted I could compete at that level. There always appeared to be a question mark. Irish people seem to be born with a curious mix of self-confidence and humility. We often give more respect to people and our competitors than we should do. In some ways, that is a sporting and a human thing to do but in the cold, hard competitive world of sport, it is not a very productive attitude. The problem I found was that, apart from Marie, I did not have many people I could share these thoughts with, particularly with regard to stepping up to F1.

I was watching with great interest and not a little concern as Mike Earle, a team owner I rated very highly, struggled with the Onyx team in trying to step up to F1. Here was a guy whom I thought could run an outstandingly good team but when push came to shove, it failed to work. There were extenuating circumstances because a Belgian sponsor who had become heavily involved ran into trouble, but that was part of the difficulty of operating at such a high level. I found that you could look at positives until you were blue in the face but you needed to have a balance in order to be realistic. This was not about talking a carpet dealer into putting a sticker on your Formula Ford car. This was commitment on a massive scale that would involve not just your livelihood but the livelihoods of others who would come to depend on you. However, in 1989, it was idle thinking. First, we had to deal with F3000.

By the time we reached Birmingham and Jean was shaping up to take the title, thoughts about F1 had become more substantial despite my initial reservations. Marie had come to realise that, deep down, I wanted to do it. Her attitude was: 'He's never going to be happy until he does it. If we lose it, we lose it. We started with nothing and if we wind up with nothing, we're not going to be any worse off.' It would not be like the old joke – 'How do you make a small fortune in F1? Start with a large one!'

Nonetheless, it had to be a worry at the back of everyone's mind. Our family was young, Zak having arrived not long before to join Zoë and Miki. Marie had a lot on her plate but, after ten years of marriage, she realised that we would always find a way. The one unspoken concern I had was just what would happen if I died for some unexpected reason. There was not a lot of money on Marie's side of the family and none on mine. Since I was not a believer in pensions, the family would be exposed. Being financially trained, I was always mindful of that, even if I did not voice those fears.

If I were to venture into F1 then, as a safety net, I would also continue with F3000. Wearing a 'sensible hat', my view was: 'We need an escape route here. If this F1 thing completely turns to shit, I need to be sure that I have a team, a job, a structure and a future for the people working for me.' That was so important at that stage. I needed to know that, if necessary, we could rekindle the fire and get going again in F3000. Certainly, by the time we reached Birmingham in 1989, it was clear that we had a handle on F3000, but what about F1?

The most obvious question was how would I make a car and, just as important, who would design it? In the hurly-burly of that street race with its temporary paddock and make-do facilities, one man stood out in every sense of the expression.

Gary Anderson is a big guy, the sort you would want on your side in the event of trouble. I knew all about that because we had travelled the roads of Europe together several years before during those glorious summers of F3. Gary's credentials were impeccable. Having completed his motor mechanic's apprenticeship in Northern Ireland, he did not take long to find his way into F1 – with Brabham, no less. It was a good move in many ways, not least because Brabham had been taken over by Bernie Ecclestone.

Gary had made a big impression on Bernie. The story goes that Bernie was in the workshop one day when he asked Gary to move one of the Ford-Cosworth engines they were using at the time. Bernie assumed Gary would put the V8 on a trolley and wheel it in the customary manner. You can imagine his surprise when Gary proceeded to pick up the engine with his bare hands.

This was in the very early days of Bernie revolutionising the running of F1, and Gary was on hand to witness the change. He grew up with the team because he started in the days when each car had just two mechanics. The entire Brabham team went to each race in a Transit van. Gary could turn his hand to anything and it was inevitable that he should want to design and build his own car, which he did – the Anson, for F3. Gary was keen to explore racing in Europe and he had a big hand in persuading me to do the same. This was how we met, while competing against each other on the one hand but working closely on the other – and when I say closely, I mean sometimes too close for comfort.

We would combine forces. Gary used a converted furniture van while I had an A-series Ford Transit with a hood. I could get my car on the back but it had to be almost vertical, which meant I had to have the biggest guy I could find to grind the thing up with a winch while others would be pushing at the back. Gary's box van did not have a tail lift, so he needed the loan of my mechanics to help push the cars up the temporary planks to get them into the van. We did not have two pence to rub together. If something broke, you would have to make bits. There was no choice. This is where Gary's practical engineering came into its own.

The Anson was a super little car, very advanced for the day. Gary would be flat out producing these cars for his customers to race and, of course, it would always be a last-minute rush. I remember one season-opening race at Vallelunga where Gary arrived with three new cars and not one of them had turned a wheel. When they were put on the scales, Gary discovered that the cars were something like 80 pounds under weight. So he had to rush off and scour the local builders' merchants for 240 pounds of lead. However, it was better to have a car under rather than over the weight limit and, as always, he got the job done in the end.

I used to tow a caravan behind the Transit. My mechanics would often travel with Gary in his truck and we would meet for dinner here and there. Once at the racetrack, Gary would park the van in the paddock and we would all pile into the Transit to head off to the nearest town at night. Gary and his team would use bed and breakfast accommodation or, if times were hard, sleep in the truck. On one occasion, I found somewhere that I thought was very reasonably priced for us all to stay. It was only later that we discovered why – the place doubled as a brothel during the day, and most of the night.

Those days were all part of the great adventure that we shared while dreaming about making a couple of quid and having fun, but beneath it all was a seriousness of intent. We both wanted to get on. Without substantial backing, Gary had to give up the unequal struggle to make ends meet as a constructor, and he went off to gather more experience in the United States, engineering for a team in Champ Car racing. Our paths crossed again when Gary returned to England in 1988 and became the driving force behind Roberto Moreno's championship-winning F3000 campaign with Bromley Motorsport.

Gary was also working with Reynard on the design of their F3000 car. I asked Adrian Reynard if Gary could come and engineer for us during the 1989 season. That was agreed and Gary was Martin Donnelly's engineer but, in reality, he was actually overseeing the team. Watching him closely at work, I realised that I had a huge belief in Gary Anderson. I thought he was underestimated and massively practical. I did not need a second opinion. It was obvious, when we gathered in Birmingham, that here was the man I needed to design my F1 car.

I took Gary to one side and asked if he would be interested in having full responsibility for the design and build of a Jordan F1 car. He said he thought I was totally mad. Beneath the banter, I could see that he was as intrigued and excited about the project as I was. Gary joined us full time on 4 February 1990.

One of his first tasks was to find somewhere to work. He would be engineering Irvine's F3000 car, at least for the early part of the season, but his priority would be the F1 car. To do that, he needed space that we did not have. The answer was to build a mezzanine in the little unit at Silverstone. We sent our carpenter, known to everyone as 'Plug', to Brackley Sawmills to buy a set of stairs. Then we bought railings and some breezeblocks, a couple of doors and one of Gary's first jobs was to help build some offices.

I would rope anyone in to help. Ross Cheever was a young driver, brother of former grand-prix driver, Eddie. Ross was good but, somehow, his career was faltering and he was looking for a drive in F3000. I told him I would consider it but, first, he could help by painting the inside of the entire factory over Christmas. He did it. We gave him some test work and, eventually, a race drive. Ross was one of those people who fits easily into the system and wanted to be part of it. That was the way things were at Silverstone. The place really buzzed.

We would torment the people running Silverstone Estates with our ducking and diving, always on the hunt for more space. We would start putting bits and pieces at the back of our workshop in places that we had no right to use. David Richards, then in the early days of his highly successful Prodrive operation, had a workshop across the way from ours. Dunlop had been involved in the Richards operation and that was good news because they had paid to have a smart mezzanine built inside. When Richards moved out, I moved heaven and earth to move in. The rules said that you could not sell-on your lease; you had to get someone to pay for the right to take it over. That led to a right old pantomime but we came to an 'arrangement' in the end. It was typical of the activity among the leaseholders, all of them racers, all of them chancers, out for the best deal.

Many funny incidents occurred but the sad thing is that quite a few of them passed over our heads because we were fighting to survive. It was madness at times as we tried to find a balance between enjoying the moment and dealing with the torment – no gain without pain. Some nights I went home feeling dizzy because of the frantic activity. The attitude had to be: 'I've got something to achieve here. This peripheral crap is not going to get in my way. People can rant and rave as much as they like. I will tackle whatever it is only when it becomes a massive crisis. But if, at the moment, it's not a crisis, then fuck them!' That was the only way to deal with the apparent drama because 90 per cent of time, it never became an out-and-out crisis.

There was no let-up. I went to the circuit café every day for lunch. That was a mad house, too. Several racing teams were based within the estate and they were involved in Formula Ford, F3, touring cars, sports cars, you name it. There might be 20 to 30 people queuing for lunch and the banter would start the minute you walked in. We would fight like hell. Someone would say, 'Jordan is doing this and that's not allowed.' Someone else would complain that Murray Taylor's truck was too big. Others would threaten to blow the whistle on whatever business scam you thought you had up your sleeve. It was an incredible atmosphere and the whole thing worked because, despite the arguments, everyone in there had one aim and a common love – winning motor races.

I knew, as 1989 moved into 1990, I would not be winning races – at least, in F1 – for quite some time. I felt sure that I could put together the people needed to make the car, but two very important aspects were outside my control. One was engines and the other was tyres.

I targeted Ford and made some inquires very early on. Dick Scammell of Cosworth Racing helped put me in touch with Michael Kranefuss, who headed Ford's motorsport division in Detroit. I made it my business to go and chat to him. It was soon obvious that Kranefuss did not want to detract from what Ford were already doing with Benetton Cosworth. On the other hand, Ford owned Cosworth and Kranefuss knew the Northamptonshire firm wanted as many customers as they could get. Cosworth and Ford had an impressive heritage in F1 that stretched back to 1967. They had, at one time or another, embraced Williams, McLaren, Tyrell, Brabham and just about any team worthy of the name.

In the end, we came to an arrangement whereby Jordan would buy engines from Cosworth on the understanding that the V8s would be at least one step, perhaps two, behind the works Benetton-Fords. The contract stage was very complicated and very difficult. There had to be different agreements about liability and who would pay for what if an engine failed. That was always the problem when dealing with engine manufacturers and Cosworth was no exception.

Initially, I was to refer to my car as a Jordan-Cosworth but that changed when Ford realised there was marketing value in Jordan being associated with Ford. Either way, I did not really care what terminology was used. I did have the choice of either Judd or Lamborghini engines but I knew the Ford-Cosworth would be perfect for Jordan at this stage. Cosworth were half-an-hour's drive away, Gary was familiar with the company and the engine could be relied upon to give us reliable and adequate performance. I was also happy to have secured the Cosworth deal because, at the time, engine manufacturers were spoilt for choice as several small teams such as Jordan were beating down F1's doors. All of them – Coloni, AGS, Larrousse – wanted the Cosworth and I considered myself fortunate. The tyre supply would not be so easy to secure.

As with the engine, I wanted a tyre that would provide a useful and consistent baseline. Goodyear had to be the first choice, particularly as we went back a long way, from when I raced karts, through Formula Ford and into sports cars. Unfortunately, Goodyear's books were full thanks to supplying McLaren, Williams and Ferrari, among others. Nonetheless, I felt I was making progress, helped a great deal by Jordan's track record. It was clear that we knew – or hoped we knew – just what we were doing and that was picked up by Goodyear's racing director, Leo Mehl, and endorsed by his man at the races, Lee Gaug, two out-and-out racing men whose support proved invaluable.

In the end, Goodyear went against the wishes of many of the established teams, who felt Jordan should stay with the rest of the small teams and run on Pirelli tyres. The Pirellis, as we shall see, had an advantage during pre-qualifying first thing on a race weekend but, in the long term, the Goodyear tyre had much better durability. With the greatest of respect to Pirelli, Goodyear knew how to win grands prix. So, now we were rolling.

How was I going to pay for this and the myriad expenses that were mounting rapidly with the F1 project? Every penny of the £5 million would have to be sunk into it but that would not be enough. This was a crucial time. The manager of the Allied Irish Bank in Northampton, Roger Donegan, was very tough with me. He was always understanding but, being a good banker, he would err on the side of caution. Roger would run through the downside rather than accept my optimistic view without question. He had a good habit of keeping my feet on the ground. It was here that I met Richard O'Driscoll, who would eventually come to work for me when the F1 team got up and running.

The bank was not overgenerous. While that could be frustrating at times, my banking background had taught me that, sometimes, an overgenerous bank was one of the worst things you could have. Eventually you have to pay the money back and, unless you have a structure in place to do that, the trouble really starts. The AIB had a very old-fashioned way. You borrowed the maximum that you thought you could pay back in a moderate time, particularly if the going got tough. The bank never wanted to know how you would repay in the good times, because anyone can do that. The trouble with this venture would be predicting just when the good times might arrive – if at all. In August 1990, the company name was changed from Eddie Jordan Racing to Jordan Grand Prix. We were committed.

## Chapter 14

# NICE CAR, NO SPONSOR

If you asked the design chiefs in any F1 team today to oversee the preparation of three GP2 cars, engineer them, test them and go racing on ten weekends while, at the same time, designing and building next year's F1 car, they would seriously suggest that you had received a bang on the head. That is exactly what Gary Anderson and his small team did during the 1990 season. The intrigue and challenge of our F1 project had tempted Andrew Green and Mark Smith to join Gary for the ride. Along the way, we went racing with Eddie Irvine, Emanuele Naspetti and Heinz-Harald Frentzen, with Trevor Foster engineering one of the cars and running the team.

It was a tall order by any standards but this was precisely the sort of hands-on adversity that Gary relished. It seemed to me that the whole thing was very Irish in its approach – absolutely no fat, unbelievably lean and immensely practical. Looking back on it now, I was not paying top F1 dollars by any means because I had to keep everything tight. When you consider that a handful of people actually achieved the seemingly impossible, I was getting away with blue murder. In the background, Bosco Quinn was tidying up loose ends and generally keeping me straight.

I had known Bosco for years. A telephone engineer from Dublin, Bosco was one of the group that had been helping me when I was a driver. A very private man – a bit of a loner in many ways – Bosco was totally dependable and a good friend. He had begun working for me in 1985. Even though Bosco had not been trained as a mechanic, one of his first jobs to was to go to Ralt in Weybridge and build our F3 car. That was the way things worked then. You did what you could, and Bosco would turn his hand to anything. He had remained with me throughout although, as the F1 project began to gather momentum, I could see he was having his doubts about staying. Bosco did not like F1. He had no feel for what he called 'the starry lights'. He really did not understand the razzmatazz but, in 1990, he was very much part of the background effort as our little group pushed on with producing the first Jordan.

Gary was extremely skilful. The key to the whole thing was that while Mark and Andrew had massive respect for Gary, they were not in awe of him. They had worked with him very successfully at Reynard and they knew what they were letting themselves in for. Of course, I was also lucky in that the experience they had gained at Reynard was second to none. Adrian knew how to build a successful car to a price. The lunatics in F1 these days have no idea because their attitude is 'money will get you out of a hole'. I don't agree with that. It never worked for me, although I'm sure some people will say that I never spent any money in the first place!

When I did have money, things never seemed as good or quite so satisfying. I have always believed that it is important to have a bit of hunger. In any aspect of life or business, you need people to push, to strive, to try to attain positions that they would not normally reach. When there is very little money, you have mind over matter – total focus. You find yourself saying, 'I'm going to build this car. I'm going to race this car. I'm going to be in Phoenix for the first race at the beginning of next year.' Gary Anderson never had any doubt. That was his belief. My job was to find the money. Compared to Gary, I had little to worry about.

Gary kept banging on about the need to use a wind tunnel. To me, that simply meant £1,500 a day that could be better spent elsewhere. My attitude changed when I went to see exactly what was going on in the wind tunnel at Southampton University. Gary was incredibly enthusiastic about the model of the F1 car and the readings he was getting. Even though I did not understand half of the technical jargon, I got his drift and it was impossible not to become even more passionate about the whole project.

This was in the early days of understanding the full importance of aerodynamics. Gary was ahead of his time and our brief forays to Southampton – we only went three or four times – were not even scratching the surface of an aspect of F1 that now calls for teams to have, not one, but two of their own wind tunnels running 24/7, and a squad of boffins to operate them. In 1990, Gary would come back from a rare visit to Southampton, pack his bag and head off with Andy and Mark to a race at Vallelunga or Pau or some such. Ask any F1 technical boss to do that today and he would think you were having a laugh.

Meanwhile, I was looking for funds. My experience on a smaller level in F3 stood me in good stead. When I put together a deal for Johnny Herbert with Stelrad, I was working with a radiator company that was part of Metalbox, a very big group. This made me become more corporate minded and focused on the wider picture. I became aware that my early years in banking and cost and management accountancy helped give me a different perspective and understanding. Looking at my career thus far, I was both lucky and unlucky – unlucky because I was very late coming into the sport as a driver and I probably suffered as a result; lucky because, when I realised that I was not going to make it as a driver, I gave up early enough to allow me to come in as a comparatively young team boss.

On top of that, I seemed to find it easy to make interesting presentations and structure a proper business plan. I could produce a spreadsheet that would show a prospective sponsor how their involvement could give them real value. I was aware that this point needed to be got across because many companies, unfamiliar with the sport, have the impression that sponsorship of motor racing is the equivalent of tipping large amounts of money into a hole.

If you explain the many facets, such as involving their staff, using the driver or team principal to come in and give motivational speeches, attitudes change. If your target company is in retailing, it is important to explain the benefit of having guests and providing hospitality at the races or, alternatively, bringing their key clients for a factory visit. Along the way, you say, 'This is what we are trying to achieve.' Then to cap it all, you say, 'If you give me twenty thousand – or whatever the figure might be – to sponsor this car and driver, I will generate five times that amount in real advertising value.' You back that up with facts and figures to show how they could generate media coverage in the area in which the company specialises. Having got the sponsor on board, at the end of the year you give another presentation showing how you achieved the promised value. It should be done on a constructive basis.

Many people continue to feel that sponsorship is a nasty, negative word. It is not. A calculating and cunning chief executive who really understands the value of advertising and the power that sport can bring, will understand that. Companies such as Red Bull are not in Formula 1 for fun. It is part of a process that has to make business sense.

In the lower formulae, such as karting or Formula Ford, if you are trying to cajole a friend, or a friend's friend, into doing something, they will only ever see it as a loss leader, money down the pan in the business sense. They tend to view it as similar to giving to charity – something they are doing because you are a mate, a 'good lad who needs a bit of support'. However, further up the ladder, you must not only make a proper case but you must also be able to justify it. Even more important, you have to believe in it. The talk must come from the heart.

Once you have presented the detail of how previously unseen and unheard of peripheral values are there to be attained, I would focus on the goodwill factor, and how this motor-racing programme can help make company members feel good about themselves, particularly if the company is growing. It is essential to convince people on the inside that they are not simply giving money, which is an impression many employees will have initially. I would always ask if I could address the firm's next staff meeting and then say to the directors, 'Don't make a decision on this sponsorship proposal until you get the feedback internally.' Nine times out of ten, the staff would say, 'We feel good about this. What Eddie Jordan says really makes sense. If we paid for advertising in the traditional way, it would cost us five times as much. And we have added value in that we're going to pull in new people who will want to come to the races and see our team – *their* team – in action.'

Those staff members loved it. It is like going to a horse race when you own or have an interest in one of the horses. Normally, you would go to the bar, have a drink, place a bet and go home. If you have a horse running, you are in the paddock, you meet the jockey and you watch every move 'your' horse makes throughout the race. It is a completely different story.

While I was searching for sponsors, the team was producing hard results. Trevor and Bosco were absolute rocks in the way they kept the F3000 operation running. Meanwhile, the work ethic of the three guys in our so-called 'Technical Department' was quite staggering. Even more incredible was the result of their endeavours. They were sharing one office and much of the work – the bodywork, for example – was drawn by hand. Certain parts, such as the suspension, were done on Cad-Cam, which was then in its infancy as far as we were concerned. I had been fortunate, through my contacts with Mugen-Honda, to receive a couple of Cad stations from Hewlett-Packard, Japan. The car was beautifully conceived, the lines perfect. Here was an F1 racer that was superb in its simplicity – exactly what we needed.

We had John Watson give the car a few laps of Silverstone and, although it was difficult to draw conclusions from a shake-down test, John was able to use his experience as the winner of five grands prix to say that, basically, the car was sound and had no vices. That was all you could hope for.

John's impartial view supported the popular theory that if a car looks right, it usually is right – and the Jordan certainly looked the part. In fact, I was thrilled. Even allowing for my obvious bias, I thought we had one of the most elegant F1 cars of the moment. Part of the attraction was that it was unpainted, left with just the stark black of the carbon-fibre chassis. Somehow this gave the car a mean and purposeful look. We had come up with this typically audacious Jordan plan in a roundabout manner.

We wanted to unveil the car officially, for the benefit of the media. Usually, such occasions have a two-fold purpose – to let everyone have a good look at the car for the first time, and to use the opportunity to introduce and gain exposure for sponsors. There was only one flaw with the second part – we did not have any sponsors.

The initial thought was to have the car appear virgin white. I was not keen on choosing a particular colour and then appearing to be tied to that scheme. I wanted to give the impression of full freedom of choice when negotiating with sponsors. In addition, I did not think it would look good if we launched the car in one colour and then, a month later, changed it. Someone – doubtless a pragmatist after my own heart – raised the question of wasting time and money painting the car at all. Why not leave it in its raw state? That appealed immediately because it was most unusual to see a car like this and, as I have said, it looked striking.

The usual form was to have a couple of hundred people from across the F1 divide turn up at some grand venue, take a look at the car for five minutes and spend the rest of the time engaged in gossip and chit-chat. On this occasion, not having much to shout about – apart from the car – we wanted to show that we actually existed and meant business. There had been a lot of speculation in the media about whether or not we had an agreement with Ford. The Larrousse team had lost their deal with Lamborghini for the supply of engines in 1991 and the suggestion was the French team would grab the V8s earmarked for Jordan. I wanted to be able to wheel out the car and say, 'Look, here is the Jordan F1 car in the flesh, with the Ford engine. The team exists, the car is ready, we're serious and we're going F1 racing.'

So we invited the F1 media to our workshop. Twenty-nine turned up and sat on plastic chairs as we took the cover off the car with the minimum of fuss. I think it is fair to say that the majority were impressed, and not a little surprised, by what they saw. Of course, this being F1, I was to discover that you cannot please everyone, particularly some of the elder statesmen of the press corps.

Gerard 'Jabby' Crombac had made the trip from Paris in his role as editor of *Sport-Auto* in France. Jabby was one of the first correspondents for the British magazine *Autosport* when it was launched in 1951, and he had been a close friend of Colin Chapman's. Very little escaped Jabby's attention. On this occasion, however, the importance to us of this car and project seemed to pass him by. In less than flattering terms, he wrote that the car looked nice but he questioned why we were bothering.

My memory is not brilliant, as any of my frustrated friends and colleagues will tell you, but I have never forgotten those words. If anything was going to galvanise me, it was a comment such as that from a highly respected journalist. More than anything, I wanted to prove exactly why we were bothering. It added to the urgency of finding sponsors, because less than four months remained before the first race of 1991.

Camel was the obvious choice. We had significant history thanks to winning the F3000 championship with an all-yellow Camel car in 1989. I felt sure that, having parted company with Lotus, Camel would want to come on board. The Jordan F1 programme was an extension of the sort of adventure we had been enjoying together, but that did not take into consideration the forces that work behind the scenes in F1.

Flavio Briatore was keen to keep Camel for his Benetton team. With support from Michael Kranefuss, Briatore told Camel that Benetton would have the works Ford engine, whereas we would not. This was perfectly true, of course. I do not know how much top spin was applied to the manner of its telling but it was enough for Camel to decide that they did not want to be associated with Jordan in F1.

Camel had received a letter at their USA headquarters from Ford in Detroit – one American company to another – reiterating Ford's total commitment to Benetton. As a result, Camel would not so much as discuss our case.

I was deeply disappointed because we had built up a special relationship with Camel. Our success with Jean Alesi had opened up massive markets in Europe. Camel France had been going crazy because of their increased sales. F1 with Jordan made sense all round.

I was so annoyed that I felt I had no alternative but to go to see the chairman of R.J. Reynolds, the parent company, in person to explain a few things. I flew economy to New York and on to Winston Salem and I refused to leave the premises until I got to speak to the man himself. They tried to get me out by promising a meeting in the future but I refused point blank to leave. I was quite brutal because this was really irritating me now. I felt I had been completely shafted.

I knew that Duncan Lee had endured enough of Lotus and he was in our favour, but I also knew that Kranefuss was desperate to make sure that Benetton had enough money to do the job. He did not want a customer team having a better sponsorship deal than Benetton. I could understand that but I felt that there had been a bond between Jordan and Camel. Naively, perhaps, I was not prepared to see that relationship cast aside and, in any case, my impression was that an agreement to go ahead together had been reached in principle.

Many things in F1 are done verbally and on a handshake with the written contracts following later. People outside this multi-million pound sport find that hard to believe. It has to be done that way because things happen quickly in F1. You do the deal and you move on. You get someone else to prepare the documentation. Eventually, you will be asked to go into a room and sign the documents. You will say, 'To the best of my memory, that's what was agreed,' and the other party will say, 'Yes, to the best of my memory, that's what it was.' Everything will be signed, you will have a drink and go home.

It's very simple – except when it breaks down. When that happens, an administrator, adjudicator, judge, or whomever it may be, finds it unbelievable that a deal of this magnitude could have been reached without notes, minutes, lawyers, secretaries and documents. They don't understand it.

With Camel, I believed a deal was there. After my speech to the chairman, Camel made a token gesture but, in truth, they could not be seen to be doing anything, particularly after that formal letter from Ford. Camel recognised my position but I had to be very mindful that Jordan were the new kids on the block. This deal was not going to happen, we were not going to get anywhere, so I had to withdraw as gracefully as possible. Win some, lose some. Now I was about to do a bit of the former – when I least expected it.

## Chapter 15

# COMING TOGETHER

Looking across the political minefield that lay ahead, it was clear to me that I needed someone to help guide me through it, someone who understood the nuances of F1 and how to work them. When I asked around, it did not take long for the name Ian Phillips to come to the fore.

I first met Ian not long after I came to England for the first time in the early 1970s. Ian was the editor of *Autosport*, a very influential position, particularly if you were a wannabe racing driver and needed all the mentions you could get in Britain's weekly motor-sport bible. I soon learned that, despite having editorial offices somewhere in the West End, *Autosport* was actually run from a pub in Camden Hill. Go into the snug bar of the Windsor Castle and the chances were you would find Phillips and his team holding an editorial meeting. At least, that was the excuse. Young drivers such as Stefan Johansson, Michael Roe, Bernard Devaney and many others used to frequent this pub because it was a well-known fact that the number of pints you bought had a direct correlation with the amount of coverage you got in a magazine run by this hippy editor with long hair.

Ian's deputy editor was Chris Witty, another semi-hooligan and passionate motor-racing fan. Chris was a man of many parts in every sense because, in the original film version of *The Railway Children*, he played the role of Jim, the young lad injured in the tunnel. I think, to this day, Chris is still living off the royalties and not much else. When I managed to arrange sponsorship from Philip Morris, Chris had connections with Marlboro and he later managed the launch of Derek McMahon's Marlboro Team Ireland programme. For most of the time, Chris seemed to be sharing a flat with Phillips.

My association with Ian continued to grow after he left *Autosport* and became general manager of Donington Park, a place that, for reasons that cannot possibly have had anything to do with the amount of partying at the East Midlands track, was very popular with the Irish drivers.

Our paths did not cross for a couple of years, particularly after I had stopped driving. Then, in 1983 when my team was doing well in Formula 3, we were invited to be part of a major onslaught on the Macau Grand Prix. Marlboro regularly sponsored a combined team for Macau, carrying the force of a couple of British outfits. This year the drivers included Martin Brundle and Ayrton Senna – and who should be representing Marlboro at this time? None other than Ian Phillips. We were reunited, but in different capacities yet again.

Macau was a big event for us, not least because we asked for plenty of money to make the trip. In fact, about 25 per cent of an F3 team's total budget for the year would be realised by going to Macau. It was always heavily sponsored and always televised live. The race through the streets was also shown in Europe, with ITV handling coverage, which was very important to the British-based teams. The race was significant because it was spectacular – a sort of mini-Monaco – and it was considered to be the pinnacle of F3 thanks to the involvement of leading teams from the F3 championships in Italy, France, Britain and Germany.

In 1983, we finished first and second. The celebrations can be imagined, and Ian Phillips led the way. He was always a good man to take for a drink because he could put them away as well as any Irishman I know – and I know several who fit that category. There were so many functions in Macau that we were worn out meeting dignitaries and fulfilling our commitments to Marlboro. It was no surprise that Sid Taylor was the man who decided to bring a welcome alternative to the formal agenda by introducing us to his Crazy Paris Show.

Sid, a great supporter of motor racing as an entrant and enthusiast, made his money from all sorts of enterprises, some of which are beyond repeating inside the covers of a book such as this. You will get a clue when I say that part of his entertainment empire included this Crazy Paris Show, a clever play on the Crazy Horse Show in Paris – except Sid's version in Macau was not quite so, how shall I say, classy. Sid had imported a number of ladies of the night from Europe to add to the on-stage entertainment. The Can-Can was the most recognisable of performances that varied from the strange to the bizarre, most of them carried out by girls in the skimpiest of skimpy costumes.

The most amazing act was performed by a girl called Jocelyn. She would climb into a massive fish tank and do acrobatic manoeuvres the like of which we had never seen before – and all of this while holding her breath for about five minutes. How she did that I will never know. It was incredible. Only slightly less remarkable – but perhaps no surprise – Phillips became very friendly with Jocelyn, a relationship that would ensure Ian's attendance at the Macau GP for years to come. Not that anyone needed an excuse to go to this fabulous event. Or to see Jocelyn, come to that.

Mind you, it was not always beer and strippers in Macau. On one occasion, my team was combined with WSR run by Kiwi Dick Bennetts and, as ever, we had a very strong line-up between us, including drivers Emanuele Pirro and Stefan Johanssen. We were in one of the best garages, which was handily located at a lower level than the rest, but that backfired on us when a typhoon blew one evening and flooded the place. Luckily, the cars were raised on stands to bring them to waist height for the benefit of the mechanics doing the preparation. Even so, water reached the axles.

I knew all about the rain, but nothing about the flooding in the garage. One or two problems had needed sorting out and when I arrived for start of business the next day and began to explain some of my own difficulties, I was rewarded with a right earful. Dick

Bennetts, now joined by Dave Price, who is outspoken at the best of times in his trademark East London accent, had been there most of the night with the mechanics, baling the place out and doing their best to have everything ready in time for practice. 'Problems!' he exploded. 'What problems? Jesus! Have you any fucking idea what's been goin' on da'n 'ere, mate? It's been like the bleedin' Titanic in 'ere. Typical bloody Jordan to miss it all…' The rest of his views on my social habits and apparent skiving from some seriously hard work do not bear repeating. Of course, this story was greeted with much hilarity by Ian Phillips, but we had the last laugh because our team was not only able to race but to win outright.

While I was working through F3 and into F3000, Ian was continuing to spread his wings, working with Bridgestone during the Japanese firm's first foray into European racing and travelling back and forth to Japan in association with Marlboro's connection in Formula 2 there. During the course of his association with Japanese racing, Ian met Akira Akagi, the owner of the Leyton House team. One thing led to another and, before he knew it, Ian was heading up the Leyton House effort in Formula 1. That was the way motor racing worked then and, to a lesser degree, in the current era. If a seemingly outrageous opportunity arose and your balls were big enough, you grabbed the chance.

It was simpler then of course because there was no requirement for an F1 team to make their own car. Leyton House commissioned March to build a chassis. Then they purchased a Judd engine, bolted it to the back and went racing. There were some very exciting times for this team, working on a shoestring, and it proved to be invaluable experience for Ian in years to come.

In between, however, he fell very ill with meningitis, which was serious given that he was not in the peak of fitness thanks to a liking for cigarettes and the occasional drink. Ian eventually returned to find the team in a mess and on the point of closure. In the meantime, and at the other end of the scale, I was about to open the door and take my first tentative steps into F1.

I distinctly remember going to Bernie Ecclestone in 1990 and saying to him, 'I probably need someone who knows the F1 ropes. Do you know anyone who can come and help me in terms of basic logistics and so on?'

'Well, you don't want anyone hanging around you too much because you need to be seen to be the front man,' Bernie replied.

'Yeah, that sounds about right.'

'There's a fella around who knows the ropes, but he's a bit ill at the moment. He'll be lucky if he sees the year out, because he can't live much longer. He's Ian Phillips. You know him, don't you?'

Know him! 'Here we go again,' I thought. 'Phillips and Jordan in yet another association.' Ian was the obvious choice because of his vast knowledge and I was absolutely delighted when he agreed to join Jordan Grand Prix and help put things together. From the word go, Ian was an absolute rock.

Two weeks after Ian joined us, another guardian angel arrived. I had always been very fortunate in having excellent secretaries because the job involved far more than taking dictation and writing letters. It was a broad-based role that included everything from being a personal assistant to a public-relations person sorting out the mess in my sometimes destructive wake.

Angela Buckland was my first secretary, in the 1980s, a member of the famous Tee family who, at the time, owned *Motoring News* and *Motor Sport*. Angela was barely out of her teens and she had to put up with a lot, including having me call her 'Green Knickers'. (During a trip in the freezing cold to an F3 race, Angela had made the mistake of joking that it was just as well she had brought her green school knickers.) Angela was completely at home in the racing environment and she fell in love with Gil de Ferran when he was racing in England before becoming a big name in the United States. They got married, raised a family and when Gil was given the top job of sporting director with the Honda F1 team in England in 2005, they bought our house in Oxford.

Lindsay Haylett, who had previously worked in the music business, knew quite a bit about F1 because she had looked after Ian's secretarial affairs at Leyton House. One of the first things Ian noticed when he walked through the door was that we had no secretarial staff at all. A call was put through to Lindsay and it was not long before she was running the show. Lindsay was the ultimate bionic woman. She would shout, 'Leave that to me! Don't talk to him, talk to me. I know what's going on – he hasn't got a clue.' This applied not just to me but to everyone on the team. When we had F3 teams in Britain and Europe, Bosco ran the outfit in Nogaro and Lindsay more or less ran the Silverstone operation single-handed. She put manners on everyone and made a formidable working partnership with Bosco.

Meanwhile, I was about to make my own luck as I sought further sponsorship. With Camel no longer in the reckoning, the obvious tactic was to switch to their rival, Marlboro, and that brought Andrea de Cesaris into the picture, a development that we were more than happy to embrace. Andrea, with no disrespect, had been through just about every team in the paddock. No one wanted to have him, but he suited our needs perfectly.

Andrea had calmed down quite a bit since the days when he terrified us all in F3. As I said at the time, there was no doubt that he was fast; it was just that he seemed to spend as much time being fast off the track as on it. Since then, he had driven in 150 grands prix and led the Belgian Grand Prix for 18 laps. His experience was just what we wanted. Jordan would become his eighth F1 team in 11 seasons.

Andrea came to the factory, looked at the car and had a chat with Gary – whom he knew – and immediately felt as comfortable with us as we did with him. Andrea was very enthusiastic. And there was an added bonus – because of his connection with Philip Morris, he would be bringing about $3.5 million, a very significant sum for Jordan Grand Prix.

We signed Andrea late in the day and that made our line-up complete. Four months previously, in November 1990, a deal had been done with Bertrand Gachot, a driver with just the sort of assets we needed at that time. Bertrand had been through the ranks and then competed in a couple of grands prix for the Onyx team as well as failing to qualify a Coloni – a dog of a car – during a brief but difficult period in F1. He was a great marketeer, probably one of the best F1 has ever had as a driver. He was bright, bilingual, had a lot of ideas and initiative, and plenty of confidence in his own ability. He was the perfect fit. Unfortunately, he was not to sit comfortably within Jordan for as long as either of us had hoped, and the first hint of his unplanned departure came at the most awkward moment imaginable.

The car had been registered as a Jordan-Ford 191. The original plan had been to call it a 911 in deference to the year 1991 and this being the first Jordan car. That seemed very neat and tidy until a writ came through the door from Porsche, pointing out the brand image that they had built up with their famous 911 sports car over the previous 20 years and reminding me of their rights to that title. I refused to change the name at first because Porsche's rights related to road cars only. We then had a bit of a discussion and I agreed to change the designation of our car to 191. Of course, it was a complete coincidence that, not long after, I took delivery of a black Porsche 911. It was only a number, after all. I did not really care what we called the Jordan. The important thing was that our racing car appeared to be quick.

Bertrand had given the car, still all black, its first serious test at the Paul Ricard circuit in the south of France. The lap times were impressive and we made it known that we were quietly delighted. The truth was that we had very little fuel on board and almost no ballast. I understood the importance of pre-season testing times from a commercial point of view. Gary came to hate it in future years when I asked him to run the car light. He knew why I was doing it but his preference was to run with plenty of fuel on board in order to learn about tyre-wear and handling in race conditions. Given our position at the beginning of 1991, I was not going to stand on ceremony. If the car looked quick, my job would be easier. A number of small potential sponsors were looking for a cheap deal and I needed to nail them down before the start of the season.

I had been looking for a theme for the 191. I have to be honest and say that I had been counting my Camel chickens by imagining the main colour would be yellow – which happens to be one of my favourites. After the rejection by Camel, that was obviously not going to be the case, which really upset me because that had been part of my mindset. Yellow would have suited Kodak, who were bringing out a new instamatic camera. They had been in NASCAR and were looking at other avenues. I had offered them a very reasonable deal and, of course, a yellow car was part of the attraction, but before I could put an alternative plan in place, a bizarre thing happened.

Chapter 16

# TALKING THE TALK

I had been thinking about 7UP as a possible sponsor. The brand had come to mind because Ireland is 7UP's biggest per capita market. You rarely see anyone drinking Sprite or Coke or Pepsi, always 7UP. We were all brought up on it. I do not know if this remains true but southern Ireland used to be the only country in the world where 7UP outsold Pepsi and Coke combined.

Through contact with John Postlethwaite, who was influential in the marketing division of 7UP, I arranged a meeting with Paul Adams, the European director. During the course of our conversation, I discovered that they were having a European marketing conference at the Carlton Towers Hotel in London. He agreed that I could come and speak about F1. If all the markets bought in to the idea, anything was possible.

I figured that it might be better if I had company rather than trying to get through this on my own. So I prepared my bullet points for the key messages I wanted to get across. Then I was going to pull a little rabbit from the hat by saying, 'Now guys, I want to introduce you to our driver. This is Bertrand Gachot. He's from Luxembourg, lives in Belgium and he is very familiar with the European market.' And off Bertrand would go, speaking English and other languages fluently and really doing the business as only he could.

Come the day and I was on my feet but there was no sign of Gachot, which was very unlike him. We will come to the reason for his absence later but, for the moment, I was well and truly pissed off – and stranded. I grabbed the bull by the horns, apologised to the delegates from Europe and said they would have to make do with an Irishman, and I ad-libbed from there. I thought this was a totally lost cause but, to my astonishment, they liked whatever it was that I said – I really cannot remember the precise content. They had a vote at the end of conference and, before I knew it, they were discussing whether they would come on board. The firm did not have a central budget; it was down to the individual markets to control their own. Since all the countries would have to contribute, the vote had to be unanimous. One or two admitted that they were not into F1 but, in the end, they agreed to do it. I could not believe it. The amount was not huge – $1.1 million plus a bonus of $1 million if we managed to score 15 points – but we had a deal. We also had a colour. It was green. My mind was working at a million miles an hour.

I was on to the Irish government in no time at all. I told them I felt so strongly about this first-ever Irish F1 team – our licence to go racing was Irish – that I was going to paint my car green. I said that I did not want to put 'Visit Ireland' on the car; I just wanted the word 'Ireland'. I was dealing with Charlie McCreevy, the Irish Minister of Sport at the time and soon to become Minister of Finance. Charlie is an understated genius who was hugely influential in the economic growth of Ireland and, later, a powerful force in charge of the Internal Market and Services in the European Commission. The Irish government agreed to my proposal – and put £1 million towards the team.

I was ecstatic. Seven days previously, I had nothing. Suddenly I had Ireland and 7UP, which was a huge brand. This was big in the sense that back-of-the-grid F1 teams had cars covered in stickers for a pasta shop here and a back-street engineering firm there. Jordan was coming in with an international brand.

Apart from anything else, this was my way of being able to say to Gary, 'I'm winning as well! You're winning with the car, I'm winning with this.' That was the way it worked between us. We had a huge amount of respect for each other but, if I was not producing the goods, Gary would let me know. And vice versa. If the car was not quick enough, Gary knew he would hear from me. It was good, competitive banter, an excellent blend that worked for us. It may not have worked for others because some people take these things personally. Gary never really did. Yes, he used to sulk but so did I, probably more than most. Nevertheless, there was an understanding and it was helpful that we were both from the island of Ireland.

There was, to put it mildly, a bit of bother in the north. With Gary being a northern Protestant and me being a southern Roman Catholic, we had our own views on the political situation and its effect on our lives. Sometimes we would have ferocious discussions about the rights and wrongs of both sides but, at heart, we were both passionate about being Irish. That was understandable from my point of view but it was interesting to discover Gary's feelings, even though he had been brought up in part of the United Kingdom and, naturally, considered himself British. For many Ulstermen – whether they liked to admit it or not – there was no getting away from the fact that, north and south of the border, we were all born on this little island to the west of Britain. It was geographical rather than religious, an ideal that was strengthened by sport.

You only had to sample the buzz at Lansdowne Road in Dublin and, particularly in recent times, Croke Park, when Ireland played rugby at home. Protestant would rub shoulders with Catholic and not give a toss about religion, in the same way that players from both sides of the border would be scrumming down together in order to take on whichever foe had dared to cross the Irish Sea. What mattered on those magical Saturday afternoons was hammering the opposition – particularly the English – into the ground and then wondering what your neighbour would like to drink rather than which church he would be attending the following morning.

It was the same for Gary and me. We would rib each other mercilessly but, at heart, there was respect for each point of view and a feeling that it was Ireland as a whole that mattered and not its political and religious parts. Our car was Irish, and by a happy coincidence, the application of green paint said as much.

On Thursday, 31 January 1991, Team 7UP Jordan was officially announced with green being the predominant colour throughout the modest press brochure. There was no sponsorship evident on the rear wing.

Despite the change of colour scheme, I was determined to continue with the plan to have Kodak on the rear wing. I went to their headquarters in the USA to present what I thought was a clever strategy. The 7UP brand was actually owned by Pepsi and, despite 7UP being considered a drink for the young market, Pepsi were not unduly concerned about being loosely linked with Marlboro on the same car. Pepsi respected Philip Morris as a massive brand name and they were quite happy with the association, particularly as they were both American companies. I would use that tactic with Kodak.

I concluded by saying, 'And what's *really* good – and this is something you're gonna love – is that we have two major American institutions sponsoring the team. Philip Morris *and* the Pepsi Group.'

The guy looked at me, and blinked. 'You've got Pepsi?' he asked.

'Well, we have in a way, because it's 7UP.'

'That's great – but 7UP is green. What's happened to the all-yellow car?'

I was ready for that question.

'Yes,' I said, 'the car will be green now, but we can do the wing and so on in your colours. It's not a problem.'

'It is a problem,' he said immediately. 'I would never get that past my marketing board. It won't happen.'

My heart sank. I barely heard what he said next, but it was enough to shake me from my momentary despondency.

'I think you've got the wrong sponsor,' he went on. 'Y'know, you're green. There's only one green photographic company and that's Fuji, and they are our biggest competitor.'

I thought I was hearing things. 'Of course!' I thought to myself. 'I'm a feckin eejit. I hadn't even thought about that – and here's the opposition telling me! Next stop Tokyo.'

Doing business in Japan is quite an experience. The serious stuff is discussed around the boardroom table during the day, but that is only half the battle. Visitors are then entertained in the evening. This is not optional. Japanese executives love expenses. They must have a system that allows the cost of entertaining, no matter how broad the term, to be reclaimed. Guests are outnumbered because members of the company concerned will come at you in droves. For instance, the entire marketing department seems to appear during what amounts to a night out on the town. When one group disappears, replacement troops materialise out of nowhere and continue to fly the company flag into the small hours. Meanwhile, the beleaguered guest has to continue drinking and eating. You can end up in a sushi place or a karaoke bar or even a steam bath and such like. Being a man of the world, I wanted to see what was going on. I mean, it would have been rude not to. I was treated unbelievably well.

The experience was made even sweeter by Fuji's interest in my proposal to have exposure on the rear wing. I had brought a model of the car and I have to confess that I had twisted Gary's arm to make the rear wing perhaps a touch larger than it should have been, all the better to show off the Fuji logo. My timing, through luck rather than judgement, was perfect. Fuji wished to increase their market share as quickly as possible and F1 was very attractive in Japan.

This was when I realised that the Japanese attach huge importance to their home market. Whereas most sales executives think about better distribution, awareness and marketing on an international level, the Japanese – even a brand as well known as Honda – will focus on home sales and acceptance as their priority. That may have changed now but in 1991 Japanese companies were governed by the strength and positioning of their brand in the domestic market. Fuji were no exception and they were aware that Canon had enjoyed a presence (with Williams) in F1 for quite some time. Most importantly, F1 was very popular in Japan and the interest had soared even further following the return of grand-prix racing to the country in 1987.

Eventually, after a visit to Japan that seemed to consist of four days and one night when in the social company of these madmen, a deal worth $1.4 million was completed. Given what was going to happen on the track, this would represent incredible value for Fuji, and the same for 7UP.

This was effectively a loss leader for Jordan Grand Prix but it gave the team an identity and credibility. I did not want the local fish shop; I did not want the local carpet shop. What I needed was a worldwide brand that would prompt people to say, 'Shit! Jordan are serious. Look what they've got. They've got the Ford engine, Goodyear tyres, and they've got 7UP and Fuji. On top of that, they've got a country – they've got Ireland on the car.'

We had three major brands. Now that we had found something to put on the car, Jordan Grand Prix had to make that car work on the track.

Chapter 17

# BY THE TIME I GET TO PHOENIX

Talk about jumping in at the deep end. The first grand prix of 1991 had been scheduled for Phoenix, which was hardly down the road at Brands Hatch or a truck journey to Italy. We were on the back foot straightaway because almost everyone in F1 had been to the street circuit in Arizona the previous year and the majority of the teams knew exactly how to plan for a so-called 'flyaway' race. They also had the money to pay for it.

The existing teams were part of a travel plan with a payout structure based on previous results and television money accrued from races in which they had taken part. Being a newcomer meant you had no claim whatsoever to the travel concessions. The irony was that fledgling teams had arguably more need of support than those with budgets five times the size of the sponsorship I had managed to pull in. Not that I was going to let such detail stand in my way.

Bernie Ecclestone controlled the finances and I had been fighting with him increasingly as I tried to release his grip on the travel purse strings. I may as well have talked to the wall. Bernie did not care because F1 was oversubscribed at the time. There were 18 teams entered, some with a single car, and a total of 34 drivers aiming for 26 places on the grid. In 2006, by comparison, there were 11 teams and 22 cars, which meant there was capacity to spare.

In 1991, Bernie would have welcomed the loss of a couple of teams. Being a stickler for neatness and order, he did not like having his paddock overrun by a rag-tag collection of teams, all demanding passes as well as handouts from the kitty. It was not in his interest to keep these strugglers going.

However, I thought I could detect, in the midst of discussions that were usually one way, a soft spot for Jordan. I think Bernie realised that, of the newcomers, here was a team with history. We had won championships in F3 and F3000; there was half a chance that we could make a go of F1. We had gained credibility by coming to an agreement with Goodyear and Ford when pundits supposedly in the know had dismissed the very suggestion.

Bernie and I had been drivers in the past and I think it would be fair to say that neither of us had been as successful as we had hoped. Bernie had bought and run the Brabham F1 team in the 1970s, so he knew how much of a struggle it could be. He could see that drivers such as Brundle, Herbert, Johansson and Alesi – all of whom were entered at Phoenix – had raced with Jordan and were, in a manner of speaking, ambassadors for the team. I liked to think that my former drivers would say to anyone who asked, 'Jordan? Don't write them off. These guys are not idiots, they know what they're doing, they prepare good cars, they have fun. They may give the wrong impression but if they catch you off-guard and you're not in tip-top shape, they'll stuff you.'

To do that, we needed to get to Phoenix. I think Jordan Grand Prix established an F1 record for travelling light. We were being charged for every kilogramme of freight, so we had to make sure we took as little as possible because we barely had the budget for that, never mind anything that we might consider a luxury. The mechanics, for instance, had to carry their own kit. The rule was if you can't lift it, you can't bring it. We trimmed everything to the bare essentials. I am absolutely certain that nobody ever carried as little weight as Jordan did to Phoenix in 1991. It was an art in terms of economy of scale.

If you look inside any F1 garage today, you will see polished floors with backdrops and overhead lighting that would not be out of place in an exhibition at the NEC. We took a couple of canvas banners for the garage walls, and that was it. Gary and Trevor noticed straightaway that our competitors had erected platforms and perches for the use of team management at the pit wall. Gary had the answer. Having worked in the USA, he called up a good mate who lived locally and they set to work designing and building a structure out of scaffolding – crude compared to some of the fancy jobs farther up the pit lane but good enough for us.

We rented a small camper van and made do as best we could with sandwiches and take-away food for the team, everyone eating beneath an awning as we discussed how we were going to get through this weekend.

The major hurdle, we all knew, would come first thing on Friday morning. It was called pre-qualifying. If we failed to get through this, we would be going home immediately. All the effort to get this far would count for nothing. In all my 35 years in motor racing, prequalifying is the most traumatic and difficult thing I ever experienced. In Phoenix, it dominated my thinking all the way through to Friday morning.

Since this was our first grand prix, I had asked Marie to come with me because I needed as much support as I could get. We were using a bed and breakfast place in town, which was very pleasant, just what we wanted, but a complete contrast to the luxury and grandeur of the Phoenician, where all the top teams and drivers were staying. I had been invited to take part in a celebrity golf tournament at this resort hotel in Scottsdale, an extremely affluent area, and among the excellent turnout of F1 people I spied Nigel Mansell and Alain Prost, among other drivers, and suddenly thought, 'Shit! I'm gonna be racing them – that's if we get through pre-qualifying.'

My mind was on pre-qualifying the entire time. I was more worried about it than I was about sponsorship, money, the car – nothing could begin to compare. It would eventually give me piles and sleepless nights. It made me very irritable. I was the grumpiest person in the paddock on Thursday because of what was coming early the following morning. I never minded stress. In fact, I think it can be good for you at times. However, distress is something very different.

Pre-qualifying was a killer in every sense because it was instant. Eight cars from Dallara, Jordan, Coloni, Fondmetal and Modena (not all teams had two cars) would have an hour in which to set a decent time, the fastest four going through to join the remaining 26 cars as the weekend began in earnest. If you didn't make it by nine o'clock on Friday morning, you were out. You were history. Your passes were removed and, if both cars had failed to get through, you would be told to vacate your garage. Immediately.

Worse than that, your sponsors would be left in limbo. There would be nowhere for them to go, and nothing you could do with them. The trouble was you could not ask them to stay away in the first place. You had to invite them along, but on the understanding that there was a risk of being unable to take any further part in the weekend after nine o'clock on Friday morning. You could forgive elements within the company, perhaps hostile to the F1 deal, asking aloud, 'Why are we sponsoring this idiot in the first place? What happens if he doesn't pre-qualify? We will be sitting in the grandstand like complete mutts watching something that we're not interested in because we haven't got any representation.' Having enthusiastically sold the idea of F1 to Pepsi and Fuji, that was my nightmare scenario. I had to perform now that I had their money.

That was another problem. I had made a reasonable amount of money from the drivers I had managed and placed in F1 teams. I had also done well racing, certainly in the last years with Camel, and by winning the F3 championship with Stelrad. This had brought some kudos and it had brought some money, but that money was gone. It had been soaked up instantly by the F1 car. Now I was eating my way through the sponsorship quicker than I felt I wanted to. Even at this early stage, I was staring quite a significant amount of debt in the face.

There were other, less obvious, pressures. This may sound a daft thing to say but I felt a certain responsibility to all the F3 and F3000 teams – particularly the British guys based at Silverstone. It was as if Jordan represented these honest grafters. We were the team to prove that small businesses such as these were doing something worthwhile and could cut the mustard, given the chance. Not making it through to qualifying at the very least would be a disaster, not just because of having the weekend cut short so unceremoniously, but because Gary genuinely felt that, once over that hurdle, we had a very good chance of qualifying among the 26 fastest – and qualifying reasonably well. But the odds stacked against us in pre-qualifying were huge.

Phoenix was a street circuit, so the track surface would be dirty and completely devoid of rubber on the racing line. In other words, there would be zero grip for the racing tyres. The situation would improve as the hour went by and more rubber was laid down. In the meantime, the drivers would have to learn the circuit and try to set up the car to deal with it as efficiently as possible. It would be a total disaster if something happened to the car – an accident or, say, a mechanical failure – during the first 45 minutes and the driver was unable to go out when the track would be at its best during the final quarter. I found that having been in racing for such a long time was working against me because I could envisage any number of problems, particularly with a new car that had only done the minimum amount of running.

Then there was the question of tyres. That was a case of good news, bad news. Having Goodyear support said much about Jordan's potential credibility and it augured well for the race – provided we could get that far. The broad belief was that Pirelli tyres would not be competitive over a race distance but – and here was the catch – they would have an immediate performance advantage during pre-qualifying because it would take longer for the Goodyear rubber to come on song. In addition, our biggest rivals, the Dallara-Judds driven by Emanuele Pirro and J.J. Lehto – good drivers, both – were on Pirelli. That, in effect, meant we would be fighting with the remaining six cars – all on Goodyear – for two places. The odds against us were mounting by the minute. After months and months of seriously hard work by a team of less than 40 people, it was distilling down to one hour of purgatory, starting at 8 a.m. the following morning. Did I sleep well on the Thursday night? Did *any* of us sleep well? Need you ask?

There was one obstacle we had neither thought nor heard of until a few minutes into the start of pre-qualifying. His name was Marlon Rauvelli. Recently released from the city's Maricopa Medical Center and hobbling on crutches, Rauvelli managed to evade circuit security and stagger across the track, right in front of Eric van de Poele's Modena-Lamborghini. It was an apparent suicide attempt. Many of us by the pit wall hoped we would not be so inclined an hour later.

The lap times began to fall and, predictably, the Dallaras were setting the pace. We were in with a shout, particularly de Cesaris, but then it all went wrong.

When pushing hard in the final minutes of qualifying, Andrea hooked second gear instead of fourth. The over-rev buzzed the engine and he coasted to a halt on the far side of the track with no time left to run back for the spare car. We watched as his lap time hovered in fourth place. Then, in the closing minute, it was pushed down to fifth – by Gachot. Good news, bad news. One car in, the other out.

Andrea was distraught. It was a simple mistake but there was no time for either commiseration or celebration. We had just under an hour in which to prepare Bertrand's car for the start of practice. At least we were still in the reckoning.

During the hour-long qualifying session on Friday afternoon, Gachot set 19th fastest time. We were OK so far and the encouraging news was that Bertrand felt there was much more potential hidden by the fact that he was struggling to make the qualifying tyres work. They were of a very soft rubber that was good for one lap but nothing more. Getting the best out of the rubber by warming the tyres up properly on the so-called 'out lap' from the pits was another phenomenon that was completely new to us – yet another item on a massively steep learning curve, which, so far, was not threatening to defeat us completely.

I hardly left our garage. It was not because I was nervous or awestruck; it was simply because there was so much to take in and do. I wanted to be on hand at all times. In any case, I did not feel a complete stranger in the pit lane and paddock. I had got to know several key people through my various dealings with drivers. I would not say that I felt their equal but, then again, I had little time to think about that. It was not a question of 'what should I be doing now – what's my position?' My position was always very clear – I needed to lead from the front. That said, Trevor was tough on me, which he needed to be as team manager and engineer. He ran the show brilliantly.

Whether they admitted it or not, everyone on the team was already partially worn-down by the tension created before and during pre-qualifying. I returned exhausted to our small room early that evening and, to my complete surprise, found a bag of golf clubs propped in one corner. I had no idea where this had come from. I opened the bag to find a full set of Ping golf clubs with my name engraved at the bottom of each shaft at the point where it goes into the club head. Ping were the clubs to have and I was bowled over by this.

After the celebrity tournament, I had been introduced to Karsten Solheim, a motor-racing fanatic from Phoenix. I had no idea who he was but we discussed F1 and my love of golf. It was only later that I discovered Karsten was the man behind Ping. There was absolutely no reason for him to go to all that trouble. I said to myself sure as hell that wouldn't happen in F3, and it certainly wouldn't happen in F3000.

I treasure those clubs and continue to play with them more than 15 years later. I also happen to have the latest modern-day Pings because I have stayed loyal to the brand ever since. That gesture made my first official day of F1 complete. Now we had to focus on second qualifying on Saturday and see where that left us for the race.

I just wanted to qualify. I was desperate to be able to say that I had competed in an F1 race. At this stage, any idea of being ultra-competitive never even came into my mind. That was something to ponder on another day. I felt that if we could get the car on the grid, it would have a huge impact.

Bertrand not only qualified, he did it handsomely by taking a place on the seventh row, right in the middle of the grid. We were ahead of a Tyrrell, a Ligier and a couple of Lolas – famous names that might have passed their best but, individually, had far more experience than Jordan. It was a fantastic boost just to have got this far. We were in the race for which a Lotus and the second Ligier – among others – had failed to qualify. We had no idea what race day had in store, but everything would be a bonus from here on in. Just to finish would be a major achievement at this stage.

Gachot did not lose any ground at the start and held 13th for several laps, moving up one place when Martin Brundle's Brabham made an unscheduled pit stop – there was no mid-race refuelling in 1991. As the field began to thin, Bertrand climbed to eighth. He had a quick spin on the debris caused by Riccardo Patrese and Roberto Moreno colliding while fighting for third place. One of them dropped out, putting us into seventh and one place away from a championship point. This was too much to take in but our racing experience warned us that anything could happen.

Gary was concerned about the state of Bertrand's rear tyres. A quick stop – our first-ever pit stop – on lap 57 dropped Gachot from seventh to eighth. We were still running, but with just six laps to go, the engine failed. A point had been made. The Jordan was competitive and we had shown that we were serious. Jordan Grand Prix had arrived. That said, the thought of failure continued to be horrific, and there was another pre-qualifying session to be got through in Brazil in a fortnight's time.

Chapter 18

# PUSHING OUR LUCK

Phoenix to Sao Paulo – the contrast could not have been more extreme. The former was a poor track surrounded by affluence. Interlagos in Brazil was a stunning permanent circuit fringed by poverty. Just to add a bit more colour and chaos, the taxi drivers were on strike on the weekend of 24 March 1991.

We were present early but not so bright on the Friday as dark clouds threatened rain – another complication we did not need. Fearing there might be a downpour sooner rather than later during pre-qualifying, Bertrand Gachot used his limited number of qualifying tyres early on. Understandable though that was, it turned out to be a mistake because the rain never came and the track, as expected under normal circumstances, got quicker.

But here was an interesting thing – Bertrand managed to hold on to third place, just a fraction slower than Andrea, our two cars sandwiched between the pair of Dallaras. This was the start of a trend as pre-qualifying became the province of two teams. So, for round two in Brazil, we had two cars ready to go through to official practice and qualifying, Gachot eventually taking an excellent tenth on the grid, a couple of places ahead of Andrea. If this continued, I might be able to get some sleep on Thursday nights.

At one stage in the race, our cars were eighth and ninth, ahead of Moreno's Benetton. Then it all went wrong when Andrea's engine began to cut out and he spun off, the trip across the grass doing serious damage to the chassis. Gachot's car, meanwhile, began to sound like a bag of nails, the resulting vibration shaking the life out of poor

Bertrand. It was difficult to know whether he was relieved or totally frustrated when he rolled to a halt with fuel starvation a few laps from the finish. The two retirements cancelled out the pleasure of getting through pre-qualifying, such was the beginning of a shift in our priorities towards bigger and better things.

The trend continued at Imola, our cars sharing the sixth row, which gave me a wry smile since we were ahead of not one but two Benettons with the superior specification Ford engine. I thought, for a pleasurable second or two, of that letter from Ford that had cut the legs from under my efforts to secure Camel's money. To my continuing delight, the two green cars were soon running in the top ten. At this rate, we might actually score a championship point far sooner than expected.

Then Bertrand spun, but Andrea made up for that by moving into sixth place. One championship point! Then the car stopped. A gearbox selector finger had broken. This component had not given a moment's bother during thousands of miles of testing and the failure was an unfair reflection on the fantastic work Mark Smith had done on the gearbox.

This was the sort of teething trouble to be expected and we had another problem a fortnight later at Monaco. Once again, we got through pre-qualifying, the prelude to Andrea doing a fantastic job by setting tenth fastest time during Saturday qualifying. So here was a Jordan in the middle of the grid at Monaco!

I could hardly bare to watch as Andrea hounded Jean Alesi's sixth-place Ferrari. You could see that Jean was struggling whereas Andrea was sitting there, calm as you like, making Alesi work for his millions. This went on for 21 wonderful laps, only for a problem with the throttle assembly to cause de Cesaris to coast into an escape road and retire. Gachot, meanwhile, having started from the penultimate row of the grid, did a solid job and, despite ramming the back of another car to the detriment of his steering, brought the Jordan home in eighth place. It was the first finish for Jordan Grand Prix, and on a circuit where you would least expect it.

Despite these various setbacks, both drivers were very positive about what they felt they could achieve. We may have been a brand new team and we may have had only four races but, in each, with a bit of good fortune, we could have scored a point. I began to have a good feeling and I was about to be proved right in the most amazing way.

Andrea and Bertrand qualified 11th and 14th in Canada – you will note I no longer need to mention pre-qualifying since, barring some unforeseen problem, the Jordans were a shoo-in, along with the Dallaras. Eleventh and 12th at the end of the first lap, our boys were never likely to be worrying the leaders, which did not matter because the guys at the front were having their own problems.

Gerhard Berger's McLaren went out after four laps. Moreno spun off in his Benetton. Senna lost third place when his McLaren stopped with electrical trouble and Boutsen was next when his Ligier's engine expired. Then Prost's Ferrari disappeared from fourth place with gearbox trouble, followed soon after by engine trouble for Alesi.

We had been having our own difficulties as Bertrand and Andrea struggled with minor problems but, at half distance, we found ourselves handily placed in eighth and ninth. De Cesaris and Gachot both passed Martini's struggling Minardi. We shuffled up one more place when Capelli retired his Leyton House, and yet another when Lehto's fourth-place Dallara had an engine failure. Two cars in the points! That was enough for me but one more treat was in store – at least for Jordan, if not for Williams-Renault.

Nigel Mansell had led the race from the start. It was going to be an easy win and Nigel, being a great showman, waved to the crowd as he went into the hairpin at the far end of the circuit on his last lap. The Williams had a semi-automatic gearbox and, while he was busy waving, Nigel did not change down through the gears. The engine revs dropped and there was no power to drive the hydraulics. The engine stalled. He was out, and we were fourth and fifth! Yes, it was lucky but I knew enough about motor racing to grab any good fortune that might come my way.

We had five championship points after just five races. This gave the team massive encouragement. The sense of relief was enormous, mainly because we were close to being free of the burden of pre-qualifying when the situation was re-assessed at the season's halfway mark – but there were three more races to go until we reached that point.

At the next race, in Mexico, we received a stark reminder that Jordan remained among F1's poor relations. Our 'pit' was a piece of grass at the end of the pit lane. I could not believe what I was seeing. It was shoddier than the worst excesses of Mondello Park or Kirkistown on a bad day.

I went straight to Bernie Ecclestone. 'This is supposed to be Formula 1,' I said. 'We're talking big crowds, big sponsors, big money. What happens if someone from the head office of 7UP or Fuji comes to visit us and there we are, camped out like gypsies on a grass verge? You charge us through the nose to bring our freight here and then you dump it by the side of the road. You're robbing me and having a laugh, aren't you?'

It didn't get me far. Bernie laughed because he knew that I was such a skinflint. I had to be because it was my money. If push came to shove, I liked to think he quietly helped our cause. Nevertheless, quite often, I could not be sure of his influence, such as on race day in Mexico.

Andrea qualified 11th and gained two places on the first lap. Then, just like in Montreal, the fancied runners began to fall by the wayside. Before we knew it, de Cesaris was fifth, then fourth. Even better, with 20 laps to go, Gachot had worked his way up to fifth, only to spin into retirement.

Andrea, meanwhile, set his fastest lap of the race. We were looking good. People often talk about their legs turning to jelly towards the end of the race while, on the surface, they try to appear calm by casually saying, 'If we get the result, well and good, but if it doesn't happen, that's motor racing.' That's rubbish. I was anything but cool. I was a wreck. The worse I became the more I shouted to Gary on the intercom. He was shouting back, telling me to be calm. I was asking if we had enough fuel. He was assuring me that we had.

As Andrea started his last lap, he was quite some way clear of Roberto Moreno's Benetton in fifth place, which was just as well. As the Jordan came off the last corner, a banked 180-degree right-hander, it rolled to a halt just short of the chequered flag. Andrea was out in a flash and, urged on by me, he began to push the car towards the line. Then Ron Dennis pointed out that this was totally illegal.

According to the rule book, we should have been excluded. Much as everyone loves the underdog, and Andrea was very popular up and down the pit lane, the rules were the rules, and I knew that Benetton and the teams finishing behind us would ensure the laws were respected. I had to come up with something very quickly if Jordan was to hold on to the three points for fourth place.

I figured the only way we could keep the place was on the grounds of safety. We claimed that, had the car been left where it was, it would have been a hazard to other drivers sweeping out of the very fast final corner. Our argument was that Andrea had no option but to push the car to the nearest exit – which just happened to be across the finishing line. That was enough to cause a bit of confusion. However, I could see that many people were not convinced and the stewards might take some persuading. In total desperation, I rang Ian, who was at home because we could not afford the budget to bring everyone to Mexico. Ian said I should talk to Bernie.

As usual, Bernie had left the circuit before the race had finished. I got him on the phone and explained what had happened. His initial reaction was, 'Jordan, I think you're fucked.' That was the last thing I wanted to hear. I did not realise that this was Bernie's way of having fun by initially painting a black picture and then, as if by magic, managing to find a cure to the problem. I hung up, expecting the worst.

I do not know what influence, if any, Bernie had on the stewards because, of course, he should have had none at all. All I can say is that the people making the decision that day bought into my claim that this had been a hugely sporting gesture on the part of Andrea. Even though he was physically exhausted after 66 laps, he was keen not to place the other drivers in danger and wanted to get the car off the track as quickly as possible. Looking back on it now, you cannot question the logic from a safety point of view but the fact that the finish line was so close was surely seen as too much of a coincidence. I could not believe our luck. I had been a bit of a chancer with the explanation to the stewards and it had come off. The irony was that Andrea did not need to cross the line because he was a lap ahead of Roberto Moreno's Benetton and we would have held fourth place in any case. Nevertheless, that did not detract from the fact that, technically, we had broken the rules. We went crazy with excitement and relief at the end result.

I hardly slept a wink on the flight home. The adrenalin was still surging though my system as I checked the championship positions and there we were in sixth place with eight points. We had scored points in two races in succession. This was serious stuff because points were awarded to the first six, not the top eight, as it is today. There we were, operating on a shoestring, having the time of our lives, embarrassing Benetton with an engine that was two editions removed from theirs. Our Cosworth may not have been as powerful but it was very reliable, very driveable, and the drivers loved it. Benetton were on Pirelli tyres and we were on Goodyear, which was a great race tyre, very forgiving. The 191 was a sweet little car and it worked – it braked well, it went round corners well. It was not the quickest thing down the straight but it was a good solid package. We were rocking! And rolling – unfortunately. Two races later, Andrea had a massive shunt – even by his colourful standard.

Having picked up another championship point in France, we could not wait to get to Silverstone. Apart from being on our doorstep, this was a track where we felt the 191 would work really well, particularly on the fast, twisting sections of the circuit. The mood was upbeat as we took part in our last pre-qualifying and got down to serious business. During the first free practice session, Andrea set fourth fastest time and backed that up with an amazing fifth fastest time during qualifying later on Friday. Only the race favourites Williams-Renault (Nigel Mansell and Riccardo Patrese) and McLaren-Honda (Ayrton Senna and Gerhard Berger) were ahead of us, and we could see no reason why this should not be maintained during final qualifying on Saturday afternoon. Then again, we should have known that motor racing is never that simple.

A fault with the wiring loom on Andrea's car meant he had to spend most of the day fretting in the garage. He had worked so hard with Trevor on finding a perfect set-up for the car – I can remember being told by other drivers that our car looked so sure-footed through the fast Becketts complex – and now he had to face the prospect of getting into the spare car that had been set-up for Gachot for this race. In the end, there was no alternative and Andrea was deeply disappointed with 13th on the grid. It was little compensation to think that six months earlier we had sat in the office here at Silverstone discussing prospects for the season, and reckoned a place in the middle of the grid was likely to be as good as it would get.

The plus point, of course, was that Andrea would have his car back for the race and he was ready and willing to use it to the maximum. Sure enough, after losing ground at the start – which must have angered him even more – Andrea took four places in as many laps. By lap ten, he was in eighth place but his meteoric progress was punishing his tyres and it was necessary to make an unscheduled stop. He rejoined in 23rd place. By lap 41 – with 18 to go – he was back in eighth place. Then disaster struck.

Coming through Abbey Curve at close to 170mph, a stud broke on the right-rear suspension, which would have been fully loaded at this point on the track. The car careered along the banking on the outside before rebounding across the track and coming to a halt a couple of hundred metres farther on. The front of the car was destroyed, the left-front wheel and suspension hanging off. Andrea, as he had done so many times before, was able to climb from the perfectly intact cockpit and walk away. Bertrand, meanwhile, had driven a really good race to come from near the back of the field and finish sixth. Another point! Jordan was sixth in the championship, one point behind Tyrrell.

We overhauled Tyrrell by finishing fifth and sixth at the next race, at Hockenheim, a trend we expected to continue two weeks later in Hungary, a tight track that should have suited our car. It turned out to be one of those weekends when we never got to grips with the track during qualifying. Our race form was good, but that was stifled by the middle of the grid starting positions, consigning both drivers to sit in traffic throughout most of the race. Bertrand epitomised our unrewarded potential by stopping for a fresh set of tyres and returning to set the fastest lap of the race six laps from the finish. None of us realised at the time that this would be Bertrand's last act in a Jordan. His world – and, less so, Jordan's – was about to take a hugely dramatic turn.

## Chapter 19

# MICHAEL WHO?

The first time I watched Michael Schumacher race, I was not particularly impressed. At least, I was not as impressed as you might imagine, given everything that Michael has done since. Perhaps the best way to put it is that Michael's performance that day in 1990 had not caused a raising of the eyebrows in the same way that Ayrton Senna had done when I first saw him race. Having come across good drivers in the past, I instantly realised there was something special about Senna. I did not have that feeling with Schumacher. He was what you might call a normal driver – very good, but nothing exceptional.

That feeling may have been compounded by the fact that I had not gone to Germany to see Michael race with the specific intention of hiring him. I was there because his manager, Willi Weber, was involved in a proposal to buy my Formula 3000 team. In other words, I could sniff a possible good deal. Michael Schumacher was of no particular interest at that time.

This had come about because the Jordan F3000 team had become an attractive proposition, thanks to our success with Jean Alesi. In earlier years, when racing F3 in Europe, I had come across many interesting people, including a successful entrant from Germany called Bertram Schaffer. He had introduced me to Weber and now Willi was expressing an interest in my team. Weber had won the German F3 championship with Schumacher but he was not pushing Michael in any way. He simply wanted to step up to F3000, with Schumacher as his driver.

I watched Michael with interest that day and I have to confess that my feelings, such as they were, were diluted when Willi then put his driver into sports-car racing with Sauber-Mercedes. Weber had gone lukewarm on the deal to buy my team but I was amazed when he diverted Michael away from F3000. This was the accepted path for any young driver hoping to get into F1. Sports-car racing, on the other hand, was a dead end, a place for either retired F1 drivers or those who were never good enough to make the cut in the first place. I just couldn't understand why Weber had done that and I suppose, subconsciously, it endorsed my feeling that Michael was good, but nothing special.

While Michael was racing for Mercedes-Benz at places such as Le Mans in 1991, Jordan Grand Prix was up and running. De Cesaris and Gachot were doing exactly the sort of job we expected of them, but Bertrand had had a red-mist moment. At the time, it had nothing to do with racing but the ramifications affected my team in a massive way.

Gachot had been driving near Hyde Park when he got involved in an incident with a taxi. The upshot was that he had an altercation with the driver and ended up spraying the man with the contents of a CS gas canister kept in his car for emergencies. Gachot claimed he had acted in self-defence and he had no idea that the use of CS gas was illegal in Britain.

This had happened in February 1991 when Bertrand was on his way to the Carlton Towers to join me as a guest speaker at the meeting of the world sales and marketing executives for 7UP. As I mentioned before, I had no hesitation in asking Bertrand along because he was one of the best drivers I have ever met with a true grasp of commerce. He knew exactly what was going on – he was very together and had a good nose for business. Unfortunately, he did not have such a good grasp of how things worked when it came to dealing with a traffic incident in London. On a day I was extolling the virtues of our team, my driver failed to turn up because the police had nicked him.

The stupid thing was that we could have sorted things out had we known about the extent of the problem. Bertrand was not the sort of guy who would go around attacking people, far from it, but rather than trying to make amends, apologising to the taxi driver and making a donation to charity, Bertrand dismissed the incident from his mind and failed to realise the possible repercussions. Suddenly, six months later, we had a court case two days after the Hungarian Grand Prix and the judge, much to everyone's total dismay, found him guilty. Expecting a fine or a suspended sentence, Gachot had planned to leave Southwark Crown Court immediately afterwards and head for a tyre-test session at Monza. Instead, Judge Gerald Butler sent him down for 18 months.

It was such a preposterous sentence that we thought it would become irrelevant. The feeling was that an appeal would be successful, if only because of how imprisonment would affect his job and his career.

The appeal was lost. The sentence was reduced to nine months but it meant he would be out of racing, starting with his home grand prix in Belgium. Having set the fastest lap in Hungary a few days before, Bertrand would be motoring nowhere.

This put Jordan Grand Prix in an unbelievably difficult position. Apart from losing a driver, we also lost the sponsorship Bertrand had brought us. The whole thing had a major financial impact on the team but the immediate concern was to find a suitable driver in the short time available. This was three-quarters of the way through the motor-racing season and any driver worth his salt would be accounted for.

Then I recalled a flight I had made earlier in the year – ironically, not long after Gachot's clash with the taxi driver – when Michael Schumacher's name had come up. I had been on a quick visit to Japan to talk to Fuji. It had been a last-minute trip, so much so that I stepped off the plane from Tokyo at Heathrow and straight on to a flight to Sao Paulo for the Brazilian Grand Prix.

I was pretty wrecked and one of the first people I met on board was Gert Kramer, the commercial manager for Mercedes-Benz cars. If you wanted a deal on a new Mercedes, Gert was the man. He was fanatical about drivers' helmets and even collected them. He was also very pro Michael Schumacher – apparently more so than Willi Weber – and he was always pushing. I remember him saying very early on, 'Eddie, I know you saw Schumacher in Formula 3 but, believe me, he is a real talent.' However, having been thinking about the financial affairs of the team and next year's engine supply, the last thing I needed on that flight was Gert Kramer banging on about this guy Schumacher. I said, 'Look Gert, I'll speak to you tomorrow.' Our paths didn't cross that weekend and there was no further mention of Schumacher. Then, in the week leading to Spa, I remembered the conversation and Michael Schumacher.

Ian Phillips and I had been casting around for a replacement. Stefan Johansson was my choice but, since he wanted to be paid, I kept looking. Derek Warwick's name had come up, as had Keke Rosberg's, despite the 1982 world champion retiring from F1 four years later. But, in the back of my mind, I reckoned that Schumacher was worth a look, even though he had not driven an F1 car. The priority was to get him into a Jordan as quickly as possible. With a week to go before Spa, time was running out.

Michael was racing sports cars at the Nurburgring that weekend and I had gone to join my family, who were on holiday in Spain. A deal was done over the phone with Willi Weber – we had a new driver and we would receive £150,000 a race. It was early Sunday evening and I phoned Ian immediately. His immediate reaction was, 'Michael who?' I did my best to ignore that and said Schumacher would be arriving at the factory for a seat fitting the following day and we were to give him a test at Silverstone on the Tuesday.

At this stage, I didn't know much about Schumacher in terms of racing an F1 car at Spa, one of the most difficult tracks on the calendar. I certainly had not realised that, even though Michael lived not far from this famous road course, he had never raced on it before in any class of car. This was not a place for the faint-hearted. When

I discovered that we were planning to put a novice in one of our cars, I was very upset because Michael had misled me. Spa's Eau Rouge is one of the most daunting corners in F1. A very good driver can learn slow corners quickly but the fast ones sort the men from the boys.

I remember, when racing in F3, I was having difficulty with Club Corner at Silverstone. With the track layout in those days, Club was an outrageously quick corner and I asked my team-mate, Stefan Johansson, how he occasionally managed to get through Club without lifting his foot from the throttle when in fifth gear. He said that he used to take his left hand from the wheel and keep it on his right knee – a sort of psychological thing to make sure he didn't lift his foot from the throttle.

As I said, Michael Schumacher was a rookie not only in F1 but also at Spa, a place with very fast corners indeed. I was concerned enough to think that I probably would have preferred Stefan to drive the car had I known that Michael had not been there before. In my view, a lack of knowledge was such a massive disadvantage at Spa.

I should have realised a few days earlier that my concern might be misplaced when I had a phone call from Silverstone following Michael's first run in an F1 car. Trevor Foster had been conducting the test on the South Circuit, which uses a small part of the northern end of the grand-prix track. It was unfamiliar to Michael but, apparently, you would not have known it. He set about driving the Jordan as if to the manner born. Trevor had to call Schumacher in after five laps and tell him to slow down – and Michael sat there, genuinely wondering what all the fuss was about. It was quite clear that he would give a good account of himself, so we continued sorting out the wording on the contract and chasing the money, which was duly paid. Michael Schumacher had become a grand-prix driver. Things were about to move very quickly in more ways than one.

Michael qualified seventh at Spa. Given everything that I have said, this was an incredible performance. Since then, of course, we have learned a lot more about Michael Schumacher, but until that weekend in August 1991, no one had much of a clue. We were over the moon because everyone was coming out of this looking good.

The mechanics could not believe what was going on. They were so excited. Until now, Andrea was a known quantity. You were going to get blood and thunder. Andrea would go as fast as he could possibly go. You never had to worry about his commitment – you got it and prayed that you got the car back as well. Talk about a cat with nine lives – I reckoned Andrea had about 90 lives – but he usually delivered.

None of us could believe what Michael had done. I would go so far as to say that this probably was the biggest surprise I had during my time in F1. I do not recall anything that blew me away so much.

I remember Michael being very calm. He didn't say much but neither did he miss much. He took it all in and focused totally on getting the job done. That was a sign of what was to come as he brought such incredible application to winning more grands prix and world championships than anyone else.

For now, though, the aim was to finish his first grand prix. If he scored points, well and good. In the event, he got no further than the first corner, where the clutch packed up, but Michael had done more than enough to confirm that he was worth holding on to, which turned out to be easier said than done. Our association with Michael did not last much longer than that clutch.

It was a disappointing weekend in more ways than one. As the years have gone by, people naturally associate Jordan and the 1991 Belgian Grand Prix with Michael Schumacher. Few remember that Jordan came close to winning that race, the 11th grand prix in the team's debut season.

De Cesaris had been eased down the media agenda from the minute Schumacher qualified two rows ahead of him but, come the race, Andrea did what had become his customary job – driving quickly and without fuss. A couple of early casualties among the leading runners and a couple of daring overtaking moves took him into the top six. When Nelson Piquet and Riccardo Patrese made unscheduled stops, we were two places farther ahead, but Andrea, in turn, dropped one place when he stopped for tyres just before half distance. Given the way we had been going, it almost went without saying that we expected a couple of championship points at the end of this. We almost got more than we bargained for.

Fourth became third when de Cesaris overtook Patrese's Williams. Then he was second as Piquet's Benetton struggled on its Pirellis. Second! Who would have believed that?

But wait. There's more. Senna in the leading McLaren was losing pace, with gearbox trouble, and de Cesaris was closing in. No one outside Jordan knew that we were having troubles of our own. Andrea reported on the radio that the water temperature was on the rise. Meanwhile, our engineers in the garage could see a worrying number of blips on the engine telemetry screen as the oil pressure began to fluctuate. With just three laps to go, the engine failed.

We could not understand it. Yes, we had experienced engine problems during various tests and practice sessions but there was no obvious reason why this should have happened. Gary reckoned that the Cosworth V8 usually consumed about a litre of oil during a race. This one had got through 5.5 litres.

It turned out to be no surprise to the Cosworth engineers. They had fitted revised pistons, and tests had shown that oil consumption would increase as a result. The pity was that no one at Cosworth had thought to tell us. This breakdown in communications had cost us a definite second place in the Belgian Grand Prix. I still do not want to think too deeply about the very strong possibility that we could have actually won it. At the time, I was about to have a really serious distraction about losing something – someone – else.

## Chapter 20

# SHAFTED

Almost immediately after the eventful weekend in Belgium, I had to leave for Japan. Bernie Ecclestone had sorted a deal for us with Yamaha for 1992, but the full significance of Bernie's part in this became uncomfortably clear in the week ahead.

Ian Phillips was looking after affairs at the factory. On the following Friday, he had a call from Willi Weber, saying that Jochen Neerpasch would be coming to our offices on Monday to sign the contract on Michael's behalf. Neerpasch had entered the picture because he was with IMG, looking after Mercedes-Benz. Mercedes had a continuing interest in Michael and were effectively paying the bills, in this case from their sports-car budget with the Sauber team. Significantly, Weber finished his call to Ian with a word of warning. 'Watch Neerpasch,' said Willi.

I returned from Japan and we waited most of Monday for Neerpasch. He arrived in the late afternoon, accompanied by Julian Jacobi of IMG. The letter of intent we had drafted and they had signed had been changed and was totally unacceptable. The amount concerned was £3 million for the season but, for that, they wanted all manner of outrageous things, such as sponsorship rights for the entire car. They also wanted the right to take Michael at any time if Mercedes came into F1. I said we needed to work on this overnight.

We agreed to meet the following morning but, in the meantime, we heard a whisper that Michael had been for a seat fitting at Benetton's headquarters, not far away in Oxfordshire. At 10 a.m. my fax burst into life. It was a single sheet with a one-line message: 'Dear

Eddie, I'm very sorry but I am not going to be able to drive for your team. Best regards, Michael.' A deal had been done with Benetton. This was two days before we were due in Monza to start preparing for the Italian Grand Prix. We were over a barrel.

It came down to a single word on a letter of intent that had been signed at Spa. Fred Rodgers had agreed to Schumacher's people changing 'we will sign "the" contract in seven days' to 'we will sign "a" contract in seven days'. So, when they arrived with a contract, it wasn't 'the' contract. I was gutted. I could not believe how underhand they had been. Neerpasch knew the significance of the change to the wording and the whole affair did not enhance IMG's reputation in F1.

I could not blame Fred because I had asked him to prepare everything in a rush. Yes, the word was changed and I suppose if you had time to consider everything carefully and in great detail, you would have picked that up, but it was not something we spent a lot of time thinking about. In retrospect, we should have done, particularly as we were dealing with IMG. Bernie would take steps where necessary to keep IMG out of F1. They considered themselves to be the biggest and best sports agency in the world. F1 represented a sport with substantial financial pickings and the largest television audience worldwide on a regular basis – and IMG were not a major player within it. I considered them to be opportunist and sly. Even today, few people in F1 have an association with IMG despite management changes within the agency.

I had learned enough about business to adopt that great piece of Irish philosophy, only go to court when you know you can't win. We tried unsuccessfully to get an injunction taken out in London. Meanwhile, Roberto Moreno, the Brazilian driver who was being bundled out of Benetton to make way for Schumacher, managed, on Fred's advice, to take out an injunction in Milan on the Thursday. The minute we arrived at Monza on the same day, the first person we went to see was Bernie who, on the face if it, was happy to help, but warned me to ensure I had all my ducks in a row.

What I didn't know was that Bernie, very keen to have a good German driver in F1, had actually advised Schumacher and Weber against staying with Jordan because we would have Yamaha engines, which were less competitive than the Ford V8s used by Benetton. Of course, Bernie knew all about my engine plans because he had set up the deal in the first place.

I have the utmost regard for Bernie but I learned from this never to assume that he will always be on your side. Flavio Briatore is one of Bernie's best friends and yet Bernie appeared to approve of what was happening in 2006 when Flavio's driver, Fernando Alonso, received the rough end of the stick. Alonso was, wrongly in my view, heavily penalised for his alleged part in an incident during qualifying at Monza. I am sure Flavio asked Bernie if he was in league with Ferrari and the FIA in order to screw Renault in the interests of keeping the championship open. I think Alonso was very badly treated and it did not matter that Flavio was mates with Bernie.

People say Bernie is a good man and it is true that he can be enormously generous and supportive. However, I think too many people have suspicions about the apparent manner in which he pulls the strings in what he regards as his show. I have to say that on the one occasion when Jordan was in with a chance of the championship in 1999, I did not notice anything untoward. Everything was dealt with in a completely fair way, but that does not get away from the fact that some of the things said about Bernie have not been nice.

Looking back on the Schumacher business in 1991, I still reserve my view on the role played by Bernie. I see now that this was part of the process of discovering that you have to have a balance when dealing with Bernie. I had very little money at the time and he covered for me on a couple of occasions – he charged interest of course – but if you complained about some of his methods, if you went in too hard and he took a dislike to you, then you had no chance. You had to push him, refuse to give in and gain his respect, but without overstepping the mark and making him see you as a threat. Do that and he would be down on you like a ton of bricks. On the other hand, if you were too soft, he would walk all over you. That was the tightrope you had to walk.

I learned a lot about Bernie in 1991. It became apparent that he wasn't just manipulating me. He was also influencing Schumacher and his people. For instance, he told me that Michael actually wanted to race with Jordan because he liked the idea that we were giving him a start and he liked the homely atmosphere within the team. Michael is a very loyal person and that is the way he has run his life in racing. It is very unusual for a driver of his quality to have just two teams in 15 years of F1 racing – not forgetting, of course, his very brief outing with Jordan. At Monza on that Thursday afternoon, I was still determined that Schumacher would race with us.

Initially, we were looking good thanks to Moreno's injunction. Roberto was a close friend of Gary Anderson's, our technical chief. Everyone was looking for Roberto, but we had him hidden in our motorhome. So, in the middle of this million-dollar tug of war, here was a grand-prix driver having to pee in a bottle because he dare not show his face.

At 6 p.m. things began to move. Ian received a call from Bernie, telling us to meet him at the Villa d'Este in about an hour. This is the five-star hotel where all the high rollers stay on the edge of Lake Como. The usual mode of transport from the paddock is a quick hop by helicopter. Ian and I bundled into our Fiat 126 hire car, minus air-conditioning, and set off on the hour's journey by road.

We got there to find Flavio Briatore and Tom Walkinshaw from Benetton, plus Bernie and Luca Birendelli, who was Moreno's agent and the man responsible for the injunction that was causing the immediate problem for Benetton.

Bernie tried to short-circuit that by telling Birendelli to forget it and go home because Moreno would not get a penny. Ian took Bernie to one side and gently pointed out that, actually, Moreno was in a very strong position because, according to the regulations, the car that Moreno was due to drive had to take part in qualifying, otherwise it would be excluded, not just from the race, but from the championship. That's when the bargaining began.

We were obviously hoping that Moreno would sit tight, in which case Schumacher would not get his drive with Benetton and would stay with us. They offered Roberto half a million dollars to go away. We told him to refuse to accept anything less than a million because he was holding all the cards. Flavio was supposed to order sandwiches, but we're still waiting for those.

The haggling went on until the early hours. During this time, Michael walked by. I could not help but reflect on how his circumstances had changed more or less overnight. Mindful of costs, we had stayed at a pretty shabby £5 a night holiday camp at Spa, where Michael had been quite happy to join us. Now, here he was in the magnificent hallway of the Villa d'Este. He looked terribly sheepish and very apologetic. He said it was out of his hands and I honestly don't think he fully approved of what was going on because he is, at heart, a very straight guy.

At 2.30 a.m. Roberto weakened and accepted the half a million. Game over. Michael would drive the Benetton.

Ian and I were shattered. We had absolutely no idea where our hotel was and, at that hour, we had no way of finding out. So we made Flavio find us a room. I had always wanted to stay at the Villa d'Este – but not under circumstances such as this, and definitely not sharing a single bed with Ian Phillips.

In the morning, we headed back to the circuit to consider our options. I had wanted to put Alessandro Zanardi in the car. Zanardi was a really promising Italian who had been doing well in F3000, but the previous evening Walkinshaw had put the block on that by saying he had Alex under contract, which he thought he did. So we had done a deal with Moreno and relieved him of £300,000 of his money for each of two races.

En route to Monza, Maurizio Arrivabene of Philip Morris pulled up alongside at a set of traffic lights and, naturally, he wanted to know what had happened. The Schumacher affair was the talk of the paddock. When we explained, he was adamant that we must have

Zanardi. Ian told him about Walkinshaw's contract and Maurizio said that Zanardi was in fact free, but it was too late because we had agreed the deal with Moreno.

Alex, who had had a seat fitting with Benetton the previous afternoon but, crucially, had not signed any contract, arrived at our motorhome in tears at 8.30 a.m. After all that promise of a drive in his home grand prix, suddenly he had nothing. And now I had to begin the business of explaining to the waiting media how we had lost Michael Schumacher. Much as I like wheeling and dealing, I can't say I enjoyed a single second of that.

When I arrived in Formula 1, Ron Dennis had greeted me with the words, 'Welcome to the Piranha Club.' Now I knew exactly what he meant. In F1, you will stop at nothing either to gain an advantage or to disadvantage your rivals. It was a minefield but I had brushed aside any advice. 'Look, I've always done things on my own,' I said. 'Sink or swim, I'm going to go that way because then I've got no one to blame.' My initial concern after losing Michael was to find a replacement immediately. I did not have time to get vicious or angry. I was simply asking myself, 'Why has this happened? Why has this happened to us? We were minding our own business and these people came along and screwed us.' I recalled an important lesson I had learned when growing up in Ireland. Never say, 'Look at what they have done'; it is better to ask, 'What was it that I hadn't done?'

I had learned a great deal about Bernie Ecclestone and the way in which he orchestrated everything. It had been clear throughout the negotiations at Villa d'Este that Flavio did not have a clue. He was new to F1 but he was learning fast. His subsequent achievements with Benetton and Renault would be nothing short of brilliant but, in September 1991, I am not sure Flavio even knew who Michael was until a few days earlier, and I do not believe he fully understood what Bernie was saying to him.

Bernie told me later, 'Eddie, I gave my word to Luciano Benetton that I would look after his team and that I would always do the best I could for him.'

'Yeah,' I responded, 'but that doesn't mean fucking me, Bernie! Which is what you've just done. You've had me over.'

Bernie would often bring that up in later years. I had to admire the way Bernie never shirked from his decision. You might like it, or you might not. On this occasion, I did not like what he had done, but there were to be other times when I was quite happy. That was the way Bernie worked and, once you accepted that, it was game on.

I was never afraid to be critical, or to tell him, 'Bernie, you are the biggest bastard I have ever met.' I have always had the impression that he quite enjoys people speaking like that because he knows, deep down, that is exactly how he operates. If anything appeared to be going too smoothly, he would throw a spanner in the works because he survived on aggravation. He is very clever and enjoys setting one person against the other – a classic exponent of divide and rule.

During the Schumacher affair, it became clear that Bernie had orchestrated it and Briatore was a puppet, listening to his every word, but make no mistake, Flavio learned very quickly indeed. Ron Dennis subsequently found it difficult to understand how Flavio could win races when he had no idea what was going on. In my opinion, Ron just did not realise that you do not need to be a mechanic, an engineer or a designer to understand F1, because this is a sport *and* a business. Flavio scores in the latter. When it comes to marketing and common sense, he is head and shoulders above anyone else. He was able to grasp the importance of gathering the right people around him, diehards such as Pat Symonds and, when they were at Benetton, Tom Walkinshaw, Ross Brawn and Rory Byrne – people who lived and breathed the sport. Flavio has proved conclusively that you do not need a background in motor sport to make a success of it. That started with Michael Schumacher as Benetton went on to win back-to-back championships.

Could Michael and Jordan have gone on to great things? I think so. With a driver of his talent, events move quickly. Jordan subsequently won races, thus proving we could do our bit. Michael had the ability to get manufacturers on side and pull in major deals and sponsors. That would have increased our clout and effectiveness. I really believe Jordan and Michael Schumacher could have built up a working relationship, because we developed partnerships in the same way as he did with Benetton. Sadly, that must remain pure speculation, thanks to just one word in a contract.

Speaking of contracts, our agreement with 7UP had, as you may recall, a clause that said we would be awarded a bonus of $1 million if the team scored 15 points in 1991. Going in to the last race, in Australia, we had 13, which was about ten more than anyone thought we would achieve. Nonetheless, the goal of 15 was achievable, particularly when de Cesaris and Zanardi, who had succeeded Moreno as our second driver, qualified in the middle of the grid, and race day dawned wet and miserable. It was one of those occasions when you knew that anything could happen.

After much debate over whether or not the race should take place, we got under way in appalling conditions. Six cars either spun or collided in as many laps. By lap 14, we were eighth and ninth, Andrea and Alex driving with more caution than some, particularly Nigel Mansell who crashed while trying to take the lead from Ayrton Senna. At the same time, two other drivers ahead of us had incidents. Suddenly, we were fifth and sixth. Three points! Three plus 13 equalled 16, which equalled a million dollars.

There was only one drawback. They had to complete one more lap in that order because, if the race was stopped – as it looked like it was going to be at any second – the count back of laps to establish the result would return to the running order of lap 14, when we were eighth and ninth. Tim Schenken, the former F1 driver who was Clerk of the Course, had Senna waving frantically to have the race stopped as he passed the pits. Ian, meanwhile, was by Tim's side, pleading with him to keep everything running for just one more lap. That was all we needed for the bonus clause to kick in.

Schenken felt he had no alternative but to show the red flag. He had the option to restart the race but none of us believed that would happen because of the terrible conditions. The results were finally declared after 14 laps. We had been less than two minutes away from one million dollars.

The money and commerce of motor racing became meaningless in 2001 when Alex Zanardi, having won the Champ Car title in the USA, was the victim of a terrible accident at a race in Germany. He lost both his legs, but he was lucky to be alive. I joined with everyone in motor racing in being delighted a few years later when Alex went racing again in a BMW touring car, a brilliant example by a lovely guy of a refusal to be beaten by seemingly impossible odds.

Chapter 21

# THE COMMITMENTS

At the end of our first season in F1 we were about to finish fifth with 13 points. Quite unbelievable. You would have thought I'd be ecstatic. I was anything but. Motor racing allows no time to bask in the light of past achievements. This was but one season and it was about to be consigned to history. Time was ticking on, 1992 beckoned, and the financial reality associated with the here and now was kicking in. I was looking at a serious amount of debt. Jordan Grand Prix was facing possible closure.

The last two races of 1991 were at Suzuka in Japan and Adelaide in Australia. I spent the weekend in between in a smart hotel overlooking the harbour in Sydney and I can honestly say that the magnificent view passed me by. My attention was diverted by phone calls and faxes, the majority of which concerned payment for the Ford-Cosworth engines that, Spa apart, had served us extremely well in our first year.

A few weeks earlier, to my surprise and horror, Cosworth had placed a winding-up petition against us. I knew I had difficulty paying for the 1991 engines and no chance at all of footing the bill in 1992. PepsiCo had agreed to sponsor Michael Jackson, which meant that the entire 7UP budget was going into the Michael Jackson tour. I continued to be very angry over the Schumacher affair and I was getting no sympathy now – not that sympathy was ever Bernie Ecclestone's way in situations such as this. He took me to one side and barked, 'Jordan, sort out your finances – you're in the shit. We want you in the family but I can't help you if you haven't got any money.' I knew I would be due money from the TV income and various other things but F1 rules had various clauses dictating that a team would not receive anything until they had been in F1 for longer than a year. There seemed to be an obstacle at every turn, painful proof of Bernie's belief that each new team had to earn its right to be there.

It is true that Bernie had engineered the deal with Yamaha for 1992. It was no coincidence that Yamaha had bought the factory Bernie had used for the Brabham team. He had placed his man, Herbie Blash, in these premises at Chessington in Surrey to run the Yamaha effort. That was typical of how Bernie was meticulous in looking after his own. Herbie, a former mechanic with Lotus, had moved on to become team manager at Brabham. In later years, he became a high-ranking grand-prix official with the FIA, the sport's governing body,

Herbie was outstanding and very helpful. He knew and respected Gary from the time they spent together when Gary was a mechanic at Brabham in the 1970s. The good news was that the Yamaha V12 engines would be free. The bad news was that they were free because they were big, heavy and no one wanted them. That was going to be a financial help in 1992 but, for now, the Yamaha deal did nothing to help pay Cosworth approximately £1 million.

Cosworth were very tough and I could understand why. I had known Bernard Ferguson, our contact at Cosworth, for many years and got on well with him, as did everyone in motor sport. But Bernard, for all his sympathy for our plight, had a responsibility to his company and its employees. There was an awful inevitability about the winding-up order.

Ironically, this had happened while I was in Japan, finalising the deal with Yamaha. Fred Rodgers agreed to represent us in court. In simple terms, we were asked, 'You have received invoices, why haven't you paid them?' There was no easy answer to that – other than, 'Well, your honour, we don't have the money.'

Fred trawled through the contracts and various other papers and established that the team had the right to buy an engine for £100,000, but in the disclosure of the invoices in front of the judge, a number of the rebuilds came to a figure in excess of £100,000 for each engine. Fred was able to demonstrate to the judge that, on that alone, we were being seriously overcharged for engines. The judge asked the Cosworth representative if a rebuilt engine might have had parts from the engine in its original form. When the answer was in the affirmative, the judge asked how it was possible for an engine made from second-hand parts to cost more than a new one. He advised both parties to get out of his court and sort this out for themselves, or words to that effect. He did not give Cosworth the winding-up petition, called an Order 14.

I began negotiations with Bernard and his people at Cosworth. It was now apparent that Michael Schumacher was going to be a big star which, in turn, would raise the value of the Jordan 191 with which he had made his debut at Spa. That car became valuable currency. We did not have any cash but we placed an astronomical value on the 191. This explains how, when Audi later bought 50 per cent of Cosworth, a green Jordan 191 found its way into the Audi museum. Vickers owned Cosworth and they did not want the publicity associated with our case because Vickers were a bit vulnerable in the City. We eventually agreed a figure and settled it over a six-month period because, by then, we were receiving reasonable sponsorship, but at the end of 1991, the Cosworth affair was causing a massive headache.

On top of that, Bertrand Gachot was very unhappy with me despite the time and effort we put in to try to keep him out of prison. Michael Schumacher may have been brilliant during practice at Spa but, prior to that, I had not wanted to change the driver line-up. I always felt that both Gachot and the 191 would go well at Spa but I am not sure Bertrand believed that as he began his time at Her Majesty's Pleasure. I was devastated when he was so unceremoniously removed from the scene and would have much preferred our driver line-up to remain the same. That may seem strange knowing what we know now about Schumacher, but at the time I knew little about Michael. Jordan Grand Prix was on a roll and I did not want to fiddle with the chemistry.

Meanwhile, while cooling my heels in Australia, I had time to contemplate having been away from home for several weeks, what with the races and flying back and forth to Yamaha in Japan. I had been on the telephone to Marie and, during the course of our conversation, she mentioned a recently released film that she had seen. It was called *The Commitments*.

I thought no more about it because I was getting ready to have lunch with Jean Alesi and some of the British F1 journalists – Nigel Roebuck, David Tremayne and Maurice Hamilton – who were also stopping over in Sydney. Our choice of a suitable venue became obvious when we found a fish restaurant called Jordans on the harbour front. It lived up to the name – a lively place in the sunshine, the atmosphere helped along by a few bottles of nicely chilled Chardonnay.

Once this lengthy lunch had finished, we took a boat trip around the harbour and then said farewell to Jean. On the way back to my hotel, we passed a cinema. It was advertising a new release – *The Commitments*. Nothing would do but for us to go and see it.

If you are not familiar with the film, it is based on Roddy Doyle's brilliant novel that tells the story of a motley bunch of lads from Dublin who start a rock band called the Commitments. The film did the book justice; it was hilarious. This was just the tonic I needed.

I had not seen the family for several weeks, the Cosworth problem was looming, I did not know who would be driving for Jordan in 1992 and I was still ticked off with Bernie over the Schumacher business. It seemed to be war on all sides. These were difficult times and I had to keep pinching myself to be strong. If anyone inside the team saw a hint of vulnerability or a lack of strength, it would percolate through the company. Someone would eventually pass this news on to a journalist and, before we knew it, the media en masse would be on the case.

There was no one I could talk to. It was not the sort of thing you can discuss with, for example, engineers because they have their own problems with drag coefficients, engine power and so on. They used to become so engrossed in their trade that I sometimes felt like telling them to get a life as they worked all hours, but that was their calling. Sorting the money was down to me and it was beginning to get on top of me but, outwardly, I remained calm. Certainly, I was totally relaxed when watching *The Commitments*. I loved it because it reminded me so much of home. My emotions ranged between tears and hysterics. At one point, I was nearly sliding off my seat and I could hardly catch my breath. I must have looked like someone on cocaine.

When we emerged into the daylight, the guys asked me if it was a true reflection of Dublin and its culture on the north side of the city. I was happy to confirm that it was a gloriously accurate portrayal, and one of the best films I had ever seen. As a corollary, I have since met Count, the saxophonist, who played one of the best roles in the film. We do the occasional gig when I attempt to play the drums to raise money for the charity Cancer and Leukaemia in Childhood (CLIC).

I remember *The Commitments* with a mix of pain and pleasure because that film reminds me of both happy and difficult times. But, as often happens in life, something comes along that redefines your priorities. The problems you thought you had suddenly pale into insignificance.

Construction of a new team headquarters had been under way throughout 1991. We had bought a plot of land directly opposite the main gate at Silverstone. Guy Austin of Ridge and Partners did the design because I had been very impressed with Guy's work at the Reynard factory. Despite the cash flow being rather slow and, at times, non-existent, the project came together really well. We had leaned heavily on the bank and I put Bosco Quinn in charge of overseeing the job and ensuring it was built to budget.

Bosco did a brilliant job. The place was state of the art with lots of chrome and matt black woodwork. We had paintwork lines that were not straight, which added to the feeling that this was a funky building, very rock'n'roll. It cost us comparatively little because different people we knew came to the aid of the party. The granite in the magnificent open-plan foyer was from Italy, thanks to a deal done through Nigel Wolheim, an Italian-speaking entrepreneur involved in various aspects of motor sport. All the cabinets for the tools, and the workbenches, came from Italian tool company Beta, which had long been associated with motor racing. I thought it looked terrific then, and nothing has changed my opinion since.

Bosco took the whole thing very seriously, as I knew he would. He said that, once the factory was open, he would leave the company and spend three years travelling through Asia. He was going to do it on his own and learn about the various countries as he went along. Bosco was a great reader and a deep thinker. He was good fun, but always in control. He would pull me aside at certain times and say, 'I don't think so! I don't think so!' It was his way of saying, 'Forget it, EJ! We don't need you in jail.' He was always very conscious of the exact location of the line between what was acceptable and what was not, and he would not let me cross it. 'I don't give a shit about you,' he would say, 'but I do care about Marie and the kids.'

The factory was commissioned and the keys handed over in early December. Bosco was planning to leave at Christmas. There were still odd jobs being completed after the handover and Bosco, as usual, had been working late. On his way home to Northampton, he crashed the car and died from his injuries. The entire team was devastated. Bosco was in his early thirties, far too young to be taken. He was a fantastic guy and I could not have managed thus far without him. His death brought an even worse twist at the end of a season that should have been characterised by joyful celebration.

We were fifth in the championship and moving into a brand new factory, but with uncertainty and sadness all around. The fact that we were the only team to have finished in the top five in their first year was a wonderful achievement but it did not seem to be helping in practical terms. We were completely independent and I was having to look at bills for travel, tyres and engines, as well as paying the staff.

Some people later said that perhaps I had been too adventurous in taking £150,000 from Michael Schumacher for that drive at Spa. The suggestion was that I was being a bit cheeky and greedy considering Michael's latent talent. I replied by saying that the money to pay the mounting bills had to come from somewhere.

A rough calculation showed that Jordan Grand Prix was five million down – 12 months before I had been five million up. It does not matter who you are or how brave you have been. If you have five million in the bank, you are a very rich man. When you owe five million, you are a very poor man and in the crap. It's as simple and painful as that. As I was discovering, there are not many people in this world who want to know you when you are up to your neck in the latter.

## Chapter 22

# ALMOST POINTLESS

It has taken several chapters to cover 1991. By comparison, 1992 will not detain us long. The honeymoon had ended and the bruising reality of racing in F1 was about to knock us for six – or just one point, to be exact. From fifth in the championship in our very first year – and I can still barely believe that statistic as I write it now – we were about to plunge to equal 11th. Rock bottom.

As a general rule, a lot more problems are thrown up in the second year. The first is easy by comparison. In fact, it is the year *before* you enter F1 that makes the difference. You have time to think and prepare. It is true that we were taking part in F3000 in 1990 but Gary, Trevor and the boys were not rushing off every other weekend to a grand prix.

When it really starts to bite is during the first season, at the point when you have to start thinking about the following year's car while, at the same time, trying to ensure the current one remains competitive. You realise there is no alternative but to keep key people at home to look after the design of the next car – easier said than done when some of your design staff are doubling up as engineers at the races.

For a novice team with a staff of just 42 people, this can be a killer. It was particularly difficult towards the end of the year with Japan and Australia on the schedule. Gary was on a return flight home as soon as the Japanese race was over and straight into work immediately after landing in London. Then he was back on a plane at the last minute and heading for Adelaide. It was a very tough schedule made possible by Gary's incredible enthusiasm, which filtered through the entire team. Meanwhile, I was working on finding a means of paying for it all.

I may have had the bank on my back but, in the credit column, the team had the instant recognition brought about by finishing fifth in the championship. Jordan Grand Prix had become a team worth talking to. That said, one sponsor wanted to pull out during the season, or at least, the new man in charge felt he needed to use his new broom to sweep Jordan and motor sport into the corner.

I had got to know British American Tobacco through Paul Adams, whom I had met at 7UP and who was now the president of BAT (Asia). The cigarette brand Barclay was already involved in F1 with Williams but that deal was coming to an end, due to the arrival of Camel at Frank's team. It was relatively easy to come to an agreement to have Barclay identification on the side of our car for 1992. The hard part came when word began to filter through that a new marketing manager with a tough reputation earned at Suchard was due to take over, a man I found so rude that he would make me appear positively saintly. This was Jimmi Rembiszewski – or 'Rambo', as he quickly became known. He was not a fan of motor racing. His first objective it seemed to me was to cancel our contract for 1992.

I went to see him. He was worse than I could possibly have imagined, the noisiest man I have ever met. He sat with his feet on the desk, spitting pips from grapes with alarming accuracy into a waste bin in the corner of the room while spluttering and shouting and waving his arms.

'Jordan! Your results are shit. Why should I give your fucking team my money?' he roared in a heavy German/Jewish accent while thumping the table with his fist. 'The only time I see your fucking cars on television is when they are on the end of a crane! Motorsport, schmotorsport! Who fucking needs it? Tell me, Jordan, you Irish idiot! Tell me who needs it!'

There was only one way to respond and that was in kind, which suited me because I had had plenty of practice although, admittedly, not on such a grand scale as that practised by Rambo. I gave him as good as I got. In the end, he agreed to continue – in fact, contractually, he had little option – and our relationship with Rembiszewski and Barclay lasted, as planned, until the end of 1993.

Along the way, we became great friends with Jimmi. You actually could not help but like him. I think he respected me because I braved it out with him and I would not entertain a settlement figure. It was not so much the money, which was very important, of course, but I could not afford to be seen having a sponsor removed from the car at this stage in our development – and I knew if that happened, Rembiszewski would be shouting about it from the rooftop.

I found his marketing philosophy very different, as you might expect, and refreshing. 'Jordan!' he would shout. 'You must never win. You get more publicity with your car on the crane or having a big accident. If you are going to win, only win very seldom because the fans will always love you. Never be like Williams who are obsessed with winning all the time and when they lose, it's shit. So, win now and again and have some terrible results now and again. That will be the best marketing position for your team.'

Jimmi was a logical marketeer in that sense, even though, in other ways, his ideas appeared loopy to me. He was an amazing character and his business methods were unorthodox, to say the least – certainly not the sort of techniques you would find at IMG, who had approached me under much more restrained circumstances not long before the start of the 1992 season.

Andrew Hampel, number two at IMG Europe, came to see me. He explained that he had a potential sponsor and the value could extend over a two- or three-year period. Naturally, I was very interested. Part of the package included having Mauricio Gugelmin as a driver. Mauricio had done reasonably well in the British junior formulae without actually setting the place alight. However, he was capable and personable, and he had four years of F1 experience with March and then Leyton House. I was not sure whether his inclusion in the proposal was because he was part of the sponsor's package or because he was a client of IMG's, but that was irrelevant at this stage. I agreed to go to IMG's office at Kew Bridge to discuss this further.

There I met a delegation from South Africa, which immediately aroused my interest because F1 was going to return to South Africa after a seven-year break. There was a lot going on in the country at the time. Nelson Mandela was out and the ANC had arrived. Cyril Ramaphosa was one of the senior ministers and he was pushing to gain identification for South Africa in a world sporting environment. F1 has always been among the first international sports to go to places when things are difficult. It would be the same ten years later when the United States Grand Prix was the first major event of any kind to take place within the borders of the USA just a few weeks after the country had been devastated by 9/11. It seemed absolutely right that F1 should be the first to recognise the new regime in South Africa. Linked to this – and the reason for my visit to IMG – was a company called Sasol.

South Africa had been forced to deal with punitive embargoes, one of which covered the import of crude oil. Clever engineers at Sasol devised a way to make their own oil from the country's very rich resources of coal. In effect, Sasol had the full blessing of the government. Every garage forecourt had a blue Sasol petrol pump, regardless of whether the franchise was held by Esso, Shell, Caltex or whomever.

This really got my attention because, traditionally, oil companies had seldom been main sponsors in motor sport. Shell, for example, had supported Ferrari for many years but the association was marked only by a few stickers on the car. Sasol were asking for title sponsorship.

I was a relatively easy target because we were in January already and I needed money. I had put up my homes in Oxford and Spain as personal guarantees against a failure to pay the Cosworth bill. I – and, in particular, my family – had never been so exposed. Things happened very quickly to everyone's benefit. Ian – who was on crutches after breaking his leg while playing football with his son, Damian – had been talking to BP about a fuel and oil deal. He was brought into the discussion with Sasol on the Tuesday. By the Friday, the deal was done. Call it Irish luck. Call it whatever you like. We could carry on racing and, for 1992, we would be known as Sasol Jordan Yamaha.

As a bonus, I became particularly friendly with Brian Mahon, the guy who had set this up as a freelance agent, acting for Sasol. His parents were from Newtownards in Northern Ireland but he had lived all his life in Johannesburg. We played golf together and I quickly discovered that Brian was not only an excellent golfer but he also had a very good understanding of the Irish way of life. He was going to need it in the weeks to come.

It turned out that Mauricio Gugelmin, who was part of the package, was a good friend of Hampel's. This came about through Mauricio's association with Ayrton Senna, who was managed by IMG's Julian Jacobi. Sasol knew nothing of this part of the deal and Andrew effectively secured Mauricio the drive for next to no money. As far as I was concerned, that was their business. I was happy with my deal with Sasol. If Gugelmin came along as well, so be it, even though I knew that Ian and Trevor, who had dealt with the Brazilian in the past, did not want him in the team. Then things became a bit tricky.

I was having dinner one evening in Oxford with Marie and Suzi and Nick Usiskin. Suzi was a magistrate and her husband was a lawyer. It was after 11 p.m. when a lawyer tracked me down and arrived unexpectedly. He had two commission agreements in his briefcase. I had already signed a contract agreeing 10 per cent commission, payable to IMG for bringing the Sasol deal to the team. He explained that they were tearing that up and, instead, there were now two contracts, each for 5 per cent. This, he said, was merely internal politics because there was an office in Cleveland and another in Monaco and I did not need to worry about the ins and outs.

I thought, 'OK, whatever – 5 per cent and 5 per cent. It's no skin off my nose. But 11 o'clock at night? In a small restaurant in Oxford? Very odd!'

During subsequent chats with Brian Mahon, I noticed he referred more than once to the good deal I had done with IMG. Eventually, I asked him what he was talking about. He said that paying IMG 5 per cent was a good deal for me. He knew about it because he was receiving half from IMG, in other words 2.5 per cent, for his role in bringing Sasol to IMG.

'Brian, hang on,' I said. 'You're making a mistake. I'm paying them 10 per cent.'

'No you're not. You're paying them 5 per cent, and I get half of it, as agreed with IMG. I've seen the contract.'

It did not take long to work out what had happened. Mahon had been shown just one of the two contracts I had signed. Brian took IMG to court. It was settled before they got that far, which was not surprising because the swapping of contracts had been carried out at 11 p.m. at night and, unwittingly, in front of a magistrate and a lawyer.

Either way, we had Gugelmin as a driver and Sasol as an excellent sponsor. We had already signed Stefano Modena in Japan at the end of the previous season. The 28-year-old had competed in more than 50 grands prix for, among others, Tyrrell. I thought the Italian was a star. We also believed that Modena would be bringing the Braun sponsorship deal with him from Tyrrell, but that never happened.

Stefano had raced with Martin Brundle at Brabham and I had heard that Modena drove the mechanics mad because he was so fussy. He wanted the car parked on a certain side of the garage, he would not allow anyone to help him fasten his belts, if they did he would get out of the car and start all over again – that sort of thing. As a result, he had gained a reputation as quite a difficult character.

I never worried about things like that. Yes, Modena was pernickety but, if we chose a driver, it was up to the team to provide him with whatever he needed. If that's what made him drive fast, so be it. I felt we could cope because we had sorted de Cesaris and others like him over the years.

In the event, we had very few problems with Stefano, although we were to discover that, to do a really good job, he needed to feel that everything was working for him. Sadly, as we were about to find out, the Jordan-Yamaha 192 would not help either Modena's cause or that of the team.

We had problems from the start because the engines arrived late and, when they came, I am not sure they were as good as they could have been. Neither, if I am honest, was our chassis. The difficulty had been caused by Jordan originally having a multi-year contract with Ford and, naturally, the initial stages of the 192 had been designed around the V8. The decision to go with Yamaha came quite late. It meant Gary's team had, in simple terms, to shoehorn a V12 into the space reserved for a V8. The balance and weight distribution on the car was always going to be a compromise in an important area that has no place for concessions.

Also, we had switched from the standard gearbox to a sequential gearshift, which meant that instead of following the traditional H pattern, the driver pulled the gearlever back to change up and pushed it forward to change down. Simple in theory but quite difficult in practice because the loading proved too great and caused all sorts of problems early on. Our pre-season testing was severely limited as a result and we seemed to be on the back foot from then on. However, if nothing else, this package gave us breathing space and allowed the team to survive.

The first race was in South Africa, which was obviously very important to us, and I asked Marie to come along. We would be meeting top people from Sasol and, in any case, South Africa is a very pleasant place to be in the spring. Paul Kruger was CEO of Sasol at that time and he and his wife Gina were a dream to work with. They loved Jordan and the entire concept of being involved with F1. Sasol could best be described as a very traditional South African business and yet they used their association with F1 better than any other sponsor we were to work with. Indeed, they sent Jan Krynauw, their head of communications, to England after three poor races for the team and signed up for another three years.

That was a major surprise, particularly after we had got off to such a terrible start. About 25 minutes into the qualifying session at Kyalami, there was not a single car in the garage. The spare and both race cars were parked out on the track with blown engines. Here we were, at the start of a new sponsorship with Sasol, in the middle of qualifying with all its supposed drama and we had 15 mechanics standing around with nothing to do. This was turning into a major source of discomfort, particularly when Modena did not qualify. Gugelmin finished 11th in the race, having run no higher than that at any stage.

We had a series of engine failures at subsequent races. In fact, we had engines blowing up right, left and centre. I think I am correct in saying that Jordan and Yamaha established a world record for the shortest engine life. The boys had been up most of the night in Brazil making an unscheduled change of engine, only for it to fail within six seconds of being started up for the first time.

There were also problems with overheating because the Yamaha required really large radiators to keep the thing cool. Gary and the design team had not appreciated the totally different running characteristics of the Yamaha V12 compared to the Ford V8. We had a succession of retirements but, throughout all of this, Mauricio Gugelmin kept his head down and pushed as hard as he could. It was just what we needed.

Modena did not finish a single race in the first two-thirds of the season. The effect on such a sensitive driver can easily be imagined. He went downhill rapidly and could not cope. Yet the final irony was that Stefano saved us from complete humiliation in the last race of the season.

In fact, he almost did it in the penultimate round in Japan. There, he was running sixth but, despite the 192 having one of the biggest fuel tanks of any car in the pit lane, the bloody thing ran out of fuel on the last lap, the Yamaha technicians having run their V12 really rich in order make it survive in their home grand prix. The fuel consumption was horrendous and, when we eventually got the car back to the garage, we found the tank was bone dry.

If you look at any picture of our cars in Australia, you will see advertising for a pasta house, which was the result of Ian spending a few days beforehand walking the streets of Adelaide attempting to sell space. Not only did he manage it, we also had free pasta for the duration. As an aside, which did not seem funny at the time, Gugelmin crashed his car spectacularly in the race and the pasta restaurant's logo was plastered all over the local papers. They thought it was terrific and supported Jordan in Adelaide for many years.

Modena narrowly missed being taken out by someone else's accident on the opening lap and this rare outbreak of luck continued when cars ahead began to drop out with various mechanical problems. Then Nigel Mansell and Ayrton Senna kindly helped by crashing into each other under controversial circumstances, which were hardly surprising because neither driver tended to do things by halves.

When Riccardo Patrese's leading Williams retired, we were sixth, with 31 laps remaining of a very tough street circuit. It seemed like a lifetime. We desperately needed that point but all you can think about at a time like that are the massive number of things that could go wrong. Every time the radio crackled we thought it was Modena about to impart some terrible news, and pulse rates shot through the roof. But Stefano was driving really well and he made it to the finish in what would be his last F1 race.

There were no celebrations, just a sense of huge relief. We were 11th in the championship. One more point would have put us into the top ten on the constructors' table, guaranteeing the subsidised travel package and other benefits for 1993. I was unable to sleep on the way home because of the feel-good factor from that single point. But there was no getting away from the fact that we had given Sasol bad value. I could see that the team did not have the same sparkle as in 1991, which was hardly surprising. In fact, 1992 would go down as the worst season ever for Jordan Grand Prix. At least we had survived, and Sasol were not discouraged. Significant changes were afoot for 1993.

## Chapter 23

# HART ATTACK

The one good thing about bumping along at the bottom of the championship is that the only way is up – but if 1993 turned out to be worse than the previous year, the doors of Jordan Grand Prix were likely to be closed for good. Whatever package we chose, it would have to work. The trouble is, you never really know whether the car in which you have invested a massive amount of time and money will be competitive until it is too late.

There was an understandable feeling of trepidation on my part when I drove Sasol's Jan Krynauw from our factory into the deserted Silverstone paddock on a cold afternoon in November, just a few weeks after the 1992 season had finished. Inside a garage sat one of the unloved 192s. It was not the car we had come to see but the brand new engine in the back of it. I had no idea whether this V10 would be powerful enough, or reliable. I could only go by instinct and the feelings of Gary and the team. This would be a gamble whichever way we looked at it and Sasol had no choice but to trust our judgement. The faith shown by your sponsor brings not just the money but also, in its own way, another turn of the screw. This new engine had better be good.

We had an agreement to continue with Yamaha for another year but, after a long discussion, I had the impression that Yamaha were as relieved as we were at the opportunity to terminate the deal. But where next? F1 engines did not exactly grow on trees.

During the course of the struggle with the Yamaha V12, we had called upon Brian Hart to act as a consultant. Brian knew how many beans made five when it came to racing engines. He had been a racer of some note in Formula 2 in the 1960s and 1970s before setting up his engine-tuning business in Essex. Brian's four-cylinder turbo engine had powered the first F1 car for Toleman (the team that became Benetton and, later, Renault).

On one particular visit to Brian's workshop in Harlow, Gary and Trevor were surprised to find he had been investing £2 million of his own money in designing and building a V10 engine, more or less in his spare time. Typically, it was a workmanlike project. Better than that, Brian understood racing. He and Gary spoke the same language and understood each other's needs perfectly – which would make a welcome change for Gary after struggling with a conglomerate such as Yamaha. Hart and Anderson would make a perfect partnership, helped along on many an evening by a mutual appreciation of good red wine.

As far as I was concerned, the language I understood best was financial and the price tag of £2.8 million for the first year and £3 million for the second, while being a tidy sum for one season in anyone's book, was good value in F1 terms. We had come to an agreement and this test hack before us in the draughty garage at Silverstone was the first product of our new liaison with Brian Hart. It was difficult to tell who was the more apprehensive – Brian or me.

Mauricio Gugelmin would do the driving although, by then, I had plans to sign another Brazilian – or, if I was really lucky, two Brazilians. For the moment, Gugelmin's feedback would give us the first indication of the likely performance of the new Jordan-Hart, due to be unveiled in the New Year. Despite a few small problems, the engine sounded lusty and, according to Gugelmin, felt as if it wanted to get up and go. That was good enough for me and, by association, Sasol. The important fact at this stage was to have an engine that would be reliable enough to allow us to go testing and improve the new car. That, in turn, would decrease the chances of something failing on the car during the races. There was also the additional benefit of allowing plenty of track time for the novice F1 driver I had in mind.

I had been very impressed with Rubens Barrichello when I first saw him in F3, winning the British Championship. Until now, I had employed drivers who, apart from Michael Schumacher, had been around F1 for a while. I was getting tired of that and felt we should go for someone younger and with a future. When Rubens and his father came to my home, I remember looking at this slightly built 20-year-old and thinking he could be my son. He seemed ridiculously young to be going into F1.

Rubens had real talent and Gary immediately took a shine to him. I had seen the magnetism Gary had with certain drivers in the past and I knew that augured well for Barrichello's first season. When you have that kind of understanding between the designer/engineer and driver, it is a very powerful combination. The icing on the cake would be the benefit Rubens would derive if I could possibly attract a team-mate who meant more to Barrichello than anyone else.

The thought of having Ayrton Senna join Jordan was not as daft as it seemed. Ayrton may have won three world championships and 30 grands prix with McLaren, but there was no question that he was unsettled by the thought of McLaren no longer having Honda engines in 1993. He may have been with the team for five seasons but his relationship with Honda was very special and he was interested in any viable alternative. I had a plan that held Ayrton's attention for long enough to have him slip across the road to see me after a McLaren test session at Silverstone.

I told Senna that I would give him 25 per cent of the team and this figure would rise to 49 per cent at the end of the second year. Since I owned 100 per cent, I would then have only half of my original holding, but with Senna on board, the valuation of the team would have risen to such an extent that 51 per cent would be worth more than 100 per cent as it stood. Ayrton would have moulded the team around him, made it his own and taken Jordan to a new level. I felt sure, for instance, that we would have got the Honda engine simply because of Senna's presence and influence. This would work to everybody's benefit. It was a no-brainer from my point of view. I loved thinking outside the box and this could be a neat solution. I was to try the same thing several years later with Michael Schumacher.

Ayrton thought long and hard about it. He made another visit to see us late at night. Even towards the end of 1992 when I was in Brazil finalising details with Rubens and his sponsor, Arisco, Ayrton would secretly run me to the airport so that we could chat further. It was the first time I had been in a Honda NSX and Ayrton made the journey entertaining by using his knowledge of the back roads to reach the airport. In the end, nothing came of our discussions. Ayrton stayed with McLaren for another season, winning five races with the Ford engine before making his ill-fated move to Williams for 1994.

Having waited as long as we could, it was necessary to fall back on Plan B. Martin Brundle had been talking to us, but he eventually chose Ligier. Our paths would cross again a few years later but, in the meantime, we settled on Ivan Capelli, a driver who had been receiving mixed reviews. The Italian had shown great form when driving for Leyton House, then under the stewardship of Ian Phillips. Ian was a big fan of Ivan's and felt that we could salvage something from a reputation that had taken a huge knock with Ferrari in 1992. I agreed that the potential was there. After all, Ivan had led a couple of races in the underfinanced Leyton House, and we felt he would be more at home with Jordan rather than enduring the huge pressure that had come with being an Italian at Ferrari. Unbeknown to us, the damage done during those 12 months at Maranello was irreparable, as we were to discover at the first race in South Africa, the home of our title sponsor.

Once again, the people from Sasol were enormously courteous and that led to a very embarrassing moment for Marie and me. Before the race weekend got under way, we were at a barbecue – or a 'braai' as they call it in South Africa – with Brian Mahon at the

Getting the opportunity to drive the McLaren F1 car at Brands Hatch in 1980 – it was about this time I began to realise I was never going to make it to the absolute top as a driver. (LAT)

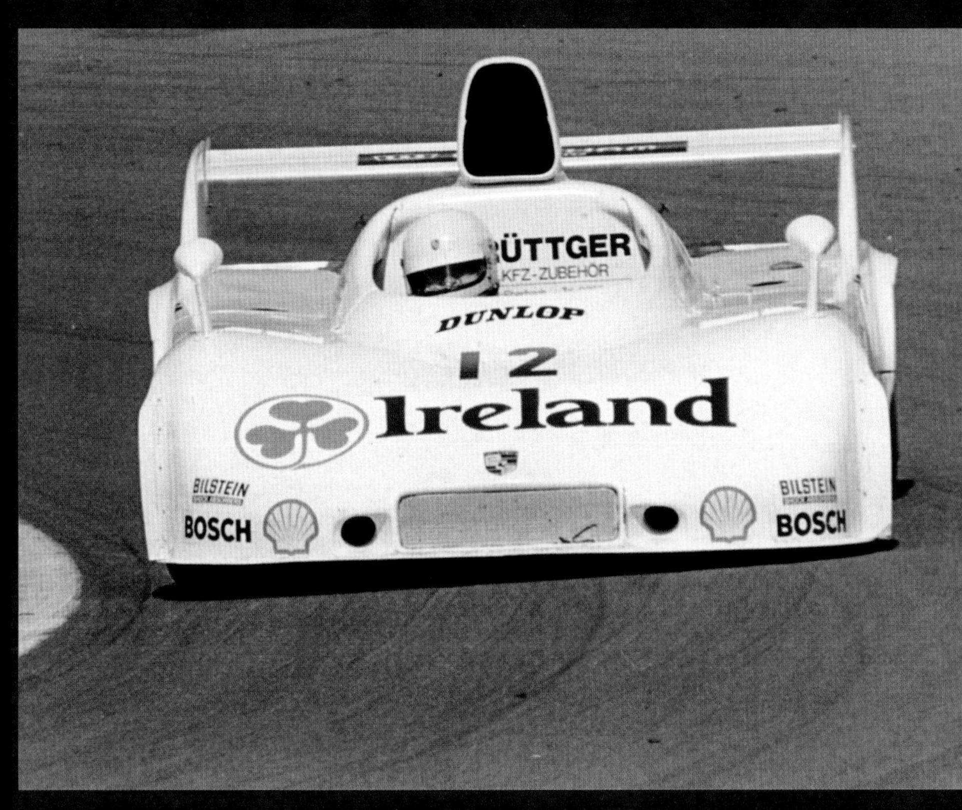


Driving the twin-turbo Porsche 908, one of the most awesome cars I ever drove.

Martin Brundle, Ayrton Senna and Davy Jones on the podium after the Silverstone F3 race in June 1983 – it was one of the most dramatic seasons in history at this level, and a sign that Eddie Jordan Racing was on its way. All three of these drivers would at one stage drive for me. (LAT)

The horrific crash involving Johnny Herbert in August 1988 at Brands Hatch in F3000. Johnny's boots were ripped off in the impact, and for a while it seemed as though his feet might need to be amputated. (LAT)

Gary Anderson and I launch our first Jordan F1 car in November 1990: 29 journalists turned up to see our unsponsored, unpainted car. Apart from that, it looked pretty good. (LAT)

The Jordan-Ford 191, in its smart green livery thanks to 7UP's sponsorship and then a link with Ireland, makes its F1 debut at the US Grand Prix on 10 March 1991, with Bertrand Gachot at the wheel. (Popperfoto)

An early wave from Nigel Mansell helped ease Andrea de Cesaris into fourth place at the Canadian Grand Prix, and with Bertrand also picking up points in the race, we had five points in our fifth race. (Getty Images)

After the briefest of spells driving for me in 1991, Michael Schumacher was on his way, but it was Jordan that gave him his Formula One debut. (Popperfoto)

Easter and the European Grand Prix of 1993, and Rubens Barrichello shot the car from twelfth on the grid to fourth after one lap. In the pouring rain, his next challenge was to make his first ever pit stop. (LAT)

I managed to lure Eddie Irvine from a lucrative career in F3000 to drive for Jordan at the Japanese Grand Prix in 1993, and on his debut he managed to infuriate the great Ayrton Senna by unlapping himself. (LAT)

As predicted live on TV by Chris Rea, Jordan won its first ever podium in the Pacific Grand Prix in 1994, with Rubens Barrichello (right) at the wheel. (LAT)

Surveying the scene with Louise Goodman, then Jordan's press officer, and one of the few able to handle Eddie Irvine (centre), at the start of the 1995 Brazilian Grand Prix. (PA Photos)

Partying with Damon Hill in 1995 after the British Grand Prix – the idea we had started of hosting an evening gig grew into a great tradition at Silverstone. (LAT)

Martin Brundle's Jordan disintegrates during the 1996 Australian Grand Prix. Amazingly, he emerged from the wreckage unscathed – it was one way to get attention for our new sponsors, B&H. (Getty Images)

Hissing Sid on the nose cone of the 1997 Jordan, driven by Ralf Schumacher, was enough to tempt John Lydon to pay us a visit at our factory. (LAT)

Ralf Schumacher celebrates Jordan's first podium in two years in our 100th race, the 1997 Argentinian Grand Prix, though the fact he hit team-mate Giancarlo Fisichella during the race meant all didn't go entirely according to plan. (Getty Images)

house of two brothers he knew well, Neil and Grant Thomas. It was a lively evening to say the least but, due to a breakdown in communications, I did not know that Marie and I were supposed to be at a dinner hosted by the board of Sasol. Eventually, Jan Krynauw tracked us down. I could tell by the desperation in his voice that all was not well.

There was no alternative but to drop what we were doing and head straight to the restaurant, even though we were in tee shirts and jeans and, shall we say, a certain amount of drink had been taken. It was a wonderfully warm evening and Neil Thomas drove us at full speed in his open-topped Mercedes. We reached the restaurant and snaked flat-out up the gravel drive – only to find the board of directors standing, solemn-faced to a man, on the front verandah waiting for their guests who were over an hour late, unsuitably dressed and half-pissed. You could read their minds – 'So, this is motor racing. And our money is going to this comedian and his team?' It was hugely embarrassing. I am not exactly sure how, but we managed to talk our way over that little hurdle, only accidentally to create another.

Despite our unfortunate start, the Sasol people were very kind indeed. In fact, they were some of the nicest people you could ever wish to meet. During the course of the evening, they explained that Sasol would be running a big boma at the race. This was a hospitality unit and they asked if there was anyone we wanted to bring along. Marie said her uncle lived in Durban and, not having been to a grand prix before, she was sure he would love to come. They said that would be no problem and asked his name. When Marie said, 'Bishop Hurley,' they went a collective shade of pale.

'What, THE Bishop Hurley? The Archbishop of Durban?'

'Yes, that's right. He's my uncle.'

'Ah right...well, absolutely no problem. Bring him along.'

Bishop Hurley was a respected voice in South Africa, but he was also very well known for his outspoken and strong views on apartheid. I would not say the Sasol people freaked, but it was clear that perhaps not all of Bishop Hurley's views matched theirs.

Nonetheless, they had no hesitation in extending the invitation. As things turned out, the bishop could not come because of other commitments and he sent his apologies and thanks.

Capelli disappointed and confused everyone, including himself, crashing because of what appeared to be the simplest of errors. When he failed to qualify for the second race in Brazil, we reached a mutual agreement not to continue. Ivan was devastated. We often talk about it now but, really, there is not a lot to be said. In my view, Capelli never recovered mentally from the hammering he received while trying to drive what was a difficult car at Ferrari.

With a novice in one car, we continued on the theme of placing an experienced driver in the other. Thierry Boutsen, with a strong reputation and a couple of wins to his name, filled that role. He also filled the car to excess, the Belgian finding difficulty fitting a chassis that had not been designed for his lanky frame and large feet. Size 12s never fitted Gary Anderson's cars very well, which is why some of our drivers had to have the tops cut out of their driving boots – a less than ideal situation.

Thierry was not happy with the car during his first race but I have to confess that the entire team was diverted that day by the progress of Rubens in the other car. We were on home territory insofar as this race at Donington had been put into the calendar as a substitute for a grand prix in Japan that had run into difficulties.

It was good to have a race not far from the factory because we desperately needed the breathing space. There had been a few problems with the semi-automatic gearbox. This forced a compromise whereby Barrichello's car would have the steering-wheel mounted paddles while Boutsen, already struggling for elbowroom, would have to cope with a conventional manual shift. That meant a lot of extra work for the mechanics. It was hardly surprising when Thierry qualified in 19th place. Rubens, on the other hand, was actually disappointed with 12th after a small mistake on his fastest qualifying lap. This may have been the beginning of April but, so far, the weather had been kind. That was about to change on race day.

Easter Sunday dawned cold, wet and miserable with no discernable pattern to the weather. Rubens loved driving in the wet and you could detect his keenness to get this race started. We may have been hopeful of a good result but I do not think anyone in their wildest dreams could have predicted what was about to happen, for both good and bad.

People still talk about Senna's amazing performance when he was pushed back to fifth place at the start of the first lap but led the field at the end of it, having sliced past Alain Prost and Damon Hill as if they were standing still. In my book, Rubens did an even more amazing job when he somehow worked his way from 12th to fourth during that crazy opening lap. We were both astounded and mightily impressed. The order was McLaren (Senna), Williams (Prost), Williams (Hill) – and Jordan. But this was only the first of 73 laps. I could not imagine this continuing, particularly as my good friend Jean Alesi was climbing all over the back of Barrichello's car.

Rubens maintained his cool and for ten laps the order at the front remained the same. The rain had eased and it was obvious that strategy and changing on to the right tyres at the right time was going to dictate everything. Here was an immediate problem for us. Rubens had never made a pit stop before.

Don't forget, this was in the days before refuelling, and in the previous two races, Rubens had retired before reaching the stage when he needed to stop and change tyres. Now, not only would he need to stop, but he would also have to choose the right moment – and the correct tyre. The rain may have ceased but the sky remained black and threatening. It was impossible to tell which way the weather, never mind the race, was going to go.

Damon Hill started the ball rolling by stopping for dry-weather slicks at the end of lap 17. That was it. The pit lane went mad with cars diving in and out. Among them was Rubens, heading for the very first pit stop for the team in 1993. Anything – and I mean, anything – could have happened. Rubens could have overshot, a mechanic could have fumbled with a wheel nut in the cold conditions, a nut could easily have been cross-threaded in the anxiety not to lose a place.

The stop was perfect, absolutely perfect, but not the weather. The rain returned five laps later. Rubens bravely hung on until the conditions became so difficult that he had no option but to stop once more for wets on lap 28 and, wouldn't you know, the bloody rain stopped almost immediately. Seven laps later, he was back for slicks. And back for wets three laps after that. While all that was going on, Boutsen was more or less mirroring Barrichello's tactics. The mechanics were working like maniacs and they had not finished yet.

The rain stopped once more but Rubens was not for coming in. He pushed on until the wet-weather rubber began to overheat on the dry line and forced a stop for slicks. Seconds after Rubens left the pits, the heavens opened. Within a lap, Rubens, along with the rest of the field, was back for wets. As he rejoined and completed another lap, I turned round to look at the TAG-Heuer computer screen. I could not believe what I was seeing – Rubens was still fourth.

This was a stunning performance in the most difficult circumstances imaginable. The boy was driving like a veteran in such elevated company. Then, with six laps to go, he moved into third when Hill made a late stop. This was too much to take in. It may have been bitterly cold, but we did not feel a thing. Was a podium finish on the cards for Jordan?

Three laps to go and the radio crackled into life. I could hardly hear what Rubens was saying but I could tell from Gary's expression that it was not good news. In barely audible tones, Rubens said the engine had died and he was parked on the grass. Third place and a podium finish down the pan.

We discovered the cause later when the car was stripped down and the fuel tank found to be empty. Traction control – new for 1993 and used to the maximum all afternoon on the slippery track – had been thirstier than anticipated. In truth, never having experienced these conditions before, we had no way of knowing this would happen. There was no car-to-pits telemetry in 1993 to give a warning.

Having been soaked to the skin, everyone suddenly felt cold and miserable. There was nothing to be said. A brilliant drive by Rubens and a fantastic performance by the team in terms of tactics and pit stops had brought us within sniffing distance of the champagne being sprayed on the podium by Senna, Hill and Prost. The motorhome was some distance from the back of the garage and that walk was among the longest and loneliest I can remember. This excruciating near-miss would become even more poignant because our season was about to go from bad to worse.

We went through a rash of niggling failures and retirements. Barrichello's best result – seventh – came in the middle of the season in France. Boutsen parted company with us after retiring from his home grand prix at Spa at the end of August. The feeling was mutual. Thierry did not feel the car was as good as he had hoped, and we thought that perhaps he was not as good as we had hoped. We did not give him a good enough package and Thierry, having been used to winning cars such as the Williams, probably asked himself, 'Just what am I doing this for?' Thierry moved on to buy and sell planes – one of his passions – and he seemed very content each time we met at Monaco, where he lives. The least said about 1993, the better.

Gary, meanwhile, was keen to take the opportunity to give young drivers a chance. We chose Marco Apicella for the Italian Grand Prix and Emanuele Naspetti for the next race in Portugal. Neither of them finished and Monza was to prove our low point when both cars collided on the first lap. With just the Japanese and Australian races remaining, Jordan did not have a single point on the board and there seemed little hope of earning one.

Other teams were attempting to lure Sasol away, which came as no surprise. That is how the business works and everyone accepts it. You can go out to dinner with a rival team principal and you are the best of friends but you know that his marketing department is working tirelessly with presentations and colour schemes for the benefit of your prime sponsor. You learn to live with that.

Taking a chance with young drivers worked in a similar way. The more successful teams could afford to wait while a novice cut his teeth with a team such as Jordan. All the learning and crashing was done at your expense. If the driver progressed well, the bigger teams would move in, offer more money and tempt the driver to leave.

Rubens had made an excellent impression in his first year but he was under firm contract to Jordan and, in any case, I do not think he would have wanted to leave at this stage, even if asked. Our other young drivers, despite fleeting moments of promise in their respective races in Italy and Portugal, did not really get the chance to impress. But everything was about to change at the next race in Japan with the explosive arrival of an Irish renegade after my own heart.

## Chapter 24

# FAST EDDIE

Eddie Irvine had taken a typically measured gamble. After struggling with our F3000 car in 1990 and winning just once with the Reynard against the superior Lolas, there was nothing worthwhile on offer for 1991 and beyond. Figuring he could make decent money racing in the Japanese F3000 series, Irvine left the hub of racing behind in Europe and headed East. By the time we began to make plans for the Japanese Grand Prix in 1993, Irvine was top of the F3000 pile in every sense. He was leading the championship and earning $800,000 a year, more than the majority of F1 drivers were taking home. Eddie was enjoying the Tokyo nightlife enormously and, by day, investing his earnings cleverly on the world's stock markets. He did not have the slightest wish to earn less money while grinding round the world on the F1 tour. However, I reckoned he might make an exception for Suzuka, and I was right.

Suzuka, with its figure of eight layout, is one of the most difficult tracks to race on, a place where local knowledge is everything. Having raced there for close on three years, Irvine knew Suzuka – wet and dry – like the back of his hand. With confidence like that, and with the skill I had seen as he drove the comparatively uncompetitive Reynard in 1990, I knew he had to be a good bet. Ian and I had met Eddie in the Hard Rock Café in Tokyo when on a visit to Fuji the previous August. After some discussion, he agreed to persuade his Japanese sponsor, Cosmo Oil, to be part of F1 for a weekend and pay for the drive. This was going to be interesting. Our press officer, Louise Goodman, would have plenty of material to work with.

This was Louise's second season with us and she was more than up to handling Irvine. It was Louise's ability to cope in a predominantly male environment that had caught my eye in the first place. I came across her while in F3000 when she was working for Ian at Leyton House. Louise was extremely capable and vibrant. Better than that, she could drink, sing, swear and act as hard as any man I knew. I had made a mental note of her name. When the time came to take what was the unusual step of employing a female press officer, Louise was perfect. She was able to give back as much as she got, a necessary attribute when dealing with Irvine.

Louise produced a press release in which I was quoted as saying that it would be good to have an Irish driver in an Irish team. Being familiar with the political problems in Ireland, I should have known better. It was not long before messages of outrage were pouring in from Northern Ireland, pointing out that Irvine was, in fact, British. We checked with people who knew about such technicalities and they advised that, strictly speaking, Irvine was actually from the UK, because British passports said on the front: 'The United Kingdom of Great Britain and Northern Ireland'.

We adapted a pair of Boutsen's overalls for Irvine and, to keep everyone happy, I had both the Union Flag and the Irish Tricolour sewn on the pockets. Of course, Irvine being Irvine and of Northern Ireland Protestant stock, he would play the fool by shoving a hand in his pocket with his index finger carefully covering the Tricolour but leaving the red, white and blue flag fully exposed. This was highlighting an age-old problem for sportsmen from Northern Ireland, born on the island of Ireland but brought up in the United Kingdom. When it comes to international rugby, boxing and hockey, just being from any part of the island qualifies you to play for Ireland. Football is the main sport that divides the two into teams from Northern Ireland and the Republic of Ireland. Irvine eventually solved the difficulty by using the shamrock emblem.

On a very different but equally serious note, we noticed, just before a photo call, that Eddie had forgotten to have the logo of his Japanese sponsor stitched on to the overalls. It was the start of what would be a colourful weekend in every sense.

Irvine was on the pace straightaway and I watched with interest to see how this would affect Barrichello. Rubens, despite being in his first season, had not been bothered by serious competition from the various drivers of the other car. Irvine was a different matter. At the end of the first free practice session, he was fifth fastest – and complaining about the car. Everyone, including the engineers, sat up and took note. Suddenly, British journalists who had not bothered with us in the second half of the season, if at all, rediscovered the location of the Jordan garage at the bottom end of the pit lane where, of course, they received a volley of cheerful insults from me.

The first qualifying session proved more difficult but changes to the car made all the difference for the second day. The increase in tempo within the team was noticeable when, for the first time ever, a Jordan topped the list of practice times on Saturday morning. This was unheard of. Irvine was fastest of all with Rubens, on his first visit to this difficult track, improving to ninth. After months of disappointment when Barrichello's best qualifying position had, bar one occasion, been in the back half of the grid, serious thought was been given to having both cars in the top dozen. Irvine got there first with a brilliant last lap that was worth eighth place. Seconds later, and definitely rising to the presence of such a precocious team-mate, Barrichello put in his best lap that was worth 12th place. It was our best qualifying as a team since Schumacher and de Cesaris at Spa more than two years earlier. After such a difficult season, I was thrilled. Irvine, as expected, treated this as an everyday occurrence. He seemed genuinely confident for the race.

I remember telling Eddie, as he got ready to climb into the car on the grid, that starting eighth would give him a fantastic opportunity to do something useful and create all the right headlines in his first grand prix. I should have known better. Irvine would create headlines – but most of them were of the controversial kind.

The track was wet at the start and Irvine immediately showed exactly the sort of experience I had hoped to see. He ran round the outside of three cars at the first corner simply because he knew there was more grip to be had on that part of the track in the wet, particularly when running slick tyres in the hope that the track was about to dry. It was an amazing move that looked simple and made Hill and Schumacher look silly. These more fancied runners eventually worked their way in front of Irvine, but he looked completely comfortable in a useful eighth place. That would become sixth when Schumacher and Hill collided. Rubens, meanwhile, had worked his way into ninth. Then the rain started to fall in earnest and the complexion of our race began to change.

Rubens was already in the pits receiving wet tyres when Irvine made a late call to come in, so Eddie had to do another lap on slicks. That meant another treacherous 3.64 miles on tyres with no treads. It was a sign of Irvine's natural ability that he managed to get back to the pits without sliding off. He rejoined in tenth place, three behind Rubens. Now the track was drying and it was a question of when to return to slicks. Irvine chose to stay out for a few laps more, and that decision had a profound effect on how the outside world would choose to view Eddie Irvine, potential grand-prix star.

Irvine caught Hill, who had stopped for slicks and was finding that Irvine's decision to stay out was the right one as the Williams slithered all over the place. Catching them both and about to lap the Jordan and the Williams was the race leader, Ayrton Senna. He passed Irvine but thought twice about lapping the Williams as Hill continued to slip and slide and almost leave the road. Irvine, anxious to put in fast times while on wet tyres, could not afford to wait. So, he unlapped himself.

It is unlikely that Senna had ever experienced such audacity before, certainly not in the hands of a novice. Senna then watched with a mixture of anger, frustration and disbelief as Eddie took Hill with a daring move into the chicane. The fact that the superior traction on the Williams allowed Damon to retake the place, only to have the two of them swap places again at the next corner, merely added to Senna's opinion that he was dealing with a mad Irishman in an Irish car.

Senna eventually lapped them both but a time bomb was now ticking in the Brazilian's head. Meanwhile, there was mayhem in the Jordan garage as the crew watched these incredible scenes on the television monitor. For good measure, a controlled drive by Rubens was about to move him into fifth place, a position he held to the end. Irvine, after a controversial incident in which Derek Warwick's Arrows spun off the road, came home in sixth place. After 14 races with zero points, we had not one but two cars in the points.

There was a brief moment of concern when Irvine was called before the stewards to discuss the incident with Warwick. When Eddie was cleared of any wrongdoing, I made a hasty departure for the airport in the belief that it was all over, which it was – bar the shouting.

Senna, meanwhile, had been addressing the winner's press conference. He complained about the behaviour of some of the backmarkers. While not mentioning Irvine by name, it was clear whom he meant. In the absence of any complaint being registered with the stewards, that seemed to be the end of the matter, which it would have been had Senna not bumped into Gerhard Berger.

Ayrton joined the Ferrari driver in the Camel hospitality unit run by another Austrian, Karl-Heinz Zimmermann, a brilliant chef with an impish sense of humour to match Berger's. A bottle of schnapps had been opened and Senna was persuaded to take a nip. Being almost teetotal and having worked hard for close to two hours, the effect of the schnapps on Senna was immediate. As he discussed Irvine's behaviour, Senna found Berger not only agreeing but also suggesting that Ayrton should do something about it. Immediately.

Suitably fortified, Ayrton marched down to the Jordan office and burst in to find Irvine, lolling on a table. The mood of both parties changed insofar as the calmer and less bothered Irvine appeared, the madder Senna became. Incensed by a perceived lack of respect, Ayrton turned to leave but took a swipe at Irvine as a parting gesture. The scenario was played out in front of Adam Cooper, a journalist who had caught the entire narrative on his tape recorder. This would soon be headline news, and I knew nothing about it.

I had thanked everyone on the team, made my excuses and left. I was feeling good for all the obvious reasons but an additional little detail had pleased me. Irvine had continued a tradition of Jordan drivers, past and present, scoring a point on their F1 debut whether they were actually driving for me or another team. Jean Alesi was one, Martin Brundle another. The same went for Johnny Herbert, and now Eddie Irvine. Pedro de la Rosa would be another. Very few drivers scored points first time out and the vast majority of this élite group had driven for me at some stage or another.

I had jumped on board a helicopter with Ken Tyrrell as we dashed to Osaka airport to catch what is known as the 'wedding flight' heading for Cairns. Marriages in Japan usually take place on a Sunday and the happy couples, dressed in their finery, head straight for Osaka and this direct flight to north Australia. The usual post-race procedure in Japan was to visit a bar called the Log Cabin and have several beers, mainly because there was little else to do. On this particular occasion, I was tired. I had been on the road quite a long time, the team was starting to improve and I simply wanted to go and play a bit of golf – just get the hell out of there.

The next morning in Cairns, I was having breakfast with Ken. He was reading the paper and suddenly let out one of his famous guffaws. 'Listen to this,' he spluttered, and proceeded to read an account of Ayrton Senna coming to blows with my driver. I was completely stunned. Having arrived at around 6 a.m. and neither heard a news bulletin nor seen a paper, I was in complete ignorance. I remembered seeing Niki Lauda sitting by the pool that morning but he had made little sense when he shouted across and asked me what the hell had been going on. Now I knew what he was on about.

I did not initially howl with laughter because I had no idea just how serious or otherwise this was. I tried to call the team but, by then, they were on the road, en route to the airport, so I called the *Autosport* office in London to find out just what their reporter had written. That was how I discovered that Irvine had become even more of a legend than I had first thought. He was to earn more publicity from this incident than if he had won the race.

As the detail gradually emerged and Berger's name was mentioned, the picture became even clearer. I figured Gerhard, who is the most notorious prankster, had wound Ayrton up. I could just imagine the crap Berger had been coming out with. 'Hey Ayrton, this young whippersnapper's first race and he's daring to unlap himself and cut you up and dive on the inside. I'd have a word with him. I wouldn't put up with that. You've gotta go and tell him who's the boss here. Doesn't he realise you're world champion?' And so on.

I guessed the schnapps had done the rest because I knew for certain Karl-Heinz would have produced the bottle out of post-race habit. That was why it was usually suicidal to venture into his motorhome, post-race. Time and again I had seen mischief emanate from there and, time and again, no less a person than Bernie Ecclestone had started it before quietly slipping away as the mayhem gathered pace. Then Bernie would ring Gerhard and ask in a conspiratorial whisper, 'What's happening? What's going on?' They were like kids, with Bernie being the elder brother sowing the seeds and Gerhard following through.

This time, however, Berger had needed no help when winding up Ayrton. Even worse, Senna was, unknowingly, about to confront a Northern Irishman who revelled in the use of sarcasm. You can imagine the effect on Ayrton when Irvine actually had the nerve, in Ayrton's opinion, to suggest that Senna was too slow and ought to have moved out of the way. Talk about lighting the blue touch paper.

It is important to remember that, at the time, the vision of Senna's yellow helmet in a driver's rear-view mirror would act like the flashing blue light on a police car. Drivers would move out of the way –

or, at least, hope Senna would pass easily. Michael Schumacher's bright red Ferrari was to have exactly the same effect. I don't care what anyone says, drivers made it easy for them to pass because they did not want to have a big ruck. In any case, holding them up would waste time because Senna and Schumacher would overtake sooner rather than later. The easiest thing was to let them by and then hang on.

Ayrton, in particular, was not accustomed to the roles being reversed and the driver in question being not in the least apologetic – quite the reverse, in fact, when Irvine had the audacity to imply that Senna was holding him up. The fact was, Eddie was quite right during that brief period in the race. Now he was about to be famous for more than 15 minutes.

The world was going mad when I reached Adelaide but, before discussing the Irvine/Senna situation, I had a little local difficulty to sort out. Someone who was angling for the Sasol sponsorship had kindly pointed out to our South African friends that the Japanese writing on Irvine's sponsorship logos actually said Cosmo, which was an oil company and therefore represented a direct clash of interest with Sasol. I answered an anxious call from Johannesburg by taking a deep breath and saying that Cosmo was a magazine. It was a white lie but we needed to keep both sides sweet. The Cosmo deal was supposed to cover Australia as well and we were obviously going to have a problem now that Sasol had been tipped off. Someone forgetting – surprise, surprise – to bring the Cosmo stickers to Adelaide saved us. That was very poor. Some people can be very inefficient…

The media wanted to know how I felt about my driver upsetting the world champion. Actually, Ayrton Senna was no longer the reigning champion because, much to his frustration, Alain Prost had recently reclaimed the crown after coming out of retirement, moving to Williams and driving what was clearly the best car. This was something that niggled Ayrton and cannot have helped his mood when he had that impromptu interview with my upstart driver in Japan.

There was nothing I could add to the debate except to say they were two grown men and they could sort out their own differences. As far as I could see, Eddie had done exactly what I would have expected. He had gone racing. I suspected, deep down, that Senna probably would have done the same, given a similar situation during his debut in 1984. Whatever the rights and wrongs, Irvine had done more that enough to prove that we should think about keeping him on board for 1994. I knew there would be the likelihood of Eddie becoming involved in controversy but I felt we, as a team, could handle that. Indeed, we would probably embrace it. None of us, however, were prepared for what was about to happen in Brazil, the opening race of the 1994 season. Eddie Irvine would become the victim of one of the most outrageous miscarriages of justices I have ever come across in F1.

Chapter 25

# AN OUTRAGEOUS DECISION

Brazil was the first race on the calendar in 1994 and, as usual, I had no idea where the time had gone between this and Adelaide four months before. For the first time since we started in F1, Gary Anderson knew we would be going into the new season with the same engine rather than having to deal with a new manufacturer. That said, there were big changes afoot technically. There had been a ban on so-called driver aids, such as active suspension and traction control, but more significantly, refuelling would be allowed during the races. Each grand prix would become a sprint between pit stops rather than a 190-mile economy run. The only major problem we had was deciding who would partner Rubens in the other car.

Eddie Irvine had been the obvious choice. We had an option, which we took up immediately after the final race of 1993, but I would not confirm his place until we had sorted the finance and I was absolutely sure he really wanted to race in F1. The Jordan-Hart 194 was launched on 11 January. We chose to do it in the factory because a lot of the space within it was, as yet, unoccupied. The plan was to fire up the engine and have the car roll into view through a haze of artificial smoke, with a smiling Martin Brundle sitting in the cockpit. This would have blown the media away because they were expecting to see Irvine and had no idea that we were in lengthy negotiation with Martin. We had also been talking to Mark Blundell and Jos Verstappen. In the event, no agreement was reached and the press kit for the 194 launch made no mention of a second driver, which meant I had a bit of talking to do when faced by the inevitable questions from, I was pleased to note, a healthy turn-out of the media.

Verstappen eventually went to Benetton to accompany Michael Schumacher, Blundell opted for Tyrrell and Martin preferred to wait to see whether Alain Prost would retire rather than accept a return to McLaren now that Senna had left to join Williams. That left us with Irvine. Eventually, Eddie agreed to come into F1 full time, even though we were not paying him a vast sum. He genuinely could not understand why he should drive for less than his earnings in Japan. Knowing Irvine's frugal nature, I felt it was quite a coup to persuade him to join us. He was such a hard guy to read. You never knew what Irvine was thinking and I always felt I would never want to take him on in a poker game. I was delighted because he would be a breath of fresh air, not just for Jordan but also for F1, and there was the added bonus that his presence in the other car would keep Rubens on his toes. Brundle's gamble, meanwhile, paid off when Prost turned down the offer to drive for McLaren-Peugeot. We were to come into contact with Martin and McLaren sooner than expected during the first race in Brazil.

As a really friendly journalist at the launch had asked me, Jordan Grand Prix had scored the grand total of four points in the previous two years and what were we going to do about it? I had replied with my usual brand of confidence and cockiness and, truth be told, I felt that we were in with a good chance in 1994. Sasol were still on board, we had been reunited with Marlboro, we had brought Steve Nichols (ex McLaren) in as chief designer, Brian Hart had been doing a lot of competitive development work on the V10 and, for the first time, we had a very strong driver pairing.

Then we went and qualified 14th and 16th in Brazil. We had become sidetracked by unexpected technical problems during practice at Interlagos, and this was the result – not a great start but we knew things were not as bad as they looked. As if to prove this was not a fair reflection of the car's potential – before the weekend started, Rubens had genuinely expected to qualify in the top six – Barrichello and Irvine made excellent starts, each driver gaining four places on the first lap. Now we were talking. Then Eddie got into a midfield battle that ended in the worst possible way.

The flywheel on Brundle's McLaren-Peugeot parted company with the engine and got itself wedged between the bottom of the car and the track. Unfortunately, this happened halfway along the back straight. Eric Bernard, following in his Ligier, was surprised to see the McLaren begin to slow and then weave unaccountably at a point where both cars should have been doing 195mph. Naturally, Bernard backed off momentarily.

Catching them both came Irvine, with Verstappen beginning to draw alongside our car on the left, the Benetton driver unaware of what was happening to Brundle's car, but very keen to trap Irvine behind Bernard. Eddie, caught completely by surprise by the slowing Ligier, was faced with an impossible dilemma. We later worked out that he was covering the ground at a rate of 285 feet every second and, during that time, he had to decide whether to dart right on to the grass and into the barrier, slam into the back of the Ligier, or move left towards Verstappen and the vacant track beyond the Benetton.

In the time available, and at the closing speed in question, hitting the brakes was never an option – regardless of the strange comments from Max Mosley when the FIA President compared this incident to a motorway accident with the responsibility lying with the following driver. Max would later admit that perhaps the FIA had been a bit too hasty with Irvine but, for the moment, Irvine was seen as the cause of what followed.

Irvine's natural instinct was to swerve left. Verstappen, keeping his foot to the floor, jinked sideways and the left-rear wheel of the Benetton went on the grass, pitching the car sideways, straight across the front of Irvine and into the back of the McLaren. That launched the Benetton into a horrifying barrel roll, during the course of which a rear wheel on Verstappen's car whacked Brundle on the head and split his helmet. How none of the drivers was seriously injured in the ensuing chaos, I will never know.

Irvine, given his controversial dealings with Senna a few months before in Japan, was identified as the troublemaker, particularly when the head-on camera shot appeared to show Eddie deliberately shoving Verstappen on to the edge of the track. He was fined $10,000 and suspended from the next race in Japan.

We thought this was a travesty. It had been a racing incident, nothing more. Although I was not with Irvine in front of the stewards, it is probably true that he did not show the right amount of contrition. A number of people did not agree with what Eddie had done in Japan. My feeling was that the one-race ban was a bit of a slap, along the lines of, 'Mr Irvine, please understand, this is not Mondello or Kirkistown. This is F1. You will behave, and here is a little reminder.'

Eddie could not cope with this and I was with him when it came to being angry at such a severe penalty. We lodged an appeal with the FIA in the belief that it would be dealt with in a fair manner, even though we knew that rarely, if ever, had an appeal against an FIA decision been upheld. However, in this case, we were confident that it would be a formality and the penalty would be reduced. We were in for a severe shock.

This was only the second one-race ban ever delivered by the FIA and we felt we had a very strong case. It was handled by Ian Titchmarsh, the one legal brain we knew who also fully understood motor racing. Ian Titchmarsh and Steve Nichols did a brilliant job and, although I was not present, Ian Phillips said they pulled the rug from under the FIA's case. However, that apparently had no bearing whatsoever. It was as if the judges' decision had been taken beforehand.

Not only did we lose our appeal but also the penalty was increased from one race to three. I could not believe it when Ian called me with the news. We were devastated. This was completely over the top. It was suggested that Eddie had probably rubbed up the judges the wrong way by appearing in the court in Paris dressed in very casual attire. In fact, he was properly dressed on this occasion, unlike the hearing over the incident with Senna when Eddie had turned up wearing jeans and a pink sweater. We had been at fault for failing to impress upon Eddie that he would be in front of senior members of the judiciary for whom double-breasted jackets, white shirts and club ties were de rigueur. Despite Irvine paying proper respect on this occasion, the judges probably thought that his modus operandi and general attitude smacked of arrogance and they were going to sort him out for good and all, which they duly did but at the expense of Irvine's reputation and our plans for the 1994 season.

I was baffled because Max had suggested that we appeal but he also believed that Irvine was in need of a sharp lesson. Whatever the reason behind this decision, it was one of the most ridiculous and harmful verdicts ever reached by a body of responsible men dealing with a very serious issue. I do however believe that Max had nothing to do with the decision.

We had thought our appeal was so strong that I had given very little thought to sorting out a replacement for the second round of the championship at Aida. We did a deal with Aguri Suzuki, and I have to say I was impressed by Aguri – and not simply because he brought a handy sum of Japanese Yen to the team. Nonetheless, this supported my view that those who are good at bringing sponsorship and are commercially astute do not always make world-class drivers. Saying that, Suzuki is, at the time of writing, the only Japanese driver ever to make it to the podium of an F1 race. Now he is a team owner in F1. I know what he is going through. Good luck to him.

There was no chance of him finishing in the first three at Aida. In fact, I think it would be fair to say that there was little chance of doing *anything* at a track tucked away in mountains in the middle of nowhere. The road access was so restricted that spectators, many team members and journalists had to be ferried back and forth on 900 coaches. Those of us who were fortunate enough to be able to avoid the traffic by staying in the only hotel at the track found it to be a mixed blessing. For the want of something better to do, I was in bed at 9 p.m. each evening. This, perhaps, was just as well because I had no part in an escapade involving our mechanics.

The social hub at Aida was a machine dispensing beer in the hallway of one of the hotel blocks. At about one in the morning, the lads, bored out of their minds, found a couple of golf buggies and decided to have a race – on the track. Three-quarters of the way round, one of the buggies ran into a gravel trap, where it became stuck fast. Eight mechanics somehow completed the lap on the remaining buggy.

That might have been OK had someone not tried to drive the buggy all the way to his room. Failing to reach his destination, the buggy was backed out, not without causing some damage, and parked across the front door of the hotel block alongside so that no one could get out. A couple of hours later, circuit security roused the boys and conducted an inquiry into how a golf buggy came to be stuck in a gravel trap and an apparent attempt to wreck the hotel. The cracks in Euro-Japanese relationships were suitably papered over in the end. However, entertainment courtesy of the Jordan crew had one more act to provide, this time in front of a grandstand full of astonished spectators.

Since this was only the second race in which pit stops were part of the routine, the team held a practice session on race morning. Tim Edwards, later to become crew chief but, at the time, one of the mechanics on Rubens' car, was handling the air gun on the left-front wheel. He noticed that his mate with the replacement wheel was holding it the wrong way round, a fundamental mistake that Tim, being a no-nonsense Australian, communicated in a very blunt manner. The mechanic, who was very big and just as bolshie – and not due to stay with the team much longer – took exception and leapt on Tim, pinning him to the ground by the throat. Spectators, sitting in polite silence, could not believe what they were seeing, particularly when this pantomime brought the overhead gantry crashing to the ground and sent air cylinders clanging in all directions. John Walton was forced to whack the aggressor repeatedly with the pit-stop lollipop in a bid to end this unscheduled entertainment. I really did begin to wonder just what sort of season this was turning out to be.

Rubens had qualified eighth. It was difficult to know what to expect because we could see that 83 laps of this not very imaginative circuit would actually be very demanding, and we suspected that a number of retirements might occur. Right enough, there were two at the first corner, one of whom was Ayrton Senna when tapped into a spin by Mika Hakkinen's McLaren. This was part of a dreadful start to Ayrton's season with Williams. The full significance of that would become apparent a couple of weeks later during an absolutely dreadful weekend at Imola.

For now, though, Rubens was up in fifth place and driving brilliantly. The Irvine nonsense in Brazil had overshadowed an excellent performance from Barrichello, who finished fourth. Straightaway, we had three points and here he was gunning for more. The only panic occurred when the engine cut out as he came to a halt at the second pit stop. For a second or two, I thought the Hart V10 was not going to fire, but it did and Rubens rejoined in fourth place. That became third when someone else dropped out – 15 laps to go and our very first podium finish beckoned.

Since it was a tight track, the lap times were comparatively slow and those final laps seemed to take forever. I could hardly bring myself to watch. When Rubens disappeared at the start of his final lap, the mechanics, as is traditional, rushed from the garage and lined the pit wall. There was a white railing at the back of the pit-wall terrace and I climbed on top, keeping my balance by holding on to the canopy overhead and hanging on to Brian Hart, who had joined me to my right. Those final 90 seconds seemed like 90 minutes.

Schumacher crossed the line to win for Benetton. Then came Gerhard Berger's Ferrari. Finally, the red, blue and green nose of the

Jordan came into view on our left. Third place! Jordan's first podium appearance! We were beside ourselves.

That reaction may have been predictable but, unbeknown to me, something far more bizarre had been going on in Dublin. A well-known musician had been interviewed on *The Late Late Show*, Ireland's premier talk show on a Saturday evening. In the middle of the conversation, this person took out three green candles and lit them. This confused everyone, not least, the programme host, Pat Kenny – a former boyfriend of Marie's sister Anne – who felt obliged to say, 'We're going off the script here! Please tell me what are you doing and what's the significance?' The musician replied, 'Quite a long way from here, I have a belief that the Jordan team will score their first-ever podium, which will be the first time that an Irish-entered car has done this in Formula 1.' Next day, the prediction came true.

When I arrived back on the Monday morning (I had managed to get the midnight flight from Hong Kong), I went to the factory bright and early and walked in to reception to find that a half bottle of champagne had been placed on each of the large tiles on the granite floor. When I counted the bottles, they matched the number of staff exactly – plus there was a magnum for me. The musician had come back from Ireland and visited the factory the previous evening. He had laid out the champagne and left an instruction that three candles, placed in a box in the centre of the floor, were to be lit when I returned. Then he sent me a fax with a poem. It was signed Chris Rea. I should have known! Chris was a great friend of the team and he wanted to share our good fortune in what could best be described as a highly unorthodox manner.

In the first two races of 1994, we had scored more points than in the previous two seasons. We were third in the championship. There were 14 races left. This being motor racing, we felt anything could happen and it was about to, but not in a manner anyone could have imagined in their worst dreams.

## Chapter 26

# THE BLACKEST WEEKEND

It was one of the biggest shunts I had ever seen. I thought Rubens was dead.

The car became airborne when Rubens ran wide at the exit of the penultimate corner at Imola during Friday's free practice for the San Marino Grand Prix. What was basically a simple error quickly became something much worse as the car was launched by the kerb and ran along the top of the tyre barrier lining the outside wall. Topping the wall was a wire-mesh fence with spectators pressed against it, and immediately behind them, the grandstand was packed. Had the car been projected a couple of feet farther to the right, there would have been a huge disaster.

I will never forget the sight of our car several feet off the ground and beginning to cartwheel before finishing on the grass, on its side and with both right-hand wheels missing. My immediate impression was that this could only end one way, and it did not bear thinking about. As I pushed my way to the circuit's medical centre, I felt certain the news would be grim, and was massively relieved to find Rubens concussed but otherwise in reasonable shape. Ayrton Senna was already by his fellow countryman's side.

I was not surprised when Rubens was taken off to hospital for observation because of concern over the significant blow to the head. In fact, I was amazed that the extent of his injuries was not more serious because the accident had looked so horrendous in terms of destruction to the car. Rubens, his confidence high after Aida, had been pushing too hard. The telemetry proved it. On the previous lap, he went through the corner at 208kph (129mph); on the lap he went off, the reading showed 223kph (138mph), prompting Gary to murmur that maybe Rubens should have tried 215kph first.

Saturday was spent gathering ourselves together and focusing on Andrea de Cesaris, whom we had called upon to return to the team and drive Irvine's car. Rubens was off the critical list and the news was encouraging. His only injuries, apart from the concussion that Professor Watkins was monitoring carefully, were a cut nose and mouth.

Everything appeared to be returning to normality until qualifying was red-flagged. Roland Ratzenberger had suffered a massive accident on one of the fastest parts of the circuit. A front wing on his car was believed to have been damaged on a kerb during the previous lap. As he reached in excess of 190mph while heading towards Tosa, the nose wing collapsed, the Simtek went out of control and slammed into a concrete wall with enormous violence. The young Austrian's neck was broken by the impact.

This was difficult to take in. Safety in F1 had reached new levels thanks mainly to the introduction of the carbon-fibre monocoque. Barrichello coming through such a big accident relatively unscathed had reinforced the rather naive view that drivers could survive most accidents. Now, for the first time in 12 years at a race meeting, a driver had been killed. It was hard to believe, doubly so because Roland had been one of the lads. He was a familiar face at our motorhome because he felt there might be the possibility of doing something with us. There was no point in Roland hanging around Williams or McLaren since he knew there was no chance of a drive, but we always made him welcome. He was a handsome guy and very good company. Two big accidents in as many days, one involving a fatality – we did not think it could possibly get any worse.

Everyone accepts that motor racing can be dangerous but, nonetheless, a fatal accident as violent as Roland's sets you back. It is as if you drop down a gear when dealing with the rest of the weekend, knowing that the business you are in can occasionally bite back. The fact that this had become a grand prix different from the norm was accentuated by having just one car being made ready in our garage – and then a huge collision on the start line. Senna started from pole but J.J. Lehto, on the third row, stalled. Most of those behind managed to miss the stranded Benetton. Pedro Lamy, starting from the penultimate row, would have been in third gear by the time he reached Lehto and, completely unsighted by the cars ahead of him, Lamy hit the Benetton full on. Neither driver was hurt but a wheel cleared the debris fence and injured several spectators. If you were not on edge before, you were now. This weekend was going from bad to worse.

Unaccountably, the officials chose not to stop the race despite debris from the Benetton and the Lotus being spread across a wide area. Senna led the queue of slow-moving cars, their tyre temperatures and pressures falling with each successive lap behind a safety car that was not up to the job.

At the restart, Senna and Michael Schumacher pulled away from the rest, these two in a race of their own. That summed up the season so far because 1994 was being seen as a fight between the former champion and the young pretender. Schumacher had won the first two races and Senna had not scored a single point, a major setback for Ayrton that was summed up by a weekly magazine carrying 'Schumacher 20: Senna 0' on the front cover. I have already mentioned Ayrton's susceptibility to pressure when racing against us in F3. It was not difficult to imagine what this was doing to him, particularly now that Schumacher's Benetton was glued to the gearbox of a Williams that even someone of Senna's calibre was finding difficult to drive.

They completed one lap like this. At the start of the second, Senna's car inexplicably veered right when going through the flat-out Tamburello left-hand curve. With its speed seemingly unchecked, the Williams went across the run-off area and into the concrete wall where the right-front wheel was ripped off and forced back and up towards the cockpit. A suspension arm, still attached to the wheel, penetrated Ayrton's helmet.

The race was stopped. After attention from the medical crew at the trackside, Ayrton was airlifted by helicopter to the Maggiore Hospital in Bologna. At times like these, rumours fly round the paddock like crazy. Some said he had a head injury but was otherwise OK; others suggested his condition was very bad.

We went through the motions of completing the race – or not, in our case, since de Cesaris retired after 49 of the 58 laps. For most of the F1 people present, that was 58 laps too many. The race was something to be got through. When it was over, I sought out Professor Watkins, knowing he had been one of the first at the scene of the accident. I also knew that the Prof and Senna were particularly close. Being typically professional, he did not say anything either way but it was impossible not to conclude that the situation was grave. In the early evening, just as we were leaving, the news came through that Senna was dead.

What can you say? We had to take on board that motor racing had just lost one of its icons and the sporting world in general one of its best-known names. I think everyone cried in different ways. Some openly wept, some didn't. Inside, there was a huge aching feeling of loss. Groping for something to cling on to, you instantly recall the memories. In my case, I thought about the recent visits to Brazil and the trips to the airport. I had also been fortunate enough to spend time at Ayrton's beach house at Angra dos Reis, a beautiful place where Ayrton treasured the peace and privacy. I cannot say I was close to Ayrton but I knew him well enough to call and ask his opinion. There had been times, particularly when doing battle in F3, that we did not get on but, since then, our relationship had mellowed. I really got to like him very much indeed and I would like to think, being the cautious man he was, that Ayrton had, at best, a guarded respect for everything that Jordan stood for in motor racing. But I never was able to feel that we had been very close. I am not sure, in fact, that he opened up to many people.

Putting personal feelings aside, this was a massive loss and the motor-racing personnel gathering that night at Bologna airport were clearly numbed and in shock at the end of a weekend of seemingly relentless horror and sadness – Barrichello's miraculous escape on Friday, the loss of a bright young star and a lovely guy on Saturday, and then the seemingly incomprehensible news that a driver who was one of the best ever had died as the result of what appeared at first to be simply another high-speed shunt. Going by the state of the cars, Barrichello's accident looked much more severe than Ayrton's.

Senna was revered. There was something about him. He may have been clinical in some respects but he was cavalier in a way that Michael Schumacher, say, could never be. Senna had panache and people liked that as much as they were drawn by the look of him. The girls thought he was sexy; the guys considered him unbelievably quick and stylish. He had presence and it was impossible not to be drawn to it. Everyone felt affected in one way or another as we stood around aimlessly, waiting for the flight to be called.

As is usually the case, the British Airways 757 back was filled to capacity with F1 personnel – as close as you will ever get to a private plane. I sat beside Olivier Panis and we said just a few words. Usually, the return trip buzzes with conversation as adrenalin continues to surge after a busy weekend, but this one was very different. Hardly a word was spoken during the two-hour trip. I am sure, like me, everyone was continuing to draw on their personal memories of Ayrton. I thought about our F3 test and, of course, that fantastic battle for the championship in 1983, but the more recent and vivid memory was of the end-of-season concert held six months before in Adelaide.

Ayrton was the star that weekend for reasons other than winning the Australian Grand Prix. He had made headlines by dating Elle Macpherson, the Australian actress and model better known worldwide as 'The Body'. When it came to the post-race concert, Tina

Turner, the star of the show, brought Ayrton centre stage as she sang 'Simply the Best'. It was a poignant moment. We were not to know that Ayrton had just scored what would turn out to be the last of his many great victories.

## Chapter 27

# POLE POSITION

The show had to keep going and no one understood that more than Bernie Ecclestone did. He was not backward in tackling the subject. 'Look,' he said to the team principals, 'whether it's me, whether it's Senna, or anyone else, no one is ever bigger than the sport. We've all got to pick ourselves up and go on. Most people thought that we could not go on after Jim Clark was killed, Colin Chapman died, or this or that. Let me tell you, the sport moves on. And it must do so now.' He was absolutely right. We had just been through one of the rare but terrible lows that can knock you for six but the momentum, like it or not, was set to start gathering again two weeks later at Monaco.

The sport was under a lot of pressure and it got worse during practice when Karl Wendlinger had a slow-speed accident that looked innocuous but put the Austrian into hospital with concussion. Certain elements of the media went over the top and the FIA had no alternative but to be seen to be doing something.

The governing body called for sweeping changes to the cars that had to be completed by the next race in Spain. The time frame was incredibly tight and it cost the teams a fortune but it was the only thing to do. On such occasions, once F1 teams are given a target, they will inevitably deliver, no matter how ridiculous the request might be. The bottom line was that you could not be seen to refuse because the next question from the initiated would be, 'So, you want another weekend like Imola, do you?' There was no answer to that, even though the cuts to the downforce-producing areas on the cars were extremely crude. It was a solution and saved the image of the sport from being tarnished. You can have thousands of very good days in motor sport but a single bad day can undo all the goodwill at a stroke. And there was no question that Imola was the saddest weekend of my 35 years in motor sport. I have witnessed some horrible events, but nothing like the sequence surrounding 1 May 1994.

Of course, no one wished to sweep the whole affair under the carpet but we knew that, with the accident having occurred in Italy, reminders of it would run and run. It was one of those things that I hated about racing in Italy, a country where somebody has to be accountable in the event of a fatality. In this instance, I knew that Patrick Head and Adrian Newey, responsible for Senna's car, would be held accountable in some form or other during what would be a long and, at times, harrowing court case. Having a manslaughter charge hanging over your head has to be the worst thing imaginable in a business with risk as an intrinsic factor.

Teams and sponsors have to sign forms accepting that the sport is dangerous. However, I could not cope with the thought that, as a family man with four children, I could be arrested and detained without trial in certain countries while going about my business in a sport that primarily entertains and brings pleasure. A member of the public could be killed in a freak accident and, for that, the team owner could be up on a manslaughter charge. I know that Max Mosley, in his role as president of the FIA, has been working hard to find an acceptable solution for the countries concerned but, until that happens, this problem will remain one of my great concerns for the teams going racing.

Meanwhile, the 1994 calendar was marching on. Racing continued and this was proving tough for Barrichello. Ayrton had been his idol and then his good friend and mentor. Rubens did a lot of growing up as his country turned to him with the unreasonable expectation that he could fill the void left by a giant such as Senna. You could see, as the season went on, a definite turnaround in the way

Rubens, having turned 21, handled himself in only his second full season of F1.

There was no question about his speed but it became clear that Rubens was at his best when everything was just right and fell into place. That was never an easy call with Eddie Irvine sharing the same garage.

Eddie got under Rubens' skin because he could never be sure just what Irvine was up to. Despite having an excellent working relationship with Gary, you could see that Rubens would occasionally imagine a worst-case scenario – Gary and Eddie, both from Northern Ireland, scheming against him. Gary, in fact, was a huge fan of Rubens', much more so than he was of Irvine.

Added to the mix was the fact that good results in the first two races had brought their own pressure by putting Rubens into the top three in the championship after being absolutely nowhere in his first season. Monaco, for various reasons, was one of his worst weekends of the season, but Rubens got back on track with a fifth place at Silverstone.

That was the perfect lead-in to what had become a very popular addition to the Silverstone programme, one that had been instigated by Jordan Grand Prix. I had always felt that the traffic problems getting in and out of the British Grand Prix let Silverstone down badly. I was not in a position to advise on traffic management but I felt we could do something to ease the problem if we staggered everyone's departure. One way to do that was to put on a gig in the evening. We arranged to have a trailer brought into the paddock. Finding a band would not be a problem because my interest in music was as strong as ever.

In my F3 days, I had become friends with Martin Chambers, the drummer who had established The Pretenders with Chrissie Hynde. Through that connection, I had got to know Chris Thomas. Chris not only produced for The Pretenders but had been responsible for production on about 80 per cent of Elton John's albums and the infamous *Never Mind the Bollocks* with the Sex Pistols. Chris's work is diverse, taking him from INXS to *The Lion King* and a recent album for U2.

I was always keen to play drums and this was a good opportunity to bring a hard core of session guys to Silverstone and have fun at the end of a weekend's work. The success of the first night went far beyond our expectations. Mika Hakkinen, Johnny Herbert, Damon Hill and Martin Brundle joined us on stage, and our gig drew guest appearances from Chris de Burgh, Nick Mason and just about any famous musician who had been attending the race. This became known as the Jordan post-Grand Prix party and grew to such an extent that Jools Holland joined us one year and brought the best part of his 40-piece band with him.

As with any impromptu evening, our raves became hugely popular. Then, as always happens, things became serious and the organisers began to arrange gigs that were more official with artists such as the Beach Boys and Status Quo. These were completely different from our thrash in the paddock but I continued to play a part, particularly after forming our own group, V10.

The idea was to link the band with the charity Cancer and Leukaemia in Childhood (CLIC) and play occasionally. Some very good musicians, session guys at the top of their trade, would join us when they could. The attraction of having us play would be the Formula 1 connection. On one occasion, we played in Stars 'n' Bars, the pub alongside the F1 paddock at Monaco. I knew that Michael Smurfit, one of Ireland's leading industrialists, was interested in coming, so I met him before the gig and asked if he would like to bring some friends who were staying on his boat, as my guests. When Michael said he would like printed invitations, I explained that we did not do such a thing because this was a very informal gig. He insisted and so I produced some invitations. When Michael's assistant came to collect them, he handed me an envelope. Inside was a cheque, made out to CLIC, for 100,000 Euros. I was absolutely staggered. It was a great start to what would be a mad night. The place was swamped.

Among the guests were Lucian Grange and Caroline Lewis from Universal Worldwide. They invited V10 to play at their forthcoming wedding. When we arrived, we were flabbergasted. This was the home of the CEO of Universal Records and we were playing in a massive marquee in front of top people. When they asked if we would do a few numbers with Lulu and Donny Osmond, we were crapping ourselves. The idea of going from our normal rock'n'roll style to performing 'Puppy Love' made us very edgy, to say the least. But we managed it and it was wonderful fun, quite unbelievable.

That sums up the path V10 have taken. We almost only play for charity, as and when we can. When I was racing, it provided a perfect release from all the pressures that came with it – such as having our drivers collide with each other at the first corner of the 1994 Hungarian Grand Prix. That did nothing for anyone's mood, particularly afterwards in the motorhome where Irvine made it clear to anyone who would listen that this had been Barrichello's fault. Rubens, however, was to have the last word during qualifying for the next race at Spa.

The Belgian track lived up to its reputation when it rained during the first day of practice. We were looking for a place on the third or fourth row if we were lucky but all the balls were thrown in the air when the rain began to ease, and then stop, during the first hour of qualifying on Friday afternoon. In 1994, the qualifying session on each day counted towards grid position. On most weekends, Friday's qualifying would amount to nothing more than a means of establishing who would be quick and who would be struggling during the final hour of qualifying on Saturday. By then, there would be more rubber on the track and the cars would have been fine-tuned. It was in the natural order of things that lap times were quicker.

For now, the track was wet with the racing line starting to dry in places. It was worth doing everything you could for the best possible time because, at Spa, there was always the chance that the weather would be even worse on Saturday. It became clear that the trick would be to try running slick tyres at the very last minute.

I remember Rubens was not convinced. He believed that the track would remain too wet. This was not the Hungaroring or some other comparatively tame circuit where a locked brake or a small mistake would cause no more embarrassment than a trip to the gravel trap. This was Spa, a fast, scary place, sweeping up and down through pine forests. Despite Rubens' reservations, Gary managed to persuade him to give it a go.

We all knew there was an element of gamble in this, but one that was worth taking, particularly if you were a team that had no other means of getting to the front of the grid. The timing had to be absolutely right. Rubens needed to start his final lap at the last possible second before the chequered flag appeared. That way he would not only experience the track at its driest but also, hopefully, he would be the last man to cross the line.

The times were coming down continually and there was little to choose between the grip offered by a wet-weather tyre on the still damp track and the superior performance from a slick tyre on the increasing number of dry sections. Rubens did two or three laps in order to get the tyres up to temperature, and did not sound convinced about the wisdom of this as he spoke on the radio about the track being too wet in places, but we were committed now.

Gary was watching the clock on the official timing monitor as it ticked towards 2 p.m. In an ideal world, Rubens would start his last lap at 13-59.59. However, as this was not an ideal world, Gary reckoned we needed to aim for about 13-59.40 in order to have a bit of leeway because, if he arrived one second too late at 14-00.01, he would have missed his chance completely. In the event, thanks to guidance on the radio from Gary, Rubens crossed the line with just eight seconds to go. Now it was down to him to do the rest – easier said than done in such a pressure situation on this difficult track.

A minor blessing, in the wake of post-Senna caution over hazards on racetracks, was that a chicane had been installed on the downhill run to the daunting Eau Rouge left-right flick. This completely cut the challenge from the corner and, on this occasion, took away the risk Rubens would have faced while trying to tiptoe through at speed on slicks. His lap was perfect – which was more than could be said for Michael Schumacher, who made a small mistake on what would otherwise have been the fastest lap of the afternoon. As Rubens crossed the line, his name shot to the top of the timing screen – a fantastic sight for us all, provisional pole, pending the outcome of qualifying on Saturday. For now, we were intent on capitalising on the moment. Gary had covered his options by having Eddie run with wet tyres, right at the last minute, and he was fastest of the 'wet' runners in fourth place. It was a brilliant job all round. You can be sure I was going to talk this up for all it was worth to ensure the team and its sponsors got maximum coverage while the going was good.

However, when we awoke on Saturday morning, it seemed we had experienced our 15 minutes of fame and that was it. There was no rain. Times were going to tumble. We set about our usual routine work in the morning. During the lunch break, we could not help but notice that it was clouding over. Then, 15 minutes before the start of final qualifying, the rain began to fall. We couldn't believe it. Never have a bunch of grown men prayed so hard for rain to continue. We knew there was nothing to be gained by going out and, in any case, why should we contribute towards drying out the track for the benefit of everyone else?

Those 60 minutes dragged by as the team stood around in the garage with nothing to do but stare intently at the monitor, praying that the lap times would not fall to our benchmark from the previous day. Towards the end of the session, the times began to tumble, Jean Alesi being the quickest in his Ferrari, but it was not enough. When the dying seconds of the hour clicked by, we knew that Jordan was about to claim a first pole position and that Rubens Barrichello was about to become the youngest driver to do it. Now we could really celebrate. We had blown away the favourites – Ferrari, Williams and Benetton – with a mix of clever tactical thinking and superb driving. It was an incredible feeling and we were intent on enjoying it.

Of course, the most common question from the scrum of journalists suddenly invading our garage was just what this meant for the race. Had we been at the Hungaroring or any other track where overtaking is next to impossible, it would have been reasonable to suggest that a decent result was on the cards, but on the wide expanses of Spa, if the track was dry, the status quo would surely be restored and that is exactly what happened. Rubens was gradually overhauled by the favourites before he eventually slid off the track. We had enjoyed our moment of glory, perched on the very front of the grid. Never had we been so happy to receive a good soaking 48 hours earlier.

## Chapter 28

# GOING GALLIC

I thought we had made it. With backing from an engine manufacturer for the first time, I remember actually saying that Jordan might sneak a win in 1995. This was not excessive exaggeration even though I might have been guilty of talking up our chances in the past. Having Peugeot on board made a big difference psychologically, never mind technically. It mattered little to me that Peugeot were actually a McLaren cast-off after just one season together. Our dismal year with Yamaha apart, this was another major step forward as we headed into our fifth season of F1. The important thing was that, even though the engine might not be perfect, Peugeot would bring other benefits to the table, such as an association with Total. That meant a proper involvement and a better class of fuel and oil because Total were spending money and making an effort to be as competitive as possible.

The only drawback was that the Peugeot deal was at the expense of our liaison with Brian Hart. We had been talking about a third year together. Our relationship had been first class but it was costing us money and there was only so far Brian could go without proper backing. Now we had a major manufacturer with technical and financial clout. The timing seemed perfect, even though the way the deal came together was less so.

Ron Dennis wanted to make a premature exit from the agreement. McLaren had scored just one podium finish with Peugeot and he wanted to clear the way for a long-term association with Mercedes-Benz. Peugeot were very upset because Ron was leaving them in the lurch, which meant he was doing all he could to ease the split and get out as amicably as possible. To do that, he had to find someone to take on the Peugeot engine and he rightly saw me as a willing party. The only problem was he was forced to carry out these preliminary negotiations in secret.

I was told to meet him at Farnborough, from where we flew to Le Bourget. Peugeot, understandably, were not happy. They thought they had a deal with McLaren and they were ending up with Jordan. In many ways, this summed up McLaren's brief and uncomfortable relationship with the French company. For Jordan, it was a godsend. I would be getting engines at no cost and, into the bargain, I was to strike up a good relationship with Frederic Saint-Geours, the Deputy Managing Director, and Corrado Provera, the Marketing Director, who later went on to mastermind Peugeot's dominance of the World Rally Championship with Sebastian Loeb.

In the months to come, I regularly flew to Paris for meetings, followed by magnificent lunches in their offices. These were part of the French way of life and I was happy to embrace it over fois gras and dishes the like of which you would never find in a boardroom in Britain, all eased down with a glass of first-class red wine. I was to find that the people from Peugeot were among the nicest I met in F1.

On the face of it, Ron appeared to be doing the entirely decent thing, helping out Jordan, ensuring Peugeot had a home for their engines and paying something like $10 million in recompense. Behind the scenes, however, Ron tried to recoup some of that money by stipulating that he would own the rights to the sidepods on our car. In other words, any sponsorship revenue accrued from such a prime site would go to McLaren. Of course, the amount involved depended on the definition of a sidepod, and my idea of where a sidepod began and ended differed from Ron's. I had sponsors whose names I placed close to the sidepod and claimed the money for Jordan. Ron felt that income should go to McLaren – which he would do because the McLaren marketing division succeeded in tempting next to no sponsors to our car.

To be fair, I could not complain about Ron, even though I wanted to. There have been times when I wanted to give him a swipe while I had the chance. Overall, Ron was usually level with me, if sometimes a bit difficult. We had very different styles but I have nothing but huge respect for his achievements.

I did not know what to expect of a new-found association with Jean-Pierre Jabouille, who was in charge of Peugeot's F1 programme. I knew him only as a former F1 driver whose main claim to fame was giving Renault their first F1 victory at the French Grand Prix in 1979. I wondered if his role was a classic case of 'jobs for the boys'. It often happens that the person involved is more personality and star name than a proper businessman and colleague.

I had heard various stories about Jean-Pierre but this was typical of any situation where people say things that are often driven by either a lack of direct knowledge or simple jealousy. I was to discover that Jean-Pierre was a 'racer' in the sense that he understood our position exactly, which was more than could be said for his successor a year later, Pierre-Michel Fauconnier, a marketing man with precious little to offer our team.

Jabouille worked very hard on our behalf and we built up a tremendous rapport – helped, once again, by some excellent lunches in Paris. We would often go to a restaurant owned by Jabouille and Jacques Laffite, a favourite haunt of French F1 drivers, past and present. It was common to find Alain Prost, Philippe Alliot and Jean-Louis Schlesser dining in what really was a nondescript place, but with a great atmosphere.

It was difficult to get my head around the French way of doing things and I found it even more bizarre when a Frenchman loosely associated with F1 for a while took out a gun and shot his wife dead after a domestic argument. He was sent to jail for just a couple of years, much of it in an open prison, because this was seen in France as a crime of passion. He received an early release for good behaviour and this, it seemed to me, was a very inexpensive way of dealing with a potential costly divorce.

There was no way I was going to break up my partnership with Peugeot. The association with Total was just as important, and just as enjoyable, thanks to key players including Serge Tchuruk, the CEO, who later moved to Alcatel, Jean-Paul Vettier, CEO of marketing, and Christian Chavane, who was Vice President of Total Competition. In terms of management skills, style and understanding, they were quite sensational. Sure, they were paying money to have space on the car and their names as title sponsors – Total Jordan Peugeot – but our relationship was not simply about the cash and what it could buy. Total would ask, 'How can we make it better?' It was not a question of, 'Sorry, that's the budget, now you eff off and sort that out!'

We created a first by launching our car before anyone else, on 27 January 1995. An extension to the factory that had been mothballed was due to become the home of the composites department, but before that happened we used the available space for the launch. Of course, our new association with Peugeot and Total was too good an opportunity to miss, so we decked out the place Gallic style, with gingham tablecloths, accordion music and French wine. Jean-Pierre Jabouille, Frederic Saint-Geours, Gary Anderson, Rubens Barrichello and Eddie Irvine joined me on the platform.

With such a heavyweight panel on stage, I genuinely felt confident as the predominantly green Jordan-Peugeot 195 made its first appearance in public. As a bonus, waiting in the wings was Enda Kenny TD, who headed the Irish Ministry of Tourism and Trade and who is currently Ireland's deputy prime minister. He had flown in specially to announce his government's continued backing for Jordan Grand Prix and to appoint me Sporting Ambassador of Ireland, something I was very proud of. We had hoped to score 20 points in 1994 and came away with 28. With our new partnership for 1995, it seemed more than reasonable to expect to exceed that total. We had set up a test team for the first time and we were ready to roll.

Pre-season tests did nothing to discourage the view that 1995 might be a turning point. We went into the first race in Brazil full of confidence but came out of it with our tail between our legs. Our testing had been carried out at smooth circuits, such as Silverstone and Jerez, but when we reached Interlagos, we discovered that the 195 did not like the bumps that are an intrinsic part of this old track. That seemed to confirm Irvine's initial feeling that the car's aerodynamics were not up to scratch. Both drivers retired – a bad omen. By the time we reached round six in Canada, we were next to bottom of the table with just two points to our name, but in the space of a couple of hours in Montreal, that was about to change.

Rubens had been struggling on a number of counts. The pressure of expectation, post-Senna, had taken its toll at Interlagos and, to make matters worse, he was being out-qualified every time by Irvine. The 195 had a two-pedal arrangement, calling for left-foot braking. Rubens was not comfortable with this and, for Canada, Gary shifted the pedals on his car slightly to the right, allowing right-foot braking. That did a lot for Rubens' confidence, particularly on a circuit with a high number of chicanes and the need for frequent and heavy braking. Irvine, meanwhile, was happy with changes to the rear suspension. We went to Canada hopeful of a top-six finish but, in all honesty, very little else.

Our optimism was damaged, along with Barrichello's car, when he slammed into a wall during practice on Saturday morning. The car looked worse than it actually was and the boys had it repaired in time for qualifying. However, a new and more unexpected drama had arisen.

Ball joints for the steering track rod had not been packed among the spares for this trip. John Walton got over the immediate problem by having the mechanics rob the joints from the spare car. This left us with an obvious difficulty should further damage be done during either qualifying or the warm-up on race morning. We needed to have extra ball joints flown from England. The only way to ensure their arrival on time was to have someone bring them on Concorde and first class from New York to Montreal.

This lovely job should have fallen to Tony Lazlo, who was always on call at the factory for this sort of thing. Having done all sorts of anti-social trips on our behalf in the past, this was his payday – except we either could not find him or, for some reason, he was unable to make the trip. He was understandably hacked off. The job fell to Simon Shinkins from the composites department. Talk about Simon's lucky day! While he was en route, Irvine and Barrichello qualified eighth and ninth with the usual suspects, including Michael Schumacher (Benetton), Damon Hill and David Coulthard (Williams) and Gerhard Berger and Jean Alesi (Ferrari), ahead of us. There seemed a reasonable chance that we might steal a point by finishing in the top six, but much would depend on others running into trouble.

It started on the first lap when Mika Hakkinen (McLaren) and Johnny Herbert (Benetton) collided. Then Coulthard spun. Rubens and Eddie were fifth and sixth. They held station for more than 20 laps but our big worry was the high fuel consumption associated with Montreal. Berger was about to prove it by creeping into the pits with a dry tank, allowing us to move both cars up a further place.

Gary was working like mad on the calculator. We were on a one-stop strategy, similar to everyone else. Our tank held 115 litres only, which meant we had to be sure that each driver stopped on exactly the right lap and that his tank was filled to the brim. Even then, according to Gary's calculations, it was going to be touch and go.

Gary instructed the drivers to lean off the engine map – and Irvine responded by turning his control switch in the wrong direction. Instead of using less fuel, he was using more until the telemetry told the tale a few laps later. That meant he had to save even more fuel by changing gear early and taking other precautions if he was to reach the finish. Then, just to add to the agony, we moved into third and fourth when Hill retired. There were 19 laps to go.

Each lap seemed to take forever. It was more like Le Mans than a grand prix. The cars may have been going as slowly as possible but our collective pulse rates soared when Schumacher's leading

Benetton became stuck in third gear with 12 laps remaining. Now we were second and third, but for how long?

The cars sounded fine but Irvine in particular was driving as slowly as he dared while he kept an eye on the shrinking gap to Olivier Panis in fourth place.

Alesi's Ferrari crossed the line first for Jean to score what would be his one and only grand-prix victory, and we had to wait half a minute – half a lifetime, more like – for Rubens to appear, followed soon after by Eddie. Two Jordan drivers had made the podium for the first time. The relief was massive.

We rushed to watch the ceremony. I felt particularly proud because all three on the rostrum were either past or present Jordan drivers. Irvine, having set the pace throughout the season thus far, did not look particularly pleased but Rubens, after such a shaky start to the year, was overjoyed. So were the people from Peugeot and I can remember Gary looking slightly alarmed when Corrado Provera rushed up and gave him a big kiss. At a stroke, we had scored ten points.

As the season rolled on, we were in position to score decent points on a couple of occasions but, each time, we were let down by reliability problems and, to be honest, Eddie and Rubens were not always working together for the benefit of the team. It was clear that Irvine was ready to move on.

## Chapter 29

# YOU OWE ME – BIG TIME

I knew Eddie Irvine well enough to appreciate that he would want a pile of money. I had given him his chance in F1 but I had been paying him next to nothing for two years. His money for 1996 was to be based on results from 1995 but, since those had been few and far between and the car had let him down on a number of occasions, it was obvious that Eddie would not be happy. Unless I could find a major sponsor, I knew there was no chance of keeping him.

When we talked about this in the summer of 1995, he said with some pride that he was close to doing a deal with Ligier. Eddie thought he was exercising a buy-out clause in his contract. It was true that such an option was included but Irvine had failed to spot the fine print, which said the buy-out could come into play only if Jordan Grand Prix agreed. In this instance, I did not agree and I told Eddie I didn't think Ligier would be interested in buying him out of his contract with Jordan. Eddie did not know what to make of that. Was I going to hold out for the money and stand in the way of his career? He could not be sure.

At least now I knew what was on his mind – and it more or less coincided with what I had been thinking. There was no point in having a driver at the end of his term – in Eddie's case, the end of 1996 – with no contract. He would say 'adios' and Jordan would have nothing to show for it.

It was clear that I had to try to place Eddie somewhere useful. Then I thought of Michael Schumacher. He was leaving Benetton to join Ferrari and it was not clear whom his team-mate would be. I knew that Eddie and his manager, Mike Greasley, had been in touch with Ferrari and, specifically, Niki Lauda, Ferrari's consultant. Lauda had stopped the discussion when he discovered I would be asking for what Niki described as an exorbitant amount to have Irvine break his contract. Nonetheless, I reckoned it was worth coming at Ferrari via Schumacher.

I gave Michael a call and said something along the lines of, 'Look Michael, you need a team-mate who is going to help you. Yes, Irvine's cheeky but he's quick and, when he gets down to it, he's obedient. Winning races will not be his out-and-out priority. I think he'd be very happy to drive for Ferrari and I think he'd do a lot of the testing and hard slog that you'd want someone to do. I genuinely believe he'll be a good team-mate.'

A meeting of team principals was held in Estoril at the start of the Portuguese Grand Prix weekend. Jean Todt took me to one side and asked about Irvine. One of his concerns was Eddie's attitude. Jean thought Eddie was cheeky and would not be the sort of driver Ferrari needed.

He asked if I knew how much Irvine would want to be paid. Jean looked a little surprised when I said I could negotiate that. We talked about various deals. When I mentioned figures of between $4 million and $6 million, Jean politely said I was obviously quite mad. Nonetheless, he asked to see Irvine.

The following night, Friday, Eddie left a sponsors' dinner early to meet Todt in his hotel, later expressing some alarm that Jean had conducted the interview in his underwear. The discussion obviously went well because, on Saturday, I was asked to have dinner with Graham Bogle, who looked after Marlboro's motor-sport affairs and, in particular, Philip Morris's dealings with Ferrari. Graham was a lovely guy but I think he found a little difficulty in dealing with the Irish. In this case, he had double trouble because there were two of us.

But Marlboro loved Irvine, a legacy of their days with James Hunt and affection for the kindred spirit they saw in Eddie. During these discussions it dawned on me that Marlboro and not Ferrari would drive the deal with Irvine because Marlboro paid the drivers' wages.

I could not help but reflect on what had happened with Jean Alesi. Marlboro had kicked him out of F3000, I had turned his career around and Marlboro had taken him back when he signed for Ferrari. Now the same thing was on the cards with Irvine, who had been with Marlboro in his early days in F3000. This might not be as difficult as I had first thought.

Things were moving very quickly. At the beginning of the following week, I went to see Ferrari's lawyer in Switzerland and felt bold enough to say that we would want the revenue from the spaces on Irvine's helmet, overalls and cap, knowing full well that Ferrari usually went to great lengths to keep that for themselves. I also talked about a bonus if Ferrari did well in the championship.

I reckoned this deal was now worth perhaps as much as $6 million in total, plus Irvine would be driving for Ferrari! And to think he wanted to earn buttons driving for Ligier and cut me out of the deal. Tom Walkinshaw was then running Ligier and the chances of Walkinshaw paying me some money were so slim that I reckoned Admiral Lord Nelson had a better chance of getting his eye back.

My immediate priority was to tell Irvine what was happening and get him to Lugano, but he was nowhere to be found. He eventually emerged, having been up until dawn in a nightclub. As Eddie slept on the floor of the private plane we had hired to get us to Switzerland, I was juggling with figures and checking the draft contract. When we arrived, I told Irvine to wait outside. He never interfered. I made full use of Marlboro's desire to have him back on board. The chain of events became quite clear: Schumacher had mentioned Irvine to Todt, who had spoken to me and then given the nod to Marlboro's John Hogan, who told Graham Bogle to sort it out.

Henri Peter was Ferrari's lawyer, based in Lugano. While I was in his office, Luca di Montezemolo, the Ferrari president, came on the phone and gave me one of his impassioned speeches, saying I was looking for too much money and claiming I had no understanding of the true value of the driver market place. When Luca finished this monologue, I said that Ferrari and Marlboro ought to be careful that Irvine did not go to Gitanes and Ligier, because they were desperate to have him. Then I waited for that mortar shell to hit home. I knew that Marlboro would not be keen to see Irvine associating with a tobacco brand that could easily increase its penetration in Britain as a result.

The discussion returned to money. I made the point that the loss of Irvine would seriously disrupt my team and I would have to pay to have a decent driver replace Eddie. After much to-ing and fro-ing, we agreed a figure of $5 million. I could hardly believe this was happening. It was daylight robbery and I was the one wearing the mask.

I went to look for Eddie and found him on a park bench alongside Lake Lugano, feeding the ducks and continuing to nurse a horrific hangover. He seemed more interested in telling me what a great bird he had been with the night before than hearing how I had got on. It was typical Irvine to give the impression that he was not completely committed to motor racing when, in fact, he was much more devoted to the job than many other drivers I could name. However, there was no denying that money and women were always near the top of his agenda, probably in that order. I had secured the deal of his lifetime. All he needed to do was sign the contract. That is when he played his ace card.

'EJ,' he said, in all seriousness. 'I get on with you, I love the team, I think I'm going to stay. I think it would be better for me. We haven't had much chance to show it yet but I think we can do a lot together.'

He looked me straight in the eye and I swallowed hard. Irvine knew exactly what was going though my mind – 'Fucking hell! He can't possibly be serious. After all the work I've done, this would be a disaster. For everyone! I've virtually spent this money in my mind.'

This was classic Irvine and it showed why he was so far ahead of his rivals when it came to being streetwise. He was very cunning and very sharp. I have never known another driver like him. By saying what he had said, he was putting himself in a position to make me reduce the commission I would be asking him to pay me for doing the deal. Eventually, we settled on a figure. It effectively cost me a million dollars to have him leave the team and still Irvine had not finished.

Before he signed the contract, Eddie tried to chisel a little bit more out of the deal by discussing such things as his driving boots and the number of promotional days he would be required to attend, something he was always fussy about because he wanted to do as little as he could get away with. Even by my standards, this was pretty outrageous. We had already broken Ferrari and Marlboro's balls by getting them to agree to us having space on the overalls and helmet – one of the first deals of its kind at Ferrari – and here was Irvine stretching their patience even further. And mine.

The deal was done so quickly that not even Bernie Ecclestone knew about it until it was almost concluded. The figures were agreed all round. Getting money out of Irvine was never an easy job. I do not want to go into the detail of what happened next but, if he reads this book, Eddie will know where to send the cheque. As I was in a habit of saying to my drivers, 'You owe me – big time.'

## Chapter 30

# YELLOW IS THE COLOUR

I reckoned Jordan really would be going places in 1996 – but not like this. Within a minute of the start of the new season, our car was torn into a thousand pieces and destined for the front pages of newspapers around the world. This was not exactly the coverage I had in mind for either the team or our new sponsor, Benson & Hedges.

We all knew F1 could be exciting but having the Jordan cartwheel through the air was beyond anyone's prediction of drama on the opening lap of the Australian Grand Prix. Looking back now, it was a suitable way to kick off the most colourful sponsorship liaison Jordan would have. As with all good things, the deal had been put together very quickly and smoothly. That is not to say the link with B&H had come out of the blue.

We had first approached Gallaher, the parent company, at the end of 1991 when I made a detailed proposal to Peter Wilson, the company chairman. The main problem was that Gallaher did not own Benson & Hedges outright, so their sponsorship plans focused on Silk Cut, and embraced music as well as sport. They liked what I had to say but, at the time, Jordan was very much a new team on the block. On the other hand, we did have a good track record with Marlboro and Camel, and rather than go to a team such as Tyrrell, Gallaher wanted something different. They liked our younger, fresher image, and, significantly, our Irishness appealed because Gallaher was a major employer on both sides of the Irish border. We did not get very far in 1991 but I was surprised and pleased when Gallaher kept in touch.

Much earlier, through golf, I had met Nigel Northridge, an Ulsterman working his way through the ranks. Nigel was into rugby and we would meet from time to time at international matches. Having been responsible for Spain, Nigel was soon back at Gallaher's headquarters in Weybridge. Since he was a marketing man – quite a spectacular one, in fact – I found it easy to talk to him about promotions, market awareness and how we could help the growth of the brand through motor racing.

A week before Christmas 1995, we heard that the ownership of the Benson & Hedges brand had been sorted out. Ian was on the case straightaway and, on 6 January, we had a preliminary meeting in our office with Nigel, now Gallaher's marketing director, and his marketing manager, Barry Jenner.

The meeting had been arranged in such a rush that the presentation was seat of the pants stuff. Ian and I ad-libbed our way through it, sowing the seed for the 'Bill and Ben' epithet that Nigel often used when referring to our double act on occasions such as this. Whatever you care to call our style, it must have worked because Nigel called us half an hour after leaving Silverstone and asked if we could repeat the performance for the chairman at Weybridge four days later. I cannot guarantee that he witnessed an identical encore but it was good enough for us to sign a deal two days later. The amount of money was not massive because Nigel's budget was already committed elsewhere, but it was very important to me to have one foot in the door at Weybridge.

Nigel was obsessed with British drivers, which was handy because we had been talking – yet again – to Martin Brundle and this time we finally did it, 13 years after Martin and Jordan had enjoyed such a great season together when giving Senna a run for his money in F3. We had actually signed Martin the day after agreeing the Irvine sale, and Brundle had been part of our pitch to Benson & Hedges. They liked the link with Martin, particularly as he had won the World Sportscar Championship in a Jaguar sponsored by Silk Cut. We were happy, Martin was happy and, most important, B&H were happy. With the first race scheduled for Melbourne on 10 March, it was all hands to the pumps and the gold/yellow paint known as Desert Storm. After all this excitement, I began to talk about our season getting off to a flying start – an unfortunate choice of words, as it turned out.

Martin had a disastrous practice in Melbourne but the guys managed to get the car sorted in time for qualifying and Martin made the grid, albeit it on the back row. Rubens added to Martin's discomfort by qualifying eighth. You could tell Martin was ready to go for it when the red lights went out at the start.

Sure enough, we could see him on the television monitor as he darted around, making up ground through the first two corners. Next thing, the Jordan launched into the air and flew over the top of several cars as the field bunched while braking for the third corner. Two cars had come together while avoiding someone else's accident, leaving Martin with nowhere to go but into the back of one of them. That had sent the Jordan skywards.

Martin came to rest, upside down, in the gravel run-off area. The car was broken in two. We feared the worst because this had been a massively spectacular accident with bits flying off the car in all directions during its crazy, barrel-rolling flight before bouncing off the concrete wall. For a brief period, we could see no movement. Then, to everyone's enormous relief, Brundle crawled out from between the overturned chassis and the gravel. When Martin stood up and looked around, it was evident that not only was he alive but also – unbelievably – he was unhurt. The car was totally destroyed.

With so much wreckage everywhere, Charlie Whiting, the race director, had no option but to show the red flag. Brundle's initial reaction was that someone had had an accident and caused the race to be stopped, not really taking in that it was his accident, such was his focus on getting back to the pits in the hope that he could take the spare car.

First, though, he had to be checked over by Professor Sid Watkins. While all Martin's limbs appeared to be working, there was no telling what unseen damage might have been caused if he had received a knock on the head. After some questions from Sid, Martin was given the all clear, by which time the boys had the spare car waiting in the garage. Talk about a lucky escape.

As far as the race was concerned, this was not to be Martin's day. After hitting another car at the scene of his earlier space flight, Martin wisely decided that was enough for one day. Rubens retired not long after.

The following morning, Brundle's airborne Jordan with B&H on the flanks was splashed across all of the local papers. Nigel, wearing his marketing hat, was delighted. Television news bulletins were continually replaying the spectacle and one thing we noticed was that the gold/sand paintwork did not show the sponsorship logos to the best advantage. The car may have looked the business in the flesh, so to speak, but it did not look in the least attractive on television.

Nigel Northridge was on the case. He brought people from the design agency used by Benson & Hedges to Estoril. They studied the effect of various colours. We could not believe the difference between the best and the worst, particularly when the car that looked very average in the flesh came out best on the video screen.

The colour was bright yellow. Taking things further, we eventually became the first team to put a metallic fleck in the yellow, creating a new colour that ICI made for us. It became so popular that we had regular calls either requesting the pantone number or asking if this Jordan Yellow paint was for sale.

When it came to adventurous thinking, I always felt that Jordan were ahead of other teams in terms of making people aware of our image. We had a growing reputation for doing mad things but, in fact, we were not as nutty as people made out. We were conscious of the fact that, while the 100,000 spectators at a race were important, to ensure the continuing support of sponsors, what mattered were the television images. Our livelihood was based on them.

We got to know that Bernie, who was definitely interested in television above all else, was receiving positive feedback concerning Jordan's perceived image among the viewers. On more than one occasion, he would send a small sponsor in our direction because he knew we would give them value for money. In addition, much of that would come from the simple fact that our car was always visible in television pictures. McLaren may have been winning races with a magnificent car but it was grey and not worth a second look on television. Parked alongside each other in the pit lane, the Jordan looked brash compared to the immaculate metallic grey of the McLaren, and it was obvious which car created the greater impact among television viewers in Hong Kong or Cambodia or New Zealand.

The business of image became even more important in Brazil, where Rubens put his car on the front row and Martin qualified sixth. That was to be the height of our weekend. Rain on race day sent our plans floating down the road as both drivers spun off. It was a massive disappointment and, although we were not to know it so early in the year, it was to be downhill for the remaining 14 races. Barrichello would occasionally find his way on to the first three rows of the grid but Brundle never came close, and seemed to struggle to get to grips with the car.

Martin went off the boil in a major way and I was never entirely sure why. Although he may not admit it, I suspect he felt subconscious pressure from having a young family plus he had to deal with the death of his father, to whom he had been very close. Martin was a very caring man. Even in his F3 days, he was calculating and calm. He was good technically but seemed to be niggled by the fact that he felt he had been as good as Senna. He kept harping back to that.

Martin had absolutely nothing to be ashamed about because no one could come close to Senna – nobody! Brundle arrived in F1 on the back of a very strong season in F3. I remember the long and detailed conversations we had at the time. I thought Martin was ahead of the game because he was in a Tyrrell whereas Senna had wound up in a Toleman. For me, Tyrrell was a better option. When

Martin scored two points in his first grand prix, he seemed on course for an impressive career in F1, but it did not happen. When Martin returned to us for 1996, he wanted to be quick. He tried really hard but the car was not quite up to it. The same, I felt, applied to Martin. The sparkle we had seen in 1983 was no longer there.

As for Jordan in 1996, we certainly did not sparkle. Nevertheless, Nigel Northridge, despite approaches from other teams, remained steadfast. We were fortunate because Nigel was just the man to have on your side at times like that. He was calm but just edgy enough for F1. We gelled despite Nigel being a Northern Irish Protestant and therefore conservative by nature, whereas I was a southern Irish lunatic. We represented both sides of the spectrum and hit it off brilliantly.

Nigel could be quite difficult in his demands because he was fastidious about attention to detail, things such as presenting the right image, doing the chat and promoting the brand. I learnt a lot from Nigel. He was quite pushy, but in a different way from the people at Camel and Marlboro. Camel had their own style, which was very American. Nigel was very British. I was not surprised when, eventually, he joined the board at Gallaher, but for now the yellow Jordans were poised to make an even bigger hit than before thanks to a very different and highly successful marketing campaign – which I disliked from the word go.

## Chapter 31

# HISSING SID

A snake? On my car? Not a chance. The Benson & Hedges design agency had come up with a scheme for 1997 to use a symbol resembling a snake or a serpent on either side of the car with a large fang running down each support to the front wing. Even allowing for Jordan's reputation for being avant-garde, this was too much for me.

I did not particularly like the emblem because, in Ireland, snakes are considered to be evil. According to folklore, our patron saint, Saint Patrick, banished snakes from the land. The more I thought about the image, the more voluble I became. I started to read passages from the bible. Nigel Northridge and David Marren – a Dubliner I had known for many years who was now head of M&C Saatchi's sponsorship division – thought I had lost the plot completely. In the end, it went to the vote. The snake sneaked in by one vote. I was not happy for a number of reasons, not least because I felt the snake image was taking up room on the side of the car that, technically, did not belong to B&H.

Against all my predictions, the snake – or 'Hissing Sid', as it became affectionately known – made a colossal impact. There had been nothing like it before in F1. The subliminal message from the team was: 'We do not care what anyone thinks. This is Jordan, take us or leave us.' Full marks to Nigel and Dave for pushing a concept that was very Jordan – rock'n'roll in the extreme. We were breaking all the rules because F1, despite its cutting-edge technology, was, and still is, a very conservative business at heart.

That was another reason why Nigel wanted to push even further by having models scantily clad in yellow drape themselves over the cars and create photo opportunities that brought consistent exposure in the daily newspapers. This venture also went some way to raising the profiles – in every sense of the expression – of models such as Melinda Messenger and Katie Price. Katie's stage name, 'Jordan', made her an obvious choice. Sam Phillips, Ian's wife, helped stage the photo shoots with models because of her experience as a fashion editor with the *Sun*. I have to confess that I was not mad keen on the idea but I could not ignore the coverage we were getting in the tabloid newspapers, an area that F1 had previously found difficult to penetrate. In many cases, our campaign took F1 from the sports pages and moved it forward in the paper.

In 1997, we were to come very close to winning despite dire pre-season predictions from pundits who suggested we would go nowhere with two young and virtually untried F1 drivers. Barrichello had left to join the Stewart-Ford team, which was due to make its debut in 1997, and Brundle had moved on to carve a tremendous reputation in television commentary. Meanwhile, I had cast my eyes east once more and liked the look of Ralf, younger brother of Michael Schumacher. Ralf, in the footsteps of Irvine and other Europeans before him, was walking away with the Formula Nippon championship.

Ralf was booked to test a McLaren F1 car and I did not realise that a pre-contractual agreement had been signed with McLaren. They wanted him as a test driver in 1997. Willi Weber, Ralf's manager as well as Michael's, was using this as a bargaining tool, which was typical of the way he operated, and I was suddenly confronted with the fact that Ralf might not be free to drive for Jordan after all. My answer to that was simple. 'I'm offering Ralf a race season,' I told Willi. 'Ron Dennis is offering him a test-drive season. If you're free to sign a contract, fantastic. If you're not, forget it and we will have wasted each other's time.'

Willi came back to me and, while I cannot remember the exact deal, part of it included something to placate Ron. I said I did not want to know about their problems with McLaren. Either Ralf was free to sign, or he was not. Willi and Ron eventually sorted their problems, by which time I was wondering if I really needed a driver and manager who gave me such grief before we even got started. The one thing that persuaded me to go ahead was Ralf himself. I really liked him, and my gut feeling proved to be correct. Even though we were to have our rocky periods in the seasons ahead, I thought – and still think – that Ralf is a fabulous guy.

Ralf was quick and there was no bullshit with him. Yes, he would make mistakes, but they were typical of any rookie. The only problem was that instead of one rookie for 1997, we had two. I signed Giancarlo Fisichella, who was under contract to Flavio Briatore. Giancarlo had taken part in eight F1 races with Minardi so, strictly speaking, he was not entirely new to F1, but joining Jordan was an upward step for him. Giancarlo was 24 and Ralf would turn 22 during the season. Whichever way you looked at it, I had taken two youngsters on board.

Of course, the pundits were having a field day. Here was Jordan, into its seventh season, the third year with Peugeot, the second with Benson & Hedges and yet we had not managed a podium in 1996, never mind a win. There seemed little chance of any improvement now that I had taken on two virtually untried youngsters.

The initial impression was that Ralf would be the stronger of the two. He qualified ahead of Fisichella for the first race in Australia and then Giancarlo hurt his knee during a heavy crash when testing at Silverstone. When Fisi crashed again during qualifying for the next race, in Brazil, I quietly asked myself if this had been a wise choice. By the end of the following race, in Argentina, I wondered out loud if I had been completely mad choosing either driver.

Ralf was ahead on the grid in Buenos Aires but it was Fisichella who made the better start and moved into fifth place. Ralf, meanwhile, had been hit by David Coulthard's McLaren and dropped to eighth. As the race settled down, we watched with rising excitement as Fisi gradually moved into second place thanks to different pit stop tactics jumbling the field. Whatever the strategy, however, we were looking good for a podium at the very least. Then along came Schumacher Junior.

Ralf had been on an incredible charge after his eventful start. He caught Giancarlo on lap 24 of the 72-lap race but, in his enthusiasm to get by, Schumacher hit Fisichella and sent Giancarlo into both retirement and an understandable Latin rage. Ralf, meanwhile, raced on and, as if to rub salt in Fisichella's wound, took third place. This was our first podium in almost two years and it was a fitting result since this had been Jordan's 100th grand prix.

The celebrations were muted, though, and none of the Jordan mechanics went to the podium to applaud Ralf. Rumours began to fly immediately. There was talk of our disgust with Ralf's move on Giancarlo. Other stories suggested that this was the mechanics' way of expressing their displeasure over an on-going discussion with me about wages. Both reports were wide of the mark.

The truth actually revealed a great deal about the camaraderie within what continued to be a comparatively modest team, recently expanded to 130 people. Andy Stevenson and Nick Burrows – the number-one mechanics for Ralf and Giancarlo respectively – had been with Jordan since before the start of our F1 campaign. They were good mates and worked very closely together. Andy and his boys felt it would be wrong to celebrate a success that had been, to a certain extent, at the expense of Nick's driver, who had been heading for a podium until the incident that brought his retirement. It was particularly hard on Andy, because this was his first podium in his first year as a number one. It was a very gracious move and a fantastic example of team spirit even if, to those outside Jordan, it conjured all sorts of stupid theories. Meanwhile, I had to do a certain amount of fire fighting behind the scenes.

I had said before the start of the season that I expected fireworks between my two young drivers, but I never thought I would be required to put out a raging inferno after a race. Naturally, Giancarlo was very upset. He had been running ahead when, in my view, Ralf misread the situation and went for a gap that Giancarlo never intended to provide.

It is true that our reactions were tempered by scoring that much-needed podium finish. However, looking back now, the collision could have had disastrous consequences for the team as a whole, because we were desperate for points. We had not scored any in the first two races. If both drivers had retired in Argentina, I might have taken a stronger view. In fact, I had reason to do just that when the European season got into its stride.

Fisi began to assert himself just as Ralf had a run of retirements. Ralf did not score another point until July when he finished sixth in France. Then he was fifth at Silverstone, with Fisichella failing to score. We had the definite impression that Ralf wanted to win the next race, which happened to be Ralf's home grand prix at Hockenheim. Fisi had other ideas.

Ralf got off on the right foot by being fastest in all of the sessions leading to qualifying. When it came to the time for the drivers to go out for the final hour of qualifying, Giancarlo could not be found. The unspoken question was whether Ralf had finally got to him. We could not have been further from the truth.

Giancarlo finally emerged from the back of our motorhome accompanied not long afterwards by 'Miss Germany'. The beauty queen had ostensibly been accompanying Ralf until she was diverted by Fisi's boyish charm. Anyway Fisi, with a notable spring in his step, marched into the garage, climbed aboard the Jordan-Peugeot 197 and hurled it on to the front row of the grid. His average starting position in the previous nine races had been eighth.

Ralf was stunned. It took the wind from his sails completely. He qualified seventh and finished a distant fifth. To make matters worse for Ralf, Giancarlo almost won the race. Had it not been for a puncture in the closing stages, he would certainly have finished second.

Into his stride now, Fisi took second at Spa and claimed a couple of fourths while Ralf had that single fifth place to his name. Now we moved to the Nurburgring and, once again, there was a feeling that Ralf was going to settle this thing once and for all.

Schumacher had it all to do when he qualified eighth, five places behind Fisichella, but he made a perfect start whereas Giancarlo made a poor one. The two of them were side-by-side on the run towards the ridiculously tight hairpin at the first corner. Ralf was heading for a gap that was narrowing all the time thanks to the presence of his brother Michael, who had qualified his Ferrari in fifth place. Any talk of brotherly love went out of the window when our cars collided and took Michael with them as all three spun into the gravel and retirement. The race was barely 30 seconds old.

I cannot begin to describe the words I used. They were so bad. What I said was ferocious. I can only liken it to when Alex Ferguson walked into the dressing room and allegedly kicked a boot so hard, it flew up and cut David Beckham's eye. When all was said and done, however, there was no getting away from this having been one of those infuriating but sometimes unavoidable motor-racing incidents. In the post-race press release, I could not apportion blame. The corner was far too tight and I pointed out that Michael Schumacher, who had much more to lose in terms of the championship, had refused to point the finger. Our mechanics were much the same. In fact, despite my outburst behind closed doors, things appeared much calmer than they had been after the incident in Argentina.

Despite throwing away potential finishes in the top six in Germany, we scored more points (33) in 1997 than during any other season, partly as a result of investing in a wind tunnel. We bought it from March, who had it at their site in Brackley. This turned out to be an excellent deal. We paid £900,000 and, as part of the negotiation, ended up with a box at Oxford United. Robin Herd, boss of March, was their chairman.

Money had to be spent upgrading the tunnel. We also expanded into an unused section of the factory – previously known as 'The Party Room' – and installed a gearbox test rig, a seven-post chassis test rig and a number of machine tools. For the first time, Gary Anderson and his technical team were able to achieve the aim of continually developing the car throughout the season – and making it reliable. During all of this, we were gaining a massive amount of publicity through the models and, I had to admit, the snake. The popularity of the team and its colour was spreading far and wide, as an incident at the factory was about to prove.

Louise Goodman had gone off to have a well-deserved crack at presentation with ITV's F1 programme. In her place we had hired Giselle Davies, daughter of the legendary sports commentator Barry Davies and formerly a press officer with Benetton. Giselle had made the most of the mileage gained by the yellow paint scheme and that controversial snake. Now we had to score on the track. We had come close to a win more than once in 1997. Could we finally make it stick the following year? We just might if we had a world champion on board for the first time.

## Chapter 32

# HIJACKING HILL

I could not believe what I was seeing. Nigel Northridge and David Marren had laid out drawings on the table showing livery proposals for the 1998 cars.

'This is something really different that's never been done before,' said David. 'We think you'll like it.'

The theme seemed to be World War II. The sides of one car had RAF roundels and camouflage paintwork with the nose bearing the flaming exhausts of a Spitfire engine. The driver was depicted as wearing battle fatigues with his scarf painted on the side, streaming in the breeze. The sides of the other car carried swastikas and emblems of the Luftwaffe. This was the car to be driven by Ralf Schumacher.

I was thinking, 'This is f***ing ridiculous.' I kept glancing at Marren, hoping to catch his eye and intimate that he should have diverted Northridge away from such a mad scheme. After all, Marren and Saatchi were supposed to be the liaison between Gallaher and Jordan, but David looked deadly serious, as did Nigel. I had discovered that Nigel was capable of making strange requests from time to time, and this idea therefore seemed par for the course for him, even if it was definitely off limits for me. What was more disturbing was that Marren and Saatchi had bought into it.

Nigel continued talking and pointed to a spike on the top of Schumacher's helmet, which was in the style of the metal hats worn by German generals in the early 1900s. The spike, said Nigel, would act as a radio antenna. He seemed really pleased with such a novel idea. Now I was becoming alarmed.

As Northridge and Marren continued to talk with enthusiasm, it seemed that B&H were intent on introducing this crazy theme on my cars. This was madness. Jordan would be a laughing stock in the pit lane. As for Ralf Schumacher, what would he and most of Germany make of such nonsense? The more Nigel talked, the more I began to panic.

Then I completely lost control. I ranted so long and so loud that, at first, I failed to notice that Northridge was chewing his fist and Marren had become red in the face as they desperately tried to suppress their laughter. Finally, they could contain it no longer. It took me a few minutes to come down from the ceiling and see the funny side. I had been well and truly stitched up.

The RAF connection had come from Nigel Northridge's continuing wish to have a British driver on board. At this stage, he wanted us to sign Damon Hill. I was not convinced. I had watched with interest as Damon won the 1996 world championship with Williams and then failed to reach agreement with the team for the following year. It supported my theory that Damon had not enjoyed a particularly easy time with Williams-Renault. In 1994, he had to more or less carry the team following the death of Ayrton Senna, which cannot have been easy, particularly as Damon did not have a great deal of F1 experience at that stage. Williams was probably the wrong place for Damon at a time like that. Frank Williams has never been sold on the idea of giving his drivers love and attention. Indeed, the Williams team seemed to think that whoever drove their car would become a world champion. There may have been some truth in that because, at the time, Williams were going through a period of fabulous performance and success.

I have no idea how much Frank paid Ayrton when he signed him for 1994, but you can be sure that it needed proper money to prise Senna away from McLaren. It would have been typical of Frank, when chasing a driver he really fancied. Frank likes drivers such as Juan Pablo Montoya and Jacques Villeneuve – drivers who are tough, hard, no quarter asked or given, drivers who really rip into the job.

Damon was not like that. I never felt that his face fitted at Williams, but if I was surprised when Frank released a driver with whom he had won the world championship, I was staggered when Damon signed for Arrows.

I never believed for a moment that Damon would consider coming to Jordan. We had worked together when Damon drove for Middlebridge in Formula 3000. My connection was that I had money from Barclay cigarettes in 1991 but could not use the sponsorship on the F1 car because of the presence of Marlboro. A deal was done with Middlebridge. I later discovered that Damon had written a vicious letter to the marketing director of BAT (parent company of Barclay), urging them not to be associated with me and more or less saying that I was a crook. We had never spoken about this but my underlying feeling was that he would not trust us as a team.

In any case, apart from the Hungarian Grand Prix where Hill had finished second, I did not think that he had done anything recently to enhance his career. It had been very brave to go from a championship-winning organisation to a team that had never won a race and barely experienced a podium finish, but that was about the height of it.

One of Nigel's arguments was that perhaps Damon needed a team with more potential than Arrows. He was keen that we should investigate. I baulked at the request because I felt we could not afford Damon. In any case, if Benson & Hedges had the funds set aside, I felt the money would be better spent on the team itself. It was explained to me that the amount of money earmarked for the team was precisely that. If I wanted to spend any on a driver, that was up to me. I think Nigel knew there was no way I was prepared to do that. We were not paying Ralf directly. He could draw income from spaces on the car and in other ways. The same would apply to Damon. I refused to allow any of the car budget to be used on a very expensive driver.

I made it very clear to Nigel Northridge and Dave Marren that, if they wanted Hill, they would need the budget to pay him. When that did not appear to deter Benson & Hedges, I thought I should investigate further whether or not Damon might be interested in driving for us. The argument was that Hill, with his experience of winning races, would bring something to the team.

Damon was living in Killiney, an area along the coast south of Dublin that was popular with celebrities such as Eddie Irvine and Bono. By chance, I was invited to a party at Damon's house. This would be a good opportunity to put out some feelers.

All sorts of local people were there, including my brother-in-law, Des Large, and Dave Pennyfather, who was very senior in Universal, a leading music company in Ireland. At one point in the evening, a few guys, led by Des, started messing around with instruments and attempting to play a few numbers. Des knew the first two lines of maybe a hundred songs but that was it. Dave Pennyfather and I shared the drums until a very slim girl in high heels asked if she could have a go. She was incredibly talented and stopped us in our tracks. I was completely gobsmacked.

Meanwhile, Des was continuing to lead as Damon and a couple of others joined in. Every now and then Des would shout at one of the guitarists, 'This is in G. It's G! OK?' The guy would nod and say, 'Oh yeah. G. Right.' This continued for a couple of songs until the guitarist suddenly broke into a huge riff of a solo that simply took our breath away. Des did not realise that he had been shouting at Charlie Burchill, lead guitarist with Simple Minds. The girl on drums was his wife. Des has not been allowed to forget it.

My initial impression, having spoken to Damon, was that he was keen to talk some more. Not everyone on the team agreed that this was the right move. Trevor Foster felt that having Damon on board would put too much pressure on us, and the team was not ready for that. His view was that it was one thing to make a world champion but quite another to have a driver who was already a world champion, particularly one who had been accustomed to working with a well-funded team such as Williams-Renault. On the other hand, Damon had chosen to drive for Arrows, which, for all the talk of the team's owner, Tom Walkinshaw, was struggling to make ends meet.

Nigel was determined to make it happen, though, and the cards fell into his hands at Monza in 1997. Damon had retired his Arrows and, by the time he returned to the pits, Walkinshaw had already departed in his private plane, leaving Hill without a lift home. When Nigel got to hear of this, he offered Damon a ride in the plane we were using. You can imagine my surprise when I stepped on board and found Damon and the B&H guys sitting in the back. Damon may have been hijacked but Nigel's plan had worked. It was at this stage that I began to realise that Damon might be serious about joining us.

We eventually decided to enter into detailed negotiations with Damon and his manager, Michael Breen. The discussions went through the night, to the point where Breen was driving me mad with his nit-picking details. He was doing a solid job for Damon but very little for the good of the negotiations between two sides that wanted to work together. Nigel kept the whole thing moving forward to the point where agreement was reached. Damon seemed very unsure from start to finish. At the end of the long and tedious discussion, however, there could be no getting away from the fact that everybody got what he wanted.

This was going to be a big story. Plans were immediately put in place to extract maximum coverage from the media. It was a complete secret. No one knew, or that was what we thought until Ian Phillips received a late-night telephone call very soon afterwards from Alan Henry, the motor sport correspondent of the *Guardian*. Alan was looking for a comment on an exclusive in the early editions of the next day's *Sun* newspaper, which said that Damon Hill had signed for Jordan. The whole thing had been blown wide open.

Ian and I were livid. Ian rang Stan Piecha, the *Sun*'s motor-sport correspondent but Stan, covering his source, would only say it had been a 'team insider'. The fact that Stan had not called us first said a lot about the way in which the story had materialised. It later turned out that word had been leaked by a close friend of Damon's. It did massive damage to what should have been a big moment for Jordan Grand Prix. It was also a bad start to an uneasy relationship with Damon.

## Chapter 33

# OH, WHAT A CIRCUS!

When it came to putting on a memorable car launch, we knew we had some tough acts to follow, most notably in the early 1980s when Team Lotus were sponsored by David Thieme and his Essex Oil company. Thieme was not averse to hiring the Albert Hall or famous nightclubs in Paris. We eventually decided on the Albert Hall, too, but we had one big trick up our sleeves that Thieme, for all his millions and his contacts, had not been able to emulate.

Some years before, I had met a juggler named Guy who, I was told, had started off as a street entertainer. He always seemed to be surrounded by the most amazing girls, most of them Brazilian. That puzzled me because Guy was short, slim and balding, but he had a dynamism and style that clearly was very effective. Some time later, at the Canadian Grand Prix, we were invited to a party at his house to the north of Montreal. That was when I discovered just how effective Guy had been and how far he had moved on since doing stand-up shows outside the bars in Covent Garden. His house was impressive.

The following winter I had rented *Douce France*, allegedly the largest catamaran in the world, for a family holiday in the Virgin Islands. Towards the end of the trip, the Belgian captain said there had been a request from the next person to charter the boat to say 'hello'. It was a Monsieur Laliberte. That meant nothing to me, but I thought it would be a nice thing to accept his offer of a drink as we handed over.

Monsieur Laliberte turned out to be Guy. He was accompanied by loads of people, including a stunning girl – Brazilian, of course – who was the mother of one of the several young children who seemed to be in the party. Her mother was there, plus Guy's mother, several nannies and other friends and relatives. Now I was to get an idea of just what this man could do.

While someone was preparing a barbecue on the beach, which was empty except for this party, Guy started building sand castles, but not the sort you would make on the beach at Margate or Killiney. I do not know exactly what he did but the shapes looked as if they had been moulded from plaster of Paris. They were sensational. Guy was well prepared and, as darkness closed in, he placed little candles in strategic places. With no other form of light, these candles flickered all evening, providing a magic touch and rounding off a special night.

By now, I knew that Guy was the driving force behind an entertainment called Cirque du Soleil. In a very short space of time, he had built up this unique show and was on the point of bringing it to London, to the Albert Hall. We had previously tried to get the cast of *Riverdance* to perform at one of our launches, but the dates were never suitable. I had also discovered that Guy was mad about motor racing, and when Ian invited Guy to dinner at the Groucho Club on the night of the B&H spoof presentation, the subject of using Cirque du Soleil at the launch came up.

Barry Jenner felt B&H did not have the budget to pay for anything so lavish but, in the event, it cost us next to nothing. I wrote to Guy and said, assuming I had the agreement of the people at the Albert Hall, I wanted to launch the Jordan 198 there. Guy responded immediately. 'Brilliant!' he said. 'I'd love to be involved. We will do you a couple of acts. It will be good for you and good for us, so we'll do it for nothing,' and he was as good as his word.

Meanwhile, we set about organising our biggest launch to date. We would have a tough act to follow, in every sense of the expression. We chose Monday, 19 January because there was very little football – or any other sport, come to that – taking place on that day, so we should have top billing in Tuesday's newspapers, provided we had something attractive and interesting to offer. I was in no doubt that we would.

Giselle Davies had been working furiously beforehand and now it was our turn to perform. Giselle had Damon and me on parade in the Albert Hall foyer at 06.25 in time for a live interview with Independent Radio News. A recording of it was offered to more than 150 local radio stations nationwide. Two hours later, we had completed 15 interviews, a mix of radio and television, and Ralf Schumacher had joined us. The process continued while, outside the front doors, journalists were beginning to gather.

We had enjoyed an excellent response from the media, doubtless keen to see just what Jordan would do next. It was a good question. How would we follow up the snake emblem? What would the latest car look like? What was on the launch programme and why had everyone been invited to such a massive auditorium? We had moved from the factory to a London hotel for the launch of the 197. In more recent days, Ferrari had unveiled their 1998 car on a fog-bound racetrack in Italy while Williams had used the corner of a chilly garage at Silverstone to reveal their latest championship contender. What on earth were Jordan up to this time?

It was easy to forget that, primarily, this was about the launch of our new car. The truth was that, not long before the event, despite these lavish preparations, we feared there might not be a car to unveil, because a major change had had to be accommodated. The Peugeot engine had been replaced by a Mugen-Honda, a switch that had been made inevitable by a mix of French and F1 politics. Those involved were actually doing Jordan a favour although, at the time, I did not see it that way.

All I knew was that I had come close to landing a deal with Alcatel, a massive global communications company, thanks to my association with Serge Tchuruk, who had joined them from Total. We were getting on even better than before but moves behind the scenes put a prospective sponsorship package beyond our control.

The key to this was Alain Prost, who was being lined up by Flavio Briatore to take over Ligier. This would be a completely French team and, since Prost and Renault were not on particularly good terms following Alain's time with them as a driver, Peugeot were seen as the most likely candidate to replace the Mugen-Honda, currently in the back of the Ligier. Government forces were at work here. Peugeot's motor-sport chief, Pierre-Michel Fauconnier, did not have a clue about how F1 worked and there was huge pressure to make the move to Prost.

Corrado Provera and Jacky Eeckelaert, Peugeot's motor-sport coordinator, fought against it, and were proved right in the long run. When Peugeot eventually withdrew from F1, having been with McLaren, Jordan and Prost, the records showed that their best results were earned with Jordan and that double podium finish in Canada in 1995. In the meantime, the rug had been pulled from beneath our feet. We needed to find an alternative engine supply.

I called upon my long-standing association (in F3000) with Hirotoshi Honda, the owner of Mugen-Honda and the son of the founder of Honda Motor. Even though Mugen were using Honda's hardware, they were independent of the main company and effectively doing their own thing. Honda had withdrawn from F1 on the crest of a wave at the end of their association with McLaren in 1992, and the rumour was that they were thinking of making a comeback. It made sense to get into bed with Mugen-Honda and, at the same time, have a foot in the door of the competitions department at Honda Motor. We reached agreement in July 1997 – plenty of time, you would think, to have everything tested and ready in time for the launch of the Jordan Mugen-Honda in January 1998. In theory, yes, but in practice, motor sport does not work like that.

Gary and his team had been working on the outline plans for the car since May 1997. Once the engine deal was in place and a mock-up of the V10 had arrived from Japan, the designers could get down to fine detail on such things as the engine cover and sidepod shapes. The first proper engine arrived in 1 December. So far, so good.

Mugen-Honda had previously used a Benetton gearbox control system when working with Prost but this was not available to us. It was agreed that Mugen would work with PI, the British company that had supplied electronic control systems to us in the past. By the time we discovered that PI were not up to the job of coping with an engine management system, time was running out. We had to drop PI and switch to TAG Electronics, with whom we would be virtually starting from scratch. So much for plans to carry out miles of pre-season testing.

The first 198 chassis was being mated to the engine on 5 January, this after the factory closing down for just two days over Christmas. Meanwhile, the graphic designers were waiting to apply the latest logo dreamed up by Benson & Hedges and Saatchi and agreed by everyone on 2 January. In place of Hissing Sid was 'Buzzing Hornet'. I liked this from the outset because it was more compact than the snake, a recognisable emblem that could be used easily as a team logo and transferred to team clothing. Now we had to await the reaction of the media at the launch a couple of weeks later.

We erected a temporary stage and screen halfway down the auditorium. Most people assumed the car was hidden behind the screen when, in fact, something completely different was lurking in the shadows. Once the formal introductions had been made and routine questions asked and answered from the stage, we moved aside for what was assumed to be the unveiling of the car. This was the cue for Cirque du Soleil to go to work. First on stage were two Mongolian contortionists who gave new meaning to being able to wriggle out of anything. That set the scene for 30 minutes of a unique blend of dancing and acrobatics that held everyone spellbound.

I have to confess that the subsequent lowering of the car from the ceiling amid smoke and dramatic music was something of an anti-climax, but we had everyone's attention and, more importantly, words of approval in the following day's newspapers. The *Guardian*'s Adam Sweeting, who had attended every F1 launch thus far, declared ours to be the best. Jordan had, once again, introduced the 'wow' factor to F1. Benson & Hedges, along with our new associates, Pearl Assurance and MasterCard, and long-time supporters Hewlett Packard, GdeZ and Speedline, were delighted.

Interestingly, little mention was made of the hornet, the sports writers preferring to home in on my declaration that, when it came to team orders, it would be every man for himself. One driver would be asked to help only if the other was in a position to win. Some critics muttered that the chance would be a fine thing, but there was no denying that our first victory had to be the principal focus and I had been quite genuine in my belief when I said that I could see no reason why that was not possible. I had told the audience that the combined salaries of our two drivers exceeded the entire budget for our first year in 1991. Now, finally, everything was in place and we were ready to win.

I really should have known better.

## Chapter 34

# LOSING THE HEAD

I did not want to talk. I did not want to be seen. I just wished the ground would open and swallow me up. Considering this was Monaco, nothing more needed to be said about the mess we were in. My boat, a Manhattan 62, was moored close by the paddock. It should have been the perfect tool for entertaining and soaking up the unique atmosphere of this glamorous harbour. On this occasion, the Sunseeker provided a bolthole below deck, a place of escape from the ignominy of our worst qualifying in the six races so far.

Our cars were 14th and 15th on the grid for the most prestigious race of the season. We had yet to score a point in 1998 and the chances were looking even less likely than before. All our sponsors were present, as well as Hirotoshi Honda and his wife. I just wished I could have stepped on board *Snapper S* and been whisked off to some far-flung corner of the Mediterranean, away from all of this.

Not a chance. On the Saturday night, Mark Gallagher, head of our sponsorship management team, had organised lightning visits to three separate dinners with sponsors – guests of Delphi were in the Hermitage Hotel; Pearl Assurance representatives were dining not far away in the famous Rampoldi's restaurant, after which it would be a short dash down the hill and on to the harbour where Denis O'Brien's Irish communications company, Esat Digifone, had hired a boat. That was the plan. What on earth was I going to say?

There could be no getting away from the fact that the car was not competitive. We had done nothing of note at any stage. Not even for one race could we have said, 'Ah, but for such-and-such an unforeseen problem, we would have been on the podium.' There was none of that. Quite often, we had been between two and three seconds off the pace set by McLaren. In Australia, Mika Hakkinen and David Coulthard had enjoyed the luxury of causing a stir by deciding among themselves who should win.

McLaren had been the cause of some trouble in Australia because of a special braking system on their cars. What had really amused me was the outrage expressed by Ron Dennis after finding a photographer in the McLaren garage in Melbourne attempting to take close-up pictures of his car. Dennis used a press conference to say that the man, under questioning, had admitted to being the brother-in-law of an aerodynamicist with a leading team, and that this amounted to espionage. I thought that was rich coming from Ron. Two years previously, at the launch of the Jordan 196 at our factory, I had caught red-handed a photographer, who did work for McLaren, sending a picture of our car to them – and using our telephone line to do it. However, such amusing tittle-tattle would be of little interest to sponsors in Monaco, who needed to know why this latest Jordan was performing so badly.

There was no point in beating about the bush. I remember saying that my mother, the Matriarch, God bless her, could have walked round the track faster than our cars. I like to think that I never misled any of our sponsors from the moment we first met. Obviously, success was the aim, but I never guaranteed it. Our job was to provide sponsors with a platform for their work while we did our work to the best of our ability. I never promised anything. That would have been crazy, even though I have to admit that the temptation was strong when a substantial deal was in the balance. Now I was receiving the pay-off because, by always being up-front and refusing to make elaborate claims in the past, I was receiving a very understanding reaction from each one of the sponsors that night in Monaco.

In any case, the point was that many of the sponsors – and, most certainly, their guests – had other agendas during a weekend in

Monaco. The enthusiasts among them, who perhaps understood our problems better than most, just wanted to be there, take in the atmosphere and walk the track. Others wanted to visit the Casino and have a flutter. Some were there purely to have fun. That was certainly the case with the crowd on the Esat Digifone boat, who were having a truly fabulous time. Priorities varied and, while the team's performance may not have been good, I was doing as much as I could on the periphery to maximise awareness.

This scenario reminded me that many people inside the sport tended to look at the results much harder than most of their guests did. For those who make F1 their business, results are everything. Sponsors' guests, on the other hand, are simply happy to be there and be part of the show.

Visitors like to have a team to support, even if that team is struggling. They are delighted to meet the drivers and have photographs taken to show that they have been on the 'inside'. Nonetheless, it was difficult to walk into each dinner, receive a warm reception and see expectant faces not once, but three times in one evening. I did not say I was embarrassed or that I was sorry because everyone, or most people, knew about the potential pitfalls and how the sport worked. I did not go so far as to recall the day that McLaren, who looked like dominating the weekend, had failed to qualify both cars. I did point out that two years earlier, Olivier Panis had qualified 14th and gone on to win the race, which I felt was a slightly positive note. However, I returned to the boat at 1 a.m., totally exhausted, in the knowledge that for all the optimism I could muster, this was going to be a difficult race.

I was proved correct when, within 18 laps, Damon and Ralf had been lapped by both McLarens. Ralf retired after clipping a barrier while Damon struggled home eighth, two laps behind the winner, Mika Hakkinen. Six races and no points. It was a complete disaster.

The walk from the pit lane to the paddock had never seemed so long and I had never felt so exposed. My discomfort was magnified because I was being filmed every step of the way. Before the start of the season I had agreed, with some reluctance, to a television documentary about the team. I thought it would be filmed over a day or two when, in actual fact, it was to cover the entire season. The film-maker and producer was Amanda Rudman, whose father, Michael Rudman, was famous in the world of theatre. Her stepmother was the actress, Felicity Kendall. With a background like that, it was hardly surprising that Amanda was a very serious operator. She always seemed to have a camera in my face and the rate at which this was driving me mental was in direct proportion to the team's increasing struggle to do anything useful. It put strain on our relationship and Monaco was the low-point. I was extremely rude to Amanda but she's a strong girl, and I think she half-expected it. As time passed I came to realise just what a professional she is but, for now, the last thing I needed was probing questions, which I knew had to be asked but which I did not want to answer. I could see the forthcoming headlines in the media: 'Jordan in Crisis'.

We had already received a mauling at the hands of sports writer Paul Kimmage, who was, at the time, working for an Irish newspaper. Paul had come to Barcelona, noted my new Sunseeker boat and the B&H girls in and around the garage, and suggested that I had lost the plot. When times were as bad as this, our critics interpreted the promotional activities as nothing less than gimmickry. It was rather like Jose Mourinho shielding his Chelsea players from the press by absorbing all the crap. Gordon Strachan did the same with Celtic. He would position himself at the forefront and take the pasting from the media. I was taking a lot of flak and the girls were taking a lot of criticism. Jordan was being labelled as a team that could not be taken too seriously.

My priority was stopping this slide with immediate effect. After the race at Monaco, I called a meeting with Gary Anderson and Trevor Foster in the truck. I lost my head. I was throwing stuff across the room while repeating the obvious. This was not good for any of us and there was added friction because Trevor and Gary were not exactly the closest of mates. Gary's view was that Trevor should be the team manager and not involved in the technical side of things. Trevor was saying that Gary was a bit too domineering and dictated too much to the young engineers, Sam Michael and Dino Toso. These two later moved to Williams and Renault respectively. I could see what was happening but felt that, sometimes, those frictions worked in a positive manner. My feeling was that you had to let them get on with things because it sharpens the competitive edge within the team. However, although frictions work well when you are competitive, when the car is poor and the performance is even worse, all hell tends to break loose.

In the meantime, I knew I would be coming under savage pressure from Benson & Hedges, who had pumped money into a car that Damon Hill claimed was not good enough. I had to believe him because he was driving it, but the engineers were hinting that perhaps Damon was not good enough. Ralf remained more or less unscathed in all of this because he was the young inexperienced driver and, in any case, he was proving to be more competitive than Hill. Part of Damon's problem seemed to be coping with the grooved slick tyres, an innovation for 1998. He did not like the feel of these tyres and his performance at Monaco, where a driver needs to fling the car around with confidence, had proved it. In addition, the television documentary had been there to record it.

Amanda Rudman was not the only person to feel the rough edge of my tongue. I was very rude to everybody because I felt under immense pressure. I was quite horrible in the things I was saying. We had another tempestuous meeting at the factory and it was agreed that Trevor should have a more influential role and Gary would miss the next races in Canada and France. I gave him enough money to design a revamped car. I felt there was no alternative because the car we had was shit. I told Gary to sort it. The tension was dreadful, particularly when we persuaded Mike Gascoyne to join the technical team and put John Davis in charge of the wind tunnel and aerodynamics.

Mike had been with McLaren and then worked under Harvey

Postlethwaite at Tyrrell. He knew all about operating under a tight budget and he made a perfect counterpoint to Gary – even if Gary did not see it that way when I broke the news. Mike was very different. Whereas Gary was probably an intuitive engineer, Mike had a way of marshalling resources. He believed in a group operation. Gary was hands-on, Mike would delegate. The problem was that the staff had grown to 165 and we were not familiar with dealing with this number of people. We had a test team; we had a wind tunnel. We had to use them more efficiently and we would be helped by the fact that Gascoyne was more of an aerodynamicist than a chief designer. He would come in as Gary's number two but the deal was that Mike would be considered for the role of number one in 1999.

In the meantime, all sorts of other thoughts were running through my head. This was turning out to be a crucial point in my life. I had been married for 20 years, I owned 100 per cent of the business and yet I had not really made any money. At this rate, the business was going down the pan because who would want to sponsor us in 1999? I would have to close the doors sooner rather than later.

I had reached my 50th birthday the previous March, and I was responsible for all the debt and loans. There was nobody else. I suddenly felt very isolated, particularly with the realisation that this could crash very easily and I could wind up with a massive amount of debt hanging over my head. It dawned on me that I was the only person who owned 100 per cent of a Formula 1 team. I had to ask myself if I was completely mad.

So I started to think about other partners, and not long afterwards, Mr Kawamoto of Honda came to visit me at Silverstone. I thought he was a great man, an inspirational figure, and arguably one of the greatest engineers of all time – and he liked Jordan. We sat down for a long discussion at the Jersey Arms in Middleton Stoney.

I mentioned to him that I would be interested in a partnership with Honda. Following our tie-up with Mugen-Honda, I thought that it might be relatively simple to form a long-term relationship with Honda. The more I thought about it, the more I realised I could offer the same sort of deal as mentioned to Ayrton Senna in 1993. If I gave Honda 40 per cent of the business, with the possibility of buying another 10 or 15 per cent over a period, then I believed that the value of the team would grow massively and, along the way, I would have a secure partner. I would have free engines, better results, better drivers and the team would be a more viable proposition all round. Every shot would be a goal. We reached a point where I thought that a deal was almost there. Then a man I had never met turned up from Honda and offered to buy 100 per cent of the team. I figured that maybe it was the right thing for the team, and asked to keep 10 per cent. Honda agreed – but on the understanding that I would not work there.

'I don't understand,' I said. 'What d'you mean "not work here"?'

Honda's reply was very interesting. 'Mr Jordan,' they said, 'your name and your brand is better known in motor sport at this moment than Honda!'

In order to replace the name Jordan with Honda, I had to be off the scene completely. They wanted everyone else to stay on board, to keep the wind tunnel and generally develop the team, but they could not risk having me there.

I said no. I am not sure if it was ego, but I asked myself why had I done 25 years of racing, dedicated my entire life to it and taken so many risks and enormous gambles that, by-and-large, had paid off. Agreed, I was suffering at that moment and felt very exposed to the point where I was asking what would happen if I died. How selfish I would be to leave four kids and a wife with a shed load of debt that they did not know about and that had nothing to do with them. How greedy, or how selfish, was that? That was the reason why I was actively looking for a partner in the aftermath of Monaco. That race had a huge effect on me.

I had good people around me, including Richard O'Driscoll who was doing a great juggling act with the money. Richard was very strong and capable of standing up to me and saying 'NO!' He wanted the team to be structured in such a way that if a buyer came in, there would be a platform that could be inspected and that would allow proper due diligence to be done. That was his belief. He wanted everything transparent, clean and very well presented.

I had Lindsay and her people, Giselle with her excellent press team, and, of course, Ian, right by my side. I needed Ian more and more as time went by. I had all these people and yet, when it came to the raw facts of the company going under, there was no one I could talk to. It was a crisis point for me. Despite everything, I felt the Honda offer or, more to the point, the demand that I no longer be a part of my team, was one step too far. The Jordan brand was too strong. In one way, that was a huge compliment. However, in another, the implications with Honda were more than I wanted to accept. That door had closed and, as often happens, another was about to open unexpectedly.

Not long after the Monaco Grand Prix, I was in the boardroom of Coventry City with the club's chairman, Brian Richardson. He introduced me to Dominic Shorthouse, who had left Morgan Stanley some years before to become head of Warburg Pincus in Europe, an American private equity business with an excellent track record. Dominic was one of those very clever people who are clearly going places. We seemed to hit it off as we enjoyed the game. It was some time later that a mutual friend got us together for a drink in London. It transpired that Dominic had been interested in a private equity partnership with Coventry City after a deal with Everton had not gone ahead. He was interested in F1 and I invited him to Budapest for the Hungarian race. Monaco aside, there are few better places to sample the flavour of a grand-prix weekend. If you are unfamiliar with F1, the whole thing seems like a whirlwind on first acquaintance. Budapest in August adds to the atmosphere with its wonderful climate and such a fine city at your disposal. The nightlife is just wild thanks to the race drawing in Austrians, Germans, Italians, East Europeans and loads of Scandinavians.

Dominic quickly realised that F1 is very different from football. It is not tribal. You can be a supporter of Ferrari yet sit down and have a drink with, say, Williams or McLaren fans. They are united, primarily, by a love of the sport. He was also impressed by the mass of fans waiting patiently outside his hotel to see not only the drivers but also the prominent people attending the race. Over dinner, we talked about the excitement of the four days and F1's global footprint. As Dominic had come to appreciate, no other sport has anything like the commercial, financial, royal and political connections. Dominic was undoubtedly smitten. We had laid down a marker for the team's long-term future.

As far as our short-term future was concerned, things had moved on since Monaco. The rebuilding mechanism had begun to take effect. Ralf scored our first point of the season at Silverstone in what was a heavily revised car, which was a huge blessing because I had begun to believe we would never get that point. We had gone eight races without scoring anything. McLaren, by contrast, had scored 80 to make our zero look miserable and useless. That sixth place acted like a kick-start.

Everything started to fall into place. Ralf finished fifth at the next race, in Austria, and took another sixth at Hockenheim, while Damon claimed fourths in Germany and, conveniently for Dominic's benefit, in Hungary. After such a desperately shaky start to the season, we were on a roll, but not even in my wildest moments of optimism would I have ever predicted what was about to happen.

## Chapter 35

# TAKING THE MICHAEL

There was no time to reach for the rose-tinted glasses and sit back and reminisce, but had I taken a moment to think about it, I would have noted that Spa-Francorchamps had been a lucky track for Jordan in the past. We may have sorted out our fundamental problems by scoring points and putting the misery of the first half of the season behind us, but life at Jordan Grand Prix seemed to be going full tilt in several directions at once.

Gary Anderson had not been comfortable with the appointment of Mike Gascoyne but they were getting on reasonably well, although Gary was not happy with the thought that I had gone over his head. Whatever may have been said, however, the plan seemed to be working. Gary had brought some very effective modifications to bear on the car and Mike, meanwhile, had been reorganising systems at the factory. More worrying was the fact that Gary had been diagnosed as having ulcer trouble. As ever, he had been working long hours and it was a major concern that this was at the expense of his health.

Trevor Foster and I had a long chat immediately after the British Grand Prix and agreed that, in his role as the team's race director, he would have the power to make more wide-ranging decisions in all areas and report directly to me.

On the domestic front, there had been a near-riot on the factory lawn during the week of the British Grand Prix when members of the Jordan supporters club – which we had established a few years earlier to cater for the worldwide interest in the team – expressed their understandable outrage over the non-appearance of the 1998 fan-club pack. We had been victims of our own success as membership reached the 3,000 mark, three times more than Benetton's club membership. Unfortunately, a well-intentioned attempt to streamline the administration with the help of our sponsor, MasterCard, had led to a complete breakdown of the system. Judging by the irate and increasingly abusive emails, our fans were not happy. It took all of Mark Gallagher's tact and patience to smooth seriously troubled waters.

Meanwhile, Ian Phillips and I had been busy attempting to deal with increasingly turbulent negotiations over driver contracts for 1999, the intention being to keep Damon and Ralf on board. The British press, searching for a story at around the time of the British Grand Prix, had gone mad with a rumour playfully spread by Tania Hughes of M&C Saatchi that we were attempting to force Damon to take a pay-cut. Having put that to rest, we reached Spa a month later to find the media carrying quotes from Michael Schumacher, saying he was advising Ralf to move to Williams because Frank ran a proper team whereas Eddie Jordan was nothing more than a money-grabber.

I was incensed. Having left messages for Michael to contact me but received no response, I decided to provoke one. It so happened that Spa had become a traditional venue for three national daily correspondents with big expense accounts, Stan Piecha (the *Sun*), Bob McKenzie (*Daily Express*) and Ray Matts (*Daily Mail*), to pursue the unusual but very welcome habit of buying dinner for Ian and myself. I decided to repay such generosity by being free with my views on Michael's comments.

I said such remarks from Michael were rich. He liked to give the impression of racing for the love of it but, in fact, money seemed to play a significant part in his life. I pointed out that he appeared to be obsessed with cash and it continued to grieve him that he had to give Jordan £150,000 for his first F1 drive, even though the sum had actually been paid by Mercedes through Sauber. The point was that, despite it not being his money, Michael did not like to be seen as a 'pay driver'.

I knew the lengths to which Michael would go to ensure he was paid properly. One of the best stories I had heard concerned his time with Benetton. Michael had a clause in his contract that stated that no team-mate – with the exception of Alain Prost, Ayrton Senna and Nigel Mansell – could receive more than him. In 1993, Schumacher's fee had been increased to $2 million while, unbeknown to him, Riccardo Patrese had been signed for the surprise figure of $3 million. Halfway through the season, Flavio Briatore had a bust-up with Patrese and wanted to get rid of the Italian even though his contract had another year to run. Riccardo reached an agreement with Briatore that if he could stay for the rest of the season, then the 1994 clause would be null and void.

Ron Dennis enters the story here. When Patrese talked to McLaren about 1994, Ron asked how much he wanted to be paid. The figure of $3 million from Benetton was mentioned and Ron, having heard about Schumacher and the terms of his $2 million contract, saw this as a way of springing Michael from Benetton. Michael got to hear the bad news about Patrese. Now we come to the interesting bit.

The people acting on Michael's behalf told Patrese they would pay $1 million simply to have a copy of his contract with Benetton, and Riccardo obliged. Who wouldn't for that sort of money? Schumacher's representatives confronted Briatore in his office. Faced with a breach of contract and the prospect of losing Schumacher, Flavio is reported to have broken down, but he gathered himself together sufficiently to take the only option remaining – he offered Michael $20 million to stay. Schumacher accepted. It was a good move. Ron must have thought he had been savaged by the same piranhas he had warned me about when Schumacher was taken from us in 1991. The really clever part of this affair was the deal to pay $1 million to Patrese and then come away with $20 million from Benetton, a net profit of $19 million.

So, I knew what Michael was capable of, even though I did not reveal this story to the journalists present at dinner at Spa. They would have had a field day if they had known. I merely gave vent to my feelings about a personal attack by someone we had helped and whom I have always respected. I explained that Jordan was as ambitious as any team and, to fulfil that ambition, we spent as much as we could of a budget that was tight when compared with our rivals. We were not penny-pinchers and part of the problem we were now facing with Ralf was the direct result of Michael's interference. I had no problem with Ralf wishing to go to Williams but I objected strongly to anyone taking personal swipes at me or the team. I do not recall the team ever saying a bad word about Michael.

As the wine flowed and I warmed to my theme, the journalists could hardly write down the words fast enough. The result made headline news on the sports pages. Michael later claimed that he had been misquoted but, although we were not to know it at the time, this was to be the prelude to another exchange over Ralf in circumstances under which it would be impossible to know whether to laugh or cry.

There was no doubt, however, that Michael's words had affected Ralf. Trevor noted that Ralf's mind seemed to be somewhere else, even during their engineering debriefs. He seemed to be either on his mobile phone or discussing the purchase of boats and planes.

Damon was on the case, however, as he revelled in both the challenge of the track and the improved handling of the car. In the closing seconds of qualifying, Hill's name shot to third in the lap times. The grid order would be McLaren, McLaren, Jordan, Ferrari, Ferrari. Who, a few months earlier, would have believed that scenario? For good measure, Ralf was eighth. Once again, anything seemed possible the following day.

## Chapter 36

# ONE TWO!

Rain on race morning was no surprise. This region of the Ardennes is noted for weather that only an Irish person might understand – four seasons in the course of one day is close to the norm. Of more concern were the unforeseen difficulties the race itself might have in store. We did not have to wait long to discover the first one – about two seconds, in fact.

Damon's clutch snatched slightly at the start and he spun his rear wheels on the wet track. He had dropped from third to seventh by the time the leaders had reached the first corner. Disappointment had barely taken hold when another surprise was waiting, literally just around the corner. The television pictures were showing mounting chaos as David Coulthard spun at the exit of the corner and car after car seemed to be piling into the McLaren. Wheels and bits of bodywork were flying in all directions, leaving the organisers with no alternative but to stop the race. Damon was going to get a second bite at the start – provided his car had not been damaged.

As the cars made their way back to the pits, Trevor and the engineers were on the radio, trying to establish what state our cars were in. It had been hard to make out anything from the television pictures, such had been the scene of total confusion. Adding to the frustration was the fact that radio contact was not consistent at Spa due to the way the track plunged up and down the valley. We could not believe our luck when Damon and Ralf eventually confirmed that neither car had been damaged. The good Spa omens were continuing.

At the second time of asking, Damon made a peach of a start. In fact, coming out of the first corner, a Jordan was leading the grand prix, having passed both McLarens! We were going to enjoy this while it lasted. We could see that Michael Schumacher, having worked his way into second place, was closing the gap to Damon but for seven wonderful laps, a Jordan Mugen-Honda controlled the race. On lap eight, Schumacher took the lead. In the light of everything that we had endured in 1998, second place would do nicely.

As for Ralf, he was stuck in traffic. Both our drivers had taken the restart on intermediate tyres but the conditions were going from bad to worse. We brought Ralf in early for his first stop and, with nothing to lose, sent him out on full wet weather Goodyears. Ralf became the fastest man on the track not long afterwards, so this had obviously been the correct call. Other teams followed suit, which allowed Ralf into third place. Two Jordans in the top three! We'll take that, thanks very much.

A win was out of the question because Schumacher was leading Damon by 37 seconds and pulling away with over half the race still to run. Everything looked to be sorted, but this amazing race was about to be turned on its head once again.

I will never forget the image on the television monitor, probably because I could not believe what I was seeing. The picture showed the leader driving towards the pits with the right-front wheel missing from his Ferrari. You had to do a double take. Sure enough, there he was, still running, but obviously heading for retirement. The rerun showed that Schumacher had been lapping Coulthard when he drove straight into the back of the McLaren. Coulthard had been doing his best to get out of the way by almost driving off the road on the right-hand side of the track. Schumacher, powering through the mist and rain, had not seen him until it was too late and bang! Wheel gone! He was out. Quite incredible.

The shock of seeing such a mistake was quickly replaced by the realisation that Damon was about to take the lead. Better than that, Jordans would be running first and second in a grand prix for the first time ever!

Each driver had one more scheduled stop. Ralf came in first and was dispatched without any problems. The team had been doing a fantastic job under such pressure, the strategies so good in such changing and difficult conditions that we got the jump on a number of people.

Then, a lap or two before Damon was due, the safety car was brought out to deal with an accident involving Giancarlo Fisichella. Damon had to be called in immediately otherwise he would lose the lead. Dino Toso tried to warn him but there was no response. Contact was made just in time. Damon dived into the pits, but his troubles were only starting. An attempt to adjust the front wing, to help deal with the wet conditions, went wrong and Damon was delayed. He rejoined, still in the lead, but the presence of the safety car meant the field had become bunched and Ralf was right behind Damon.

Now we had a beautiful but totally unexpected dilemma. Ralf, who had yet to win a grand prix, had set up his car for the wet conditions whereas Damon had gambled on a drier track. Ralf had the faster car – and he knew it. Damon, on the other hand, had done all the hard work. The grand prix was not simply about what happened during a couple of hours on a Sunday afternoon, it was also about the preparation and effort put in from the start of business on Friday. On that score alone, Damon deserved this win.

At the pre-race briefing, we had never in our wildest imagination believed we would be running first and second. This scenario had never been discussed and, if it had, the person raising the subject would have been considered certifiable.

We did not have a number one and a number two driver. As I had outlined at the launch in the Royal Albert Hall, it was every man for himself. However, to prevent incidents such as the collision between Ralf and Fisichella in Argentina the previous year, we had agreed that whoever was in front with only a few laps to go, would stay there. Above all else, we did not want a fight between the two drivers. They would be asked to hold position. The other consideration was that

Jean Alesi was third, very keen to show his skill in the wet and bring Sauber their first F1 win.

There were five laps to go when the safety car disappeared. Ralf was weaving every which way in Damon's mirrors. Damon came on the radio and said he was pushing as hard as he dared in order to stay on the road and give Jordan its first win. He said it was up to the team to call the shots. He was very calm and very measured but the implication was very clear. He was effectively saying, 'Call Ralf off. Don't force me to do something stupid and risk everything.'

Damon did not trust too many people. He gave the impression that he was a little bit sceptical, a very private man who was holding back and not letting you see all of Damon Hill. There was no doubt that he had his suspicions about Michael after the collision in Adelaide that had cost Damon the 1994 world championship. Now you had the feeling that those suspicions had spread to Michael's younger brother.

I understood the rules of engagement. So did Damon, but what about Ralf? When told to defend second place from attack by Alesi, Ralf did not reply. Here we were with a one-two finish on the cards and I had one driver threatening to run to his own agenda and possibly cost us everything.

Damon came on the radio and said someone on the pit wall had to make a call, otherwise this might end in tears. Sam Michael, Ralf's engineer, told Ralf to hold position. There was no response. Sam repeated the message and reiterated that it was an instruction. Silence. Sam asked Ralf to respond. After a short pause, Ralf replied, 'Yes. I hear you.' That was all he said.

There was no question that Ralf was the quickest driver on the track at the time. He had made a statement, but he stayed where he was during those very long last laps. No one said a word as we watched the fuzzy pictures on the little television monitors on the pit wall. The track was still very wet in parts. Eddie Irvine had spun off when he simply put a wheel of the Ferrari on a slippery, damp kerb. The same thing could happen to our boys with the slightest moment of inattention.

I cannot begin to describe the sense of relief as we saw the two yellow cars appear out of the gloom to our left and take the flag. At the 127th attempt, and after almost eight dramatic seasons of highs and many lows, we had achieved what we set out to do – and not just a win for Jordan Grand Prix, but a clean sweep.

Spa had a curious arrangement for presentations because the podium was nowhere near the pits. It was part of a permanent building located on the run down to the second corner. I could barely speak and did not know where I was supposed to be or what I was supposed to do. I seemed to be swept along by euphoria and, in the midst of it, someone ushered me towards a waiting minibus for the brief journey to the podium.

When I got there, someone said they did not have the Irish national anthem – which was a major cock-up on the part of Formula One Management because Jordan was an Irish-registered team. Our first win was to be marked with the wrong national anthem. This was outrageous. Nonetheless, the British version was the next best choice because the team was based in England and the majority of the workforce was British. It was a huge moment for us all.

It was also Damon's way of sticking up two fingers to critics who said he had only won races in the past because he had been in a Williams. Ralf, meanwhile, had made his point. I told him that he had gone up 100 per cent in my estimation and that I was massively impressed. He seemed happy enough because his family and friends were present and this marked his emergence as a serious contender. I remember being saturated, not just from the rain, but also the champagne. That did not matter in the slightest because the only seriously damp part of the weekend was about to hit me once I got back to the motorhome.

Michael Schumacher arrived, as I thought to congratulate the team that had given him his F1 break at this very circuit, but he did not have it in him to do that. He was quite arrogant about me not allowing Ralf to win. It was true that he had endured a miserable day when a win that would have put him at the top of the championship for the first time in 1998 had been denied by an incident that he clearly continued to believe was not his fault. He had been guilty of having a major go at David Coulthard in the McLaren garage and now he was having a go at me. I was very disappointed in him. The way I ran the team was none of his business and, in any case, this was not the time to discuss it. Within a few seconds of returning to the spontaneous party outside the motorhome, I had forgotten Michael's petulance – for the moment.

I have to admit that I did have a drink or two while dealing with seemingly endless interviews. It was more civilised than glugging champagne straight from the bottle and having it come back down my nose while standing in front of everyone on the rostrum. Once the formalities had started to die down, one of the first moves I made was to visit 80 staff members who happened to have organised a coach trip and had watched from opposite the podium. Their state of delirium can be imagined.

Throughout the celebrations, one very major piece of sadness affected not only me but also a number of the more senior personnel on the team. Gary Anderson had not been present to see his first F1 victory. This car was all his work and he had not been there to appreciate it. Andy Stevenson and Nick Burrows, the number one mechanics for Damon and Ralf, rang Gary later that evening and had, by all accounts, an emotional conversation. We all knew that we would not have achieved any of this without Gary.

I rang Marie. Everyone was so emotional that I wanted to get back to Oxford as quickly as possible, but how? Marie had intended to fly to Spa on race day but the weather was so bad that the helicopter had been grounded. Now Ian and I had no way of getting home. As we sat in traffic on our way to Brussels, it seemed a hopeless cause. Then I remembered our sponsor, GdeZ, and my old friend, Brian de Zille.

In my early days in F3, one of our rivals had been a team called Pegasus, founded by Brian de Zille. The girlfriend of Nick Burrows, who came to work for me eventually, was an administrator for Pegasus. She also made the most amazing bacon butties, which would be served with coffee at the races. Since then, we had gone our separate ways. Brian had founded the Sweater Shop and I had started Jordan Grand Prix.

One day Brian phoned the office but I was very busy and could not take the call. He tried a couple of times and finally left a message to say that I really ought to talk to him. I did so eventually and discovered that Brian was living in Jersey. He said he wanted me to fly across to see him. I said that would be impossible because I was up to my eyes. He insisted. Brian said he would have me picked up from Coventry early in the morning and I could be back by late morning. I was curious now because I discovered that he had two planes and a helicopter.

I flew over and we had breakfast in a small place near the airport. He simply wanted to be part of the team and would give me some cash in return. It transpired he had sold the Sweater Shop for more than £140 million. We put together a deal that included the use of one of his planes. Brian was the perfect gentleman. He would turn up at the occasional race and stand quietly on the sidelines, sit in the motorhome and have a couple of glasses of champagne and simply be part of the scene. We had no contract, only the scribbles on a paper tablecloth from the café. I eventually bought the Hawker 125 plane from him and we would use his Twin Squirrel to fly across to Ireland. It was a wonderful arrangement, built on Brian remembering me from the early days when I was a chancer, blagging my way into his motorhome in search of coffee and bacon butties. Now was the moment to ask a favour.

I called him. 'Brian, you and I, we've been through some shit since Formula 3, back in Silverstone when you used to cook me those bacon butties and support our efforts. Now we've gone and won a grand prix!' He was weeping with joy.

I explained that we needed to get home. His response was immediate. Ian and I were told to get ourselves to Liège airport. Somehow, at very short notice, Brian managed to scramble one of his aircraft and pick us up there. The next problem would be landing at Oxford, more or less unannounced, but the staff at Oxford airport, accustomed to racing people such as Frank Williams, Tom Walkinshaw and Flavio Briatore coming and going at all hours, were terrific. Ian called Lindsay and the airport officials agreed to reopen if we accepted that there would no cover from the fire brigade.

Ian's wife, Sam, collected us from the airport and gave me a lift home. I arrived at about 10 p.m., stinking of sweat, champagne and booze. Inside, more than 20 people were celebrating with all their might, and Amanda Rudman was waiting with her camera. The film company had more or less given up on Jordan. Here was a team that had started out with great expectations and a flash launch at the Royal Albert Hall, only for the team boss to utter profanities and not want to talk because things were so bad at Monaco. The team could not even score a point, never mind win a race. Things had improved slightly since Monaco but Amanda had decided to give Spa a miss. Suddenly, she had a film-maker's dream and she filmed the whole thing. For the first time since the start of the season, I was happy to see her camera.

I was asked if this was the biggest and best thing that had ever happened to Jordan. The answer was 'no'. Survival was the best thing that ever happened. Winning at Spa was second best and the sense of achievement that afternoon merely highlighted the huge stress, strain and pain that had been necessary to get us that far.

## Chapter 37

# BACK TO REALITY

The post-race debrief had become a tradition within the team. Good race, bad race, it did not matter. Trevor Foster and I – and sometimes Gary Anderson or Richard O'Driscoll – would make a habit of addressing everyone at the factory on the Monday after each race. I would explain what we did well, how we screwed up, what parts had failed, how the latest developments had worked, outline the general performance and how we intended to do improve it. It was a means of involving everyone in the team, particularly those who had not been to the race but wanted to know the detail. Many of the meetings were difficult but that was never going to be the case as the race team returned to Silverstone on Monday, 31 August 1998.

Many people think that on occasions such as a grand-prix win – particularly the first one – I would be off my head. That may be my reputation but, in fact, I'm exactly the opposite. I am not a big drinker, having been put off by terrible hangovers in the past. Ian and I had a few beers on the flight to Oxford and I sipped some champagne at various times, but that was it. Ian and I actually fell asleep for a brief period on the plane.

Once the initial euphoria had died down, my overriding feeling was one of calm as I allowed the effects of this momentous result to sink in. That was my mood as I walked from my office on the first floor and headed for the door leading to the workshop. The usual procedure would be to go down the metal staircase to the factory floor, where everyone would be waiting – but not this time. I had barely gone three paces along the walkway leading to the stairs, when the place erupted. It was a fantastic moment. Even when I think about it now, my pulse rate quickens.

I was holding the trophy for the winning team and just the sight of it was enough to trigger clapping, cheering and chanting. 'One two! One two! One two! One two!' It grew louder and louder. From the oldest to the youngest members of staff, they were applauding themselves because, as I was about to tell them, this had been a team victory thanks to their efforts and their belief. No one had expected us to win and this result showed how difficult it was to categorise Jordan. One minute, we were struggling; the next, we were finishing one two.

I had difficulty speaking because, in many ways, this was much more emotional for me than winning the race. The strange location of the podium at Spa meant that not so many of the usual familiar faces from the pit lane had been there, looking up. Here at the factory, each and every person standing below had put sweat and effort into attaining this result, and a number of the faces had been part of Jordan for more than 15 years. It was like having a huge family and every member of it was overjoyed. You do not get many moments like that. I will never forget it.

Despite most of the day disappearing rapidly in a haze of telephone calls and a long lunch at The Green Man pub, we were aware that F1 waits for no one. Spa was history. Monza was next.

We were reminded of that when Willi Weber put out a statement saying that Jordan had withdrawn from negotiations with Ralf for 1999. This was plainly not true and we had to issue a press release that evening refuting Weber's words. It was clear, though, that Ralf wanted to leave. Michael was ready to pay whatever it cost. Come what may, Ralf would take us to court if necessary. We went so far as preparing a case, but it did not get that far.

Personally, Ralf's attitude hurt me a lot. Nevertheless, to this day, I feel as close to Ralf as to any other driver that I have had. He is one of a small bunch of people I would consider to be amazing fun. It was true that Ralf had mood swings, but when he was on the case, he was deadly quick. Unfortunately, that was not going to happen for much longer in a Jordan.

It was September and we had to start an immediate search for a replacement. Heinz-Harald Frentzen was known to be parting company with Williams – another driver who had endured a less than happy time with Frank Williams and Patrick Head. We knew Heinz-Harald from our time together in F3000 but word was that he was going back to Sauber, the team that had given him his F1 break in 1994. I called his manager, Ortwin Podlech, and discovered that negotiations with Sauber were not going smoothly. Within a couple of days, we had agreed a deal – concluded on the telephone while I was playing golf at Sunningdale.

That allowed me to feel comfortable about accepting an offer to terminate Ralf's contract. Michael had asked Bernie rather than IMG to negotiate the release of Ralf's contract. Unlike Michael's departure from Jordan in 1991, it was done with some decorum and style. I could have been an absolute bastard and said no but the money involved amounted to more than I would have had to pay Ralf the following year. This was a windfall because I would not be paying Frentzen anywhere near as much, so it made good financial sense.

No sooner had all that been sorted out than I had to deal with a domestic crisis within Jordan – Gary had handed in his notice. I was sad about that, too, but not altogether surprised. It would be the end of a fantastic partnership, one without which I really think Jordan would not have enjoyed such a successful entry into F1. To my mind, the Jordan 191 remains one of the most beautiful racing cars ever made, and it is Gary who we have to thank for that and the amazing success that came with it. However, the time comes in a relationship, particularly in a business such as this, when both sides perhaps grow apart. We agreed the wording of a press release and issued it just over a week after Spa.

The following day, another release confirmed that Ralf would be leaving at the end of the season. It was brief and to the point because I was unable to say what I really felt. I was sure that Ralf wanted to stay and there was no doubt that we were happy to go along with that. Michael poked his nose into something that was none of his business. We had invested time and money in Ralf. Spa had done wonders for his reputation and I felt sure we were going from strength to strength. Then Michael whispered in his ear and he was off. So be it. At least we had Frentzen coming and, of course, Damon would be staying, or so I thought.

On the night before we were due to fly to Monza for the Italian Grand Prix, I went to Anfield to watch a midweek match between Liverpool and Coventry. At half time, I had a call from Ian. He felt there was trouble looming with Hill because neither Damon nor Michael Breen were taking calls even though everyone knew that Benson & Hedges expected to confirm the contract for 1999 at Monza the next day. There had been all sorts of rumours, one of which concerned British American Tobacco and their wish to have Damon join Jacques Villeneuve at BAR-Honda. We flew to Monza anticipating a difficult weekend. Spa and its success seemed from another era.

I was due to appear at an offical FIA press conference and when I told Damon that I would be announcing our intention of keeping him, Damon became extremely uptight. By a stroke of good fortune, Nigel Northridge had brought two guests who happened to be lawyers. Their professional services were called upon immediately and we thrashed out an agreement, but it was not reached until Sunday morning. So much for the lawyers having a few days off but at least B&H could confirm that Hill was staying – much to the relief of Nigel Northridge, who had become a huge fan of Damon's and the professional manner in which he dealt with sponsors and the media.

It was a relief for me too because I was having to face some difficult questions at the British media breakfast, a Friday morning tradition started by Louise Goodman and happily embraced by Giselle. This was a very informal way of staying in touch with our friends, although I always felt sorry for any newcomer to the media ranks visiting the Jordan motorhome for the first time on a Friday morning. I would specialise – without too much difficulty, it must be said – in arriving through the front door and immediately launching a verbal assault on whichever hapless journalist caught my eye first. It did not take long for the guys to get in the mood and the banter was often hilarious. It was a great way of building upon what I liked to think was an already strong relationship with some great people, although the look of shock on the face of any media novice had to be seen to be believed. The craic was wonderful.

Much of the abuse directed my way at Monza suggested that Spa had been a fluke and we were about to receive our comeuppance. This was said in jest but I was aware that one or two in the paddock might actually believe it. We were very confident about being able to banish such a thought.

Mike Gascoyne had been at work in the wind tunnel, the cars at Monza showing the resulting modifications to the sidepods. Our confidence increased when Ralf qualified sixth and Damon might have joined him near the front but for a mistake on his best qualifying lap. As a result, the plan was to have Damon start with a light load of fuel from 14th and see how far he could get in the early stages. It worked perfectly as he gained several places.

Ralf was fifth for most of the way and then moved into fourth when Villeneuve spun, and third when Mika Hakkinen's McLaren dropped back with brake trouble. That made it two podiums in a row for Ralf, with Damon adding to the feeling of well-being by scoring a point for sixth, for which he worked hard. This was the sixth race in succession in which Jordan Mugen-Honda had claimed points, which was difficult to believe after spending several races simply trying to score a single point. It was business as usual as far as those of us inside Formula 1 were concerned, but in some respects, that business was totally divorced from the world outside.

At the races, we had reminders of that each day as pictures from Sky News were received in the motorhome. A month earlier, we had been stopped in our tracks when news came through of a bomb in the streets of Omagh. Watching the terrible scenes of devastation in the Northern Ireland market town added to our feelings of helplessness as we pursued a sport that, compared to this latest atrocity, seemed nothing but a game, a complete folly.

It affected Jordan more than most, given the Irish presence in the team. Gary Anderson, Mark Gallagher, Nigel Northridge, John Boy, David Marren, Richard O'Driscoll and I all came from Ireland. Damon lived near Dublin, Michael Breen was from Belfast and at least one member of the British media came from Northern Ireland. There was nothing we could say at the time but I did wonder if there was something we could do. I had no idea what. Then a letter arrived not long after.

It was from the neighbour of a young boy, Alister Hall, who had suffered appalling injuries at Omagh. Alister had lost a leg and yet the first thing he had wanted to know when he regained consciousness was how Jordan had got on during qualifying in Hungary. Another letter arrived from his surgeon to the same effect. It brought a lump to my throat and I vowed we would do something other than simply send an autographed cap. A chance arose immediately after Monza.

Damon and I were due to take part in a charity VIP golf match in Ireland with Darren Clarke, the professional golfer, who is from Dungannon, not far from Omagh. I arranged for Brian de Zille to fly us North in one of his helicopters and land at Altnagelvin Hospital, a major facility dealing with many of the Omagh casualties. The entire event was low key but, with Damon's win at Spa still fresh in everyone's mind, the place was buzzing when he stepped from the chopper in the hospital car park. We found Alister and also visited other kids who had lost limbs. They were overjoyed. Typical of children, these brave patients did not think they were as ill as they obviously were. It made us all realise that, in places such as this around the world, there are much harder battles being fought than anything we might endure in our sport.

## Chapter 38

# A BRILLIANT VICTORY

Fourth in the 1998 Constructors' Championship – that was our best-ever result and it led to the obvious question. What next? Winning the championship was the obvious answer. We were under no illusions that this was a very tall order but, in the event, we were to get closer than I had ever dreamed possible.

Financially, things had never looked better. Dominic Shorthouse, the managing director of Warburg Pincus, had been carrying out due diligence on Jordan, part of which involved me having a medical. As it turned out, Dominic was doing me a favour in many ways because the medical showed my cholesterol to be very high. I was in good shape thanks to training every day, so this was a surprise. Otherwise, everything about the company was considered fit.

Dominic had been sold on two things – the value of race teams was increasing and he would make many useful connections through F1. Having a significant minority stake in an F1 team, particularly one with a profile such as ours, would open doors throughout Europe. I reckoned Dominic was making a bold and clever move on two counts – he was looking at this as a pure investment and he was seeing his involvement as a platform for a sales pitch. In November 1998, we agreed that Warburg Pincus would buy 49.9 per cent of the holding company.

Our value in terms of respect and potential on the racetrack remained an open question. There continued to be doubters who wondered aloud about our ability to raise our game. Questions were asked about how we would cope without Gary, particularly when we did not replace him. Mike Gascoyne would continue on probation, the Jordan 199 being his first car, albeit a logical development of the one that had done so well in the last half of 1998. That was part of the problem, of course. So much effort and resource had been poured into the car at the end of 1998 that work on the 199 had suffered.

I spent the winter watching with interest to see how we would get on without Gary's powerful presence in the drawing office and on the shop floor. Trevor Foster, in his role as managing director, was confident that we had an excellent technical team. Mike was backed up by Mark Smith (head of mechanical design), John McQuilliam (in charge of composite design), John Illey (head of aerodynamics), John Davis (head of R&D) and our two race engineers, Sam Michael and Dino Toso. We had restructured to allow each department to have more responsibility, a move that would work better than anticipated.

There was a further change of philosophy on the driver front. By hiring Heinz-Harald Frentzen, we were demonstrating serious intent by entering, for the first time, a new season without a 'pay driver' to bolster our finances. I had every faith in Frentzen but the doubters were pointing to the fact that he had scored just one grand-prix win during two years with Williams. Many reckoned he was demoralised and on the scrapheap. I did wonder why Williams had let him go. I asked myself if Frank knew something that I did not because I reckoned Heinz to be very good. The first race in Australia was going to answer many questions.

Unlike previous seasons when all the hype and hope of winter testing had been banished by disappointment in the opening races, 1999 was completely different. We hit the ground running, Heinz qualifying fifth and finishing second – albeit it on a day when the favourites, McLaren-Mercedes, retired both cars. When he finished third in Brazil and looked like repeating the result at Imola until caught out by oil from an exploding Ferrari engine, our intentions were clear. Then the sport, as it frequently does, bit back.

We had mechanical problems in Spain and Canada, the latter hurting in every respect. Frentzen had been heading for a well-deserved second place when a brake disc shattered, a rare problem but one that sent the car into the barrier and caused a leg injury. It was painful enough to have Heinz do no testing between Montreal and the next race in France. Any doubts were dispelled when Frentzen showed his continuing confidence by qualifying fifth, the perfect place from which to run a fantastic race in wet/dry conditions, helped greatly by 'Big Dave', our secret weapon.

Big Dave generally helped with whatever needed doing. He would do odd jobs such as security at night. On the morning of the French Grand Prix, he was in early because the team needed to start the packing process as quickly as possible. As the start of the race approached, Dave asked if there was anything he could do. I had a lot on my mind at that moment, particularly with regard to Damon's progress, or lack of it, and the last thing I needed was to find something to keep Dave occupied. I thought about it for a second or two.

Teams such as Ferrari and McLaren were wired into satellite stations and employed expensive ways of predicting the weather. We would spend 5p on a telephone call to the local airport and receive a forecast. On this occasion, I was not sure that would be adequate. Dave could be just the man to help.

'Listen Dave,' I said. 'You could do me a favour. Can you see the way those dark clouds are coming from the direction of Magny-Cours village? It's dry now but we haven't got a clue what's going to happen. I'll tell you what you can do. You go down the road and go into a field or find some vantage point directly in line with the way the clouds are coming across the circuit. You need to make contact with Andy Stevenson. If you can see the rain's coming, we'll need to know how far away you are, how strong the wind is and, most important of all, how long you think the rain's going to last.' Dave nodded and headed off with a mobile phone and an umbrella. I thought no more about it.

In the opening laps, Frentzen was handily placed in fourth and hanging on to the leaders. Like most teams, we had decided on two stops but we were eyeing the sky. It was getting gloomier by the minute and it was evident that anything could happen. We needed to be on our toes because there was a chance to pinch a good result if we got our tactics just right. There was plenty to think about.

Someone tugged my trouser leg as I sat on the pit-wall perch and I thought, 'Jayzus, not now! Can't you see we've got to concentrate on this race?' But I glanced down to see Andy, beckoning me to listen.

'Dave's been on. He says it's pissing down and there's no likelihood of a let-up.' That was the key – 'No likelihood of a let-up.'

Normally, I would not get too involved in strategy but I grabbed Trevor.

'If the track's wet and the pace is slower, how many laps d'you reckon we can do with the tank full to the brim? D'you think we could get away with stopping just once?'

As the boys worked like mad on the computers to come up with the required information, it began to rain quite hard. Ten cars, including the leading six, came in to the pits at the end of lap 22 for fuel and wet-weather tyres. We knew we would never beat McLaren or Ferrari in a straight fight. We had to look for something different, and we had to do it now!

At the last minute, the instruction went out to fill Heinz-Harald's car to the brim. Even though 50 laps remained, the plan was to see if we could make it home without stopping again. Judging by the shorter time taken by the rest of the leaders during their stops, it was obvious they were relying on the rain easing and a change back to dry-weather tyres at the time of the second stop. We knew better. We had Dave, soaked to the skin in the middle of a field somewhere and convinced 'there's no likelihood of a let-up'.

Dave was proved accurate in his definition of 'it's pissing down' when the rain intensified. The track was awash in parts with cars spinning in all directions. It was only a matter of time before the safety car appeared. It could not come quickly enough as far as we were concerned.

Despite the longer stop, Heinz had maintained fourth place. However, he was finding the car very difficult to drive with such a full load of fuel. When he saw Alesi spin like a top in front of him, Heinz began shouting on the radio for us to call for the safety car. It appeared on lap 25 and stayed for 11 laps. This was exactly what we wanted because that represented a considerable fuel saving while droning around behind the official car. Now it would be a question of the track staying damp enough to allow Frentzen to continue all the way on wet-weather tyres.

Alesi's spin in his Sauber had put Heinz into third place and that became second when Mika Hakkinen spun his McLaren when trying to take the lead from the Stewart-Ford of Rubens Barrichello. Then we were third again when Michael Schumacher, on a serious charge in his lightly fuelled Ferrari, came through and eventually took the lead from Rubens, but not for long. A problem with the steering wheel on the Ferrari meant an unscheduled stop and we were second again, but also not for long. A recovering Hakkinen forced his way past our car before he, too, took the lead from Barrichello.

We were reasonably certain that the two cars in front would need to stop for fuel during the 12 remaining laps, but the question was could Frentzen make it to the finish? He had been driving at a steady pace, saving fuel where he could. Would that be enough? The weather – and Dave's prediction – remained in our favour, as did our tactic as both Hakkinen and Barrichello dived into the pits together. Heinz led the race for the first time.

There were seven laps to go and Sam Michael talked Heinz through every one of them – 'Ease back, you used too much fuel on the last lap,' and that sort of thing. Luckily, the track was still wet enough to prevent Barrichello and Hakkinen from fitting dry-weather tyres. We were looking good. In fact, the rain returned briefly in the closing laps and Heinz actually extended his lead before backing off on instruction from Sam. He crossed the line 11 seconds ahead of Hakkinen.

What a brilliant way to win a race! We were over the moon. Our tactics had worked and, as ever, the pit crew had done a brilliant job under pressure. As for Heinz-Harald, he had driven faultlessly on a day when several of the leading lights had spun off. Bear in mind that Heinz-Harald could hardly walk without lingering pain from that shunt in Canada. Fortunately, he was comfortable when sitting in the car and, most important of all, his throttle foot had been as delicate as ever in those treacherous conditions.

We were third in the Constructors' Championship with 26 points. Damon had scored just three of those points, and this race was a typical example of the troubles he was experiencing. He never ran higher than 14th before retiring with an engine-related problem.

The front cover of the following week's *Autosport* summed up our situation. Under the heading 'Joy and Despair', one picture showed a jubilant Heinz-Harald while the other caught a lonely and dejected Damon as he walked away from his car and told ITV that was the last time he would be seen in a Formula 1 car.

## Chapter 39

# A WIN FOR THE TAKING

Even now, I find it difficult to pinpoint what went wrong with Damon Hill in 1999. He had been excellent the previous year and formed a great partnership with Ralf, Damon's win at Spa being exactly what you would expect from such a serious and seasoned campaigner. However, almost from the start of 1999, Damon was not happy with the car. Had Heinz-Harald not been doing such a fantastic job, we might easily have panicked and made unnecessary changes to the 199, but Heinz's performance was, in fact, turning the screw even tighter on Damon. He had a mini-crisis in both Monaco and Canada and then failed to qualify in France. We got him into the race somehow but, to be honest, we may as well not have bothered.

There was no bad feeling. We told Damon that we would go along with whatever he felt he had to do. The last thing we wanted was to pressure him. When he got out of the car at Magny-Cours, he was adamant he wanted to stop, with immediate effect. That meant we had to get to work finding a replacement for the next race at Silverstone. Usually the French and British Grands Prix were a week apart but, fortunately, in 1999 there was a two-week gap. Nonetheless, as soon as the chequered flag fell at Magny-Cours, Ian and I had to leave immediately. We had a meeting scheduled that evening with Jos Verstappen and his manager, Huub Rothengatter, at my house in Oxford. Instead of celebrating a fantastic win, Ian and I were locked in conversation with two Dutchmen, one of whom drove us mad.

It was agreed that Verstappen would drive our car that week during the big pre-grand-prix test at Silverstone. We also ran Mugen-Honda's test driver, Shinji Nakano. When Verstappen turned out to be just three-tenths of a second faster than Nakano, who was no more than a journeyman driver, I knew we had a problem. Meanwhile, Hill was having second thoughts – which suited us because we were stuck for a driver. Damon received a last-minute call to come and test, which he did, and posted fifth-fastest time, a couple of seconds quicker than Verstappen. Now everyone was confused, not least, you suspected, our star driver.

It was clear that Damon was no longer enjoying it and, come what may, he planned to retire at the end of the year. Damon just did not look happy in the car, which was difficult to understand because Frentzen was going so well. Something happened inside Damon's head and only he knows what that was. We were trying everything – fresh engines, the opportunity to drive Heinz-Harald's car – but nothing seemed to help. If Damon had been on a race-by-race contract, he would have been sacked. Now the media were on his back.

Whatever happened, it was important that a former world champion should retire with dignity, and Damon felt that he really had to take part in the British Grand Prix. Fair enough. We were happy to go along with that. In fact, Bernie Ecclestone had agreed to a parade of F1 cars, including Damon's and those driven by his father, Graham. In many ways this would be the perfect place for Damon to sign off. After all, Graham Hill had done exactly that at Silverstone during the International Trophy non-championship race in 1975. We arranged for Damon to sign some papers on the Tuesday before the British Grand Prix. He failed to turn up. We then discovered that he wished to continue until the end of the season.

Almost everyone I spoke to felt that was the wrong move. I don't know precisely what was behind Damon's thinking but I believe he got the wrong end of the stick after reading an interview I had given to James Mossop for one of the Sunday papers. Damon had the impression that I would somehow make money out of his early retirement. That was not the case at all, but I could just imagine Damon steaming as he sat at home thinking I was stitching him up. I thought back to that vitriolic letter he wrote to BAT in 1991. The irony was that the media concluded that Damon was staying on for the money – which he was, but not for the reasons everyone thought. It was a great shame because Damon was a total gentleman, a very honourable man who was perhaps wrongly influenced by others.

A more pressing problem for the team was that we were looking at defending third place in the championship with the equivalent of one arm tied behind our backs. However, Damon turned in a much better performance, finishing fifth at Silverstone, one place behind Heinz-Harald. Heinz went on to score more points in Austria and in Germany but, whereas Frentzen finished on the podium at Hockenheim, Hill ended his race amid controversy after going off the road twice and then parking the car because he was not happy with the brakes. I was not in the car, so I took his word. Nevertheless, you could tell by the looks etched on the faces of his mechanics that they were disappointed.

Both drivers scored points in Hungary and Belgium but, on each occasion, Frentzen was drilling Hill. At the start of the season, we had expected it to be the other way round. Nonetheless, we were still third in the Constructors' Championship with Frentzen now equal third in the drivers' title race. Next thing we knew, Heinz was talking about winning it!

After putting our car on the front row at Monza, Frentzen drove a beautifully controlled race, looking after his brakes and tyres in the early stages and then setting about closing the gap to Hakkinen's leading McLaren. It was one of those classic situations where McLaren knew we were likely to be having a longer first stint and Mika therefore needed to build up a healthy lead. Each time Hakkinen put in a fast lap, Frentzen responded. If anyone had doubted our pace, this was proving once and for all that the Jordan 199 was a serious contender.

The McLaren engineers urged Hakkinen to push harder, which he did. Then, unbelievably, the Finn selected the wrong gear and spun off. You may remember the incredible scene as he climbed from the McLaren, threw his gloves on the ground and hid behind a bush to have a good weep. While he was doing that, Frentzen took the lead and never looked back. Two wins in as many months!

Ron Dennis was never one to give away too many compliments to his competitors but immediately after the race at Monza, he pulled me to one side and said, 'Well done, Jordan. At least you've won one race by merit.' I was offended at the time and responded with a remark about his parentage but Ron was always one to keep you on your toes. In any case, he could hardly say anything else because we had forced the error that lost McLaren the race. People thought I had no respect for Ron – a point of view encouraged by Ron suggesting that I was never serious enough – but, deep down, I would like to think there was mutual respect for our different approaches to the same job. Not many people realised that Ron and I often had detailed conversations, in either his motorhome or mine. Now here we were, on the point of having our drivers square up to each other in the championship.

With three races to go, Heinz was just ten points behind the joint leaders, Hakkinen and Eddie Irvine, neither of whom had had a distinguished race at Monza. This was quite staggering. McLaren may have had almost twice as many points as Jordan in the Constructors' Championship but Frentzen had a genuine chance, helped by the fact that Michael Schumacher had ruled himself out of the equation by breaking a leg at Silverstone. That may have been fortunate from our point of view but it did not hide the fact that we had beaten Michael before his accident.

Frentzen and the Jordan Mugen-Honda were consistently quick – everywhere. Heinz proved it by qualifying first at the Nurburgring. People tend to forget that – a pole position for Jordan under the most difficult circumstances. After a lot of problems with the car, Heinz had limited running and yet he had the confidence to wait until the very end of qualifying when the track would be quickest. Nine minutes from the end Heinz had not done enough to qualify. You can imagine the pressure but, calm as you like, he went out and produced a brilliant lap. That was a measure of the guy in 1999.

In the race, he was leading comfortably, on a day when Hakkinen and Irvine were not figuring. It was too good to be true. Leaving the pits after another clean stop by the boys, the engine cut out on the run to the first corner. An identical problem had put Damon out at more or less the same place on the first lap. We were devastated. A problem with the anti-stall device was to blame. It needed to be turned off as soon as the car got going from rest. Each time, without fail, Sam would say to Heinz, 'Press cancel, press cancel,' as a reminder. On this occasion, he simply said, 'You've 4.5 seconds on Ralf. Bring it home first.' No sooner had Sam said that than we heard Heinz reporting that the engine had cut out. It was the most sickening feeling to see the pictures of our car rolling to a halt. Hard to believe, but we had almost expected a win, our third in 1999.

A win would have put Frentzen in with a very serious chance of the championship going in to the last two races. Certainly, the final round at Suzuka was right up his street because Heinz-Harald had been one of the many European drivers to race in Japan and he knew the circuit well. So, for that matter, did Eddie Irvine. Yet, for some unaccountable reason, Eddie was having trouble with his car.

The story was that Michael was back in the cockpit but out of the championship running following his accident at Silverstone. Ferrari had not won the drivers' title since 1979 and now Irvine was in with a chance of finally bringing it home. The impression some of us had, rightly or wrongly, was that Ferrari were not that keen on Eddie becoming the hero when, of course, Michael was the star, the man around whom the team had been built. So at a track around which he should have flown to pole and walked off with the race, Irvine suddenly discovered that Ferrari were having trouble with the floor on his car. Very strange.

Eddie's disappointment added to the feeling of anticlimax evident within Jordan. Yes, we finished third in the championship but the fizz seemed to go out of that last race because we knew we could not win the title. Everyone was depressed, but we had no reason to be. McLaren won the championship, Ferrari were second, Jordan were third. That was fantastic. We had done brilliantly for a team that had started less than ten years previously. We had hauled ourselves up in a very short period from being no-hopers to having a crack at the world title. Now there could be no excuses.

## Chapter 40

# A TOUCH OF THEATRE

Giselle Davies came to me one day and explained that a record company had requested a factory visit for one of their leading artists. The conversation went like this:

'Yeah, no problem, Giselle. Who is it?'

'I can't tell you.'

'Pardon? What d'you mean?'

'I don't know who it is.'

'Well, forget it. We need to know who's coming for security reasons and, apart from anything else, it's just good manners to let us know who we're being asked to give up our time for.'

'I agree, but they weren't prepared to tell us. They said we had to trust them, otherwise they couldn't trust us not to take photographs.'

'Look, I'm not happy about this. Not happy at all.'

A couple of weeks later, I looked from my office window to see a very large limo struggling to get through the narrow entrance.

'Who the hell is this?' I shouted to no one in particular, only to be told jointly by Giselle and Lindsay to be quiet. Everything was in hand and I would soon find out.

Now I was riled and feeling out of control. I started shouting at all and sundry but my mood changed dramatically when I saw a famous figure step from the limo. I went from being stubborn and rude to a mix of excited schoolboy and enormously grateful music fan. It is not every day that Johnny Rotten visits an F1 team.

I was down the stairs like a shot. Here, outside my front door, was a music legend, a groundbreaker in terms of musical appreciation.

This man had created the punk era with the Sex Pistols. Their album *Never Mind the Bollocks* had been engineered and produced by Chris Thomas, who later became a member of my V10 band. Chris will tell you that, to this day, he does not know how he made *Never Mind the Bollocks* because the four musicians were on a different planet when they cut the album at Air Studios in Oxford Street. You either loved the Pistols or you hated them. If you loved them, you adored them.

Johnny Rotten's real name, John Lydon, has Irish connections. Sure enough, I discovered that Johnny hailed from Wexford, the same town that Marie's parents came from. He has an Irish passport. We were obviously going to get on famously.

Delighted as I was to see him, I was puzzled over exactly why he had chosen to visit Jordan. When I asked, he grinned, said nothing but pulled off a beanie hat to reveal hair that was exactly the same colour as our car. This explained why his agents had been mysteriously pestering us for the pantone number. Johnny wanted a photograph of his face alongside the car to be used on an album cover, and he spent a lot of time working on an angle that also showed the snake in its semi-aggressive state. He felt that suited his style and image perfectly. He was so excited about the whole idea.

You could never describe Johnny Rotten as being soft, cuddly and adorable. It simply does not fit. A hard-looking, tooth-missing, aggressive image is more like it, and it was a massive thrill for me to help him portray that with our car. In subsequent years, Johnny would be our guest at Indianapolis. He was excellent company, although you learned to expect the unexpected. On one occasion in a restaurant, we had a small row, which blew over as quickly as it had started but proved there was a slightly freaky side to the boy. Nonetheless, I was delighted to have got to know this legend with the Irish background. Too bad Johnny did not drive racing cars as well as he created music.

Thinking about our successful association with the Schumacher brothers and Heinz-Harald Frentzen, I found it surprising that

Jordan had not taken any benefit out of having German drivers. This occurred to me at the Essen Motor Show, where I was picking up a prize for finishing third in the championship. The thought was prompted by a strange call received by Ian on the previous Saturday. Michael Williams, an agent in Germany, wanted to know if he could doctor a picture of our car to show the Deutsche Post symbol on the engine cover and ask the question if the telecommunications company was coming into F1. He said if we allowed him to do that, he would introduce me to someone important in Essen.

I could not see what we had to lose, so I agreed. In the event, I was not so keen. I had been up since the early hours, visited the show and now I was aiming to catch the last flight home. Talking nonsense with a man who simply wanted to meet someone from an F1 team was the last thing I needed. I told the agent that I had to be very sure that there was something of interest we could actually talk about. Then again, since I was in Germany, I thought it would be silly not to make the most of whatever was on offer.

I was asked to go to what turned out to be a small bedroom on the 12th floor of a hotel. Some water and a few sandwiches were provided. It was very uninviting and immediately clear from the first person I met that these people, whoever they were, knew nothing about motor racing. While waiting to see the man in charge, I made a quick call to Ian and said I really did not know why I was there, but I was still aiming to catch the last flight home and would keep him posted.

I eventually got to meet the man who was clearly going to do all the talking – Dr Gert Schukies, the Managing Director of Corporate Communications at Deutsche Post World Net. He wanted to investigate the possibility of being involved with an F1 car – but it had to be yellow because that was the Deutsche Post colour. Now he had my attention. Suddenly, a number of things clicked into place. There had been a rumour that Jackie Stewart was close to doing a deal with Deutsche Post to sponsor the Jaguar team, which had taken over Stewart-Ford. However, Jaguar's corporate colour was green and if

Deutsche Post were insisting on yellow, I was going to work that angle for all I was worth.

I also knew that Jackie would not have been doing things on the cheap. Bolstered by this, I began talking large numbers and moving the discussion onwards and upwards from merely sponsoring parts of the bodywork. I could sense that the engine cover was not going to be big enough for the image Deutsche Post would want to portray. I abandoned plans to catch the last flight home.

We spent all evening in that room discussing different scenarios and objectives as well as learning more about each other. I discovered that Dr Schukies was massively keen on bicycles and the Tour de France. He knew all the top cyclists and had their support for charity days that he held across Germany. Dr Schukies had just come back from a cycling tour in the Sahara. I explained that I loved that sort of thing and had actually gone cycling in the Sahara for the charity CLIC.

We finished at around 2 a.m., having had nothing but water and the rather dodgy sandwiches. I could hardly believe what was happening as I recounted everything to Ian, who was in a Soho nightclub with Nell McAndrew and Richard Dunwoody. His immediate response was, 'Forget it. You must be mad. Deutsche Post are with Stewart. You will not be able to break into that.' However, Ian did concede that his spies had told him that a contract had not been signed. The colour yellow could decide this one way or the other. Dr Schukies had certainly made it clear to me that Deutsche Post on the car without their corporate yellow would be of no use. Strong identification was everything. This was a company on the move. They were about to buy Postbank, DHL and a couple of other very closely aligned businesses throughout the world.

Dr Schukies agreed to bring some of his key management and marketing people to see us later that week and when they arrived, I noticed that Dr Schukies was carrying a massive briefcase. My initial reaction was that he had prepared a huge piece of artwork and that this was going to be a long and drawn out negotiation. Then he opened the big bag and removed a special edition Sahara Tour lightweight bike for me as a present, irrespective of what happened in our impending discussion. That was the first real indication that a good impression had been created at our initial meeting.

Deutsche Post were not able to enter into long-term contracts but they wanted an option for the next two years. I explained that they could not have an option without paying for it and, since this was the way they preferred to organise it, they agreed. Ian and I looked at each other. Nothing needed to be said about such a great deal and the way it was taking shape so quickly and easily compared to some. Ian prepared a contract and it was signed on the Monday – a six-day negotiation and $22 million at the end of it. I have always believed that the best deals come together smoothly whereas protracted negotiations have a habit of going sour over time.

This was to be a fantastic programme and, appropriately, we added international flavour by signing Jarno Trulli to join Heinz-Harald Frentzen. I had been watching Jarno closely in F3 and during his two seasons in F1 with Prost. He had led the Austrian Grand Prix for a while and looked very confident even though, strictly speaking, he had no right to be there. I thought he was worth a try. Not everyone agreed with me.

Frentzen and Trulli would be driving a Jordan Mugen-Honda EJ10. The car was so-called to avoid confusion. Under the previous numbering sequence, the 2000 car would have been referred to as the 100, which didn't seem a good idea. 'EJ' was incorporated for obvious reasons and '10' represented our tenth year in F1. The next car would be an EJ11, and so on.

The EJ10 was launched at London's Drury Lane theatre, another first for Jordan and one that involved theatrics that I knew nothing about. Something I was aware of was the inclusion in our launch of an act by Jean Butler from *Dancing on Dangerous Ground*. Jean, principal dancer in *Riverdance*, was hugely popular, not just in her native Ireland but globally, so when Michael Aspel suddenly appeared on stage carrying his big red book, I thought Jean was his target. I had it in my mind that *This is Your Life* tended to focus on entertainers rather than sports personalities, although I was rarely at home to see it on TV. I also believed that the programme tended to select British subjects, mainly from the point of view of convenience of research, finding guests and arranging travel and accommodation and so on. When Michael presented the book to me, I was thrown completely.

Marie and Lindsay had been hard at work behind the scenes but, with the launch coming up, I had not noticed. I did not have the time to sit down and realise that two plus two made four. That is where the programme makers and my people at Jordan were so clever. It was the perfect chance to spring the surprise because everyone – friends, sponsors, family, team members – was in place. It really was a fantastically slick piece of organisation.

The usual procedure is to go straight into the show. However, we had a launch to complete and the plan was to go to the television studio and record the programme there. My initial reaction was that I did not want to go through with it. In fact, I seemed to recall that there had only ever been one refusal and that was from an Irishman, international footballer Danny Blanchflower. Then I realised that the show was more or less ready to roll and there would be many very disappointed people if it did not go ahead. As time went on, I began to look forward to it, although I was a little nervous about what might happen, and whom they would dig out from my past.

A chauffeur-driven car was waiting to whisk me I knew not where, but turned out to be Teddington. They did not tell me anything. Marie was taken away and the only person I had with me in the special room at the studio was Mark Gallagher, our head of marketing, and he would not give anything away. Unknown to me, the guests were having a great time drinking and chatting in another room and, for once, knowing far more than I did.

They started the show by having me walk on to the stage through sliding doors. A number of familiar faces were already there – the oldest members of the team, others from my racing past whom I had not seen for years, right up to the present, including Jarno. I really did not expect to see him, having said goodbye at Drury Lane.

My Mum, of course, and my family were on the front row. It was a fantastic experience for them. *This is Your Life* is a huge programme in Ireland, mainly because the great Eamonn Andrews was the original host. He was a wonderful TV personality – perhaps one of the first. We always viewed him as a total professional.

The show started with a filmed tribute from Murray Walker. I thought he was absolutely fantastic and was very touched by what he said. Then came a stream of guests. I may not have looked it, but I was relaxed all the way through. Of course, I was apprehensive. It is daunting to have to sit there not knowing whose voice you are going to hear next – and what they might say. I likened it to being a passenger on a bobsleigh, which I was once. You are not in control. Someone else is in charge – and I don't like that. Being on *This is Your Life* was a kind of verbal equivalent.

The surprises came thick and fast, not least the appearance of Margaret Nevin and her brother Liam, 'Big D' Derek McMahon, George Mackin, Brian 'Red' Hurley, Eddie Irvine, David O'Leary, the then manager of Leeds United, and Richard Dunwoody, the then champion jump jockey, having won more races than anyone else at that time, followed by Darren Clarke and Lee Westwood, heroes of the Ryder Cup. When Mike Rutherford of Genesis, Chris Rea and Nick Mason of Pink Floyd suddenly appeared together, it backed up the feeling that the choice of guests was perfect. When you look back on your life, there are so many crossroads that didn't seem that important at the time but, on reflection, were absolutely crucial. The nice thing about the programme was that all the people who had been standing at those various crossroads were present in the studio. I could not think of a better way of saying thanks.

When the recording had finished, we adjourned to the studio bar and restaurant and then moved on to the Soho House club, followed by early morning coffee in Bar Italia – a Ferrari stronghold in the West End. I remember falling out of there at about 3 a.m. All told, it was a fantastic experience.

Seeing Eddie Irvine in person was one of the many surprises, mainly because they had previously shown a recorded film clip in which Eddie passed on his usual rude greetings. Our relationship had never been better. He would slag me off and I would slag him off. He was very clear – he said he wanted to beat Jordan in 2000. That was fine by me. I was genuinely confident we could give Eddie and his new team, Jaguar, a hard time.

Michael Schumacher and Ferrari would finally go on to win the world championship for the first time. Jordan would go backwards, falling from third to sixth in the championship at the end of a hugely disappointing season. I may have got my sums wrong because I was very optimistic about the car in the beginning – we led the first race in Australia for a while – and we made good progress, but a number of things happened. BMW came in as a works team with Williams, as did Jaguar. So, the emphasis was changing regarding factory engines. Having a customer engine, as we did, was never going to be an easy task.

That was no excuse, though. The fact was that our reliability was not good. Our drivers had some very good potential finishes taken from them through clashes in racing incidents. We were the only team to break the front-row domination of Ferrari and McLaren when Heinz-Harald was second quickest at Silverstone and Jarno qualified a brilliant second at Monaco and Spa. Monaco was a good example of what went wrong. Jarno was denied a possible win when gearbox trouble – our Achilles heel all season – put him out when he was lying second behind Michael, who later retired from the race.

Meanwhile, management changes were afoot at the factory. Mike Gascoyne had received an offer from Renault and would be leaving at the end of the year. I was sorry in many ways. I had hoped he would make a good partnership with Gary but, on the other hand, I understood why that had not worked and Gary felt he had to go. The thing was that, at the time I hired Mike, I could not afford to let the moment pass. He had come on the market very cheaply when the Tyrrell team was bought out and, to my amazement, BAR did not take

Mike. I needed him to strengthen the team and I thought he and Gary would complement each other and make an awesome duo. As it turned out, Mike was in charge for a couple of years and he won races with us – which was more than he did at Tyrrell and, later, at Toyota.

When he left, Mike took no fewer than 29 people with him. His move was very disruptive in more ways than one. He had given many of our engineers their head, so he knew what they were capable of and he was able to cherry pick those whose contracts with Jordan were coming up for renewal. It was frustrating, but you cannot stand in the way of people who feel they want to go. There was some discussion over Mike being required to take so-called 'gardening leave', but Flavio Briatore and I were able to come to an agreement. Fortunately, Tim Holloway was there to hold everything together in the technical department. He did an excellent job while we awaited the arrival of Eghbal Hamidy as technical director.

By this stage, I had received some money from my new partner, Warburg Pincus. I felt like a new man and wondered why I had not done it earlier. I had secured money for my family as well as investing in the infrastructure of the team and looking to its future. We were about to spend £100,000 on an expansion within the factory by adding two mezzanine levels to accommodate storage and manufacturing for composites and to allow the relocation and doubling in size of the fabrication shop and hydraulics department.

Staff numbers were about to rise from 175 to 250 and we would also be finding room for 25 engineers from Honda, assigned to work with the team now that we had agreed to move on from the Mugen-Honda – which, for all its excellent service, was getting long in the tooth – to a works Honda V10. It was a necessary step because competition was increasing along the length of the pit lane.

Gone were the days when people could say, 'You're just an assembler. You're not a proper manufacturer of F1 cars.' They made out that we ordered the stuff from an outside source, put it together and called the result a Jordan. Now we were making our own chassis with Dave Price, plus items such as uprights and suspension parts.

That was why staff numbers were on the rise.

This was getting scary for a number of reasons, not least because the wages were very high. It was time to bring in extra management because, in truth, I never saw myself as a manager. I was more of a seat-of-the-pants operator. I liked to know everyone's name and everything that was going on. This was no longer happening. I began meeting people in the corridor whose faces I would recognise but whose names were beyond me. That horrified me. I felt I was losing touch. I began to think, 'I'm not enjoying this any more. This is hopeless. How can I go back to where I was?' Of course, the answer is that you can never go back.

That led to the arrival of John Putt as Chief Operating Officer. John knew what he was letting himself in for since he had acted as our management advisor in 1996. He began telling me that we needed systems everywhere, and that I needed to do this and I needed to get that. It was becoming a Catch 22 situation. If the team had stood still, we would not have attracted key people. Now I had to delegate even more and I began to feel that parts of the team – my team – no longer had anything to do with me. Instead of having frequent meetings and wandering through to the design office and sitting down with Gary for a chat, I found that everything was much more structured. Now we had a two-car test team. Whatever next? There was even talk of two test teams. That meant more trucks, more drivers, more people. It was never ending and seemed to be getting out of hand.

That was the start of a period during which I felt that the stress levels were too high, and the income was not enough to withstand that kind of expenditure. I recalled the words of Rambo – 'Jordan, you're a brilliant brand, you're a brilliant idea. But remember, Jordan should not be winning more than they need to. Leave the winning to McLaren and Ferrari and Williams.' But the scene was shifting and there was no way of stopping it. The manufacturers' influence was increasing. Firms such as Toyota had arrived and were spending huge amounts of money. Yet we had to remain competitive if we were to survive.

## Chapter 41

# CUT BACKS

Sacking one of our drivers two-thirds of the way through the season did little to help what was turning out to be a disastrous year. We had started 2001 on the right note by scoring points in the first five races. Trevor had set a target of 50 points, which we reckoned would be good enough for fourth place, if not third, and we seemed to be on our way to achieving it. Then reliability problems struck again and we were destined to collect just three points in the next eight races, which was a hopeless return for the massive amount of effort that was going in.

A lot of activity was going on behind the scenes. There was pressure on Honda to get rid of us because BAR felt they should be the works team, the 'chosen team'. They had big commercial deals with British American Tobacco, particularly in China, and that happened to suit Honda, who wanted to expand their sales in that part of the world. I needed to find a way of keeping Honda because this was our lifeblood. To do that, I had to agree to take Takuma Sato.

I did not want to get rid of Heinz but there was no denying that his performances had dropped off. He had started the season very well but it seemed to affect his motivation when Jarno was consistently the quicker of the two during qualifying. Heinz was also more affected than he cared to admit by a shunt in the tunnel at Monaco for the second year in succession. He had been knocked unconscious and I am not convinced that he had fully recovered.

Heinz had an option on his contract that he took up on the weekend of the French Grand Prix. The crunch came two weeks later at

Silverstone where, ironically, Frentzen had one of his better qualifying sessions by taking fifth place. Even then, Trulli had been faster. I had to bite the bullet in the interests of the team. I could not afford to wait until the end of the year and risk losing Honda. Changing to a different engine for 2002 would have meant designing a car to take it, which would have been very difficult, if not almost impossible, at that stage in the season. In any case, there was no other engine that I wanted. I was happy to stay with Honda.

Bridgestone had talked to us about Takuma Sato. He was quite a story because only a few years earlier he had been racing pushbikes and yet here he was winning the F3 championship in Britain. Arguably, it was too early to bring him into F1 but Honda were desperate for a Japanese driver. Agreeing to take Taku put me in their good books – I had been tipped off that it would help secure the engine if I did that. It was very harsh on Frentzen and not something I wanted to do but it was in the best interests of the team. I felt guilty. With the German Grand Prix next on the schedule, I knew we were in for a rough ride at Hockenheim.

It actually became quite hostile. Signs hung from the grandstand opposite our pit inviting me to 'F*** Off' and making personal remarks. As it happened, this was a big race for not only Deutsche Post but also Benson & Hedges because Nigel Northridge had invited a number of City analysts for a working weekend. Benson & Hedges had always been big on sponsoring sport but, at this time, their involvement with golf and cricket had diminished, which meant F1 had become an even bigger platform. Keith Wood, the Irish rugby captain, had come to Hockenheim, along with a number of other big lads. We appeared together in a number of places and the Germans automatically thought Keith and the boys were my bodyguards.

I did not fully appreciate how vociferous the crowd had become until we tried to leave the circuit after the race. The intention was to make a quick exit by helicopter for a flight that would take us to Ireland and the Galway races, stopping off at Oxford to pick up

Richard Dunwoody, Pete Burrell and Charlie Feather. Since we were leaving immediately after the race, the minibus taking us to the helipad got stuck in traffic and the mass of spectators heading for the car parks.

One of the fans recognised me. The shout went up and suddenly the minibus was being rocked from side to side quite violently. I was sure that the vehicle was going over on its side, in which case there would be fuel everywhere and goodness knows what might happen after that. Keith started shouting at them and looking menacing to no avail but, fortunately, we got moving again before things got completely out of hand. The Frentzen story had been big news in the German papers and I have to confess I was glad to get out of there.

There had been little to celebrate in Germany. We had replaced Frentzen for this race with our test driver, Ricardo Zonta, but both cars had failed to finish. This was to be one in a run of five successive retirements for Trulli, which was typical of a disappointing season for him. He had been qualifying consistently in the top seven, the 'best of the rest' outside the top three teams – Ferrari, McLaren and Williams – but we had been having massive quality control problems with certain suppliers. On top of that, Honda eventually admitted that they were lagging behind in terms of power. There was one highlight, however, when Trulli finished fifth at the penultimate race in Indianapolis. Even then, we had to fight to keep the points, a dispute that would have the most bizarre ending imaginable.

Jarno had crossed the line in fifth place but the scrutineers later excluded our car because of a technical irregularity. Trevor Foster put our case to the stewards but a subsequent FIA bulletin stated that the penalty still stood. We had lost fifth place and two points.

Not long afterwards, I received an anonymous call suggesting that we take a close look at the signatures of the three stewards who had signed the bulletin. Trevor said he had addressed two stewards, and it became clear that the third, Roger Peart, had already left the circuit, yet his signature was on the subsequent bulletin. In any case, Tim Holloway and our technical guys were convinced that the car had contravened the regulations for genuine reasons beyond our control. We decided we had ample grounds for an appeal.

It so happened that the FIA had decided to allow the media to be present in their appeal court and our case would be the first to be heard in this new spirit of openness. Only one journalist, Maurice Hamilton, bothered to turn up, and he found himself witnessing an extraordinary event.

When the court asked those representing Jordan to identify themselves, we had a stranger to F1 among our number – Mike Ansell, an authority on forensic handwriting. However, before anyone could hear what Mr Ansell had to say, the General Secretary of the FIA declared immediately that the decision of the stewards at Indianapolis had not been in order because Trevor had given his explanation to a panel of two judges when, in fact, there should have been three. This did not constitute a proper hearing. We were given our fifth place back on the spot and everyone went home. We never did find out how a signature purporting to be that of the third steward, Roger Peart, had found its way on to the bulletin, particularly since Peart had been on a plane back to Canada at the time.

Whatever the rights and wrongs of the actions of the FIA and their stewards, this was only the second time in recent history that an appeal had been successful. It was hugely important for Jordan because the points moved us back into fifth place in the championship – ahead of British American Racing. It was worth about £2 million in prize money and fringe benefits, including a better place in the pecking order for 2002.

The mood was lifted in the latter part of the season when we arranged for Jean Alesi to come from Prost and drive for us as a replacement for Frentzen during what would be Jean's final races in F1. It felt like a homecoming because we had raced with Jean in F3000 and helped him into F1 with Tyrrell. It was great to have him on board, even though his arrival brought more work for the team. They made a new seat for him and adapted the car to suit the fact that Jean did not use his left foot for braking. He scored one point at Spa but ended his career by colliding with Kimi Raikkonen's Sauber in Japan. It was hard to imagine Jean making his exit in any other way.

As ever, Jean had been good value for our sponsors. Despite our problems, Benson & Hedges remained loyal and Deutsche Post were becoming even more enthusiastic about their involvement with F1. Talking to Dr Schukies, it became clear that Deutsche Post were intent on turning a national post office into the world's largest logistics company and, along the way, as mentioned before, they had acquired DHL.

At first, we had some difficulty in featuring the two brands together because initially Deutsche Post did not own the majority of DHL's shares. We worked out a solution by having DHL on the sidepods. I presented the car in yellow with the brown DHL insignias, but this led to a problem because, at the time, the DHL background colour was white, not yellow. They wanted white. They said it would be a massive job, for instance, to change the thousands of DHL vehicles from white to yellow. Jordan needed to stay yellow simply because of our association with Benson & Hedges.

We worked hard on convincing DHL that yellow was a more striking colour. We chased every possible argument, even pointing out that if they wanted to grow in the United States, they should remember that the FedEx colour was white. 'Look at what UPS did,' we said. 'In order to get away from FedEx white, they chose brown. Ugh! That's shit! Yellow is your colour. It's vibrant, it's young, it's different.' There was, incidentally, a ridiculous irony attached to Ian and I pleading this case because we are both completely colour blind, although we could not admit that to DHL.

In the end, DHL went for it. I think we can be safe in saying that the yellow (now the red) of DHL became one of the most recognisable brands in the world and that is largely down to their association with Jordan Formula One. It was a major move for DHL. I am really quite proud of that. DHL and Deutsche Post were wonderful to be with and, interestingly, they said they did not want to be with

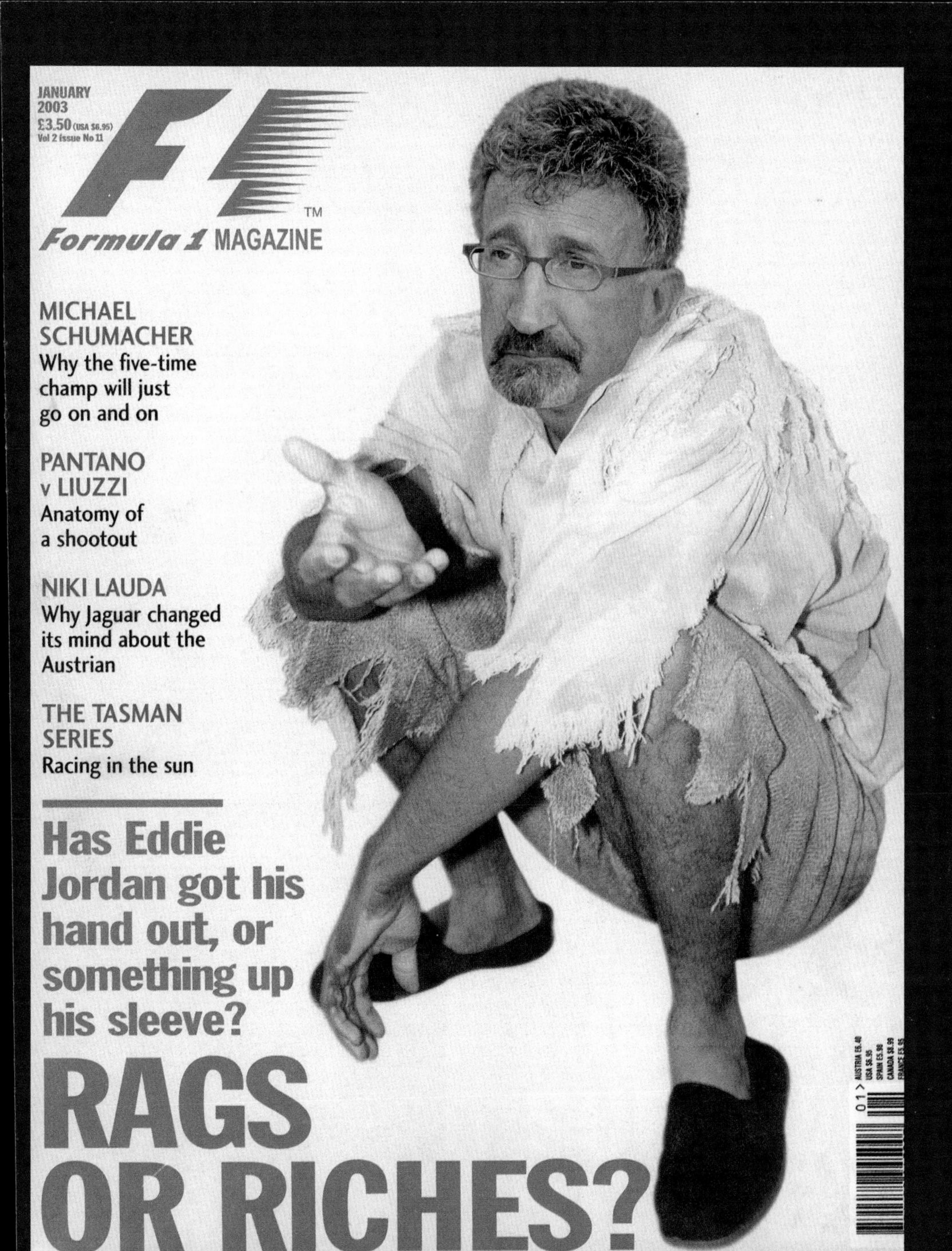


Bernie's joke: a special cover that he mocked up for me. Anyone would think I was always asking for favours!

The Jordan team. (Top) Me with Mike Gascoyne (left), who knew how to work to a tight budget, and race director Trevor Foster. (PA Photos) (Above left and right) Gary Anderson was one of the longest-serving members of my team; while Ian Phillips, the commercial director, was always a key figure. (Getty Images/PA Photos)

(Above left) Sponsorship and PR are vital if a team is to have any chance. So I had much to be grateful to Giselle Davies for her PR work, while (above right) Fiona Cranfield ensures that Nigel Northridge of Gallaher gets the best of treatment. (PA Photos)

John Walton, team manager of Jordan for many years. (PA Photos)

On a rainy August day in 1998, Jordan achieved its first ever grand prix win, with Damon Hill leading the way, closely pursued by Ralf Schumacher (above); it was a proud day for all of us on the podium (left) – and who cared if it was the rain or the champagne that soaked us. (LAT)

Two more wins: Heinz-Harald Frentzen and I celebrate two more great victories: (above) in France and (below) in Italy, 1999. Going into the last few races, he still had a shot at the drivers' title. (Getty Images/LAT)

Giancarlo Fisichella holds off the challenge of Ralf Schumacher on the way to securing Jordan's fourth and last grand prix victory, in Brazil in 2003. Because of a bad crash late on the race was abandoned, and there was controversy as to who would be declared the winner. (PA Photos)

Sharing a joke with Ron Dennis of McLaren after the 2003 Brazilian Grand Prix. He thinks he's won; I know we have. (PA Photos)

Deep in conversation with Bernie Ecclestone. Working out how to get his support in the many issues that arise in Formula One is always a challenge. (Getty Images)

With Flavio Briatore, one of the more colourful characters in the paddock. (LAT)

The Jordan factory HQ. (LAT)

With Damon Hill and Heinz-Harald Frentzen and the Jordan team during the 1999 season. Between them they won three of our four grands prix, and gave me some truly special memories. (PA Photos)

any other team, not even when we continued to struggle in 2002.

Whatever the reason – be it 9-11 or a general fall in confidence – an adjustment in the stock market meant it hit an all-time low. We were faced with a massive downturn in the economy. When that sort of thing happens, motor sport is usually among the last to be affected. That is because most contracts are in place and the money continues to flow, even when bad times are affecting the world outside. Conversely, when the market recovers, it takes a while for the money to filter back into motor sport.

In our case, we were hurt sooner than our rivals because we rarely had long-term contracts in place from the outset. B&H, for example, could not commit themselves because of the continuing issues over tobacco advertising. We were hit very hard financially and, at the same time, Dominic Shorthouse was leaving Warburg Pincus to set up his own business, which meant I was unsure of the level of support we could expect from our equity partner. They could see that the market had turned and the value of the team was no longer what it was. We were no longer in the £120 million range. It would be a matter of managing the downside.

It was proving increasingly difficult to find sponsors. Benson & Hedges were staying with us but not increasing the financial value of their support. I consulted with Warburg Pincus. Looking at our forecast and setting this against the escalating level of salaries we were now paying to stop our people from going elsewhere, it was clear that I had no alternative but to reduce the staff level from 265 to 200. That was a very harsh and difficult judgement to make. I had never faced this sort of thing before. It had to be drastic and across the board, each department being asked to make a sacrifice. Along the way, we lost Trevor Foster and Lindsay Haylett. It was a desperate time, but it was either this or close the team.

I knew that other companies were in similar trouble and I wanted to avoid, at all costs, the messy ending that would affect one particular British-based team when the doors were closed and loyal members of the workforce, never mind outside suppliers, were owed money. The 50 people we made redundant received a package that was above the prescribed financial level. In most cases, they found work with teams such as BAR and Toyota, who were expanding. Some started their own satellite sub-assembly businesses. Some, from the Antipodes, decided it was time to return home. Considering the difficulties and the pain involved, particularly for people who had devoted much of their working lives to Jordan, this went as smoothly as it was reasonable to expect. I would like to think that it contributed to the fact that, in all my time as a team owner, I never once received a letter from a disgruntled member of staff.

As the team was reduced in size, one welcome addition was Gary Anderson, who returned to become Director of Race and Test Engineering. This was the sort of role that I knew Gary enjoyed. Eghbal Hamidy had left and Gary would work with both Henri Durand, the ex-McLaren man, who would be Director of Design and Development, and our stalwart from the engineering department, John McQuilliam. As you would expect, Gary found that he was returning to a team that had changed in many respects. Reading between the lines, I could tell he was not impressed with a car that, by the time he arrived in December 2001, was well under way.

At least one known quantity was Giancarlo Fisichella, who returned to us in place of Jarno Trulli, who had gone to take Fisi's place at Renault. Takuma Sato was on the driver strength, of course. Eyebrows continued to be raised, particularly when Taku seemed to spend more time off the road than on it during the early part of the 2002 season, but he was an absolute hero at the final race in Japan, where he produced a fantastic drive into fifth place. Taku was a legend in Japan and the two points earned that day allowed us to leapfrog into sixth place in the Constructors' Championship, overtaking two teams. One of them was BAR-Honda, which I found particularly satisfying. That result saved Sato's career. It also ensured that Honda insisted he drive for BAR the following season, which was a sign that Jordan might no longer have Honda engines.

BAT had continued to put Honda under a lot of pressure, and there was an additional complication. BAT, for reasons I could never understand, were against Benson & Hedges, even though Gallaher and BAT were under the same ownership umbrella. In a market place such as Australia, how could BAT ignore the fact that, due to the many Anglo-Irish connections, Jordan were popular there? How could they dismiss the marketing expertise and style of B&H combined with Jordan? Melbourne was of very little value to Gallaher because they did not own a brand in Australia. However, BAT owned a brand and yet they would not contribute in any shape or form to our budget, and neither would they use us for entertaining.

Every year we had to request them, on bended knee, to use B&H there. That was how ridiculous it had become. Here was a free offer to make use of a brand that they already had. I do not know why the chief executives of public companies could not have said, 'Hang on. You, Gallaher, are paying Jordan. Thank you very much for that. Let's use that and we will return the compliment in some other way, somewhere else.' It happens in other sports when various brands work together. How could these great companies not work with each other when they knew each other so well? The bottom line was that BAT did not want to help us because, in the end, that would possibly contribute to Jordan being even more successful than their team, BAR-Honda. At least, that's how it seemed to me.

It was clear from my conversations with Hirotoshi Honda that this would be a difficult decision. Honda knew that BAR had all the facilities, and yet they could not manage to win a race. I always felt that BAR never had what I would call real passion. The team had no history and did not seem to possess a racing soul. Now the call was out to have the Jordan thorn removed from their side.

I went to see Honda in Japan and told the new president, Takeo Fukui, that they could not end our association. We had a great deal of support from Mr Kawamoto, the legendary former president, and Fukui understood that Honda had history with Jordan. We had won races together. Honda's ideal game plan seemed to be the eventual ownership of BAR but, in the meantime, they wanted to continue supporting Jordan. Yet I had the feeling that all was not well and we were about to be axed. That was all well and good, but I had a contract that said otherwise.

There was confusion over the structure of this contract. One view was that it was for two years with an option for a further three; the other was the reverse, three years with a two-year option. I believed it was three plus two, but the Japanese version of the contract favoured the other interpretation. We had been together as a works team for two years. I told them that, contractually, they could not leave us.

Honda said they would contribute towards an engine for 2003 even though, at that stage, we were unsure which engine that might be. I told them that I felt that I had no alternative but to seek legal advice because I wanted to stay with Honda. No matter how hard I tried, I could not win. The feeling I came away with was that a deal had already been done with BAT.

They treated me impeccably. We reached a very generous settlement. To allow Honda to give up one year of our contract and further options, we would receive $22 million that had to be used towards future engine contracts. It was a huge figure and I should have been grateful. However, we wanted to win races and there was no doubt in my mind that the way forward should have been with Honda. A very happy and successful era had ended.

Meanwhile, another reminder of how difficult and sad 2001 had been came in November with the news that George Harrison had succumbed to cancer. George, a motor-racing fan, would frequently hang out in our motorhome. I was delighted that he should want to do that and it was only after a period of time that I realised he must have been drawn to us because of his Irish background. It turned out that his maternal grandparents were from the same village that Marie and John Lydon came from in County Wexford. His father's lineage could be traced back to County Sligo. Whatever the reason was, we got on famously. Marie and I often visited his house in Henley-on-Thames, particularly if he was recording in his studio there. Our families spent Christmas and New Year together and we visited George and Olivia at his place on Hamilton Island on our way to the grand prix in Australia. George had suffered for some time with cancer but that did not detract from the terrible sense of loss.

One of my greatest thrills had been introducing George to *Riverdance* when the Irish step-dance show made its debut in London. *Riverdance* had exploded on the scene as the interlude entertainment during the 1994 Eurovision Song Contest and I had been asked to take care of 20 VIP tickets for the show in Hammersmith. As well as George and Olivia, I also invited Nick and Annette Mason, Bernie and his wife, Slavica, Mike and Angie Rutherford, Piers Brosnan, Flavio Briatore and Christina Estrada, and the Danish supermodel, Helena Christensen.

The music for *Riverdance* was a captivating and emotional sound that was sweeping the world. I was sitting beside Helena Christensen and I was surprised to see that she was fiddling with her mobile phone during the performance. I thought she must be bored. It was only later that I discovered Helena had called her flat in Paris and recorded the show on her telephone answer machine just in case there was no DVD available. That summed up a wonderful Irish performance that said so much for the emergence and acceptance of the Celtic culture. I remember hoping at the time that Jordan Grand Prix would be able to do their bit on the racetrack. Certainly, that had come to pass in 1998 and 1999, but what would 2003 hold?

Chapter 42

# WINNING AND LOSING

It was typical that we should win a grand prix at the start 2003 and finish the year near the bottom of the championship. Jordan never did things by halves. Before we could do anything, however, we had to find another engine. Various opportunities presented themselves but Cosworth seemed to be the only choice, although my relationship with Ford was to plummet before the end of the first year of our two-year relationship. By moving from Honda, I found that I had gone from one extreme to the other. There could be no comparison, and that was indicative of a very difficult season, probably the blackest of my time in F1.

We were hurting badly because of the shortage of manpower and yet, as ever, the team worked wonders to have three new cars ready for the first race in Australia. Sitting in one of them was Ralph Firman Junior. It was actually quite a tight fit because Ralph was tall and gangly. Even though, in my experience, tall drivers had never been successful in one of our cars, I was very keen to give Ralph his chance for a number of reasons. Nigel Northridge had wanted Eddie Irvine, who was not happy at Jaguar, and we also tried to sign Felipe Massa. In the end, we opted for Firman. He had been successful in the nursery formula before following in the steps of famous names, many of them Jordan drivers, by winning the Formula Nippon championship in Japan.

Along with just about everyone in motor sport, I knew and respected his father, Ralph, and his mother, Angie, who was from Naas in Ireland. I felt very attached to that family, as did many young drivers who had beaten a path to Ralph's door at Van Diemen, the ultra-successful manufacturer of racing cars for the junior formulae. Ralph always liked to help Irish drivers in particular and, since his son had an Irish passport, it was good to be able to return the favour.

Ralph Junior was a delightful, caring man but caring, kind people rarely win grands prix. He had a very tough time with mechanical failures in two of the first three races, and just when it looked as though things might be coming together, he had a sizeable shunt during practice in Hungary. While he was recovering, Hungarian driver Zsolt Baumgartner came in, but when Ralph returned, the momentum seemed to have been lost. This was a bitter disappointment. I thought it would work and, now that the business market was rebuilding confidence, we might have been able to tap into Irish industry in particular.

One of the problems Ralph had to deal with was comparison with Fisichella in the other car. That was never easy and became more difficult as Giancarlo's confidence and natural ability blossomed when he finally won his first grand prix, albeit under the most bizarre circumstances in Brazil.

Giancarlo qualified eighth at Interlagos but grid positions became largely irrelevant when it poured – as it can only in Brazil – on race day. The start was delayed and the opening laps eventually run behind the safety car. We figured that, if the weather persisted and the conditions remained so hazardous, they would stop the race at three-quarter distance. If it was stopped before then, half points would be awarded, and knowing the officials as I did, my gut feeling was that they would prefer to have the race count in full rather than mess around with half points. Trying to second-guess people such as Charlie Whiting and Herbie Blash was not difficult. They were hardened, professional racers.

Our plan was to stop early and carry just enough fuel to get us to lap 54, three-quarter distance. If the race ran its full course, we would lose but, applying the law of averages to our usual practice of taking a gamble, it might turn in our favour. As had happened in

France in 1999, going against the perceived logic of the front runners was the only way we could beat them. Giancarlo was the first driver to stop and refuel and he rejoined next to last.

The conditions, if anything, got worse. Cars were spinning and crashing all over the place, and the pit lane was a busy place as cars came and went. The safety car appeared twice more. Giancarlo kept running. By lap 40, he was sixth. Then he was fifth when Alonso's Renault made a pit stop, fourth when Barrichello's leading Ferrari retired, and third when Ralf Schumacher stopped his Williams. The race looked like going to David Coulthard until he almost ran out of fuel and had to come in to the pits on lap 52. Now we were second and closing on Kimi Raikkonen's leading McLaren. It was lap 54 and, in a crucial move, Giancarlo passed Raikkonen just before the end of the lap. The track was beginning to dry and the Michelin wet-weather tyres were losing their edge. The race was at the point where we hoped it might end. Then all hell broke lose.

Mark Webber crashed heavily coming on to the pit straight. With debris all over the place, the safety car was deployed yet again. At the same time, Alonso came over the blind brow at the start of the straight and smashed into Webber's wreckage. There was no alternative but to bring out the red flag, stop the race and declare a winner. But who?

We were certain it was Giancarlo. McLaren felt sure it was Raikkonen, even though he was heading for the pits when the red flag was shown. The situation was made more complicated by the so-called 'count-back' rule that said results should be settled on the order two laps before that on which the race is red-flagged. In our view the red flag was shown on lap 56, so the order should be taken at the end of lap 54. For some reason, the timing people handed the officials the order at the end of lap 53. Everyone went to the podium – and the trophy was handed to Raikkonen.

Gary insisted that we should ask the officials to re-examine the printouts, but they said they did not have the relevant detail. In fact, we were able to provide the evidence. Back at the factory, Mark

Cormican, our excellent IT guy, had devised a way of downloading the timing pages during the race. We put the relevant information on a CD and sent it to Charlie Whiting.

There was now no doubt about the result but it was not until the following Friday that Fisichella was declared the winner, too late to have the Irish national anthem played on the podium and too late to give Giancarlo due credit for a beautiful drive. He had stayed on the road in atrocious conditions on a day when Michael Schumacher, on the same Bridgestone tyres, and several other leading lights had either spun or crashed. In a small ceremony at the next race, at Imola, McLaren and Raikkonen sportingly handed over the trophy. It was not the same, of course, but that did not detract from the fact that we had employed a clever piece of strategy on a crazy day in Brazil.

Unfortunately, his first victory did not help persuade Giancarlo to stay. I think he had made up his mind early on that he was treading water and he was looking for an alternative. He was determined to go. I would be sorry to lose such an extremely talented driver who had a very nice way with him. Marie and I had spent great holidays with Giancarlo and his wife-to-be, Luna, and their kids. Yet, somehow, things had changed since Giancarlo's previous spell with the team. He had grown up in some respects, become harder. I was to do the same after seeing the unpleasant side of Jordan's relationship with Ford, or, to be accurate, one person in particular.

Richard Parry-Jones was Ford's group vice president of global product development and chief technical officer. He was responsible for, among other things, Cosworth, Jaguar and Ford's F1 programme. Ford had bought into F1 by paying Jackie Stewart for his team, which seemed a strange thing to do since they had helped fund it in the first place. Stewart-Ford had been renamed Jaguar and Parry-Jones helped to fund it by using money raised by the sale of Cosworth customer engines.

Coincidentally, F1 was going through one of its periodic tugs-of-war over who controlled what. On this occasion, manufacturers including Ford and Mercedes had threatened to run a breakaway championship known as the GPWC. Part of the negotiating process to stop this happening included an agreement, signed by the manufacturers, that they would supply independent teams, such as Jordan, with engines costing no more than 10 million Euros each for a season. In return, they would be allowed to keep much of the advanced technology that the governing body wanted to ban on the grounds of cost saving. Whatever the reason behind it, the 10 million Euro engine sounded good to me.

At Imola in the spring of that same year, I had an exploratory meeting with Norbert Haug, the competitions boss of Mercedes. We had discussed the possibility of having customer Mercedes engines for the following season, 2004. It was an interesting proposal. Mercedes owned Smart and they were wondering how best to promote this range of small cars. The plan was to badge our engines 'Smart' and, as part of the deal, we would provide a drive for the McLaren-Mercedes B List driver Gary Paffett. It was a neat plan that would be inexpensive for us and provide us with a good engine.

We went so far as to produce drawings for the Jordan-Smart and outline a plan. Smart saw Jordan as the perfect partner, a sort of wacky outfit in keeping with their image. Mercedes liked it because their chairman, Jurgen Huppert, could tell his board that not only were Mercedes supporting another team, they would be earning money and, at the same time, promoting one of the company's other brands. Everyone would be a winner.

In late July, at Silverstone, Huppert came to see me and asked why I had not told him that we had a contract with Ford for 2004. In fact, we had a contract with release options and I pointed out that a get-out clause would shortly come into force. Ford, who did not know about the Mercedes option, were delaying settling on a deal for 2004 in the hope that, late in the day, we would have no alternative, by which time they could ask for, not 10 million Euros, but 18 million Euros. I told Huppert there would be no difficulty in switching to the Mercedes/Smart engine and proved it by showing him the relevant part of the Ford contract at the next race at Hockenheim.

Meanwhile, Parry-Jones was under pressure from Ford in Detroit. The Jaguar team were haemorrhaging money, looking unlikely to win a race and paying Eddie Irvine $10 million a year. Jaguar had the best technology but the team seemed to lack passion and commitment. Parry-Jones had responded to none of my letters. I would reach a new level of blasphemy when I found out just what Parry-Jones had been up to behind the scenes.

On race day at Hockenheim, Huppert told me that Mercedes would be unable to do a deal for the supply of engines. I was informed that Parry-Jones had threatened to pull Ford out of the GPWC and hasten its possible collapse if the remaining manufacturers did not agree to Ford supplying all of the independent teams with engines, and not at 10 million Euros each. The manufacturers, in a captive position, agreed. Our deal with Mercedes had been scuppered by Ford's tactics.

I wrote to Irish Prime Minister Bertie Ahearn, to Max Mosley and to Massimo Monti of the EU and now Italian prime minister. I took legal proceedings against Ford, which were still ongoing in 2007. The irony was that Ford, a stalwart of the GPWC, were the first to pull out. Parry-Jones gave me seven minutes' notice before announcing to the world in September 2004 that Ford would be quitting F1. It was a terrible way for my relationship with Ford to end. I had dealt originally with Martin Whitaker and Martin Leech, two proper and honourable men, both of whom were racers and whose business methods and understanding were flawless. I could not say the same for Richard Parry-Jones, nor for David Haines, a representative of Vodafone.

I first met Haines in 2001. We made contact with Vodafone when it became clear that the telecommunications company was interested in F1. I had been to their headquarters in Dusseldorf to make a presentation. The timing was right because Benson & Hedges were thinking of winding down due to tobacco agreements and pressure from governments. Vodafone was attractive because they were looking for title sponsorship. On the one hand, B&H were not keen to accept a secondary role; on the other, they did not want to stand in our way. That was a measure of the rapport and friendship between the two sides. Unfortunately, there would be no danger of that with Vodafone after developments with Haines, their global brand director.

We knew that other teams were in the mix, notably Ferrari, McLaren and Benetton/Renault, but we were hopeful because we knew we could meet Vodafone's wish to have title sponsorship and a red car. Negotiations had gone back and forth until the early evening of 22 March 2001. That was when I received a phone call from Haines saying the deal was ours. We believed we had a three-year contract worth $150 million.

On 25 May, Ferrari announced that they had a three-year deal with Vodafone. We claimed damages from Vodafone for breach of contract. It led to a hearing presided over by the Honourable Mr Justice Langley in the Royal Courts of Justice in August 2003. We lost our case. In fact, we came out if it badly, Mr Justice Langley saying in his summing up that our claim was false and some of our evidence fanciful.

Haines never denied the conversation. It was a conference call and Ian heard it all. Haines said, 'You've got the deal.' Vodafone claimed that Haines was not empowered to agree to any sponsorship deal and, in any case, the judge found it difficult to accept that a phone call, involving such large amounts of money, could constitute a contractually legally binding agreement. As I have said before, this was the way it worked in Formula 1. Did I have an actual contract in place when I did the deals with DHL, Deutsche Post and Benson & Hedges? No, I did not. We always did everything on a handshake initially. Perhaps the lesson was that F1 needed to change its ways in that respect.

We had done all the preparatory work, most of which had been agreed to the point where, when Haines said we had a deal, I knew exactly what that meant in F1 terms. I have no doubt that Vodafone, encouraged I believe by Bernie Ecclestone, then changed their minds in favour of secondary sponsorship with Ferrari. Perhaps wrongly, I chose to pursue this.

It was my first time in court. I was there every day and I found being cross-examined by a skilful QC the most harrowing experience of my life. Some people are used to it; I was not. Haines was very plausible in court. The defence ran rings round us and the conclusion of the court was very damaging.

I could not get my head round the decision. I rode my bike back to Oxford and stopped at The Perch, a small pub by the river. I sat for some time, watching the water and asking myself where I had gone wrong. Perhaps I made a mistake going to court, but it is not my style to give up. Perhaps I thought Vodafone would make an offer because they knew what had happened. But Haines had been very convincing in court. I had to face defeat.

I was upset for Ian because the judge had been very harsh about us both. Ian was an employee who had done what he thought was right. He knew every detail of the case and offered to stand strong in court and confirm his memory of the facts. I have never known a more strong-willed or loyal member of the team. We were both devastated. I believed it was a fully binding contract. However, as I've said, the judge found it difficult to accept that this was the way it usually worked.

In our view, everything was in place. The title sponsorship had been agreed, the colour of the car and the artwork completed. Everything had been presented and discussed prior to the phone call. There was never a question in my mind that we had the deal. I truthfully believed what we had agreed.

If Haines had come to us and said, 'Eddie, look, I've made a mistake. I'm going to go with Ferrari but I'll do a small deal with you with some of our sub-contractors or another brand,' everyone would have been happy. I felt I had to follow it through in court. Would I do it again? Despite the hardships caused, yes I would. Who knows, perhaps at some time in the future I will meet senior people from Vodafone and we can lay this unhappy episode to rest.

Life is about experiences. Now I can say I have been to the High Court and I know what it is like to get a pasting. I am not afraid to talk about it or to mention it. There have been no repercussions in any of the business dealings I have had subsequently. I wrote and explained everything to our existing sponsors. Every single one stood by us.

## Chapter 43

# SLIPPING AWAY

Our media kit for the 2004 season was cleverly designed in the shape of a cover for a vinyl long-playing record. The introduction said 2004 marked the start of a fight back for one of the very few privateer teams left in a sport dominated by motor manufacturers.

In the eyes of some outside the team, this amounted to no more than brave talk. They thought the Vodafone affair would have brought us to our knees. Not in the least. The media kit noted 21 sponsors – Benson & Hedges, in our ninth and final season together, headed the list – and I was about to add a 22nd sponsor, arguably the most significant in terms of novelty and value for money.

I had become friendly with Crown Prince Salman, having met him a number of times at grands prix when we offered him the use of our motorhome because, typically, there was nowhere for the Prince and his staff to go in the paddock as they learned more about F1. At Monza, the Prince said he knew how tough things were for small teams and he would make a few phone calls to see if he could help.

The next time I saw him was at Zuma restaurant in London, where he tapped me on the shoulder as I was paying my bill. He said he had something to discuss and I should meet him for breakfast the following morning. I had been giving him credit for plans to bring a grand prix to Bahrain in 2004, saying it was unique for a country to be supporting motor sport with the sort of enthusiasm he had shown. Now we had an idea to extend that further.

I had been involved on the fringe of a deal to bring the world-renowned College of Surgeons from Dublin to set up a satellite in Bahrain. The humanitarian aspect was close to Prince Salman's, and particularly his mother's, heart and I suggested a scheme that was not simply sponsorship but a method of extending his country's reputation for compassion, involving a vision that could be changed every two weeks. I suggested that he use the engine cover on our cars to feature a different charity at each race, representing a cause that would be chosen by a key figure from the host country. He liked the idea.

On the weekend of the Grand Prix in Bahrain, I felt like Jackie Stewart must feel as I looked after dignitaries attending a function hosted by Prince Salman. I used the occasion to ask Prince Albert which charity he would choose for display on our car at Monaco. Similarly, I asked Prince Andrew which cause should benefit when we ran in Britain later in the year, and he said he would consult with his sister, the Princess Royal.

The charities eventually ranged from children, to cancer, to AIDS/HIV, as supported by Nelson Mandela and signified on the car by his prison number, 46664. This was the first time space on a car had been funded by one country for other country's use. It was magnanimous, sporting and, strategically, a very clever move as Bahrain extended the hand of charity and peace beyond their border by supporting these charities abroad.

We had an outstanding evening when the race team was invited to dinner on board HMS *Grafton*, a Type 23 frigate deployed in the Persian Gulf. You can imagine Marie and me walking up the gangplank to a full naval welcome. The United States and British ambassadors were on board, along with an admiral of the US Navy. Having received permission to fly the White Ensign after sunset, we watched as the flag was furled with due ceremony later in the evening by the US admiral. It was wonderful recognition for the team to be asked to be a part of this. We were treated brilliantly – too well, in fact. To say that the measures of gin were generous would be an understatement. I finished the evening playing the spoons while standing on a table in the officers' mess. They loved it, I think. The officers said that this had to be the first time in the history of the Royal Navy that an Irishman had stood on a table in the mess and let rip with Irish republican songs.

The media kit did not carry the name of Gary Anderson. He had left at the end of 2003 and that blow was made doubly difficult because we did not have the funds for a replacement. John McQuilliam faced the almost impossible task of pulling the engineering and design side together and he was helped by some fantastic people who were sticking with us, including Mike Wroe, the electronics genius who had got us out of many difficulties in the past, and Tim Edwards, who had worked his way through the ranks of mechanics to become team manager, his place as chief mechanic being taken by Andy Stevenson. Richard O'Driscoll, meanwhile, had become Chief Operating Officer in 2003. This was going to be a hard slog for all of them.

The green light for the new car could not be given until November, because of the shortage of money, and this impossibly late start had a massive knock-on effect all the way through the season. It started at Melbourne, the EJ14s arriving there having done only a handful of laps beforehand. That desperate situation was made worse by tyre development having progressed during the winter and we had no experience of it.

We had signed Nick Heidfeld to drive for us, a move that helped us both because his career was on hold after a disappointing few years with Sauber, and we could not afford to pay him. It turned out to be a happy compromise. We also signed Giorgio Pantano, an Italian with incredible credentials from racing in F3000. Giorgio was a bit wild at first. He settled down eventually, but not before we had to 'rest' him in Canada because of a dispute – which had nothing to do with us – between his family and manager over payment of sponsorship money. His place was taken by Timo Glock, who went on to finish sixth and join the long list of Jordan and ex-Jordan drivers who had scored at least one point in their first grand prix.

Glock had been doing great work as a test driver on the Friday of each grand prix – and that amounted to most of the testing we would do during the year. That's how bad things were. We finished the season next to last with five points. Under the circumstances, our drivers, particularly Nick, had done a tremendous job.

I wish I could say the same for the engine, Cosworth having to run a low specification to stop the V10 from blowing up. We reckoned it was about 70bhp below the engine used by Jaguar, but Cosworth were more concerned about avoiding failures. They didn't want Cosworth engine failures to be seen on television because the company was up for sale. So, for that matter, was Jordan.

Money was becoming more and more difficult to come by. Dominic Shorthouse's replacement at Warburg Pincus, Joe Schull, a top corporate banker, did not have quite the same enthusiasm for motor racing. Dominic had used contacts fantastically well. It is important to know who to see and to understand the deals that are happening. You cannot simply cruise in and cruise out of the occasional race. Joe did not have the same feel for the race team, which did not help when he looked at numbers that were not great.

I did not want to lose Warburg Pincus. They had an excellent image as one of the best private equity houses but, if the opportunity arose to sell on, I decided I would take it and, just before the start of the 2004 season, the Warburg Pincus 49.9 per cent stake in the team was bought by Merrion Capital. I was aware that perhaps the time had come to sell the team as a whole.

I had to look in the mirror and ask where the team was going and could it ever win in its present state? The answer, as we sat parked at the end of the paddock, alongside Minardi, was patently 'No'. Toyota were into their stride, writing cheques; Honda were spending huge sums and about to buy all of BAR; BMW were showing interest in buying Sauber. We did not have anything like that amount of money. There was a chance that we might get lucky, but

I was not prepared to wait another four years for a win. As it stood, Jordan had no chance of being successful.

In the meantime, we had to find a replacement after being left high and dry in such a scandalous manner in September 2004 by the Ford Motor Company and its representative, Richard Parry-Jones. Fortunately, we had built up a relationship at team meetings with John Howett and Mr Tomita of Toyota. They had been in F1 for almost three seasons by this stage and it was fair to say that they had been struggling to achieve the expected results. Toyota had a very good budget and they remained a team doing things their way – but in Germany. I had always thought it was a mistake to set up the F1 operation in Cologne, where their rally operation had been established many years before. My feeling was that Toyota should have come to the UK, a country with a much better motor-racing infrastructure and a culture established over decades of success in F1 and just about every other formula you can think of.

John was not a racer as such, but a very stylish businessman who understood the commercial implications. He may not have had what you might call hard-core motor-racing experience, but I found him to be a caring man who was willing to listen, even though, at the time, Toyota were not really in a position to supply engines.

Nonetheless, negotiations with Toyota, through no one's fault, took us right up to the deadline. Ian and I had arranged to meet Tomita-San and Howett in their office at Suzuka at 9 a.m. on the Saturday morning of the 2004 grand prix. Unfortunately, this coincided with the arrival of a hurricane that caused practice and qualifying to be cancelled. When we reached the paddock half an hour early, the place was locked and full of water. The only person we could find was the security man at Sauber and he kindly made us a cup of coffee.

When Howett and Tomita arrived, they explained that a decision had not yet been made in Japan regarding the supply of a second team. They asked us to wait, so Ian and I hung around in the storm with nothing to eat or drink. At around midday we were finally summoned and told that the answer was yes. There was still a lot of detail – such as cost – to be sorted but, appropriately on such a wild, wet day, we had been thrown a lifeline. Ironically, if everyone concerned had not been forced to have a day off, the deal might never have been done. Red Bull and Minardi had also been lobbying Toyota and, as it was, we only managed to sort the final detail on the afternoon of the November deadline.

Toyota understood the cost situation; it would not be as expensive as the Cosworth deal and we would be receiving a comprehensive service. I was very impressed because, in truth, Toyota could have done without having to supply a second team. However, it meant that we could plan from a racing point of view in the short term. Now I could focus on the long-term future of the team as a whole.

The paradox was that the arrival of large manufacturers, such as Toyota, had meant less sponsorship being spread among the smaller teams. Blue-chip companies, such as Panasonic, were being lured into associations with major manufacturers because they had more to offer. My feeling was good luck to them. If I were in their position, I would have done exactly the same.

I had begun to feel disillusioned for the first time ever because, whichever way I looked at our situation, there was no way Jordan could win another race. When we had won in the past, we did it by designing, building, developing, testing and racing our own car. Now I could see the writing on the wall. It was beginning to look as if the small teams could exist only by running a car provided by a major manufacturer. How could that small team ever expect to win a race with control from a manufacturer's team being exerted over them?

I did not want to race in F1 without the hope and dream of being successful. It seemed that the GPWC had killed that dream. Despite the manufacturers signing an agreement in April 2003 to supply engines for 10 million Euros, this was not happening because the GPWC appeared to be circumventing FIA rules. The day of the constructor appeared to be over as more and more manufacturers began seeing private teams as an outlet for their old cars and a means for developing young drivers for the bigger teams. That would not be Jordan's way. I am an optimist by nature but reality seemed to be setting in. I was getting older but was I losing the bit of bottle I had always had? Was I choking?

I hoped I was doing neither. Circumstances had changed. My priority now was to protect my family, and the staff and suppliers who had been so loyal. The last thing I wanted was to be a bankrupt hero. I somehow needed to ensure a future for Jordan. It had been costing me nearly half a million dollars a month to keep the team going during the final third of 2004. I cannot say I was a poor man. Nonetheless, I did not want to see a free fall of cash into something that was uncertain, and would continue to be that way unless steps were taken to secure the team's future.

This was turning out to be a traumatic year. In July, we had been stunned by the news that John Boy had died of a heart attack. He had been running the Minardi team, spending most of his time with Louise Goodman, living in Faenza where the team was based. While Paul Stoddard may have owned the team, it was John Boy who used all his experience and charm to make it work and look after the day-to-day running on a shoestring.

In the mad rush to get from the French to the British Grand Prix, the teams had agreed to take part in an F1 demonstration on the streets of London, a hugely successful promotion that Bernie had asked me to become involved with as the link between the teams and Harvey Goldsmith, the promoter, and Mayor Ken Livingstone. John had collapsed on the evening of the demonstration and was rushed to St Thomas' Hospital. As we prepared to start practice on the Friday at Silverstone, we heard the shattering news that John had passed away.

The world of F1 was completely devastated. Given John Boy's time in the business, nearly everyone either knew him or had been touched by his presence. The funeral in Oxford was hugely emotional. Louise wanted to have it in England to allow his many friends to come together. The turnout was huge, as you would expect.

John Boy had adored the work of folk singer Finbar Furey. When they played his song 'Lonesome Boatman', it ripped everyone apart. I gave a short address, one of the most difficult things I have ever had to do. I had become consumed by the whole thing because there were so many great memories of John Boy running around in my head. I recalled all the things we had done together, the massive contribution he had made, the friendship we had, that wicked smile and the 'come-to-bed' eyes, the lovely sense of humour and the pure Irishness of the man. John had enjoyed a great life but to have a heart attack at the age of 47 seemed insufferably cruel. The loss was immense.

## Chapter 44

# SAYING GOODBYE

There were alternatives on the horizon. Interest had been expressed by Belgravia, an investment group set up by Duncan Hickman in 2000 after he and his partner had sold the successful hedge fund, Liberty Ermitage. The deal was that I would retain 20 per cent of the business and continue to manage it, which was perfect from my point of view. I would be responsible for 20 per cent of the debt. Instead of half a million a month, I would have to raise $100,000, which was easier to deal with. Belgravia would find the necessary capital to allow the team to continue. They had very good contacts, particularly in the Middle East, and word was that the company was a front for Sheikh Ahmed Bin Saeed Al Maktoum, the ruler of Dubai. The Emirates deal was a possibility.

Belgravia were already involved in motor sport, handling the management of Jenson Button among other things. I checked them out. They seemed to have a huge amount of revenue coming in and appeared to be a perfect partner. I was very comfortable about this. It would be a new Jordan and I would be able to go ahead with other plans, such as putting together a motor-sport museum in Ireland. Here was a company prepared to take on 80 per cent of the debt. This would be even better than any restructuring deal that I could do. I was pushing hard in this direction.

At the same time, interest came from both Slazenger and Christian Horner, who reputedly had support from family and friends and backing from Hong Kong Hutchison Wampao. Discussions continued for three or four months but, since Christian made it clear that

I would no longer be required if he took over, he found that the price remained high! Christian eventually ran the Red Bull team.

Kleinwort Benson had an offer on the table from a consortium in Australia but, while a lot of effort went into investigating all these potential buyers, none of the negotiations was happening quickly enough. One week was dragging into the next. Another month meant a request for another million, and we were heading towards Christmas, which is by far the worst time for any race team. Sponsorship has stopped, there is no money coming in and, in our case, Benson & Hedges were seeing out their contract, Nigel Northridge pledging £1 million from his sick bed. The tobacco gravy train was coming to a halt and yet we had to build a new car. That needed to go ahead because I felt there was a chance to do something useful now that the team had the Toyota engine. Yet, with each passing week, I had the feeling that things were beginning to spiral out control. We were in survival mode.

I was not panicking but I was not myself. This was not the Eddie Jordan I knew. For the first time in my life, I felt I was not in communication. I felt apprehensive. Normally, I would have had my finger on the pulse of the young driver market and I would have known all about the up-and-coming talent. At this particular point, I had no enthusiasm for any of the young drivers. Similarly, I had been good at finding ways of financing equipment, such as the wind tunnel and the autoclave, and yet I no longer had the resources to keep them running. Time was flying by, the debt was mounting and we appeared to be going nowhere. The Belgravia negotiations had dragged on for 11 months and then they announced a deal with McLaren – which ultimately never happened, just as their much-vaunted interest in Newcastle United some time later came to nothing.

I had a call from Bernie Ecclestone, asking me – no, telling me – to visit his office in Knightsbridge. He sat me down and spelled out his thoughts. 'I don't really care about you, Jordan,' he said. 'I have much more interest in your family and your team. I'm concerned that you are putting everything at risk without them knowing. Jordan has done remarkably well. It has surprised everyone, including me. You have brought great credit to yourself and to F1. But I don't want to see that go up in smoke.'

At first I was unsure whether he was blowing smoke up my backside, having fun or being serious. Then he got up and led me to the Playboy Room, so-called because of the magazine covers lining the walls. This is where I met Alex Shnaider for the first time. Bernie explained that this Russian-born Canadian was interested in the team. After an initial discussion, I went back to Bernie's that night for tea and we talked it over. In effect, he said beggars could not be choosers. He pointed out that I had been asking for television money in advance but he failed to see how that would save us. Quite often, Bernie would say such a thing in order to wind me up but this time I could tell from his expression that he was perfectly serious. He was not playing his usual game, particularly when he mentioned the undignified exits made by other down-at-heel teams in the past. He underlined what I had been thinking but did not care to admit. The bottom line was that if I continued as I was going, the team would probably collapse. I knew he was right.

Shnaider sent 12 representatives to Silverstone the next day. On the following Saturday, Ian and I met Colin Kolles, Shnaider's right-hand man in racing, and their sponsorship advisor, Christian Geisdorfer, in our office. A deal was concluded two days later.

The plan was to complete on, 23 December 2004 and I delayed my departure for a break in Barbados. Due diligence was executed and included with the sales and purchase agreement (SPA), the document that guides each party through the journey of sale. It is quite a complex process but, thanks to my banking experience, I understood most of it. I knew about the tax warranties and the litigation warranties and all of the different objectives. We agreed the detail of what was included, and what was not included. For example, my pieces of Irish art were to be excluded and I wanted the Jordan F1 cars for my planned Irish museum.

We did not finalise everything until 21 January 2005. I told the staff, which was an emotional experience because I was suddenly faced with the raw reality of what I had done. Richard O'Driscoll was the only member of management at any level who said he could not stay. He had joined Jordan and he could not see himself working for anyone else. I could understand that. I could also appreciate that Shnaider and his Midland group would not wish to keep the head of finance of the previous company. It was the end of era. Richard was a tough guy, who was prepared to stand up to me. It was black or white with Richard and I usually discovered that he was right. By Christmas 2004, he had come to terms with the fact that he would be leaving.

I had spoken to our suppliers and everyone on the staff and reiterated that their jobs were secure because that had been a key aspect of the negotiations. No one would be made redundant, at least up to a certain period because you cannot legislate for the future. Midland agreed to take on all the staff as well as promising that all the benefits or options would remain.

Above all, I was going to miss working with Ian Phillips. We had been involved in some incredible deals together. We would often reach a point where I would not need to say anything to Ian because he understood exactly and could have replied on my behalf. It was almost telepathic. I would make a point and then Ian would appear to contradict me by saying, 'Well, maybe we should look at it this way,' and give the impression that this had not been pre-arranged – when, of course, it had. Nigel Northridge would often come to the end of a negotiation, raise his hands and declare, 'We've just been had over by Bill and Ben. You boys are fleecing us again! Our trousers are round our ankles!'

When things got tough I would always ask Ian's opinion. Invariably, I would go along with what he said because he had a very sharp mind and a balanced outlook. He did not suffer fools gladly. In fact, he formed opinions very quickly, which could be either good or bad depending on whether he liked or disliked you. He could be extremely serious and 15 minutes later become the biggest party animal imaginable. There was just no knowing.

What I liked most was that he had a very good spirit, a lot of style, and he was intelligent. He came from a good background. I am not saying I understand a lot about wine, but Ian taught me all I know. We finally got him off the cigarettes and I was overjoyed to see that he stayed with the team when Midland took over. That was a very difficult time for him but, in 2005, the bonus for Ian was that he joined BBC Radio 5 Live and commentated so brilliantly on the races in an outstanding partnership with Maurice Hamilton. Ian loves radio and this was the perfect medium for him to exercise his incredible fund of knowledge and display a remarkable enthusiasm that has not dimmed in the slightest – and, believe me, there must have been times when I tested his patience and that enthusiasm to the absolute limit.

Meanwhile, there had been a major hiccough in terms of 'financial assistance', a term used in SPAs. It was not permitted to use certain assets to prop up parts of the business; the job had to be done with real money. Trucks, cars, motorhomes, land and the wind tunnel were no longer part of the deal. They would remain the property of Jordan Grand Prix with options for Midland to buy them at a later stage. As a result, the purchase figure was not as much as we had expected. Midland were buying the main factory and the team with all the necessary rights to go forward. However, as soon as proof of funding had been established, they could – and did – buy most of the remaining assets.

It was important to be sure that Midland could handle this on their own. The last thing they wanted was to have me around the place. It would have been bad for them and bad for me.

I had mixed feelings. On the one hand, I was extremely sad. On the other, I was glad the negotiations were over and the future of the team seemed to be assured. I had done all I could. The risks I had taken in the past, irrespective of how big they had been at the time, now seemed tiny compared to the uncertainty leading to this.

The timing was right. I had a contract, a sale, and a gradual earn-out in terms of its purchase. It was very satisfactory. In the end, the one item not purchased by Midland was our motorhome. Bernie bought that – as if to prove the old motor-racing adage that there is always a deal to be done. Now I had done my last deal in F1.

In February 2005, I went to Moscow with Schnaider and Kolles, who would effectively run the team in Alex's more or less continual absence. It was an extravagant affair with the car on show in Red Square. I thought it was significant that Bernie turned up. Bernie does not do things like that unless there is a reason. On this occasion, it amounted to the newcomers with Russian connections receiving Bernie's blessing. If he was playing F1 politics, Bernie was in the right place because the great and the good of the Politburo made an appearance. I am not sure if the relationship between Bernie and Schnaider remained as good as it was, but the trip to Moscow was a memorable one for me. That was appropriate because it was my last official function with what I had to accept was no longer a team known as Jordan Grand Prix.

## Chapter 45

# CLIC: ANOTHER LIFE

Adrian Reynard did me a great favour when he showed me the property we eventually bought in Oxford. As well as making a wonderful home, this house also brought us into contract with a neighbouring family who would have a major effect on our future.

Having previously lived in Westbury in the Buckinghamshire countryside, we were not accustomed to neighbours, but when Marie returned from Spain with Miki in 1988, she quickly got to know Suzi Usiskin, who lived across the road. As mentioned previously, Suzi was a magistrate and her husband Nick was a lawyer. They had three girls and a boy, very close in age to Zoë, Miki and Zak. We became great friends, so much so that we would regularly be invited to eat with them on a Friday and be part of their Jewish Shabbat family meal.

I was amazed to discover that Suzi had been born and brought up in Belfast. This must have been a bizarre situation for her – a Jew living in the middle of a country torn by ill feeling between Catholics and Protestants. Perhaps the understanding that grew from that about the Irish way of thinking helped cement our friendship. Certainly, we all became very close. We would use the gym together, go cycling and play tennis. The Usiskins came to our christenings and we attended their Bar Mitzvahs. Occasionally, I would attend the synagogue with the family.

During the course of all this, I met an extraordinary character, Rabbi Shmuel Boteach, an American-born Orthodox rabbi. He was the resident rabbi at Oxford and responsible for the L'Chaim Society, which I believe is now the second largest student organisation in Oxford's history. The lectures he organised attracted world figures, including Mikhail Gorbachev, Bill Clinton, Diego Maradona and Michael Jackson.

We had some very lively discussions, particularly when I got on to Irish politics and he started talking about the holocaust and Jewish ideals. It became quite heated on many occasions. I would be shouting and he would be roaring back at me. I tried to antagonise him as much as I could, but he was far too intellectual for me. I always felt he could have been an interesting match for the Reverend Ian Paisley.

My first experience of Oxford University from the inside was hearing him speak. The Union president asked me to do the same in the main hall of the student union. I thought, 'Jayzus, what am I going to say?' Obviously, they wanted me to talk about Formula 1, but I also wanted to do something different.

Rather than use a lectern, I chose to sit on a stool and have them bring me pints of Guinness. I felt like Irish comedian Dave Allen. In a way, that was the relaxed style I wanted to portray. I also decided not to talk for as long as expected, saying at the finish that I had a surprise in store. With that, the screen behind me was removed to reveal our band, ready to play.

It was amazing to see the effect on the audience. Having sat quietly, taking in every word about a sport that, clearly, they were passionate about, the students got to their feet and let go on what had now become a dance floor. It was not only one of the best gigs we have ever done, we were also creating a piece of history – no speaker at the Union had ever finished off in this way. In this case, the speaker, having talked at length to some of the most intellectual young people in Britain, had suddenly begun to act like an idiot while beating six bells out of a drum kit and playing songs with robust titles such as 'For Fuck's Sake I Can't Concentrate'. They had never seen anything like this before. It went down extremely well.

Suzi Usiskin was in the audience. By this stage, she had given up her magistrate's role to concentrate on charity work, a move that intrigued me. At one Bar Mitzvah, Suzi had introduced me to her uncle, a titled man who was also the Mayor of Cork. I simply could not believe it. There seemed no end to the extraordinary connections this woman had.

One day, Suzi asked if I would mind helping her out. The charity had been let down by someone who was due to visit and sign autographs. I had no hesitation in agreeing. In fact, I wondered why I had not done it before for such a worthwhile cause. I had heard of Cancer and Leukaemia in Childhood (CLIC) in relation to the suffering Barry McGuigan's daughter, Danika, had gone through, the same having affected Gary Lineker's son, George. This would be my formal introduction to the charity. I discovered how little I knew.

I had heard the term 'play nurse' before, but without really understanding what it meant. Now I was to learn at first hand that a play nurse becomes the child's absolute best friend. The child will confide in the play nurse and say things the parents would never hear because of the embarrassment involved. The play nurse becomes one of the most important aspects of the welfare of the child. In the process, they become incredibly close, which makes it very tough on the play nurse when, as often happens, the child dies. I do not know how play nurses do the job because it must rip them apart when a child does not make it. You have to be a certain calibre to do that job.

The CLIC nurses look after the medical care of the kids, particularly when monitoring the dreadful effects of chemotherapy. CLIC nurses are vital, but the play nurse has an equally important role, which also embraces dealing with the parents, helping them understand the medical treatment and consoling them if the worst comes to the worst.

All of this was new to me. With Suzi's help, I discovered more about the work done in the CLIC centre attached to John Radcliffe, the excellent teaching hospital in Oxford. Marie had been talking to me for some time about making a commitment to CLIC. Since I was still running the F1 team at the time, I did not feel I would be able to devote the necessary effort but I would do what I could to help raise money.

One of the various schemes that came along was a sponsored bike ride through the Negev desert from Tel Aviv to Elat, passing Petra along the way. That turned out to be a very emotional experience, going far beyond dealing with the physical effort involved. The party was made up of a variety of people – play nurses, doctors, care nurses, a couple of teenaged kids in remission, parents of children who were either ill or who had died. After the death of a child, the parents are usually surrounded by well-wishers who want to help, but that often stops after a couple of days. People tend to stay away for fear of intruding too much, or maybe they cannot handle the pain, or do not wish to understand it. Many bereaved parents need to be with people who understand. Talking to some of them ripped me apart. It is so difficult to know what to say when you have been blessed with four healthy children of your own.

Miki had suffered from very bad asthma but we were fortunate to be able to take her to Spain where the warm climate helped ease the problem. There is always an upside to everything and that period in Sotogrande allowed Miki to become fluent in Spanish and add this to the French and Italian learned while she studied at Marlborough.

What must have been a wonderful period as a student at Trinity College, Dublin, included an Erasmus Year that took Miki to Nice and Turin. Three of the months in Italy were spent working at Juventus and this, added to work experience with our team and with the Marlboro hospitality people at the grands prix, encouraged Miki's love of sport. After completing her degree in the summer of 2006, Miki spent three months in the Ryder Cup office helping to put together one of Ireland's most successful sporting events. After that, she spent two months running two events at the Asian Games in Doha.

Miki was a prefect at school and pretty much a model pupil, unlike her elder sister. Zoë was captain of the hockey team at

Marlborough and only just managed to keep her place at the school after the headmaster did not take kindly to having this lively pupil moon at him from the back window of a bus. Zoë was full of surprises, not least when she completed a business degree and chose to go into the banking world. Two years as a bond trader with HSBC in New York led to Zoë being headhunted by Credit Suisse to run a pan-European equity desk in London.

As often happens, all four children are very different, the only common denominator being that none of them has any interest in working in motor racing. Zak, who is tall, like his mother, was approached by Storm to do model work but he preferred to go to Quebec and earn his licence as a snowboard teacher. That helped him become the Irish universities freestyle snowboard champion while at UCD. Zak also played for the Ireland B Lacrosse team, a sport that people think is just for women but which, believe me, is tough as hell.

Our youngest boy has been known as 'Killer', almost from his first days at school because people are unfamiliar with Killian, the Irish version of Kyle. Kyle went to Stowe but avoided the trouble caused by Zak, who was caught breaking into the teacher's desk to find the key for the tuck box. Both boys like to do a deal where possible. When working with Marlboro and Benson & Hedges, we would have plenty of promotional samples lying around. In the early days, we would trade in packs of 200 for food at the village store. Latterly, Zak was reprimanded for selling cigarettes at school. I was upset that he had pinched them from our samples but quietly amused to note that he was selling them for above cost price, his reason being that it was due to market forces because the boys had little choice.

Kyle is rather like Zak, but with even more front. He loves being the centre of attention and you can never be sure what he is going to say next. One occasion springs to mind when Flavio Briatore came to dinner. Kyle appeared in the room to say goodnight and when introduced to Flavio, his immediate response was, 'You cheated!'

Suggestions were circulating at the time that the Benetton team had been engaging in dubious tactics.

Zak would not have had any takers for his cigarettes in the Negev. A cigarette was the last thing you wanted on a cycle ride across the desert. One guy, Des, was a complete pain in the arse. The organisers said to me, 'Look Eddie, there's no one here really strong enough to handle this guy. Can you do anything with him?'

I made a point of cycling with Des, a tough-looking bloke who had more tattoos than I had ever seen on one person. My language can be colourful from time to time but I was a complete novice compared with him. I needed to understand why he was there if he hated the ride and everyone associated with it, and discovered that he was from Newcastle and his friend from Birmingham had simply said, 'We're off on a bike ride. And you're coming.' He had no idea where he was or what he was doing. All he knew was that he was doing it to support a friend whose family had suffered bereavement though leukaemia.

Part of the healing mechanism is to have the parents take turns in standing in front of everyone after dinner round the campfire and talk about their child. It can be a very emotional experience for everyone but it is a successful way to release feelings that otherwise get bottled up. Some of the parents or relatives are very strong; some of them are terribly upset.

You may ask why anyone should want to spend a week on a bicycle, in stinking hot weather and generally living rough. At many of our overnight stops, there was no running water, for example. It was very basic but that only seemed to strengthen the camaraderie. There were many plusses. I would never have visited extraordinary places such as the ancient settlement of Petra in Jordan, the only difficult bit being the steep climb out of the city. I was determined to get to the top – and just made it. You can imagine the effect the climb had on Des.

He was cursing, sweating and swearing. I used similar language to tell him to keep control of himself. I said some members of the party had to cope with enough grief without having to listen to him. Being aggressive was the only way of communicating. I could see him looking at me, trying to size me up.

I had no idea what his reaction might be. He could have jumped on me or smashed into me with his bike. He said nothing but it was clear from his expression that I was not his favourite person. Slowly, however, he began to come round. There was the feeling of being in this together when dealing with the difficult bits of desert where there was no option but to carry your bike in the heat. It was very hard indeed.

Des eventually admitted that this trip was worse than he could ever have imagined. I also discovered that he had spent more of his life inside jail than out. I wondered if I could persuade him to tell us a bit about his background. At first, he would not hear of it. Then, on the penultimate night, he agreed.

Des stood up and said that he had hated every minute in the beginning. However, listening to the various talks from the bereaved and the suffering, and seeing the kids in remission, had led to a change in his priorities. He said his story should be used as an indication that you must not do what he had done. He had made a mess of his life through violence and drink. He confessed that, as the days had gone by, he had begun to understand why his friend had cajoled him into coming.

Apart from finding out more about himself, Des also understood everything about CLIC. He vowed that he would spread the word about the charity and the kids it served. It was not the most articulate speech, but it did not need to be. It was from the soul, from the heart. Here was a man who did not realise he could be loved. He had never been involved in anything like this before. It was an amazing speech from a guy who had been so foul-mouthed and unpleasant just a few days earlier, and he had one more surprise.

We had a celebration on the last night when we reached Elat. This was our first opportunity to have a decent shower and start to get the sand out of our skin, a process that took weeks because the pores had been open for so long in the heat. We dressed up as best we could in the few half-decent clothes we had brought with us, and gathered for a party. Des stole the show with the best impersonation of Elvis Presley I have ever seen. I have been on many bike rides for charity but this was the best end-of-cycle party, thanks to Des.

Despite the hardships, I would recommend the ride across the desert to anyone. Sleeping under the stars in the Negev is an unbelievable experience. You feel ten times closer to the sky than anywhere else in the entire world. It is impossible to describe the feeling you get from seeing that vast expanse on a warm, still night, and at the end of it, money has been raised for a good cause.

Not long afterwards, I had a phone call from *Hello* magazine, saying they wanted to do a feature. I told them I was not interested in having photographers wandering around my home. Some time later, at one of the CLIC centres, I met Bryony, a gorgeous 15-year-old who was in remission. She called me and said, 'Look, *Hello* are happy to have me in a picture with you and I would really love to do it.' However, when they said they would double the price and give all the money to CLIC, I agreed, suddenly detecting the hand of Marie and Suzi behind this.

In the event, *Hello* did a good job at our house in Oxford. They spent lots of time on Bryony's make-up and she looked sensational. Her parents were present and we all went to Browns restaurant afterwards. I have never seen Bryony look so happy or radiant. When the pictures were published, she sent me a beautifully written letter.

A few months later, I had a phone call asking me to go to High Wycombe. It concerned Bryony and I had to be there. I arrived on my motorbike and went into a large room full of kids dressed in pink. They were singing R. Kelly's song 'I believe I can fly'. It was a celebration of the life of Bryony. She was in an open coffin in the centre of the room.

The effect of her death on everyone can be imagined. During the church service, they read out letters from Bryony to her teacher, to her CLIC nurse, to her play nurse, to her mother and her father. She had known what was coming but no one else, apart from her consultant, had a clue. The cancer had come back a million times more aggressively than before and she was gone, just like that.

I was devastated, and I was not alone. Bryony had touched many people. It is very important, when involved with a charity, to keep individual cases at arm's length and not get emotional. However, Bryony was different. Now that I was free from motor racing, she was to be the catalyst for our commitment to a very worthwhile campaign.

We had discovered that there was a dire need for funding in connection with University College London Hospital. UCLH is one of the largest paediatric oncology centres in the UK and over two-thirds of children are referred from outside Greater London, but there is nowhere close to the hospital for these children and their relatives to stay. Those receiving outpatient radiotherapy treatment often have to travel for up to four or five hours daily. Many children have to stay in the hospital for weeks or months, with family members trying to sleep in a chair alongside the bed in a ward. Essentially, families are separated for all that time although research has shown that children have a much better chance of survival if they can stay with their families. If what we referred to as a 'Home from Home' could be found nearby, the children could attend hospital every day and yet lead a more normal existence. The idea was to have a special room for each child and their relative.

I investigated the opportunity of buying three houses close together in north London, in the vicinity of London's University College Hospital. The new home will provide 15 family bedrooms with en-suite facilities, five self-catering kitchens and dining areas, two communal sitting areas, a children's playroom, TV and computer rooms for teenagers, a laundry and lift for disabled access. All the facilities offered will be free to families. The total cost of the project is £5 million – £2.5 million to purchase the site; £2 million for conversion costs; and £500,000 for furniture, fixtures and fittings. Marie and I committed ourselves to raising the money.

The timing was perfect because I was now in a position to put my mind to it and focus on how to find the funds. One of the first steps to was draw key figures on board, including Gary Lineker, Barry McGuigan and Keith Wood. They would be great ambassadors for the project, helping to demonstrate that leukaemia no longer kills 80 per cent of those who contract it. With investment, research and proper care from CLIC nurses and play nurses, the figure has been gradually falling to around 30 per cent, which is remarkable. In addition, we think the 'Home from Home' scheme will help children and parents tackle the illness mentally as well as physically. That has nothing to do with my fellow fundraisers or me. Due praise must be given to the NHS, which has been first class in terms of helping us get to grips with this problem. Our job is to raise the money.

One of the first things we did was organise a race meeting at Windsor. The owners gave us a Monday night free, with all the proceeds going to CLIC. I found sponsors for the races and we had a charity auction, run by Charlie Ross, unquestionably the best charity auctioneer I have ever come across. Rock'n'roll band Bogus Brothers contributed to a wild night. It was complete mayhem. People just did not want to go home at the end of a glorious summer evening.

About 80 VIPs attended, including many top sports people. Their unselfish actions proved to me yet again that while sports personalities are ridiculed from time to time about their excesses, they do not receive enough credit for the unbelievable things they do for charity. Australian cricketer Shane Warne and England players Freddie Flintoff and Kevin Pietersen turned up at a function in aid of CLIC. I find that sort of gesture so rewarding. Many sports people give up their valuable time. They are incredibly busy and yet they do it freely, with pride and pleasure.

It is important to say that we do not push CLIC. It is not a charity that requires us to browbeat prospective sponsors. When we organise a function, our guests buy a table and it is up to us to put on an amazing night that more than justifies the cost. One of my biggest thrills was raising £700,000 at La Dolce Vita Ball in December 2006.

The auction at Windsor raised a lot of money but the most poignant moment came when Bryony's mother said a few words. It was very soon after her daughter's death and I was blown away by how composed she was. She explained that, on the one hand, she was devastated. On the other, she had recognised that Bryony was very ill and, in the end, the way she had died was so elegant – if you can describe anyone's passing as elegant. We knew exactly what she meant. Inside, she felt huge sadness but massive pride as well. It was very moving.

We laid plans for another race meeting at Windsor in 2007 and this, combined with a summer La Dolce Vita Ball in the Royal Albert Hall in July, should help us reach the £5 million target for 'Home from Home'. There could be no better tribute to a beautiful girl who epitomised the battle being fought by so many brave young people.

## Chapter 46

# DRIVING WITH A DIFFERENCE

When I was growing up in Ireland, golf was not considered élitist. Anyone who wanted to play would turn up at a golf course and have a game; it was as simple as that. There were golf clubs all over the place, utilising anything from scrubland to downs beside the sea. Playing golf was as much a social phenomenon as anything else, the clubhouse being a meeting place and somewhere to have a drink, particularly in the days when the licensing laws were stricter than they are now and the pubs were closed more often.

My mum and dad were members of a seaside golf course in Bray and I was a junior member almost from the moment I was tall enough to swing a club. I have to confess that playing a round of golf was not my priority. My mother and father would tee off while I pretended to be playing with the juniors. I would finish early, steal the keys of my dad's car from his locker and go for a drive without him knowing.

We had a new Anglia Super, maroon with a cream top – very racey in the 1960s. The Ford had a 1200cc engine, which was too fast for me on the day that I lost control in a big way. Previously, I had got away with returning the car bearing the odd scratch mark, but not even I could explain away the fact that, this time, the car had been turned on its side on a twisting road near Powerscourt, which was used as a special stage on the Circuit of Ireland Rally.

Even though golf was not a top priority when I was in my teens, I was good enough to play off a single-figure handicap and qualify for the Leinster Junior Boys. My mum and dad were quite proud of me playing at that level. I found it came effortlessly. Racing took over, though, and I more or less gave up golf for 25 years or so. I was never able to regain the feel and fluidity that I had when I was younger, but that does not detract from my enjoyment of a good game.

My interest was rekindled thanks to buying a place in Spain. That came about through my friendship with John Fitzpatrick, the former British Saloon Car Champion. In the early 1980s, he ran a sports-car team from a unit near mine at Silverstone. Fitz was so keen on golf that, at one stage when he was younger, he had attempted to turn professional.

We were in Spain when John invited Marie and I to play at an incredibly difficult course that was to become known as Valderrama. Fitz was playing off about five, I was back on 12 because this was just as I was returning to the game, and Marie was a complete novice. You can imagine our delight when we discovered that the fourth player would be Tony Jacklin, winner of the British and US Open Championships in 1969 and 1970. He was a very good friend of Fitz's and we joined them for lunch at a beach club. I was in high spirits after returning from a successful trip to Macau, where we had won. Tony was mad about cars and he loved all the stories Fitz and I had to tell.

In those days, Tony was in the building business. We were joined eventually by Fernando Montoquo, a bit of a lunatic who was the sales and marketing director of Sotogrande Estates. He put a plan on the table and began a sales pitch, trotting out the usual stuff about access to the beach, the villa facing south, the magnificent view and the marina that was planned nearby. He then came out with the classic line that he had a special deal for me. I said we were not interested, but he persisted.

Slightly tongue in cheek, I said I would only be interested for a sum considerably less than he was asking. Cutting a long story short, and after a few more drinks had been taken, I rang our bank manager, Roger Donegan, and told him to sort out a mortgage and find a deposit because I had just bought an apartment. Roger immediately demanded to speak to Marie, saying I was a nightmare and had clearly had too much to drink. He instructed Marie to stop me from buying anything. Marie replied that the deal actually looked sensible. That was how we came to start a happy association with Sotogrande, which was a great place for the kids and many good rounds of golf.

Now that I am no longer running a race team, golf plays an even greater part in my life. When we sold our house in Oxford, we could hardly get closer to the game because we bought a house in Wentworth, where Marie and I became members. Marie loves the game, plays off eight and is the Sunningdale matchplay champion and also the foursomes' champion with Ali McGinley, wife of Paul, the Ryder Cup star.

In the summer of 2006, IMG approached us on behalf of their client Tiger Woods. He had entered the HSBC World Matchplay and wanted to rent a local house. I refused initially. Then I thought about it and agreed, on one condition – the money should be doubled with half going to CLIC and the other half to Tiger's Foundation in memory of his recently deceased father. We had to go through a bit of red tape but, in the end, it was worth it because the charities received all the money, Tiger used our home and everyone was happy. Tiger brought his wife, a housekeeper, a chef and his caddy, Steve Williams – who, on seeing my motor-sport books, revealed that he was a motor-racing fanatic and ran a Formula Ford team in New Zealand.

Tiger's dedication to the game is extraordinary. He practised on the fifth green, which is nearby, and insisted that he hit 100 five-foot putts before he could leave. If he missed one, he would do another 100. He just kept knocking them in. By this stage, he had a huge following of admirers and it was amusing to watch what happened when he finally walked off the green and disappeared into the trees. People assumed he had gone for a pee. Little did they realise that he was heading for the back gate of our house, through which he would disappear, not to be seen until the match itself. That was one of the reasons why he liked to stay in a local house rather than a hotel.

It is not unusual to bump into famous golfers in and around Wentworth and Sunningdale because many of them live nearby. The golfer I know best is Paul McGinley. One of the things I wanted to do after retiring from F1 was to see other sportsmen at the cutting edge of their profession and it struck me that Paul was the very man who could help me do that in the world of golf. I had played with big names in Pro-Am matches, but that is far removed from the pressure of an actual tournament. The professionals rarely play at their best in Pro-Ams. Indeed, pro golfers will tell you that they have a terrible fear of winning a Pro-Am because tradition has it that if you succeed in the fun match, you will not win the important game that follows.

I was talking this through with Paul and mentioned that I wanted to caddy for someone at a significant tournament. When Paul asked if I would like to do that with him at the BMW Masters in Munich, I did not need a second invitation. Then I thought about the consequences. He was having a good season and a lot would be riding on this tournament. I reckoned my caddying for him might bring added pressure he did not need, but he insisted it would work.

There is a similarity between golf and motor racing insofar as they are both team sports. In F1, there are managers, engineers and mechanics but, when the lights go out at the start, the driver is on his own. The golfer has his caddy and physio but, when he steps on to the tee, it is just him and that ball. I did not want Paul to think that he would have to look after me. He would have enough on his plate without that. I talked to many of the caddies, particularly J. P. Fitzgerald, who had worked with Paul and Darren Clarke and later became bagman for Ernie Els. I asked about any quirks, likes and dislikes that McGinley might have. I said to Paul that he had to understand that we were in this together and I wanted to win as much as he did.

*

Paul brought me to the pre-tournament barbecue in Munich, where I got an awful slagging from Colin Montgomerie and Padraig Harrington, but we all knew that the jokes would stop as soon as play started, or so I thought. When I went to go out on the first day, I could not believe the weight of Paul's bag. It took a while to discover that Ian Poulter and a few of the caddies had filled the bottom of the bag with stones and cans of Red Bull.

Once I had sorted what should really be in the bag, I had to make sure there were enough golf balls bearing Paul's marking – a green and an orange dot with the white of the ball in between, representing the Irish colours. His tee peg carries the green and white hoops of Celtic football club.

I marked everything very clearly in terms of yardage in my little notebook. It was remarkable to witness how pumped the players become with each passing day. I might say, 'Ninety-four to the front of the green and the pin is twenty-one farther on. In other words, one hundred and fifteen all up.' Paul would hit it, say, 112 yards on the first day, then maybe 115 yards the next day, but 118 yards on the final day. No matter who the caddy is, Paul always lines up the putt – which was a weight off my shoulders at the time.

When it came to the final day, I witnessed a different golfer. This is what I wanted to see. I wanted to be inside the ropes. I wanted to be discussing the clubs he might use. As the days went on, we had got better and better.

When golfers finish their round, they do not have many people to answer to. Once he had dealt with the press, I wanted Paul to tell me everything and go through some of the shots in detail. I was not inquisitive or pushy, but I was trying to get inside his head. I kept saying, 'Paul, remember, I want to win this, too.'

One evening, we had dinner with Ian Poulter, an outstandingly funny man and a great player. I discovered that golfers are very honest with each other and they are very happy to talk about their bad shots. That is not something that occurs in motor racing. A driver only ever thinks about how he made a good start, how good he was in this corner and how he had out-braked someone into that corner. Golfers are much more honest and extraordinarily friendly to each other.

It was a very different environment in many ways because, going from one tournament to another and playing together, they are familiar with each other. I did not want Paul to lose his friendships with people but my feeling, rightly or wrongly, was that it should not extend to when he is practising or on the course. That is easier said than done, though, for a player as popular as Paul.

We would sit down and talk for half an hour before he went out to play each morning – rather like a pre-briefing before a motor race. I would say, 'Right, today Paul, if we're going to win this tournament, we need to be six under par for the round. So that means every third hole we need to have a birdie and you cannot afford to drop a shot. On every green, on every tee box, you need to be confident beyond any doubt that you'll make par at worst.'

A player should not drop shots on a regular basis in the same way that a great football team should not give away weak goals. Any team that leaks goals has to score twice as many to win. I made the point that every birdie would be like a goal.

Paul needed to birdie the last hole, a par five. He hit a cracking drive. Then his second shot caught the top of the greenside bunker. He needed a tricky up and down to make it to the World Matchplay the following week, where he was the beaten finalist. Then he won the Volvo Masters to finish in the top three of the Order of Merit in 2005. I was delighted. To me, that was the equivalent of finishing third in the world championship. It had been a fantastic experience. I loved every second of it. Paul had made my wish come true.

A game of golf is not as important as it used to be in Formula 1. Time, or a lack of it, is the obvious reason. When we went to places such as Magny-Cours, Silverstone or Jerez, I would regularly meet with Alain Prost or Nigel Mansell for a game on the Wednesday or Thursday. I would grab whatever chance I could, even though it led to Ron Dennis and others making remarks such as, 'Where's EJ? Oh, he'll be on the golf course...'

F1 became so time-consuming that you arrived at the circuit on Thursday morning and hardly left your motorhome until Sunday afternoon. I found it increasingly depressing that F1 was becoming so intense. It got to the point where you would not see another team manager unless it was in a meeting. You could actually go to a grand prix and hardly see a driver from another team. Yet when we used to go to Estoril for the Portuguese Grand Prix in the early 1990s, we'd have a game of golf and then enjoy dinner together.

I really do not believe that the F1 show today is the better for those involved being more serious and wound up about what they do. There is a feeling that you have to be seen slogging your heart out non-stop to impress a prospective sponsor. The argument against that is that most of the sensible CEOs and marketing directors welcome a game of golf. They see it as part of the business mechanism when it comes to wheeling and dealing. Besides, I am sure they prefer to have an F1 team principal who is a keen golfer rather than someone who is perceived to be boring and one-dimensional.

Priorities have changed since my first season in 1991. I remember arriving in Australia for the final race and having time for a round of golf at Royal Adelaide with Jackie Stewart, Nigel Mansell and Alain Prost. Needing to rent a set of clubs, I went to the shop, where the resident pro came rushing over and shook me by the hand.

'My name is Pete Ormsby. I'm so pleased to meet you,' he said. I wondered what was going on because, in the process, he was ignoring my three distinguished playing partners. 'I'm a very big Formula 3 fan,' he continued, 'and I've called my son Jordan.'

'Fine, yep,' I thought. 'Another lunatic.'

We had our game of golf and when I went to return the clubs, Pete insisted I keep them.

'Thank you. You're incredibly generous,' I responded, 'but I can't accept them. For a start, I've nowhere to put them and I'm flying back on Sunday after the race. It's very kind of you, but I'll have to say no.'

Pete then insisted that the clubs would always be there for me. I had another round before leaving Adelaide and, sure enough, the clubs were waiting. When I returned the following year, it was the same deal. That was a nice gesture. If none of the F1 people were available to play with me, he arranged to have a couple of the young pros join me for a round. In the meantime, I organised tickets for Pete and his wife and son Jordan to go to the race.

This continued until our final race in Adelaide in November 1995. Meanwhile, Jordan began karting and the family used to send me his results with the occasional card about how they were getting on. Then, one day, the set of clubs turned up at the factory with a note from Pete saying he no longer had any need for them and he wanted me to have them.

Fast forward to 2005 and the BMW tournament at Wentworth. McGinley was playing very well, lying second behind Angel Cabrera. I was following his progress along with Marie and Ali. After watching Paul play the 12th hole, we were about to leave and take a short cut when, suddenly, a huge shout came from behind me. 'Eddie! Eddie!' That is not normal on a golf course. People do not shout. I was mortified. I turned round to see one of the players running towards me. I had absolutely no idea who he was, but he certainly seemed to know me, which added to my feeling of confusion and embarrassment. He rushed up, stuck out his hand and said, 'Eddie! I'm delighted to see you. This is unbelievable. Wait till I tell my dad. I'm Peter Ormsby's son. I'm Wade!'

It took a second or two for the penny to drop. I had known all about Jordan Ormsby but next to nothing about his baby brother – and here he was, lying third in the BMW tournament. We became good friends and Wade would use our house in Sotogrande when playing in Spain – a good example of how golf has been such an important part of the fabric of my life.

## Chapter 47

# BREAKING AND ENTERING

When leukaemia strikes, it draws a family together and brings them even closer than they might have been before. In 2005, I became involved with a project at the opposite end of the domestic spectrum when I worked with boys from broken homes.

When I finished in F1, I drew up a list of things I wanted to do or, at least, try to do. Among them was taking a look at working in television. I had no idea what that might entail but an idea started to take shape when I met Victoria Edwards. Victoria felt I might be good at working with kids and we organised a trial in Hyde Park, where they filmed me chatting to youngsters. That seemed to work and it was helped greatly by the fact that no one knew anything about my background. They accepted me totally as a complete stranger. Now I had to think of a format and, just as important, find someone to make the programme.

I was put in touch with a company called ZigZag Productions. We came up with the idea of having a probation officer, or someone working in socially deprived areas, nominate eight teenagers who had either been released from prison or were doing community service. We would set up a garage in south London and find a wrecked car. The plan was to give the boys a focus – perhaps for the first time in their lives – by teaching them the basics of mechanics. We would rebuild the car and prepare it for a stock-car race. There would be a deadline and they would have to be disciplined in order to meet it. That was the proposal.

We were presented – I had no say in the choice – with eight boys between the ages of 17 and 22. They were a mix of Afro-Caribbean, English and Asian, and between them they had amassed over 100 convictions. Clearly, they were not saints. The producers found a classic location under a railway arch in Deptford and we added a severely clapped out and well-stuffed car. The deadline was set for a stock-car meeting four months later in Essex. Our car had to be ready by then and one of the boys would be the driver. My job during this time would be to get to know and understand the lads and attempt to marshal them into a half-decent team – easier said than done.

I spent time in their homes and assisted, where possible, in the garage but I really needed to see how they would react as a team when under duress. We organised the unexpected, such as military and activity courses. Usually, they would have the weekend off but on one occasion, I told them to bring rough clothes and report at 7 a.m. on a Saturday. It was freezing as we set off for a training yard, where the boys were given the job of mucking out all the stables. By midday, the head stable girl reported that the boys had done a good job but she noted it was obvious that none of them – bar one – had ever seen a horse before and they were understandably nervous in the presence of the animals.

Having no idea what was coming next, the boys were ushered into a room and kitted out in new suits and white shirts – but with different coloured ties so that they did not look like a boy band. We moved on to a race meeting at Kempton Park. I had arranged with jockey Mick Fitzgerald to take the lads to a fence and talk them through the skills involved, giving them the inside line on the sport.

The boys were impressed and, at times, amazed. That may have been predictable but what I did not expect was the reaction when food was served. A magnificent spread had an interesting mix but the boys did not touch any of it. Couscous, for example, was of no interest whatsoever. Neither was the more traditional and basic fare of vegetables, ham and chicken. The only thing they wanted – indeed, the only thing they felt capable of eating – was burger and chips.

In case the story of the visit to Kempton gives the impression that all was sweetness and light, you can be assured that was far from the case. Right from the start, the boys had been trying to undermine my position through intimidation, particularly when they were together. I decided I would have to deal with them individually, where possible.

A case presented itself easily when one of the boys, Miff, was due to be sentenced for some misdemeanour. On the night before the hearing, I went to see him and asked to be taken through a normal evening in his life. We went to the local youth centre, where he knew quite a lot of people. A couple of things struck me immediately – the kids were hardly bothered by the presence of a television camera, everything in the surrounding area was boarded up and everyone seemed to have a dog.

I played Miff at ping-pong and treated him – or tried to – as if he was my son. We moved on to the pool table and I was beginning to think that he was like any other teenager. If this was what he did most nights, he could not be as bad as everyone was making out.

Then he suddenly said, 'Look, I'm bored. I wanna go.'

'OK,' I said, 'but I need to know what you'd do now, if I wasn't here.'

'I'd probably steal a car. Monday nights get a bit boring because there's not a lot to do. Everyone's at home, I don't have a mother or a father. I've got a sister whose boyfriend doesn't like me.'

Now I had a problem. I did not know what to do next because the obvious alternative was worrying, to say the least. I thought about it for a couple of seconds, before saying, 'Do remember, I'm here to understand what you do, and to do the things that you do with you. If you're telling me that you would steal a car, while I'm not encouraging you to do it, I want to see how you would do it.'

He nodded and headed down a nearby lane to a small car park. He chose a particular car, used a small screwdriver to lever open the top of a window, just enough to allow him to pull it back while, at the same time, jumping up and gaining more leverage by putting his feet against the door. The window did not break but he had the door open in an instant. I could not believe what I was seeing. Once inside, it was a moment's work to pull the steering column box down, break the steering lock and short-circuit the wiring. One minute and 14 seconds after Miff had put his mind to doing this, we were driving away.

I asked him why he took such a risk. He did not see it that way. His view was that if they were going into town from Deptford and there was no bus, they would nick a car and drive it there. Then they would either bring it back or, in his words, 'torch it'. I played dumb and asked him to show me what tools they had to do that. The answer was frighteningly simple. By somehow adapting a cigarette lighter, it had become a flame-thrower. A couple of seconds playing this on upholstery and the car would be alight.

Strictly speaking, I was aiding and abetting this theft. It was an alarming experience, witnessing the ease with which Miff had taken this car.

Prior to sentencing, we had put a case in Miff's defence, saying he was an important part of a film that, among other things, was investigating the background behind the behaviour patterns of boys such as this. In Miff's case, he should have gone to jail, but he was fined and given community service instead. When he failed to turn up at the garage for the next two or three days, we thought he must have been celebrating. In fact, the opposite turned out to be true.

Miff eventually came back and said that he wanted to go to jail. His brother had given him a hard time for not taking his punishment. Jail was looked upon as something that would have added to Miff's street credibility, but in truth, he had no idea about the reality of being locked up. With help from the governor at Brixton prison, we took Miff inside and showed him. We were allowed to film as the shock clearly registered. After the programme had finished, Miff moved to Manchester, where he did work experience in a well-known Audi dealership and made good progress as an apprentice mechanic. That was rewarding for everyone, but it had been a hard slog getting that far.

I had some very tough times in the beginning. Being of a suspicious nature and refusing to trust anyone, the boys thought there was a catch and the programme would portray them as being even worse than they actually were. Once they understood our aims, they calmed down and mellowed, and with each day I was learning more and more about their way of life.

One of the Caribbean boys puzzled me. He had been inside for beating up an old woman and stealing what little money she had. He took me to visit his mother on the 14th floor of a block of flats. There were two other children present and his mum had gone to the trouble of baking me a tiny cake. It was a really touching moment in one way and confusing in another because I wondered just what had driven her boy to commit such a terrible crime.

An important part of the bonding process occurred on St Patrick's Day. It had been very cold and we had spent a long time filming outside in Norfolk. That can be tedious when you have to re-do it again and again and again. It had been a long day, made worse by the drive back. As we passed through Edgware in the early evening, I told them that, as this was the 17th of March, any decent Irishman had to have a pint of Guinness on such a special day. We stopped at the next pub. I knew this could be a bit tricky because a couple of the boys were under age, which meant I could not buy them a drink. I told them they could do whatever they wanted if I was not watching – which, of course, they would have done in the normal course of events.

When we went inside, by a stroke of luck, three girls were playing Irish music and one of them knew me. That set the scene perfectly. Before we knew it, I was playing the spoons and joining in. It was great craic. Then the boys came into their own. One of them, Richie, began rhyming and rapping over the top of the Irish music. The effect was sensational. More than that, it helped build the relationship between us, just as a day at a kart track would do some time later.

All the boys considered themselves to be aces at the wheel and the karting not only helped us choose the driver for the stock-car race but also showed the lads just how good they really were – or not, in some cases. Once the boys appreciated how tricky it was to find the final couple of tenths of a second, I said I would show them how it was done. I was taking a risk because it had been many years since I had sat in a kart and it was important not to lose face in front of such a critical audience.

I would not say that I cheated, but I did wait until the track was at its driest on that day. I also knew that I would have to cut the corners, a tactic that I had seen some of them use. I was brutal with the kart while setting the fastest time. I did not beat them by a massive margin, but just enough for this old racer to get their attention. That had a big effect. I was not asking them to do anything that I would not or could not do. It had been the same when we did blindfold driving, which required total trust in the co-driver and his instructions. It was the same when mucking out the horses. I had been happy to do it and slowly build up the respect that is so important to youngsters.

After much drama, which included sacking the boy I had chosen to be team leader, the remaining boys had the car ready for the race. I did not know what to expect any more than the lads did, although I suspected, from experience, that the competition would be tough. I was right. We were absolutely pasted. In one way, that was a good thing. If we had won, it would have looked like a put-up job. In addition, the result allowed the boys to come to terms with defeat, but in an acceptable way.

I think the programme had a calming influence on almost everyone involved. Statistics show that 82 per cent re-offend. Almost a year after the programme had been made, five of the eight had not done so. That argument failed to appease one or two critics, who asked why eight hooligans should be given such a chance when there are so many honest and straight people who would love to have a similar opportunity.

It is a perfectly valid argument. However, I had come face to face for the first time with individuals from socially deprived backgrounds. A typical example might be a girl in her late teens, having perhaps been abused by her parents or relatives, arriving in London, working in a bar, meeting a guy, becoming pregnant and wanting to keep the baby whereas the father could not care less. The child has to go into care, even though the mother is still in love with her offspring – but the baby does not know this, particularly when put up for adoption, or fostering, or remaining in care. Now that child's life has become a mess.

That was the case with most of the team. Yes, I can understand why people might disagree with the boys receiving what amounted to privileged treatment, but my question is this. What are you going to do with these boys? It is hardly their fault that they do not have a father, or perhaps their mother has done a runner. It is hardly their fault that the environment in which they have been brought up revolves around either jail or a lack of work. They become caught in a vicious circle involving crime, which leads to a criminal record. The programme's objective was to highlight this growing problem in the community and show that, while the country in general is getting richer, it is also becoming poorer in other respects. Money is not the solution and neither is jail. The boys need, in my view, to be given a chance to do something with their lives.

From a personal point of view, I enjoyed doing the programme. It was much more difficult than I had anticipated. When I was in racing and confronted by a television camera, I would say my piece. The job would be done in one take and finished in a matter of minutes. A programme such as this involves a lot of work. I refused to use a script, preferring instead to think about what I wanted to say and then let the words flow. Occasionally the producer would suggest that I follow a script in order to make a point in a particular way. I did not enjoy that because I had to learn my lines and that did not feel natural. It was not me. Some very bright editors managed the programme – Tom, Oscar and Anna – and I thought they did a brilliant job. Certainly, I found that working to camera was not a problem at all.

I did it for free and because I wanted to. Here was an opportunity to try something different and it turned out to be fun. There was huge interest in the show. Trans World International (part of IMG) purchased the rights and brought the show to Mifcom, which is the equivalent of the Cannes Film Festival for video and television. The programme has been shown in 26 countries, as far afield as South Africa, Poland and Chile. Some places have bought the rights to do a similar programme in the same format. It seems that we touched a chord that runs through most countries. Filling that need was as satisfying as doing the programme itself.

## Chapter 48

# BERNIE AND THE NO. 414

In the 1980s, Harvey Pallett used to come to Silverstone in an Aston Martin. He owned Savoir Fayre, a company that provided hospitality and backed James Weaver when he drove our F3 car. Harvey was an eccentric man. Standing 6' 6" tall, he had a passion for opera and reared prize donkeys, a bizarre combination to say the least. He was also vice president of Coventry City Football Club and he encouraged me to go to see his team play. At the time, Coventry were in the First Division and being managed by Jimmy Hill.

I continued to support Coventry over the years, and got to know Gordon Strachan. Subsequently, through contacts in football, I became good friends with Irish international players Roy Keane, Robbie Keane, Paul McGrath, David O'Leary, Liam Brady and Shay Given.

Coventry were one of the first teams to provide corporate hospitality in their so-called Vice President's Club, a practice that eventually spread to all sports, including motor racing. Much as I appreciated the hospitality, I was there for the football and enjoyed many good games. However, when it comes to recalling a heady atmosphere, there is none to equal the day Ireland beat Italy in a World Cup group match in America on 18 June 1994. That was one of the greatest footballing occasions I can remember. I suppose I would say that – but the drama and passion that engulfed the Giants Stadium in New York that afternoon make my pulse race, even when I think about it now.

The Irish prime minister and most of his government seemed to be in the Plaza bar beforehand. Leaders of Irish industry, bishops and priests, artists and musicians were there, and everyone appeared to be getting trashed. We were warming up because, this being New York, we expected to be overwhelmed by Italians but when we got to the stadium, we discovered to our amazement that the Irish vastly outnumbered the opposition in the 75,000 crowd.

I was with Bono and the whole of U2, J. P. McManus, Dermot Desmond and Ossie Kilkenny in a magnificent box owned by Universal Records. We had a great view when Ray Houghton scored for Ireland after just 12 minutes. We waited for the inevitable retaliation from the Italians but the boys in green managed to hold on to the lead until the end. It was the most extraordinary night, never to be forgotten, even though the Dutch knocked the Irish out in the next round. Nonetheless, I did not miss the opportunity to mention the Italy result when I saw anyone from Ferrari or Minardi at the next grand prix in France. They had the last laugh, however, when Italy got through to the final.

Based on this performance and others, Jack Charlton's status in Ireland as demi-god and manager was guaranteed for the rest of his years. Jack was a smart boy. When he returned to Ireland, he would pay for everything by cheque in the knowledge that the majority would not be cashed because the recipients wanted his signature more than the cheque it was written on. There would not be such a demand for memorabilia eight years later when Ireland became bogged down in internal squabbling during the World Cup in Japan and Korea.

By playing in various charity golf matches, I had got to know Mick McCarthy, who succeeded Jack as Ireland manager. Mick found himself at the centre of a storm when Roy Keane walked out of the 2002 World Cup campaign after a row over the way the Irish team was run. Roy wanted everything just so – he was a thorough professional – and he did not feel the team was properly prepared.

Roy came home. I tried to get in touch with him before he left Saipan because there was a window of opportunity for an apology all round. Roy's country needed him. It was above private issues. It had taken Ireland forever to get this far and the Irish fans were being let down. My view was that no one person was greater than his team or his country.

In the end, I began negotiating with Mick in Japan while Kevin Moran, a close friend, fellow Irishman and former Manchester United player, was jumping over Keane's back fence in Manchester and trying to negotiate a settlement. We reached a point where we thought we were really close to having useful communication between the two sides. However, progress became slower and slower, and then it broke down completely. This was like the United Nations and we needed to get a deal done. Mick and Roy were probably as difficult as each other but I did not feel that the attitude of Michael Kennedy, the solicitor who looked after Keane's affairs, helped the situation. In the end, Ireland was the biggest loser. The team, predictably, got no further than the last 16. In fact, I was amazed they reached that far, given the battering to everyone's morale.

When I bought a flat in London's Fulham Road, I suddenly had access to Premiership games, particularly in midweek. One of the first things I did was buy a couple of season tickets for Chelsea. This was in the days before Abramovich, and the number of F1 people I used to meet regularly at Stamford Bridge, notably Patrick Head and his wife Betise, Dave Price and Peter Digby of Xtrac, the transmission company, surprised me. Occasionally, Bernie Ecclestone would be there. I met Ken Bates several times. While I thought he did a lot of good for the club in certain ways, there is no doubt that the death of Matthew Harding in a helicopter crash had a major effect on the club and its fans. Chelsea had begun to progress before Roman Abramovich came along but there can be no denying that Jose Mourinho has transformed everything and done a brilliant job with some fantastic players.

I have an interest north of the border, too, being a shareholder in Celtic. That association took me to Turin for a Cup match in which

Celtic were beaten by Juventus. After the game I was in a local restaurant with Dermot Desmond, the Irish business magnate and also a shareholder at Celtic Park. Jean Alesi's manager, Mario Miyakawa, was also involved with Alessandro del Piero, the star player at Juventus. Mario knew we would be in this particular restaurant, which was packed. Suddenly, the entire place seemed to come to a standstill. I looked round as del Piero came in and walked straight to our table. To my amazement – and that of our fellow diners – he said, in perfect English, 'Evening, lads. How are you?', handed Dermot the shirt he had been wearing when he scored that evening, had a quick drink, got into his car and buzzed off. Our status rose instantly from mere diners to visiting celebrities.

A less enjoyable but equally memorable trip took us to Tehran to see Ireland's play-off against Iran in the 2002 World Cup qualifiers. We went in a new Gulfstream owned by Denis O'Brien, a world player in terms of growing businesses such as phone technology. We stopped for the night in Istanbul and drove into a city jumping with football fever because Turkey was also in a play-off, with Austria.

After a very lively night, we reached Tehran the following day to find a hideously hostile environment. We had to be escorted into an open stadium packed to capacity with 120,000 raving fans. I will never forget the intimidating atmosphere as the Irish supporters were herded together in the middle of a mob chanting to the Ayatollah. We were in a pen made of scaffolding, reminiscent of a jail, complete with security guards outside. The crowd was vindictive, to say the least, because the Republic of Ireland was defending a 2–0 lead from the first leg played in Dublin.

Missiles rained through the open top of the pen. At the end, when Ireland looked like going through, these so-called football fans were pissing into the bags they had used to carry their food and throwing them into the pen. It was one of those experiences that you make light of after the event but, at the time, seemed very intense and threatening.

Thankfully, despite the sometimes cruel chanting, you can never say that about a night at Stamford Bridge. Certainly, Bernie enjoys his occasional visits. He joined me for Chelsea's 100th anniversary function, held opposite the ground. I had arranged for a car to pick us up. Along the way, Bernie asked the driver if he had children. When the man replied that he had young kids, Bernie told him not to bother waiting for us but to go back to his family and we would make our own way home.

Of course, when we eventually left the function, it was very busy and there were no cabs. After a short while, a No. 414 bus pulled up. I got on, telling Bernie I was not prepared to wait any longer for a cab. To my surprise, Bernie followed me. Neither of us had been on a bus for longer than we cared to remember. Bernie immediately told the driver that he was a pensioner but insisted that I did not qualify for any concessions and the driver had to make sure I paid.

After about ten stops along the Fulham Road, Bernie suddenly got up and rapped the driver's window.

'I just need you to turn right here and go round the square,' he told the driver. 'It's worth a score.'

Being a money man since he was in short pants, Bernie always talked in terms of 'scores' and 'monkeys'. Unfortunately, the driver was Asian and did not know that a score was £20. The poor guy probably thought a 'score' was something to do with drugs. He said he was sorry, but he could not turn right, as requested by his belligerent passenger. You could see that he had become very confused when this grey-haired pensioner in a tuxedo had asked him to deviate from the bus route and go completely the wrong way. At the next stop, I told Bernie I had had enough, and jumped out. Bernie followed me and we both walked home.

That was typical of Bernie. He rolls a smoking bomb under the door and walks away. I find that people outside the sport want to know more about Bernie than they do about the drivers. I am being asked continually, 'You must have worked with Bernie. What's he like?' It is a very difficult question to answer because he can be all things to all men. He can be hard, he can be soft, he can be goddamn miserable, and he can be generous and kind. He has the ability to move from one side to the other with incredible speed, so much so that you are taken by surprise – which, of course, is exactly what he wants.

He has the ability to divide and rule. If he decides that too many factions are getting together and posing a threat, he will cut them down before they realise it. In my opinion, too many people are in awe of him and bow down to him. He knows they would do anything for him and he will use that. There is no question that everyone should have respect for Bernie and all that he has achieved, but many people go beyond that. Bernie has created a reputation for being clever and having great vision – and there is no doubt that is true. People want to be associated, or seen, with him. Many will wait for weeks, sometimes months, to get an appointment with him and then rush around telling everyone. That is the effect he has.

Bernie can be hard, but there is a caring side to him as well. When Ian Phillips was sick, he arranged for Professor Watkins to make sure he was available all the time in case of need. He has done something similar in any number of instances – the serious accidents that befell Frank Williams and Martin Donnelly, to name just two.

Bernie remains in the background, but his influence is far-reaching. He may not have the physical presence of Harvey Pallett, but Bernie Ecclestone is one of the biggest men motor sport has ever known. I consider it a massive privilege to have known and worked with him.

Chapter 49

# BACK TO DEALING

Even before I had finished with F1, I had met a number of interesting people from the financial world, an area that was of particular interest. David Yarrow, a founding partner of Clareville Capital, is one of the best hedge-fund managers I have ever met. We gradually built a relationship, largely, I have to admit, through enjoyable evenings having dinner at Carpaccio's. I took the opportunity to invest in companies such as Destiny Wireless, a company specialising in improving business process flow. I also became a director and investor in Debrett's, one of the oldest publishing brands in the world, and I was about to become involved at director level with a fascinating company called Betbrokers.

Betbrokers see themselves as a new and efficient way of placing bets by helping the punter save time and, hopefully, money. A good example at the beginning of 2007 was the betting on one of the favourites for the Ballymore Hurdle race at Cheltenham. The price to the outside world appeared to have gone skinny at 7–2 and yet I was able to place a reasonable bet at 4–1. Betbrokers take 3 per cent of the stake but, even allowing for that, the punter will be ahead because of the increase in winnings that usually comes from dealing with this company. I am on board as a non-executive director and it was to be excellent experience for me, particularly as we spent nearly a year bringing the company to the market.

When it came to old friends, I had none better than Michael Tunney. Michael joined the Allied Irish Bank a few years after I started with the Bank of Ireland. After the strike in 1970, we both got hooked on motor racing. I started in karting and Michael, because of his size, found saloon cars more accommodating. We worked as a team in that I would make money from buying and selling cars and Michael would use it to prepare our karts and cars for racing. Like me, Michael later raced Formula Ford in Ireland but his true talent was in finance. He became well known in Ireland for buying out and expanding companies that had been in trouble. He is an extremely bright guy. We had remained close friends and Michael would come to the occasional grand prix as my guest.

Meanwhile, I was keeping in touch with friends from F1, particularly Nigel Northridge. Nigel had been very astute when he became CEO at Gallaher. He bought into a huge part of the tobacco industry in Russia and was emerging as a very serious player. I remember going, some years before, to a ceremony in Shanghai where Bernie was cutting the first sod at the circuit that would eventually host the Chinese Grand Prix. To my surprise, I bumped into Nigel in the middle of a big hotel in the centre of Shanghai. He confided that he was putting together a deal with Shanghai Tobacco. During the course of dinner, I had a call from Mouse Morris, the legendary trainer in Ireland. I had a share in Rostropovich, a horse that had won a number of big races. Mouse rang to say that the horse had broken down.

During the conversation, Mouse said he knew of a magnificent young horse and asked if I want a piece of it. Since we were celebrating the successful conclusion of Nigel's deal with Shanghai Tobacco, I said this was the right moment to take an interest in this horse. In the end, four of us were involved – a leg each, you might say – and the deal was done. The other legs were owned by Tony Kilduff, my regular partner at horse racing, and J. P. Fitzgerald, now Ernie Els's caddy.

The horse was untried and unbroken, a complete punt on our part. Nigel said because we were in Shanghai, that ought to be the name of the horse but, when we later tried to register Shanghai with the Turf Board, they said the name had already gone. I rang Nigel and told him we had been shanghaied, or stuffed. Almost as one, we said, 'That's what we'll call the horse.' Just before Christmas 2006, Shanghide won its first race at Punchestown in Ireland. Meanwhile, I was getting into my stride with investments that I had long since started in other areas.

When David Yarrow offered an involvement in Clareville, I was delighted. This was exactly what I needed. I wanted to be busy. I needed to have my mind focused on a different kind of dealing. I wanted to use the skills I felt I had for putting deals together knowing that, if you were wrong, then you were wrong and there was no way back. However, if you were right most of the time, the buzz had no equal. With all of these activities going on, I had neither the time nor the inclination to go to a grand prix. The one exception, perhaps predictably, was Monaco.

I wanted to keep a low profile. That may seem a strange thing to say when I chose to stay as a guest of Philip Green on a boat that was moored a few paces from the back of the swimming pool. However, it was perfect because it was easy to slip in and out unnoticed and yet be close to the action. Having been racing here for the best part of 20 years, I wanted to see the other side of Monaco. I went to the Amber Lounge, Jimmy'z nightclub, Sass Café and other haunts that I had previously only visited briefly and usually on business with sponsors. It was great craic and reaffirmed just why Monaco is massively attractive.

I was very reluctant to venture into the pits and paddock. I knew what it was like to be going about your business as a race team, only to be distracted by old friends with plenty of time on their hands. People forget that the pit lane is the equivalent of an F1 team's office. Regardless of the glamorous setting, it is a place of work.

Eventually I ventured in and was pleasantly surprised. Everyone was welcoming, many people keen to know what I had been up to. It struck me that there was a purpose behind the questions because many of the top people were in their late 50s and perhaps beginning to wonder how they would or should approach life when the F1 shutters come down. Given my unique qualifications, I reckoned I could set up a business as a counsellor.

It felt very strange to be hanging around, dressed only in tee-shirt and sun shorts when, ordinarily, I would have been wearing the full team kit festooned with sponsors' logos. I felt and probably looked like a tourist, feeling strangely naked in what had been my working environment for so long.

I had been apprehensive for many reasons. One of them, if I am truthful, was the possible discovery that I had not been missed in the slightest. I would bump into people in London or elsewhere and they would say, 'Eddie, you brought something extra to F1. We really miss you.' But did they? Would I walk in and be swept aside by the very business that I had known so well?

It did not feel like that. I experienced genuine warmth from the team principals, the drivers and the fans. It was a good feeling but it did nothing to change the thought that I had made absolutely the right decision to quit. I had been a chancer and got away with it. Now I could move on.

## Chapter 50

# CONCLUSIONS

Almost from the start of my days in motor sport and, certainly, when I formed the F1 team, my philosophy was to remain totally independent. Looking back across three decades, I am very happy to be able to say I achieved that.

However, as with everything in life, there were downsides. When I reached the age of 50, I began to realise that my preoccupation – my obsession, almost – to succeed in F1 was actually being unfair to my family. What if the whole thing collapsed, or I died? That would leave the family terribly exposed. I had no other shareholders. Mine was the only name above the front door.

As I have recalled, I had offers to buy the team lock, stock and barrel, but I turned them all down because, after such a long struggle, I wanted to remain a part of the team that had consumed so much of my life. Selling shares to Warburg Pincus in 1998 allowed me to put some money away for the family and plan a structure in case the unthinkable happened. It was rather like a pension, even though it was a bit late in the day.

In the early years, particularly when starting the F1 team in 1990 and 1991, I had taken huge risks. The closest call had undoubtedly been the winding-up petition from Cosworth at the end of our first season. Once we had survived that, I felt better equipped to handle things but harsh times were ahead.

It was not until 1995 that we, as a team, began to feel more secure thanks to having bigger sponsors on board. One thing led to another and the high point had to be 1998 and 1999 as we won our first race and went on to challenge for the championship. This brought a gradual change in attitude within the team. I knew we had a number of ambitious people at Jordan but it was only when we became really competitive that I realised just how ambitious they were.

These people were spending money, much of it without my authorisation. I did not object to that because I knew they were doing it for the right reasons. However, they were spending money that was not actually there. To counteract that, I began to put 10 per cent of our income aside into a fighting fund, without saying anything about it. I had to do that because racing people, by their very nature, will always spend whatever it takes, not just to get the job done, but to do it better than anyone else.

Trevor Foster, for example, was only concerned about the team's performance. That could cover anything from the wind tunnel to spare parts. Trevor was not interested in whether the money was there or whether the team was in profit or not. That was not his problem, and that was the way it had to be. Trevor pushed me, and I have to thank him for that. He knew that, if pressured to find the money, I would somehow manage it. That was why I needed the fighting fund. Trevor and people like him thought they were fooling me; I thought I was fooling them. The truth was no one was fooling anyone because it balanced out in the end.

The usual form for teams is to have marketing departments focused on raising money. I did most of my deals – Camel, Pepsi, DHL, for example – on the hoof. MasterCard was a classic example. The credit card company had done a deal with the Lola team at the start of the 1997 season, but I always thought the prospects of Lola making it in F1 were not good. Sure enough, the team failed to turn up for the race in Brazil. I got the telephone number of MasterCard's CEO, Bob Surlander, from Bernie Ecclestone.

I called Bob and said I knew he had a number of important guests in Brazil with nowhere to go. I offered to look after them on the condition that I would fly to New York and see him on the Monday after the race. Mark Gallagher and I gave a presentation and the long and the short of the story is that MasterCard came on board with Jordan and formed a great relationship with the team. This was a major coup. MasterCard had previously favoured the sponsorship of events rather than teams and people but, thanks to this spur of the moment decision to get in touch, we had made it work.

It was a similar story when I met Bob Druskin at a time when the CEO of Citibank was in Shanghai after the company had just bought 200 retail outlets in the country. I suggested it would be a good idea to have Citibank's logo on our car for the first Chinese Grand Prix. Bob agreed and a successful deal was done, more or less on the spot.

When it came to juggling the finances, a large part of that had included finding the right mix of drivers. By that I mean having a driver who could bring the results and partnering him with someone who, without perhaps recognising or admitting it, was better suited to finding sponsorship than driving. Invariably, that worked. When I first started out as an entrant, I would tell drivers how much it would cost them to drive the car. The aim, of course, was to move into the position where I could pay my drivers.

When it came to drivers finding sponsorship, particularly for F1, I would pay them about 10 per cent of the money they brought to the team. That would be their salary. If they brought, say, £2.5 million, they might get 12.5 per cent or 15 per cent. Everyone was happy because the driver could be receiving perhaps £300,000 in wages – peanuts by today's standards but that was how it worked in the early 1990s. Figures like that provided the incentive for drivers to bring money, but they could not have the drive without contributing to the sponsorship budget.

I think it is fair to say that most of the drivers did far better with Jordan than they had done with the teams they had been with before. Our drivers would generally punch above their weight when they were with us, and I think much of the motivation came from being with a team unique for its wacky and slightly mad way of doing things. The drivers never knew what was going to happen next. We would tell them that they were getting new bits for the car, that the performance was going to improve and, as a result, they would be faster and better drivers. They became pumped, believed they were quicker – and they *were* quicker as a result.

This added to a sense of mystery that caused people, including members of other F1 teams, to ask, 'How the hell can Jordan achieve the results they are getting and yet behave the way they do?'

I loved that. It automatically encouraged the rock'n'roll image that seemed to be a part of the team and was growing with us. Traditionally, motor racing at the top level is quite a sombre experience. Williams, Benetton, McLaren and Ferrari had been doing most of the winning. They were serious teams that deserved their success. You can imagine the effect when a loud and brash team such as Jordan came along and won the odd race. Here was a team that was defying all the accepted parameters, given its status, finances, drivers, equipment and image. Added to which, Jordan appeared to have a very flaky team boss. That was the impression we were giving out, but in reality, we were operating like a very committed, hard, determined and ruthless bunch of Paddies.

I always felt a strong sense of 'Irishness' in connection with everything we did. Our time in F1 coincided with the emergence of Ireland through *Riverdance* and leading on to the huge success of the Ryder Cup in 2006. I was massively proud of what Bono and Bob Geldof had achieved both musically and for charity. There was also the emergence of the 'Three Amigos': Dermot Desmond, who is a major shareholder of Celtic, National Hunt owner J. P. McManus and John Magnier, the legend of Coolmore, arguably the finest breeder of Flat racers on the planet. It was a great feeling to be a part of this important transitional period for Ireland.

Naturally, we had a number of Irish people in the team. There were also South Africans, Kiwis and Aussies. Half of them were desperate for a job, in need of work experience, or looking for a work permit. We never took on staff without permits, but we would do the applications for them. It meant we had really good people for less money. Then they would become established and be headhunted by the bigger teams. That was the system and you worked it to your advantage.

There was an increased reluctance to leave Jordan as we made more money, the spirit within the team rose further, the results improved and the wages increased. If things went well, the money would rise accordingly. If things were bad, the team members would be earning a pittance but they would stay because, I would like to think, the atmosphere was exciting. Jordan was a good place to be. A number of personal relationships sprung up within the team. Tim Edwards, our crew chief, married Trudie, who looked after our catering. It was that kind of atmosphere. However, while Jordan was a free and easy place, there was one unspoken rule – have your fun but make sure it does not interfere with our performance. The car and the team *always* come first. Do whatever you like after that.

I have to admit that the team was being run by man who was a cross between a schizophrenic and someone with a huge attention deficit disorder. I could remember everything I wanted to remember but nothing that I believed to be unimportant. I could, and still can, see all the scenarios and everything that is likely to happen. It is like a sixth sense. Something would happen and I would have a feeling of *déjà vu* because I had already envisaged it.

When you have a person in charge who does not want to delve into the past and whose only wish is to choose one of several options to jump to next, there is no orderly sequence of events. Yet, despite that, the team was formed, it worked, the car was competitive, we won races – but only because I had a team of people such as Gary Anderson and Trevor who made sure it happened. We were unique on several counts, not least the fact that the team actually got up and running – and survived.

Is it possible for someone to emulate me today? I'd like to meet him! I am not saying it is impossible, nor am I suggesting that I was totally stupid and the whole F1 project was so mad that no one else could do it. There are plenty of people like me, but they need to be very brave. The manner in which we would spend money before we had so much as a sniff of it was suicidal. We were making promises and I never wanted to let anyone down. That had been the subtext to the way we worked, right from the start, even before F1. In 1983, we had that dramatic season in which Martin Brundle and Ayrton Senna duelled for the F3 championship. We had enormous highs and the terrible low of the accident to the truck in Austria, and I had the continual worry that the team was insolvent most of the time. It was touch and go all the way.

At times like that, you need support. Women have played a very important role in my life and the most influential of these have been my mother, Eileen, and my wife, Marie. My mum has been the wise, all-seeing, all-knowing source of encouragement. When possible, I would call her every day at around 8 a.m. Sometimes the call would be brief, sometimes in lengthy detail. Mother liked to know what was going on. I always knew she was there for me.

It was the same with Marie, the complete opposite to me in temperament and an absolute rock. While I may rant and roar, Marie remains calm and quiet. Perhaps that is what makes the partnership work so well. Whatever the reason, Marie deserves several medals for being a companion, friend, mother, counsel and lover for more than 28 years.

While Marie would take care of personal and home affairs, I was also very fortunate in having a wonderful team to guide me through the PR minefield that is such an important and tricky part of being in F1. Louise Goodman set the standard and it was matched by Giselle Davies and Helen Temple, while Lindsay Haylett and Lynda Sotham somehow kept me on the straight and narrow in the office. It can't have been easy. I must have tested their patience on a daily basis, but when the chips were down, I knew I could rely completely on the girls and the rest of the team. As I said, the tragedy in 1983 was a case in point. The way in which everyone rallied round to have Brundle on the grid for the next race was a humbling experience.

Martin was one of the most professional drivers I had the pleasure to work with in terms of his preparation and really wanting to win that F3 title. He did not have the talent of Senna but that actually prompted him to dig very deep. Damon Hill was another in the same mould and who is to say that any driver like that should not receive more respect than a complete natural who does not need to try so hard?

Of all the drivers I have seen and worked with, even for the briefest of periods, Senna and Michael Schumacher were electric. They were complete in every area – natural ability, dedication, determination, single-mindedness. Johnny Herbert, on his day, could, in my view, match Schumacher and Senna in terms of dazzling natural talent, but he lacked the application. He made too many mistakes that were unnecessary. He was scatty, but when it came to car control and raw ability, Johnny was among the best I have ever seen.

If Martin Donnelly was fast, solid, calm and very laid back, then Johnny was horizontal. Johnny would not know or care at what time the race started. Unless you had him on a lead, you would not know where he was as the start of the race approached. Once in the car, though, he was on a par, if perhaps slightly better, than Tommy Byrne – another massive talent that was squandered by a lack of the dedication that was second nature to Senna and Schumacher.

Jean Alesi almost went the same way. When we first met, he was a hopeless mess – very Latin, prone to be hysterical. More than any other driver I came across, Jean benefited from the system of racing in the United Kingdom. A driver had to be disciplined in order to survive and win in such competitive company. Jean was cavalier, using only his right foot and it seemed rarely engaging his brain. He was hopeless in the beginning. His fitness was as appalling as his English but we helped to put both right when he came to live with us. Barry Grinham, a personal trainer, not only worked wonders on Alesi but he also did a brilliant job on Giancarlo Fisichella and Eddie Irvine, arguably the most unfit drivers I have ever had in F1.

On his day, Irvine could be unbelievable but, like Johnny, there was no attention to detail. Eddie could not concentrate on anything for more than a millisecond. He was very similar to myself in that and other respects. He had great flare, understood business and had a Midas touch that has brought great wealth since he retired from F1. Eddie wins the award for getting the most out of motor racing for the least amount of effort. He is the world champion in that respect. There is simply no contest.

Irvine had one target and that was to make as much money as he could without spending a penny. When he won a F3000 race with us in 1990, you could see that such an important victory was tainted by the fact that he had promised his engineers a watch if he ever reached the podium. Eddie then devoted most of his time to trying to blag a couple of watches without having to pay for them. Yet I admired him because he was completely up front about how tight he was. He is a very honest man.

Jarno Trulli was one of the fastest drivers we ever had. He was nice to work with, very courteous and kind. Fisichella was the same but we seemed to spend most of our time trying to persuade Giancarlo to have the self-belief he was due. Fisi was very good for us. He always provided a useful benchmark because he could eclipse his team-mate by a small margin, just enough to keep the other guy on his toes. Yet Giancarlo liked his comfort zone. Whereas Michael Schumacher, for instance, was always looking for new heights, always wanting to raise the bar, Fisi would rise to the occasion only if his team-mate proved to be faster.

When it came to flashes of absolute brilliance, few were capable of matching Heinz-Harald Frentzen. Heinz should have won a lot of races at Williams before he came to us but he could not deal with the massive pressure to perform. He was so calm and the environment at Jordan suited him far better.

Being happy at your work – and working to make sure that is the case – is such an important part of a driver's make-up. Schumacher is a classic example. Michael was one of the greatest people I ever met in F1. I was so proud and privileged to have him in our car, even though it was a brief stay and the entire episode came close to bringing us to our knees.

I was happy to see him quit F1 with such dignity at the end of 2006. Going out the way he did in Brazil was unbelievable. Rejoining at the back after stopping to change a punctured tyre, and then driving through the field to an eventual fourth place was awesome, arguably one of the greatest drives Michael has ever had without winning. He had no need to dig so deep at that stage in his career but that drive showed immense character and style. Michael could not have left a more impressive stamp on the sport he had dominated for so long. I will bow to his brilliance every time and, although we had our differences, I refuse to hear a bad word against him. Michael was stunning from the first day to the last. I was so happy to be a part of that era.

Michael's retirement was part of the never-ending movement within F1 as young drivers come in, mature, win and then retire. At the start of the 2007 season, a number of young names were poised at the back, waiting to shove the established stars off the front. That, for me, is part of F1's enduring attraction.

On the other hand, I have never been happy about the escalating costs necessary to keep the show running. I would prefer it if the finances in F1 were curbed. That said, I am appalled by what appears to be a two-team structure whereby one team can more or less give their car to another. The rulebook as I understand it has never been interpreted in this way before. When I was planning our entry to F1, it would have been so easy to take the Lotus chassis that was on offer, put the Ford engine in the back, call it a Jordan and go racing. That would have eliminated so much of the pain and the cost associated with the torture of building your own car – particularly in the knowledge that Lotus was ready to do a joint deal with Jordan.

However, Gary Anderson was right when he persuaded me not to go down that route. To allow one team to use another team's chassis is fundamentally wrong and goes against the spirit of F1. It will be a big problem in the future. Teams receiving a chassis from another team will have to agree not to pass that team on the track and to stand in line and do this, that and the other. That is wrong. You cannot have that level of inequality and unfairness. Free spirit is essential. Could you have imagined me getting on the radio and saying to Eddie Irvine, 'Listen, Eddie, you must not pass that guy in front because his team supplied the chassis you are sitting in'? The reply would have been unprintable.

It is fundamental that each F1 team must be able to design, build, test and race its own car. That brings its own challenges, but they are worth it in the end. I came in on a wing and a prayer. I don't think I had a single day off mentally, and that applies to everyone in F1. The unseen cost was summed up recently by my daughter Zoë. I reminded her what a good Dad I was but she simply looked at me and said, 'Dad, you've only just turned up.' It was a sobering moment.

That said, everyone had great fun along the way. At this moment, only five teams have won multiple grands prix in the past 20 years. Jordan is one of them and I am proud of that, particularly as I did it as an independent man.

# INDEX

A1 Grand Prix, 2
Abramovich, Roman, 370
Acheson, Kenny, 44
Acorn computers, 77
Adams, Paul, 126, 172
Adelaide, 164, 179, 198, 212, 359
Aer Lingus, 9
AGS, 107
Ahearn, Bertie, 323
Ahmed Bin Saeed Al Maktoum, Sheikh, 335
AIB *see* Allied Irish Banks
Aida, 204-7
Ainsley-Cowlishaw, Mick, 34
Aintree Car Club, 29
Air Studios, 299
Akagi, Akira, 121
Albert, Prince, 328
Albert Hall *see* Royal Albert Hall
Alboreto, Michele, 91, 94
Alcatel, 255
Alesi, Jean
- joins Jordan team, 89–91
- moves into F1, 91–6
- and Jordan's move into F1, 100
- F1 races, 95, 141, 142, 187, 220, 227, 228, 275, 290, 311–12
- and Marlboro, 231
- brief references, 99, 101, 116, 133, 148, 167, 196, 371

Alesi, José, 89, 91
Alfa Romeo, 65, 79
Allied Irish Banks (AIB), 41, 107–8
Alliot, Philippe, 224
All Stars Club, Bray, 7
Alonso, Fernando, 157, 320
Altnagelvin Hospital, 285
Anderson, Gary
- before joining Jordan, 102–4
- designs Jordan-Ford 191, 104, 109, 110–11
- and pre-season testing, 124
- good working relationship with EJ, 127–8
- and 1991 season, 134, 136, 139, 143–4, 171–2
- and Herbie Blash, 165
- designs Jordan-Yamaha 192, 177, 178
- and Brian Hart, 182
- and Rubens Barrichello, 183, 209, 216, 219, 226
- at launch of Jordan-Peugeot 195, 225
- and Montreal race, 227, 228
- continual development of car, 246
- designs Jordan Mugen-Honda 198, 256
- friction between Trevor Foster and, 262–3
- and Mike Gascoyne, 264, 268, 305
- health problems, 268
- and Jordan's first F1 victory, 277
- hands in his notice, 282
- departure from Jordan, 286–7
- returns to Jordan, 314
- and result of Interlagos race, 320
- leaves Jordan, 329
- brief references, 85, 107, 123, 130, 158, 181, 186, 188, 189, 200, 220, 280, 285, 382, 386

Andrew, Prince, 328
Andrews, Eamonn, 304
Anfield, 283
Angra dos Reis, 211

Ansell, Mike, 311
Anson, 102, 103
Apicella, Marco, 189
Ardennes, 272
Argentina, 242–3
Arisco, 184
Arrivabene, Mauricio, 159–60
Arrows, 91, 95, 249, 250–1
Ashford, Paul, 7, 38
Asian Games, 344
Aspel, Michael, 302–3
Audi, 166
Austin, Guy, 168
Australia, 1, 44, 162–3, 164, 167, 171, 179, 196, 198, 242, 260, 287, 305, 315, 318, 358 *see also* names of places
Australian Grand Prix, 3, 212, 234
Austria, 267, 294, 383
Austrian Grand Prix, 45, 75, 302
*Autosport*, 39, 115, 118, 119, 197, 291

B+I Ferries, 24–5
B&H *see* Benson & Hedges
Bahrain, 3, 327, 328
Ballymore Hurdle race, Cheltenham, 374
Bank of Ireland, 13
BAR (British American Racing), 283, 305, 308, 311, 314, 315, 316, 330
BARC (British Automobile Racing Club), 68
Barcelona, 262
Barclay, 172, 173, 249
Bar Italia, London, 304
Barney, 17
Barrichello, Rubens
  joins Jordan team, 183
  1993 season, 186, 187–8, 189, 190, 193, 194, 195
  1994 season, 202, 206, 208–9, 212, 215–16, 218, 219–20, 221
  at 1995 car launch, 225
  1995 season, 226, 227, 228
  1996 season, 236, 237, 238
  leaves Jordan, 241
  1999 season, 290
  2003 season, 320
  brief references, 184, 200, 201
BAT *see* British American Tobacco
Bates, Ken, 370
Baumgartner, Zsolt, 319
BBC Radio 5 Live, 339
Beach Boys, 217
Beamish, 36
Beckham, David, 245
Belfast, 33–4, 341
Belgian Grand Prix, 123, 153–4
Belgium, 294 *see also* Spa; Zolder
Belgravia, 335, 336
Bell, Derek, 49
Benetton
  and Camel, 115–16
  Johnny Herbert drives for, 227
  Jos Verstapper drives for, 201, 202
  and Michael Schumacher deal, 155–6, 157, 158–9, 160, 161
  Michael Schumacher drives for, 206, 210, 227, 270
  Michael Schumacher leaves, 229
  Nelson Piquet drives for, 154
  Roberto Moreno drives for, 140, 142, 144, 145
  Roberto Moreno ousted by Schumacher deal, 156, 158–9
  Roberto Moreno accepts money from 159
  Toleman bought by, 82
  brief references, 34, 85, 106, 141, 162, 182, 220, 246, 257, 324, 346, 381
Benetton, Luciano, 160
Bennetts, Dick, 69, 74, 79
Benson & Hedges (B&H)
  Jordan gains sponsorship of, 234–5
  and Damon Hill, 249–50, 251, 283
  and logos, 240, 257
  and problems with car, 263
  and Hockenheim race, 309
  and BAT, 315
  winds down sponsorship, 323–4, 336
  heads list of sponsors, 327
  brief references, 237, 242, 248, 254, 258, 312, 313, 345
Berg, Allen, 63, 71, 75, 76, 77
Berger, Gerhard, 64, 75, 142, 146, 195, 197, 206, 227
Bernard, Eric, 202
Beta, 169
Betbrokers, 374
'Big Dave', 288, 289
Birendelli, Luca, 158
Birmingham Superprix, 95, 101, 102

Bishops Court, 20, 25
Black and Tans, 6
Blanchflower, Danny, 303
Blash, Herbie, 165, 319
Bleekemolen, Michael, 61, 62
Blundell, Mark, 200, 201
BMW, 163, 305, 330
  M1, 48
BMW Masters, 355, 359
Bogle, Graham, 230, 231
Bogus Brothers, 350
Bologna, 211, 212
Bono, 250, 369, 381
Boteach, Rabbi Shmuel, 341
Boutsen, Thierry, 142, 186, 188, 189
Bowden, Kate, 75
Bowden, Rob, 75, 76
BP, 175
Brabham, 102, 106, 133, 139, 165, 176
Brabham, Jack, 46
Bracey, John, 56
Brackley, 41, 245
Brackley Sawmills, 104
Brady, Liam, 368
Brady, Michael, 33
Bramach, Katrina, 39
Brands Hatch, 85–6, 91
Branson, Richard, 82
Braun, 176
Brawn, Ross, 161
Bray, 5–8, 352
Brazil, 44, 139, 140–1, 178, 184, 186, 199, 200, 201–3, 211, 225–6, 238, 242, 287, 319–20, 321, 379, 386
BRDC *see* British Racing Drivers Club
Breen, Michael, 251, 283, 285
Briatore, Flavio, 115, 157, 158, 159, 160, 161, 242, 256, 270, 279, 306, 317, 345–6
Brick In The Wall concert, 48
Bridgestone, 121, 309
Bristol Bar, Jersey, 14
British American Racing *see* BAR
British American Tobacco (BAT), 172, 249, 283, 294, 308, 314–15, 316
British Automobile Racing Club (BARC), 68
British Avon, 70
British F3 Championship, 40, 44–5, 46, 53, 70, 71, 77, 79, 183
British Grand Prix, 39–40, 42, 96, 216, 268, 269, 292, 293
British Racing and Sportscar Club (BRSCC), 68
British Racing Drivers Club (BRDC), 54, 68, 69, 71
Brixton prison, 363
BRM, 31
Bromley Motorsport, 104
Brosnan, Piers, 317
Brown, Hamish, 71
Brown, Jimmy, 54, 68, 69
BRSCC (British Racing and Sportscar Club), 68
Brundle, John, 68, 69
Brundle, Martin
  and F3, 63, 68, 70, 71, 72, 74, 75, 76, 119
  and EJM, 88
  and Tyrrell, 93
  at Phoenix, 133, 139
  drives for Ligier, 184
  and plans for launch of Jordan-Hart 194, 200
  drives for McLaren, 201, 202–3
  and Jordan post-Grand Prix party, 217
  signs with Jordan, 235
  1996 season, 236–7, 238
  goes of the boil, 238–9
  television career, 241
  professionalism, 383–4
  brief references, 176, 196
Bryony, 348–9, 351
Buckland, Angela (later Angela de Ferran), 122
Budapest, 266
Buenos Aires, 242–3
Burchill, Charlie, 250
Burgh, Chris de, 217
*Burrasca*, 2
Burrell, Pete, 310
Burrows, Nick, 243, 277, 278
Butler, Judge Gerald, 150
Butler, Jean, 302
Button, Jenson, 335
'Buzzing Hornet' logo, 257
Byrne, Gay, 10
Byrne, Rory, 161
Byrne, Tommy, 53, 63–5, 71, 88, 384

Cabrera, Angel, 359
Cad-Cam, 113
Cadenet, Alain de, 50–1
Cadwell Park, 46
Cairns, 196
Camel, 83–4, 85, 91–2, 94, 100, 115–17, 125, 135, 172, 234, 239, 379
Camel France, 116, 123
Camel Trophy, 92
Canada, 80, 142, 226–8, 256, 263, 288, 292, 329
Canadian Grand Prix, 253
Cancer and Leukaemia in Childhood *see* CLIC
Candy, Vivian, 31, 33–4
Canon, 130
Capelli, Ivan, 142, 184, 186
Captain America, 31
Carlton Towers Hotel, London, 126, 149
Celtic, 370–1
Cesaris, Andrea de, 44–6, 123, 137, 140, 141, 142, 143–4, 144–5, 145–6, 149, 153–4, 162, 209, 211
Chambers, Martin, 216
Champ Car, 80, 104, 163
Chapman, Colin (Chunky), 47, 84, 93, 115, 214
Charlton, Jack, 369
Chavane, Christian, 225
Cheever, Ross, 104–5
Chelsea, 370, 372
Cheltenham, 374
Chessington, 165
Chevron, 46
B28, 34
China, 308
Chinese Grand Prix, 375, 380
Chosen Few, The, 7
Christensen, Helena, 317
Christian Brothers, 10
Circuit of Ireland, 27, 352
Cirque du Soleil, 254, 257
Citibank, 380
Clareville Capital, 374, 376
Clark, Jim, 214
Clarke, Darren, 285, 355
CLIC (Cancer and Leukaemia in Childhood), 168, 217, 301, 343–51, 354
sponsored bike ride in Negev, 301, 344, 346–8
Clinton, Bill, 342
Clowes, Tim, 53, 76
College of Surgeons, 328
Cologne, 331
Coloni, 107, 124, 135
Colonna, Philippe, 54
*Commitments, The*, 167, 168
Constructors' Championship, 286, 291, 294, 295, 314
Coolock, 52
Cooper, Adam, 196
Cork, 39
Cormican, Mark, 320–1
Cosmo Oil, 191, 198
Cosworth, 106–7, 154, 164, 165–6, 167, 174, 318, 321, 330, 378
Coulthard, David, 227, 242, 260, 272, 273, 277, 320
Count, 168
Coventry City Football Club, 266, 368
Crazy Paris show, 120
Credit Suisse, 345
Croft, 25
Croke Park, 128
Crombac, Gerard 'Jabby', 115
Crossle
20F, 19
25F, 19, 29

*Daily Express*, 269
*Daily Mail*, 269
Dallara, 80, 135, 136, 137, 140, 142
Daly, Derek, 19, 24, 25, 40
*Dancing on Dangerous Ground*, 302
Dandelion Green, Dublin, 22, 23
Danielsson, Thomas, 85
Dartry, 8
David Price Racing, 56, 120
Davies, Barry, 246
Davies, Giselle, 246, 255, 266, 283, 298, 383
Davis, John, 263, 287
Debrett's, 374
Delphi, 259
Dennis, Rob, 160, 161
Dennis, Ron, 144, 222–3, 224, 241, 242, 260, 270, 295, 358
Derby, 34
Des, 346–7, 348

Desmond, Dermot, 369, 371, 381
Destiny Wireless, 374
Detroit, 80, 106
Deutsche Post, 300–2, 309, 312–13, 324
Devaney, Bernard, 24, 44, 118
Deveney, Donny, 7
DHL, 301, 312–13, 324, 379
Digby, Peter, 370
Dijon, 56, 57
Docking, Alan, 41
Doha, 344
Dolce Vita Ball, La, 351
Donegan, Roger, 107–8, 353–4
Donington, 43, 53, 119, 186–9
Donnelly, Martin, 22, 85, 86, 87, 89–90, 91, 95, 96–7, 104, 373, 384
Donnelly, Mr, 22
*Douce France*, 253
Doyle, Roddy, 167
Drogheda, 17
Drury Lane theatre, 302–3
Druskin, Bob, 380
Dubai, 2, 3, 335
Dubai Open, 2
Dublin, 128, 167, 168, 207
  EJ in, 5, 8–13, 20, 21–8, 30, 31–3, 36–7, 38, 39, 40, 52
Dunlop, 105
Dunwoody, Richard, 301, 310
Du Pont chemical plant, 27
Durand, Henri, 314
Dusseldorf, 323

Earle, Mike, 101
Earls Court, 48, 50
Ecclestone, Bernie
  and Colin 'Chunky' Chapman, 47
  and James Weaver, 54
  and finances in F1, 62, 73, 132
  and Ken Tyrrell, 93
  and Gary Anderson, 102
  recommends Ian Phillips to EJ, 122
  does not like too many teams, 132–3
  attitude to Jordan, 133
  and EJ's complaints about facilities in Mexico, 143
  and breaking of rules by de Cesaris, 144
  and Jordan's deal with Yamaha, 155, 165
  and IMG, 156
  and Schumacher affair, 156–7, 157–8, 160–1, 167
  and Jordan's finances, 164–5
  and Gerhard Berger, 197
  after Senna's death, 214
  and Jordan's image, 237–8
  negotiates release of Ralf Schumacher's contract, 282
  agrees to parade of F1 cars, 293
  and F1 demonstration in London, 333
  concerned about future of Jordan, 336–7
  and football, 370, 372
  EJ's bus journey with, 372
  EJ's opinion of, 372–3
  brief references, 233, 317, 325, 340, 375, 379
Ecclestone, Slavica, 317
Eddie Jordan Management (EJM), 87–9, 91, 96
Eddie Jordan Racing *see* Jordan
Edwards, Tim, 205, 329, 382
Edwards, Trudie, 382
Edwards, Victoria, 360
Eeckelaert, Jacky, 256
EJM *see* Eddie Jordan Management
Elat, 344, 347
Els, Ernie, 355, 375
Esat Digifone, 259, 261
Essen Motor Show, 300
Essex Oil, 253
Estoril, 230, 237, 358
Estrada, Christina, 317
European Championship, 63, 70
Eurovision Song Contest, 317
Eustace, Joe, 21–2
Everton, 266

FI *see* Formula 1
FIA, 90, 157, 165, 202, 203, 214, 215, 283, 310, 311, 332
F2 *see* Formula 2
F3 *see* Formula 3
F3000 *see* Formula 3000
Faenza, 333
Falls Road, Belfast, 34
Fauconnier, Pierre-Michel, 224, 256
Feather, Charlie, 310
FedEx, 312

Ferguson, Alex, 245
Ferguson, Bernard, 165
Ferran (*née* Buckland), Angela de, 122
Ferran, Gil de, 122
Ferrari
  Alain Prost drives for, 142
  Eddie Irvine's move to, 230, 231–2, 233
  Eddie Irvine drives for, 275–6, 296
  Gerhard Berger drives for, 206, 227
  Ivan Capelli drives for, 184, 186
  Jean Alesi signs with, 96
  Jean Alesi drives for, 141, 220, 227, 228
  Michael Schumacher drives for, 198, 229, 245, 273, 290, 296, 305
  Rubens Barrichello drives for, 320
  Shell supports, 174
  and Vodafone, 324, 325
  and weather prediction, 288
  1998 car launch, 255
  brief references, 91, 99, 107, 157, 271, 289, 297, 307, 310, 381
Fildes, Ken, 30
Fiorio, Cesare, 96
Firman, Angie, 318
Firman (Junior), Ralph, 318, 319
Firman (Senior), Ralph, 318–19
Fisichella, Giancarlo, 3, 242, 243–4, 245, 274, 314, 319, 320, 321, 384, 385
Fitzgerald, J.P., 355, 375
Fitzgerald, Mick, 361
Fitzpatrick, John, 353
Flintoff, Freddie, 350
Flooring Centre, The, 22, 30
Foitek, Gregor, 85
Fondmetal, 135
Ford, 106, 114, 115, 116, 131, 133, 141, 157, 177, 184, 318, 321, 322, 323, 331
Ford Anglia, 19
  Super, 352
Formula 1 (F1)
  Nigel Mansell moves into, 47
  and payment arrangements, 62, 73
  Eddie Jordan Management enables drivers to move into, 91–7
  Jordan prepares for racing in, 99–131
  1991 season, 132–54, 162–3, 164
  and IMG, 156
  rivalry, 160
  rules, 165
  1992 season, 171, 177–80
  1993 season, 186–99
  1994 season, 200–21
  safety, 209
  1995 season, 225–8
  1996 season, 234, 235–9
  1997 season, 242–5
  1998 season, 259–64, 268, 271, 272–7, 284, 286
  Dominic Shorthouse's interest in, 266–7, 286
  1999 season, 287–91, 292, 294–7
  2000 season, 305
  2001 season, 308–12
  2002 season, 314
  2003 season, 318–21
  and threat of breakaway championship, 321–2
  2004 season, 329–30
  demonstration in London, 333
  2005 season, 1, 2
  and golfing opportunities, 357–8
  EJ assesses his career in, 378–87
  *see also* names of teams, sponsors and individuals associated with F1
Formula 2 (F2), 121
Formula 3 (F3), 16, 25, 44–6, 53–81, 99, 100, 111, 119, 123, 133, 135–6, 183, 383
Formula 3000 (F3000)
  Eddie Irvine in, 97, 191, 385
  and Jordan, 77, 80, 82–6, 89–90, 95, 99, 100, 101–2, 113, 115, 133, 135–6, 148, 171
  and Michael Schumacher, 148, 149
  and Reynard, 78, 80, 104
  brief references, 91, 192, 231, 249
Formula Atlantic, 30, 31, 34, 39
Formula Ford, 16, 19, 21, 22, 24–5, 27, 29, 30, 31, 34, 66, 77, 375
Formula Nippon, 241, 318
Foster, Trevor
  and F3000 team, 82, 113
  in Phoenix, 134, 138
  and Michael Schumacher's test drive, 152
  opposed to inclusion of Gugelmin in team, 175

and Brian Hart, 182
and Damon Hill, 250
friction between Gary Anderson and, 262–3
increased responsibilities, 268
and Ralf Schumacher, 271
and post-race debrief, 280
confidence in technical team, 287
target for 2001 season, 308
and penalty in Indianapolis, 310, 311
and staff reductions, 313
and financial issues, 379
brief references, 109, 146, 171, 272, 289, 382
France, 145, 189, 224, 244, 263, 288–91, 292 *see also* names of places0
French Grand Prix, 91, 224, 288–91, 292, 308
Frentzen, Heinz-Harald, 97, 109, 282, 283, 287, 288–9, 290, 291, 292, 293, 294, 295–6, 302, 305, 308–9, 310, 385
Fuji, 129, 130, 131, 135, 150
Fukui, Takeo, 315
Fullerton, Terry, 16
Furey, Finbar, 334

Gachot, Bertrand, 124, 126, 137, 139, 140–1, 142, 143, 146–7, 149–50, 166
Gallagher, Mark, 259, 269, 285, 303, 379
Gallaher, 234, 235, 239, 247, 315, 375
Galway, 17, 21
Galway Rally, 27
Gascoyne, Mike, 263–4, 268, 284, 287, 305–6
Gaug, Lee, 107
GdeZ, 258, 277
Geisdorfer, Christian, 337
Geldof, Bob, 381
Genesis, 304
German Grand Prix, 309
Germany, 148, 163, 245, 267, 294, 300, 309–10, 331
Giants Stadium, New York, 368–9
Gibson, Gary, 24
Gitanes, 232
Given, Shay, 368
Glock, Timo, 329–30
Goldsmith, Harvey, 333
Goodman, Louise, 192, 246, 283, 333, 334, 383
Goodyear, 107, 131, 133, 136, 145, 273
Gorbachev, Mikhail, 342
Gorne, Rick, 77, 78, 79, 80, 81
GPWC, 322, 323
*Grafton*, HMS, 328–9
Granby Bar, Dublin, 52
Grand Prix Ball, 55
Grange, Lucian, 218
Greasley, Mike, 230
Great Western House, London, 31
Green, Andrew, 109, 110
Green, Philip, 376
Green Man pub, near Silverstone, 80
Greystones, 37
Grinham, Barry, 384
Groucho Club, 254
*Guardian*, 251, 257
Gugelmin, Mauricio, 173–4, 175, 176, 178, 179, 182
Guyana, 44

Haines, David, 323, 324, 325
Hakkinen Mika, 206, 217, 227, 260, 261, 284, 290, 294, 295, 296
Hall, Alister, 285
Hamidy, Eghbal, 306, 314
Hamilton, Duncan, 69
Hamilton, Maurice, 167, 311, 339
Hamilton Island, 317
Hammersmith, 317
Hampel, Andrew, 173, 175
Harding, Matthew, 370
Hard Rock Café, Tokyo, 191
Harrington, Padraig, 356
Harrison, George, 316–17
Harrison, Olivia, 317
Hart, Brian, 181–2, 201, 206, 222
Haug, Norbert, 322
Hawkridge, Alex, 82
Haylett, Lindsay, 122–3, 266, 279, 298, 303, 313, 383
Head, Betise, 370
Head, Patrick, 215, 282, 370
Heidfeld, Nick, 329, 330
*Hello* magazine, 348
Henley-on-Thames, 317
Henry, Alan, 251
Herbert, Johnny, 79, 80, 82, 83, 84, 85–6, 87, 99, 100, 111, 133, 196, 217, 227,

384
Herd, Robin, 245
Hermitage Hotel, Monaco, 259
Hewlett-Packard, 113, 258
Heysham, 16
Hibernian Bank, 13
Hibernian Hotel, Dublin, 39
Hickman, Duncan, 335
Highgate, 88
High Wycombe, 348
Hill, Damon
1993 season, 187, 188, 189, 194, 195
and Jordan post-Grand Prix party, 217
1995 season, 227
joins Jordan, 248–52
and launch of Jordan Mugen-Honda 198, 255
1998 season, 261, 263, 267, 271, 272–3, 274, 275, 276, 284
contract for 1999, 269, 283
visits Omagh bomb victim, 285
1999 season, 291, 292, 296
decides to continue to end of 1999 season, 293–4
brief reference, 384
Hill, Graham, 293
Hill, Jimmy, 368
'Hissing Sid' logo, 240
Hobbs, David, 49, 50
Hockenheim, 97, 147, 244, 267, 294, 309–10, 323
Hogan, John, 231
Hogan, Tommy, 30
Holland, 59–60
Holland, Jools, 217
Holloway, Tim, 306, 310–11
'Home from Home' scheme, 349–50, 351
Honda, 122, 183, 256, 264–5, 266, 306, 308, 309, 310, 314–15, 318, 330
Honda, Hirotoshi, 256, 259, 315
Hong Kong Hutchison Wampao, 335
Horner, Christian, 335–6
Horrigan, Ed, 92
Houghton, Ray, 369
Howett, John, 331
HSBC, 345
HSBC World Matchplay, 354
Hughes, Tania, 269
Hungarian Grand Prix, 218, 249
Hungary, 147, 150, 266, 267, 294, 319
Hunt, David, 77
Hunt, James, 50, 51, 77, 230
Huppert, Jurgen, 322–3
Hurley, Bishop, 185–6
Hurley, Brian 'Red', 10, 304
Huysman, Harald, 77–8
Hyde Park, 360
Hynde, Chrissie, 216

ICI, 237
Illey, John, 287
IMG (International Management Group), 87–8, 155, 156, 173–4, 175, 176, 354
Imola, 141, 206, 208–11, 215, 287, 321, 322
Independent Radio News, 255
Indianapolis, 299, 310, 311
Interlagos, 140–1, 201–3, 226, 310–20
International Management Group *see* IMG
International Trophy, 293
INXS, 217
IRAC, 31
Iran, 371
Ireland, 126, 127, 128, 131, 192, 207, 225, 240, 250, 369, 375, 376, 381
EJ lives in, 5–40, 352
and Marlboro sponsorship, 31–3, 43
Ireland football team, 368–9, 370, 371
Ireland Under 21s basketball team, 38
Irene, The (dance hall), Dublin, 52
Irish Formula Atlantic Championship, 34, 40, 43
Irish Sisters of Charity, 9
Irish Sisters of Charity Bank, 13
*Irish Times*, 90
Irvine, Eddie
racing career before entering F1, 96, 97–8, 109, 191
enters F1 at Suzuka, 191–9
joins Jordan team, 200, 201
1994 season, 202, 203–4, 218, 220
difficult relationship with Rubens Barrichello, 216
at launch of Jordan-Peugeot 195, 225
1995 season, 226, 227, 228
and Ferrari deal, 229–33
1998 season, 275–6
1999 season, 295, 296
and *This is Your Life*, 304–5

earnings at Jaguar, 323
character, 384–5
brief references, 104, 250, 318, 387
Isle of Man, 16
Istanbul, 371
Italian Grand Prix, 156, 189, 283
Italy, 63–6, 69, 190, 208–11, 215, 255, 344
Italy football team, 368, 369
ITV, 119, 236, 291

Jabouille, Jean-Pierre, 224, 225
Jacklin, Tony, 353
Jackson, Michael, 164, 342
Jacobi, Julian, 155, 175
Jaguar, 68, 69, 235, 300–1, 305, 318, 321, 323
Japan, 98, 121, 129–31, 150, 155, 165, 167, 171, 178–9, 186, 190, 203, 312, 314, 315, 318, 331, 369, 370 *see also* Aida; Suzuka
Japanese F3000 series, 191
Japanese Grand Prix, 191
Jardine, Tony, 92
Jenkinson, Tom, 37
Jenner, Barry, 235, 254
Jerez, 83, 97, 226, 357
Jersey, 14–15, 278
Jersey Electricity Company, 14
Jocelyn, 120
Johansson, Stefan, 43, 44, 46, 57, 118, 120, 133, 151, 152
John, Elton, 216
Johnnie Fox's pub, 25
John Radcliffe hospital, Oxford, 343
Johnson, Alan ('The King'), 16
Jones, Alan, 30
Jordan
known as Eddie Jordan Racing, 53
and Formula 3, 53–81
funding from BRDC, 69
and Formula 3000, 77, 80, 82–6, 89–90, 95, 99, 100, 101–2, 113, 115, 133, 135–6, 148, 171
obtains sponsorship from Camel, 83–4
prepares for Formula I racing, 99–108
name changed to Jordan Grand Prix, 108
first season in F1 (1991), 132–54, 162–3, 164
and Schumacher affair, 155–62
financial difficulties, 164–6, 170
new team headquarters constructed, 168–9
sponsorship for second season, 172–6
1992 season, 171–80
1993 season, 181–99
1994 season, 200–21
sponsored by Peugeot, 222–5
sponsord by Total, 225
1995 season, 225–8
Eddie Irvine leaves, 229–33
1996 season, 234, 235–9
image, 237–8, 240
snake logo, 240
newspaper exposure, 241
drivers signed for 1997, 241–2
1997 season, 242–6
Damon Hill joins, 248–52
production and launch of Jordan 198, 253–8
1998 season, 259–64, 268, 271, 272–7, 284, 286
partnership discussions, 264–5, 266
supporters club, 268–9
negotiations over driver contracts for 1999, 269
factory response to victory, 280–1
Ralf Schumacher leaves, 281–2, 282–3
Heinz-Harald Frentzen joins, 282, 287
Gary Anderson leaves, 282, 286–7
agreement with Damon Hill, 283
affected by Omagh bombing, 285
Warbury Pincus buys 49.9 percent of, 286
1999 season, 287–91, 292, 294–7
Johnny Rotten visits factory, 298–9
negotiations with Deutsch Post, 300–2
Jarno Trulli signs with, 302
2000 season, 305
management changes, 305–7
2001 season, 308–12
departure of Frentzen, 308–9
Takuma Sato becomes driver for, 309
DHL becomes associated with, 312
financial problems 313
staff reductions, 313–14
Gary Anderson returns to, 314
2002 season, 314

end of association with Honda, 314, 315–16
BAT's attitude to, 314–15
2003 season, 318–21
problems with Ford, 321–3
negotiations with Mercedes, 322–3
and Vodafone, 323–6
sponsorship from Bahrain, 327–8
management changes, 329
2004 season, 329–30
EJ considers future of, 330–1, 332–3
negotiations and deal with Toyota, 331–2
negotiations and sale of, 335–40
EJ's assessment of achievements, 378–87
*see also* Jordan cars

Jordan (Katie Price), 241

Jordan, Eddie
early life, 5–13
employed by bank, 13
works in Jersey, 14
karting, 14–17
injured in karting accident, 17
transferred to Galway, 17–18
purchases first cars, 19
begins to take part in motor-racing, 19–20, 24–5
returns to Dublin, 21
money-raising efforts, 21–4
social life, 25–6
and rallying, 26–8
injured in motor-racing accident, 29
takes part in Formula Atlantic races, 30–1, 34
obtains sponsorship from Marlboro, 31
and George Macken's visits to Dublin, 32–3
in Belfast, 33–5
and the Large family, 36–7
meets Marie, 37–8
relationship with Marie, 38–9
annual visit to Silverstone, 39–40
wins Irish Formula Atlantic Championship, 40
marries Marie, 40
early married life, 41–2
Marlboro continues to sponsor, 43–4
takes part in British F3 Championship, 44–6
begins to take part in sportscar racing, 48
takes part in Le Mans 24-Hour race, 48–50, 51
at Pink Floyd concert, 50–1
begins working relationship with John Walton, 52
stops racing, 53
runs Formula 3 racing team, 53–81
becomes member of BRDC, 69
makes move into Formula 30000, 77, 82–6
buys house in Oxford, 81
obtains sponsorship from Camel, 83–4
management, 87–98
prepares to move into F1, 99–131
searches for sponsors, 111–13, 115–17, 126–7, 129–31
first season in F1 (1991), 132–54, 162–3, 164
and Schumacher affair, 155–62
financial difficulties, 164–6, 170
sees *The Commitments*, 167–8
and construction of new team headquarters, 168–9
encounter with Jimmi Rembiszewski, 172–3
approached by IMG, 173–4
makes sponsorship deal with Sasol, 174–5
commission agreements with IMG, 175–6
obtains drivers for 1992 season, 173–4, 175, 176–7
and 1992 season, 171, 177–80
Brian Hart works for, 181–2
chooses drivers for 1993, 183–4, 186, 191–2
and Sasol hospitality, 184–6
and 1993 season, 186–99
and 1994 season, 200–21
loses appeal to F1A, 203–4
organises gig at Silverstone and forms band, 216–18
and Peugeot, 222–5
and Total, 225
and 1995 season, 225–8
obtains deal for Eddie Irvine, 229–33
negotiations and deal with Gallaher/Benson & Hedges, 234–5

and 1996 season, 234, 235–9
concerned with image of team, 237–8
dislikes snake logo, 240
signs drivers for 1997, 241–2
and 1997 season, 242–6
shown drawings, 247–8
obtains Damon Hill as driver, 248–52
and production and launch of Jordan 198, 253–8
and 1998 season, 259–64, 268, 271, 272–7, 284, 286
partnership discussions with Honda, 264–5, 266
meets Dominic Shorthouse, 266–7
negotiations over driver contracts for 1999, 269
responds to Michael Schumacher's comments, 269–70, 271
returns to Oxford, 277–9
at the factory after victory, 280–1
and Ralf Schumacher's departure, 281–2, 282–3
obtains Heinz-Harald Frentzen as driver, 282, 287
and Gary Anderson's departure, 282
reaches agreement with Damon Hill, 283
and Omagh bombing, 285
visits Omagh victim, 285
has medical, 286
agreement with Warburg Pincus, 286
and 1999 season, 287–91, 292, 294–7
and Damon Hill's intentions, 292, 293–4
discussions with Jos Verstappen, 292–3
and Johnny Rotten's visit, 298–9
negotiations with Deutsche Post, 300–2
signs Jarno Trulli, 302
features in *This is Your Life*, 302–4
and 2000 season, 305
management changes, 305–7
and 2001 season, 308–12
and departure of Frentzen, 308–9
agrees to sign Takuma Sato, 309
and association with DHL, 312
and financial problems, 313
makes staff reductions, 313–14
and Gary Anderson's return, 314
and 2002 season, 314
and end of association with Honda, 314, 315–16
and attitude of BAT, 314–15
and George Harrison, 316–17
and 2003 season, 318–21
problems with Ford, 321–3
negotiations with Mercedes, 322–3
and Vodafone, 323–6
obtains sponsorship from Bahrain, 327–8
attends dinner on HMS *Grafton*, 328–9
and 2004 season, 329–30
considers the state of his company, 330–1
negotiates and makes deal with Toyota, 331–2
and death of John Boy, 333–4
involved in negotiations with various companies, 335–6
meeting with Bernie Ecclestone, 336–7
sells company, 337–40
activities during opening of 2005 season, 1–4
friendship with Usiskin family, 341
meets Rabbi Boteach, 341–2
speaks at Oxford University Union, 342
involvement with CLIC, 343–4, 346–51
children, 344–6
and golf, 352–9
involved in television project with boys from broken homes, 360–7
and football, 368–72
bus journey with Bernie Ecclestone, 372
opinion of Bernie Ecclestone, 372–3
investments and financial interests, 374–6
attends grand prix at Monaco, 376–7
assessment of his career, 378–87
Jordan, Eileen (EJ's mother), 8, 383
Jordan, Helen (EJ's sister) *see* McCarthy (*née* Jordan), Helen
Jordan, Kyle ('Killer') (EJ's son), 345–6
Jordan, Lilian (EJ's aunt), 5, 7, 8
Jordan (*née* McCarthy), Marie (EJ's wife)
meets EJ, 37–8
relationship with EJ, 38–9
marries EJ, 40
early married life, 40–2
in Monaco, 55
in Spain, 80

home in Westbury, 81
and EJ's decision to move into F1, 101
in Phoenix, 134
sees *The Commitments*, 167
in South Africa, 177, 184–5
unable to attend race at Spa, 277
and *This is Your Life* programme, 303
and George Harrison, 316–17
attends dinner on HMS *Grafton*, 328–9
and EJ's holiday at beginning of 2005 season, 2, 3
friendship with Suzi Usiskin, 341
and EJ's involvement with CLIC, 343, 348, 349
and golf, 353, 354
and purchase of house in Sotogrande, 354
marriage relationship, 383
brief references, 50, 175, 321
Jordan, Maureen (EJ's aunt) *see* Rectrus, Mother
Jordan, Michele ('Miki') (EJ's daughter), 26, 80, 81, 101, 341, 344
Jordan, Zak (EJ's son), 26, 81, 101, 341, 345
Jordan, Zoë (EJ's daughter), 42, 55, 101, 341, 344–5
Jordan cars
Jordan-Ford 191, 102, 104, 106–7, 110–11, 113–15, 124–5, 144, 145, 154, 166, 282, 285
Jordan-Yamaha, 192, 177, 178–9, 181
Jordan-Hart 193, 182
Jordan-Hart 194, 200
Jordan Peugeot 195, 225
Jordan-Peugeot 196, 234, 236, 237, 238, 260
Jordan Peugeot 197, 240, 244, 255
Jordan Mugen-Honda 198, 254–8, 259–60, 263
Jordan Mugen-Honda 199, 287, 292, 294, 295
Jordan Mugen-Honda EJ10, 302
Jordan EJ14, 329
Jordan Grand Prix *see* Jordan
Jordan post-grand Prix party, 216–17
Jordan's restaurant, Sydney, 167
Judd engines, 106, 121
Jury's Hotel, Dublin, 32, 37
Juventus, 344, 371

Kawamoto, Mr, 264, 315
Keane, Robbie, 368
Keane, Roy, 368, 369–70
Kempton Park, 361
Kendall, Felicity, 262
Kennedy, David, 24, 25, 31, 40
Kennedy, Michael, 370
Kenny, Enda, 225
Kenny, Pat, 207
Kilduff, Tony, 375
Kilkenny, Ossie, 369
Killiney, 250
Kimmage, Paul, 262
Kinaine, Gerry, 34
Kinsella, Austin, 16
Kirkistown, 20, 34
Kleinwort Benson, 336
Knopfler, Mark, 2
Kodak, 125, 129
Kolles, Colin, 337, 340
Kramer, Gert, 151
Kranefuss, Michael, 106, 115, 116
Kruger, Gina, 177
Kruger, Paul, 177
Krynauw, Jan, 178, 181, 185
Kyalami, 178

Lady of Lourdes hospital, Drogheda, 17
Lafite, Jacques, 224
Lafosse, Jean-Louis, 49, 50
Laliberte, Guy, 253–4
Lamborghini, 106, 114
L'Amie, John, 34
Lamy, Pedro, 210
Langley, Mr Justice, 324
Lansdowne Road, Dublin, 128
Large, (*née* McCarthy), Ann, 39
Large, Des, 36, 37, 39, 250
Large, Gill, 36
Large, Mrs, 36–7
Larrousse, 107, 114
*Late Late Show, The*, 207
Lauda, Niki, 196, 230
Lazlo, Tony, 226–7
Le Bourget, 223
Lee, W. Duncan, 83–4, 85, 91–2, 116
Leech, Martin, 323
Lehton, J.J., 136, 142, 210
Leicester Royal Infirmary, 29
Leinster Junior Boys (golf), 353

Le Mans, 48–9, 69, 149
24-Hour Race, 48–50, 51
Loeb, Sebastian, 223
Leopardstown, 37
Leslie, David, 53
Lewis, Caroline, 218
Leyton House, 121, 123, 142, 173, 184, 192
Liberty Ermitage, 335
Liège, 279
Ligier, 95, 139, 142, 184, 202, 229, 231, 232, 256
Lincoln Place, Dublin, 13
Lineker, Gary, 343, 350
Lineker, George, 343
*Lion King, The*, 217
Livingstone, Ken, 333
Lola, 139, 191, 379
London, 126, 149, 156, 254, 302, 327, 349, 360, 370
London Hospital, 97
Longridge, 24, 25
Lotus, 47, 83, 84, 85, 92, 93, 96, 115, 116, 139, 210 253
Lotus 61, 19
Lotus 69, 30
Lugano, 231
Lulu, 218
Lydon, John (Johnny Rotten), 299
Lynch, Peter, 37, 38

McAndrew, Nell, 301
Macau Grand Prix, 119–21
McCarthy, Ann (later Ann Large), 39
McCarthy (*née* Jordan), Helen (EJ's sister), 9, 21
McCarthy, Marie *see* Jordan (*née* McCarthy), Marie
McCarthy, Martin, 27
McCarthy, Mick, 369, 370
McCarthy, Neil, 21
McCreevy, Charlie, 127
McGarrity, Patsy, 20, 34
McGinley, Ali, 354
McGinley, Paul, 2, 355, 356, 357, 359
McGovern, Terry, 30
McGrath, Paul, 368
McGuigan, Barry, 343, 350
McGuigan, Danika, 343
Macken, George, 31, 32–3, 304
McKenna, Siobhan, 10
McKenzie, Bob, 269
McLaren
Andrea de Cesaris drives for, 45
Ayrton Senna drives for, 142, 146, 154, 183, 184, 187
Ayrton Senna leaves, 248
Belgravia makes deal with, 336
David Coulthard drives for, 242, 260, 272
Gerhard Berger drives for, 146
Jean Alesi drives for, 95
Kimi Raikkonen drives for, 320, 321
Martin Brundle drives for, 202, 202
Mika Hakkinen drives for, 206, 227, 260, 261, 284, 290, 294, 295
and Peugeot, 222, 223, 256
and photographers, 260
Ralf Schumacher has agreement with, 241, 242
and weather prediction, 288
1998 season, 260, 261, 267, 271, 272, 273, 284
wins 1999 championship, 297
brief references, 31, 99, 106, 107, 238, 263, 270, 287, 289, 305, 307, 310, 322, 324, 381
McMahon, Derek, 44, 119, 304
McManus, J.P., 369, 381
Macpherson, Elle, 212
MacQueen, Alastair, 76
McQuilliam, John, 287, 314, 329
Madgwick Motorsport, 79
Maggiore Hospital, Bologna, 211
Magner, John, 381
Magny-Cours, 288–91, 292, 357
Mahon, Brian, 175, 176, 184–5
Maktoum Hasher Maktoum al Maktoum, Sheikh, 2–3
Mal, 55
Mallory Park, 29
Manchester, 363, 370
Mandela, Nelson, 174, 328
Mansell, Nigel, 2, 44, 45, 46, 47, 96, 134, 142, 146, 162, 179, 270, 357, 358
Maradonna, Diego, 342
Maranello, 184
March, 46, 47, 82, 121, 173, 245
March 74B, 30
Marlboro, 31–4, 43–4, 56, 77, 89, 91, 119,

121, 123, 129, 201, 230–1, 232, 233, 234, 249, 344, 345
Marlboro Italy, 44
Marlboro Team Ireland, 33–4, 43, 44, 119
Marlboro World Championship Team, 44
Marlborough, 344, 345
Marren, David, 240, 247, 248, 249, 285
Martini, 80
Martini, Pier Luigi, 63, 65, 142
Mason, Annette, 317
Mason, Nick, 48, 217, 304, 317
Massa, Felipe, 318
MasterCard, 258, 269, 379–80
Matts, Ray, 269
Meek, Dave, 22, 23, 24
Mehl, Leo, 107
Melbourne, 1, 3, 236–7, 260, 315, 329
Mercedes-Benz, 149, 151, 155, 222, 322–3
Merrion Capital, 330
Messenger, Melinda, 241
Metalbox, 111
Meteors, 38
Mexico, 143–5
Miami Showband, 7
Michael, Sam, 263, 275, 287, 290, 296
Middlebridge, 249
Middle East, 335
Midland, 338, 339, 340
Mifcom, 367
Miff, 362–3
Milan, 156
Minardi, 142, 242, 332, 333
Misano, 63–6
Miyakawa, Mario, 371
Modena, Stefano, 176–7, 178–9
Monaco, 53–6, 57–8, 59, 141, 189, 214, 216, 217, 259, 260–2, 263, 265, 279, 292, 305, 308, 328, 376
Monasterboyce, 16–17
Mondello Park, 20, 25, 27, 30
Montezemolo, Luca di, 231–2
Montgomerie, Colin, 356
Montoquo, Fernando, 353
Montoya, Juan Pablo, 248
Montreal, 80, 226–8, 253
Monza, 48, 85, 95, 150, 156, 157, 158, 189, 251, 281, 283, 284, 294–5, 327
Moran, Kevin, 370
Moreno, Roberto, 85, 104, 139, 140, 142, 144, 145, 156, 158, 159, 160, 162
Morris, Mouse, 375
Moscow, 340
Mosley, Max, 202, 204, 215, 323
Mossop, James, 293
*Motoring News*, 122
*Motor Sport*, 122
Mourinho, Jose, 262, 370
Mouti, Massimo, 323
Mugen-Honda, 113, 255, 256, 257, 264, 293, 306
Muller, Cathy, 64
Muller, Herbie, 48
Mullingar, 15
Mullingar Karting Club, 15–17
Munich, 355, 356

Nakano, Shinji, 293
NASCAR, 125
Naspetti, Emanuele, 97, 109, 189
Neerpasch, Jochen, 155, 156
Nelson, Brian, 20, 34
*Never Mind the Bollocks*, 216, 299
Nevin, Liam, 24, 27, 304
Nevin, Margaret, 24, 304
Newcastle United, 336
Newey, Adrian, 215
New York, 368–9, 379
New Zealand, 44
Nice, 344
Nichols, Steve, 201, 203
Nielsen, John, 63
Nissan, 36
Nogaro, 123
Northern Ireland, 7, 16, 20, 27, 33–5, 192, 285
Northridge, Nigel, 235, 237, 239, 240, 241, 247, 248, 249, 251, 283, 285, 309, 318, 336, 338, 375
Novamotor, 65, 66, 69, 70, 79
Nurburgring, 48, 151, 245, 295–6

O'Brien, Denis, 259, 371
O'Briens's pub, Dublin, 32–3
O'Byrne, Eddie, 6
O'Dea, Dennis, 10
O'Dea, Donnacha, 10
O'Donaghue's pub, Dublin, 32
O'Driscoll, Richard, 108, 265–6, 280, 285, 329, 338
O'Flaherty, Michael, 31–3

O'Leary, David, 368
Oliver, Jackie, 95
Omagh, 285
Onyx, 101, 124
Oreca, 89
O'Reilly, Mona, 38, 39
Ormsby, Jordan, 358,l 359
Ormsby, Pete, 358–9
Ormsby, Wade, 359
O'Rourke, Steve, 48
Osmond, Donny, 218
Osterreichring, 75
O'Toole, Fran, 7
Oulton Park, 44–5, 46, 72, 91
Oxford, 81, 91, 122, 174, 175, 279, 325, 333–4, 341, 343, 354
Oxford United, 245
Oxford University, 341–2

Paffett, Gary, 322
Pallett, Harvey, 368
Palmer, Jonathan, 94
Panasonic, 332
Panis, Olivier, 212, 228, 261
Pantano, Giorgio, 329
Paris, 90, 223, 224
Parry-Jones, Richard, 321, 323, 331
Parsons, Richard, 19, 24, 34
Patrese, Riccardo, 139, 146, 153, 154, 179, 270
Pau, 91
Paul Ricard circuit, 95, 124
Pearl Assurance, 258, 259
Peart, Roger, 310, 311
Pederazzani brothers, 66, 69
Pegasus, 278
Pennyfather, Dave, 250
Pepsi, 129, 135, 164, 379
Perini Navi, 2
Persian Gulf, 1, 3, 328
Peter, Henri, 231
Petra, 344, 346
Peugeot, 222–3, 224, 225, 228, 242, 255, 256
Philip Morris, 31, 118–19, 123, 129, 159, 230
Phillips, Ian
  before joining Jordan, 118–21
  joins Jordan, 122
  and appointment of Lindsay Haylett, 123
  EJ phones about Michael Schumacher, 151
  and Schumacher affair, 155, 158, 159
  and Alessandro Zanardi, 160
  and Tim Schenken, 162
  discussions with BP, 174–5
  discussions with Sasol, 175
  opposed to inclusion of Gugelmin in team, 175
  attempts to sell space in Adelaide, 179
  and Ivan Capelli, 184
  meeting with Eddie Irvine, 191
  and appeal to F1A, 203
  and Benson & Hedges deal, 235
  and signing of Damon Hill, 251
  and Guy Laliberte, 254
  and driver contracts for 1999, 269
  return journey from Spa, 277, 279, 280
  meeting with Verstappen and his manager, 292
  and Deutsche Post negotiations, 301, 302
  and Vodafone case, 325
  and negotiations with Toyota, 331–2
  and deal with Shnaider, 337
  good working relationship with EJ, 338
  character, 338–9
  joins BBC Radio 5 Live, 339
  and Bernie Ecclestone, 373
  brief references, 144, 266, 283, 300, 312, 324
Phillips, Sam, 241, 279
Phoenician hotel, Phoenix, 134
Phoenix, 95, 132, 133–9
Phoenix Park, 20, 39, 52
PI, 257
Piecha, Stan, 251, 269
Piero, Alessandro del, 371
Pietersen, Kevin, 350
Ping golf clubs, 138
Pink Floyd, 48, 50
Piquet, Nelson, 68, 153, 154
Pirelli tyres, 107, 136, 145, 154
Pirro, Emanuele, 63, 120, 136
Podlech, Ortwin, 282
Poele, Eric van de, 137
Pollock, Jay, 24
Porsche, 30, 124
  Porsche 908, 48

Porsche 911, 124
Porsche 956, 49
Portaferry, 20
Portavogie, 20
Portugal, 189, 190
Portuguese Grand Prix, 358
Portumna, 21
Postbank, 301
Postlethwaite, Harvey, 263–4
Postlethwaite, John, 126
Poulter, Ian, 356
Powerscourt, 352
Premiership games, 370
Preston, 24
Pretenders, The, 216
Price, Dave, 55, 56, 57, 73, 121, 306, 370
Price, Katie (aka Jordan), 241
Price Waterhouse, 40
Prodrive, 105
Prost, Alain, 134, 142, 187, 189, 198, 201, 224, 256, 257, 270, 357, 358
Provera, Corrado, 223, 228, 256
Pulchinellas restaurant, Monaco, 55–6, 57
Punchestown, 376
Putt, John, 307

Quebec, 345
Quinn, Bosco, 89, 109–10, 113, 123, 168, 169

Racing for Britain, 54
Raikkonen, Kimi, 312, 320, 321
*Railway Children, The*, 118
Ralt, 46, 53, 66, 74–5, 79, 81, 99, 110
Ramaphosa, Cyril, 174
Rampoldi's restaurant, Monaco, 259
Ranelagh, 8
Rathfarnham, 12
Ratzenberger, Roland, 209
Rauvelli, Marlon, 137
Rea, Chris, 207, 304
Rectrus, Mother (EJ's aunt), 9, 13
Red Bull, 88, 332, 336
Reid, Tommy, 20
Rembiszewski, Jimmi ('Rambo'), 172–3, 307
Renault, 3, 82, 157, 160, 182, 224, 256, 263, 305, 314, 320
Reynard, 77, 78, 79, 80, 82, 84, 85, 89, 90, 99, 100, 104, 110, 191
Reynard, Adrian, 77, 78, 79, 80–1, 82, 104, 110, 341
Reynolds, R.J., 83, 116
Richards, David, 105
Richardson, Brian, 266
Richie, 364
Ridge and Partners, 168
Riley, Brett, 55, 58
*Riverdance*, 254, 302, 317, 381
Rock, Dickie, 7
Rodgers, Fred, 88, 156, 165–6
Roe, Michael, 118
Roebuck, Nigel, 167
Rosa, Pedro de la, 196
Rosberg, Keke, 151
Rosie's Bar, Monaco, 57
Ross, Charlie, 350
Rostaprovich (horse), 375
Rothengatter, Huub, 292
Rotten, Johnny (John Lydon), 298–9
Royal Adelaide, 358
Royal Albert Hall, 253, 351
Jordan Mugen-Honda 198 launched at, 254–5, 257–8, 279
Royal Irish Constabulary, 6
Rudman, Amanda, 262, 263, 279
Rudman, Michael, 262
Rushen Green, 66
Rutherford, Angie, 317
Rutherford, Mike, 304, 317
Ryder Cup, 344, 381

Saatchi, 240, 247, 257, 269
St Brelade's Bay, 14–15
Saint-Geours, Frederic, 223, 225
St Joseph's Church, Terenure, Dublin, 40
St Kevin's Gardens, Dublin, 8
St Mary's Hospital, Sidcup, 86
St Thomas' Hospital, 333
Salman, Crown Prince, 327, 328
Sandford Park school, Dublin, 37
Sandro Sala, Maurizio, 79
San Marino Grand Prix, 208–11
Sao Paolo, 140–1, 150
Sasol, 174, 175, 176, 177–8, 179–80, 181, 182, 184, 185–6, 189, 198, 201
Sato, Takuma, 308, 309, 314
Sauber, 149, 155, 275, 282, 290, 312, 329, 330
Savoir Faire, 368

Scammell, Dick, 106
Schaffer, Bertram, 148
Schenken, Tim, 162–3
Schlesser, Jean-Louis, 224
Schukies, Dr Gert, 300, 301–2, 312
Schull, Joe, 330
Schumacher, Michael
  EJ's first impressions of, 148, 149
  and Willi Weber's discussions with EJ, 148
  and sports-car racing, 149
  comes to Jordan as replacement for Bertrand Gachot, 150–1, 166–7
  drives for Jordan at Spa, 151–3, 170
  Jordan loses contract with, 155–60, 161–2
  1993 season, 194, 198
  1994 season, 206, 210, 220
  1995 season, 227
  and Irvine's move to Ferrari, 229–30, 231
  1997 season, 245
  advises Ralf Schumacher to leave Jordan, 269
  EJ's response to comments of, 269–71
  1998 season, 273, 276–7
  and departure of Ralf Schumacher, 281, 282, 283
  1999 season, 290, 295, 296
  2000 season, 305
  20003 season, 321
  brief references, 34, 166, 167, 184, 201, 212, 275, 384
Schumacher, Ralf
  signs with Jordan, 241–2
  1997 season, 242, 243, 244, 245
  1998 season, 261, 263, 267, 271, 272, 273, 274, 275, 276, 284
  and Michael Schumacher's intervention, 269, 271
  departure from Jordan, 281–2, 282–3
  brief references, 247, 248, 249, 255 277, 292, 320
Scottsdale, 134
Sears, David, 53
Senna, Ayrton
  test drive at Silverstone, 66–7
  in F3, 68, 69, 70–1, 72, 74, 75, 76, 119, 383
  in 1990 F1 race at Phoenix, 95
  1991 season, 142, 146, 154, 162
  1992 season, 179
  discussions with Jordan, 183–4
  1993 season, 187, 189, 194–5, 195–6, 197–8
  and Barrichello's accident, 208
  death, 210–12
  EJ's memory of, 212–13
  brief references, 16, 79, 148, 175, 199, 201, 206, 214, 215, 238, 248, 265, 270, 384
Serra, Chico, 44, 45
7UP, 126–7, 129, 131, 149, 162, 164, 172
Sex Pistols, 216, 299
Shanghai, 375, 380
Shanghai Tobacco, 375
Shanghide (horse), 375–6
Shankill Road, Belfast, 34
Shaw, Dennis, 15, 16
Shell, 174
Sherry, Jim, 24
Shinkins, Simon, 227
Shnaider, Alex, 337, 338, 340
Shorthouse, Dominic, 266–7, 286, 313, 330
Sidcup, 86
Silk Cut, 234, 235
Silverstone
  EJ's annual visits to, 39–40
  EJ buys house in, 41
  Senna's test drive at, 66–7
  and F3, 70–1, 72–4, 75,76
  1989 season, 90
  Jordan workshop at, 94, 104–5
  1991 season, 145–7
  Club Corner, 152
  new Jordan headquarters built at, 168–9
  post-Grand prix party, 216–17
  1998 season, 267
  factory welcome for EJ, 280–1
  negotiations with Shnaider at, 337
  brief references, 123, 136, 181, 182, 183, 226, 242, 244, 255, 292, 293, 294, 295, 305, 309, 322, 353, 357
Silverstone Circuits, 68, 71
Silverstone Estates, 105, 113
'Silverstone Sid', 71, 73
Simple Minds, 250
Simtek, 209

Skegness, 46
Sky News, 284
Slazenger, 335
Smart, 322
Smith, Alan, 34
Smith, Ian, 29
Smith, Mark, 109, 110, 141, 287
Smurfit, Michael, 217
*Snapper S*, 259
Soho House club, London, 304
Solheim, Karsten, 138
Sotham, Lynda, 383
Sotogrande, 344, 354, 359
South Africa, 174, 177–8, 184–6
Southampton University, 110–11
Spa, 95, 151–2, 156, 159, 166, 170, 189, 218–21, 244, 268, 269, 271, 272–7, 279, 281, 283, 284, 292, 305, 312
Spain, 80, 81, 83, 95, 174, 214, 288, 344, 353, 359
Spanish Grand Prix, 97
Speedline, 258
Spiess, 79
*Sport-Auto*, 115
Stamford Bridge, 370, 372
Stanley, Wyatt, 56, 57
Stars'n'Bars pub, Monaco, 217
Status Quo, 217
Stella house, Dublin, 38
Stelrad, 111, 135
Step Inn, Stepaside, 25–6
Stevenson, Andy, 243, 277, 288, 289, 329
Stewart, Jackie, 11, 92, 300, 301, 321, 358
Stewart-Ford, 241, 290, 300, 321
Stoddard, Paul, 333
Stoop, Joe, 63, 64
Storm, 345
Stowe, 345
Strachan, Gordon, 262, 368
Straits of Hormuz, 3
Strangford, 20
Strangford Lough, 20
Suchard, 172
*Sun*, 241, 251, 269
Sunningdale, 354, 355
Super Aguri, 34
Surlander, Bob, 379
Suzuka, 164, 191–6, 296–7, 331
Suzuki, Aguri, 204
Sweater Shop, 278
Sweeting, Adam, 257–8
Switzerland, 231
Sydney, 164, 167
Symonds, Pat, 161
Synge, Robert, 79
Synge Street School, Dublin, 10–11, 12

TAG Electronics, 257
Tassin, Thierry, 77
Tauranac, Ron, 46, 74, 75–6, 78
Taylor, Murray, 53, 63, 106
Taylor, Sid, 119–20
Tchuruk, Serge, 225, 255
Teddington, 303
Tehran, 371
Tel Aviv, 344
Temple, Helen, 383
Templelogue Inn, The, Dublin, 9
Thackwell, Mike, 44
Thieme, David, 253
*This is Your Life*, 303–4
Thomas, Chris, 216–17, 299
Thomas, Neil and Grant, 185
Thruxton, 53, 74–5
Tiger Woods Foundation, 354
Tip Top bar, Monaco, 57–8
Titchmarsh, Ian, 76, 203
Tobago, 44, 56
Todt, Jean, 230, 231
Tokyo, 191
Toleman, 82, 182, 238
Tomita, Mr, 331
Toso, Dino, 263, 274, 287
Total, 222, 225
Tour de France, 301
Toyota, 65, 69, 79, 306, 307, 314, 330, 331–2
Trans World International, 367
Tremayne, David, 167
Trinidad, 44
Trinity College, Dublin, 344
Triumph 2–5pi, 27–8
Troubles, the, 19, 20, 33
Trulli, Jarno, 302, 304, 305, 308, 309, 310, 314, 385
Tunney, Michael, 16, 374–5
Turin, 69, 344, 370–1
Turner, Tina, 212–13
Tyrell, 91, 92, 93, 95, 100, 106, 139, 147, 176, 201, 238, 264, 305, 306

Tyrell, Bob, 94
Tyrell, Ken, 85, 91, 92–4, 94–5, 196

U2, 217, 369
UCD, 345
UCLH (University College London Hospital), 349
United States 129, 163, 174, 312
United States Grand Prix, 174
Universal, 250
Universal Records, 218, 369
Universal Worldwide, 218
University College London Hospital (UCLH), 349
Usiskin, Nick, 175, 341
Usiskin, Suzi, 175, 341, 342–3, 348

V10, 217, 218, 299
Valderrama, 353
Vallelunga, 89, 90, 103
Van Diemen, 319
Vauxhall Viva 2000, 26
Verstappen, Jos, 200, 201, 202, 203, 292, 293
Vettier, Jean-Paul, 225
Vickers, 166
Villa d'Este hotel, Lake Como, 158, 159, 160
Villeneuve, Jacques, 248, 283, 284
Virgin Islands, 253
Vodafone, 323–6, 327
Volkswagen, 79
Volvo Masters, 357
Vos, John, 59

Walker, Murray, 304
Walkinshaw, Tom, 68, 158, 159, 160, 161, 231, 251, 279
Wallace, Andy, 77, 79
Wallace, Brian, 36
Walton, John ('John Boy'), 52, 55, 56, 58, 59, 60, 62, 206, 226, 285, 333–4
Walton, Mrs, 52
Warburg Pincus, 266, 286, 306, 313, 330, 378
Warne, Shane, 350
Warren, David, 84
Warwick, Derek, 91, 95, 96, 151, 195
Warwick, Paul, 91
Watkins, Professor, 97, 209, 211, 236–7, 373
Watson, John, 113
Weaver, James, 53–4, 66, 368
Webber, Mark, 320
Weber, Willi, 148, 149, 151, 155, 157, 241–2, 281
Wendlinger, Karl, 214
Wentworth, 354, 355, 359
Westbury, 81, 341
Wexford, 299
Weybridge, 235
Whitaker, Martin, 323
Whiting, Charlie, 236, 319, 321
Williams
  Alain Prost drives for, 187, 198
  Ayrton Senna drives for, 184, 201, 206, 210–11, 248
  Barclay has deal with, 172
  Damon Hill drives for, 187, 194, 195, 227, 248, 249
  David Coulthard drives for, 227
  Heinz-Harald Frentzen drives for, 282, 287, 385
  Jean Alesi drives for, 95
  Jim Wright works for, 88
  Nigel Mansell drives for, 142, 146
  Ralf Schumacher wishes to move to, 269, 271
  Ralf Schumacher drives for, 320
  Riccardo Patresi drives for, 154, 179
  Sam Michael drives for, 263
  brief references, 99, 106, 107, 130, 189, 220, 250, 276, 305, 307, 310, 381
Williams, Frank, 95, 96, 172, 248, 249, 255, 269, 279, 282, 373
Williams, Michael, 300
Williams, Steve, 354
Wilson, Peter, 234
Windsor, 350, 351
Windsor Castle pub, Camden Hill, 118
Winston Salem, 116
Witty, Chris, 44, 118–19
Wolheim, Nigel, 169
Wood, Keith, 309, 310, 350
Woods, Jim, 24
Woods, Tiger, 354–5
World Cup, 368–9, 371
World Cup of Motor Sport, 2
World Rally Championship, 223